8|28

W9-DGJ-366

THE RESISTANCE IN AUSTRIA,
1938-1945

Principiis obsta!

THE RESISTANCE IN AUSTRIA, 1938-1945

RADOMIR V. LUZA

University of Minnesota Press
Minneapolis

LIBRARY
COLBY-SAWYER COLLEGE
NEW LONDON, N.H. 03257

D
802
·A9
L89
1984

10/85

Copyright © 1984 by the University of Minnesota.
All rights reserved.
Published by the University of Minnesota Press,
2037 University Avenue Southeast, Minneapolis, MN 55414
Printed in the United States of America.

Library of Congress Cataloging in Publication Data

Luža, Radomír.
    The resistance in Austria, 1938-1945.

    Bibliography: p.
    Includes index.
    1. World War, 1939-1945—Underground movements—
Austria. 2. Austria—History—1938-1945. I. Title.
D802.A9L89 1983   940.53'436   83-6714
ISBN 0-8166-1226-9   .

The University of Minnesota
is an equal-opportunity
educator and employer.

96785

For my Czech, Slovak, and Austrian
Resistance Companions

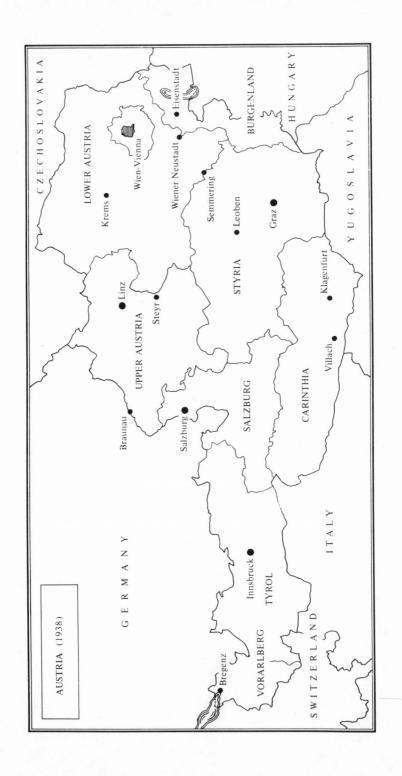

AUSTRIA (1938)

Contents

Abbreviations

Archives

BA	Bundesarchiv, Koblenz
DÖW	Dokumentationsarchiv des österreichischen Widerstandes, Vienna
IfZ	Institut für Zeitgeschiche, Universität Wien
NA	American Historical Association, American Committee for the Study of War Documents. National Archives, Washington, D.C.
OM	Privatarchiv Otto Molden. Zur Geschichte der österreichischen Widerstandsbewegung gegen Hitler 1938-1945. Deposited at the IfZ
ÖS-AV-RW	Österreichisches Staatsarchiv—Allgemeines Verwaltungsarchiv. Der Reichskommissar für die Wiedervereinigung Österreichs mit dem Deutschen Reich

Journals, newspapers

ÖGL	Österreich in Geschichte und Literatur
RGBl	Reichsgesetzblatt
VB	Völkischer Beobachter
VfZ	Vierteljahrshefte für Zeitgeschichte

Organizations

Abwehr	German Military Intelligence Service
ALÖS	Foreign Bureau of the Austrian Social Democrats
AVÖS	Committee of the Austrian Socialists Abroad
BS	Besonderer Senat (Special Senate)
CC	Central Committee
CSP	Christian Social Party
CTU	Christian Trade Unions
DAF	Deutsche Arbeitsfront (German Workers' Front)
FTU	Free Trade Unions (Socialist)
GB	Gewerkschaftsbund (United Trade Union Association, 1934-1938)
Gestapo	Geheime Staatspolizei (Secret State Police)

GSAW	Generalstaatsanwalt (Attorney General)
HJ	Hitler Jugend (Hitler's Youth)
HS	Heimatschutz (Home-Front) or Heimwehr
JV	Österreichisches Jungvolk (Austrian Young People)
KJV	Union of Communist Youth of Austria
KP	Communist Party
KPD	Communist Party of Germany
KPÖ	Communist Party of Austria
KSČ	Communist Party of Czechoslovakia
KZ	Concentration camp
LG	Landgericht (Provincial Court)
NSDAP	National Socialist German Workers' Party
NSV	National Socialist Public Welfare Organization
ÖAAB	Österreichischer Arbeiter- und Angestelltenbund (Austrian Association of Blue- and White Collar Workers)
ÖBB	Österreichischer Bauernbund (Austrian Peasants' Union)
ÖFF	Austrian Freedom Front
OLG	Oberlandesgericht (Supreme Provincial Court)
OS	Österreichische Sturmscharen
OSS	Office of Strategic Services
ÖVP	Austrian People's Party
ÖWB	Österreichischer Wirtschaftsbund (Austrian Economic Association)
PCF	Communist Party of France
RH	Rote Hilfe (Red Relief)
RKG	Reichskriegsgericht (Reich War Court)
RMdI	Reich Ministry of the Interior
RMdJ	Reich Ministry of Justice
RS	Revolutionary Socialists of Austria
RSHA	Reichssicherheitshauptamt (Reich Security Main Office)
SA	Sturmabteilungen (Storm Troops)
SAJ	Socialist Workers' Youth
SB	Republican Schutzbund
SD	Sicherheitsdienst (Security Service)
SG	Sondergericht (Special Court)
SOE	Special Operations Executive
SPD	Social Democratic Party of Germany
SPÖ	Social Democratic Workers' Party of Austria
SS	Schutzstaffel
VF	Fatherland Front
VGH	Volksgerichtshof (People's Court)
Wehrmacht	German Armed Forces

Others

AS	Anklageschrift (indictment)
Hauptmann	Captain
Oberleutnant	First Lieutenant
RM	Reichsmark (a monetary unit)
U	Urteil (verdict)

NOTE: The author uses the terms Lower- and Upper Austria. In 1938 the Nazi authorities substituted the names Lower- and Upper Danube for the historical terms and changed some of the provincial boundaries.

Preface

The history of Austria during the era of National Socialist rule 1938-45 is not well known. In particular, the anti-Nazi underground that many Austrians have dismissed as historically irrelevant has not been sufficiently studied. The Nazis spread their efforts everywhere. Their rule continued for seven long years and involved the entire society. It was a searing ordeal that brought Austrians together as a people and created their national consciousness. Concerned with the impact of the National Socialist regime on the Austrian people, I set out to write a case study of the development of the resistance movement in Austria. I do not treat other themes such as the activities of exile groups and individuals living abroad, or the experiences of prisoners of war or inmates of the concentration camps and prisons. Nor do I discuss at length the Nazi security apparatus or the technicalities of clandestine life.[1]

My interest in the Resistance originated in my own experience during the six years I fought in the Czechoslovak Resistance. There I acquired insight into the nature of underground work, later realizing that the resistance activities in the Nazi-occupied countries were in many ways similar. At the outset, I must say that I had initially approached the subject with much skepticism and was ready to dismiss many of the claims of the Austrian Resistance as irrelevant or exaggerated. After the initial years of research—mainly concerned with examining source material—I abandoned my reservations.

I have based my study on an examination of documents, wartime records, and secondary accounts, as well as on the recollections of a number of activists. Of course, in many respects the study is incomplete, for missing records obscure a great deal of what happened. Similarly, because of the nature of clandestine work, many actions were never recorded. These are but some of the methodological problems that confront the historian seeking to illuminate an area so shrouded in secrecy.

In describing those personal and collective experiences that define the Resistance organization, the historian sometimes implies causal connections where none might have existed. The evidence on which one depends in writing about political movements does not exist in the case of the Resistance, where sources are of varying reliability, such as ephemeral underground publications, personal accounts, and police and court files. In particular, police and court files are often dangerously deceptive. Officials tended to exaggerate the importance of the conspiratorial movements, if only to show their own effectiveness in combating the hostile forces. Their accounts necessarily had to be adjusted by the often one-sided recollections of survivors.

Yet another methodological problem is that although it is difficult to find out how many activists there were, it is almost impossible to learn who they all were. We know much about the resisters who were arrested and tried but little about those who were not caught, who left no accounts, and who kept no files. Such a paucity of evidence makes the underground difficult to describe.

The absence of material is also symptomatic of another problem in describing the Resistance—the contrast between the self-serving, often ambiguous, personal accounts of marginal activists and the actual conspiratorial practices of the elusive but genuine underground core itself. As always, the historical reality is much more complicated than the myths or self-serving accounts. Because of the sudden origin and abrupt end of the Resistance phenomenon of 1938-45, the emotional individual experiences are marginally historical, and the tangible but anonymous achievements of clandestine cohorts and individual resisters are rarely sufficiently documented. What Jonathan H. King stated on the nature of the French Resistance can be applied to the Austrian Resistance also:

> The resistance was an unexpected and unlamented phenomenon. It had, initially at any rate, . . . no roots outside personal impulse and chance affinities. Hardly born, it disappeared. It threw up men unknown before [1938] and buried them virtually without trace in [1945], when, its most tangible goals accomplished largely by others, its intangible aspirations rejoined the mainstream of ideological history and thereby lost their identity.[2]

Despite the many methodological problems, I believe that thanks to the evidence on the underground movements available at the *Dokumentationsarchiv* of the Austrian Resistance (DÖW) in Vienna and at other institutions, it is possible to present a reasonably satisfactory account and to offer some conclusions.

Beginning with the Anschluss, I have, in the main, arranged the topics chronologically, threading the narrative through chapters divided according to the spread of political movements and resistance organizations and their regional patterns. I deliberately emphasize the organizational and political aspects of clandestine work and only occasionally include in the narrative the more glamorous individual exploits, which are, however, not necessarily typical of the work of many thousands of activists. Furthermore, I have attempted to draw a distinct line between the genuine resisters and those who engaged in individual acts of opposition. I devote some space to a computer-assisted social analysis of the membership in the former group.

The limits of space prohibited not only the study of individual resisters but also the inclusion and enumeration of all the groups and their achievements. Consequently, the narrative concentrates on discussing the cadres of militancy in order "to disentangle a myriad of individual and collective exploits into intelligible patterns" (M. R. D. Foot). This survey often makes for depressing reading, reminding the readers of the frightful suffering which the National Socialists inflicted on so many persons who either belonged to the Resistance elite or were victims of the regime's pervasive repression.

Although I alone am responsible for its shortcomings, the study is very much the product of collective efforts. Among my unwitting collaborators I must first mention my companions from the Czechoslovak Resistance. They have contributed more than they could imagine to my understanding of the ephemeral and intricate nature of the Resistance, at once highly personal and individualistic and dominated by its insistent, almost strident, attachment to the virtues of morality and national sovereignty.

To the staff of that admirable depository for the files of the Austrian underground, the DÖW, to its director Professor Dr. Herbert Steiner, the late Professor Friedrich Vogl, Herbert Exenberger, the late Dr. Selma Steinmetz, Christoph Kopeszki, Trude Benda, and their colleagues, I owe a special debt of gratitude. Above all, Dr. Wolfgang Neugebauer generously gave me his invaluable advice and commented on the manuscript. Colonel Dr. Ferdinand Käs offered me his support. I wish to thank the staff of the Institut für Zeitgeschichte of the University of Vienna, particularly Dr. Anton Staudinger, Dr. Karl Stuhlpfarrer, and Dr. Peter Malina, for their hospitality and help. I would like to express my gratitude to the staffs of the Howard Tilton Memorial Library, Tulane University; the Franklin D. Roosevelt Library, Hyde Park, New York; the National Archives and Records Service, Washington, D.C.; the Bundesarchiv, Koblenz; the Flugschriftensammlung of the Österreichische Nationalbibliothek; the Österreichisches Staatsarchiv, Kriegsarchiv; the Verein für Geschichte der Arbeiterbewegung; and the Österreichisches Statistisches Zentralamt. I am grateful for advice to Franz Klar of the Österreichische Widerstandsbewegung.

My study profited handsomely from summer research grants from the American Philosophical Society (the Penrose Fund, 1975 and from the Tulane University Senate Committee on Research (1976). A special grant from the Committee on Research (1977) covered the cost of the computer operations at Tulane Computer Laboratory, to which I am especially obliged for assistance. I have received valuable aid from my former colleague Professor Samuel M. Kipp, who guided me in working with computers. I am deeply indebted to a Tulane graduate student in history, Edward A. Allen, for reading the manuscript, giving me his suggestions, and helping me handle the computer work. Although I have designed the codebook, coded the source material, and selected the questions, he compiled the computer program and ran the data. It is my great pleasure to express my sense of gratitude to this able young scholar for his skill and thoroughness. My appreciation goes to Professors Ronald Batchelder and Jefferson Frank for their advice. Professor Robert S. Robins generously helped me and took time to read the section on the profile of the Resistance. For his interest in my research I am especially grateful to my good friend, Professor Herman Freudenberger, who always responded generously to my requests for advice.

I should like to express a special word of thanks for their valuable comments and observations to Dr. Neugebauer and Dr. Steiner, who read large parts of the earlier version of this book. My appreciation goes to Professor Bruce Pauley who greatly assisted me by reading the final draft of the study. I am deeply grateful to Barry McCarthy for his editorial help. I acknowledge with gratitude the permission to reprint a passage from my article "Nazi Control of the Austrian Catholic Church, 1939-1941," *The Catholic Historical Review* 63 No. 4 (October, 1977): 537-72.

So many persons assisted me in my research that a complete list would be impossibly long. I was very fortunate in obtaining valuable information and cooperation from former members of the Austrian Resistance. I am indebted to Erwin Altenburger, Herbert Baumann, the late Father Ludger Born, S. J., Antonia Brůha, Hans Christian, Dr. Herbert Crammer, the late Karl Czernetz, Hofrat Dr. Franz Daniman, Dr. Johann Dostal, Johannes von Eidlitz, Alfred Ellinger, the late Professor Anselm Grand, Dr. Wilhelm Grimburg, Dr. Karl Gruber, Dr. Otto von Habsburg, Professor Walter Hacker, the late Karl Hartl, Theodor Heinisch, Josef Hindeis, Alois Hradil, the late Hofrat Anton S. Hyross, Hofrat Dr. Hubert Jurasek, Msgr. Dr. Alfred Kostelecky, Julius Kretschmer, Leopold Kuhn, Hermann Langbein, the late Dr. Franz Latzka, Bertha Lauscher, the late Josef Lauscher, Hans Leinkauf, the late Dr. Ernst Lemberger, Univ. Prof. Dr. Franz Loidl, August Lovrek, the late Karl Maisel, Dr. Alfred Maleta, Hans Marsalek, Heinz Mayer, the late Dr. Alfred Migsch, Fritz Molden, Dr. Otto Molden, Rudolfine Muhr, Frieda Nödl, Dr. Wolfgang Pfaundler, Msgr. Josef O.

Pinzenöhler, Dr. Bruno Pittermann, Hofrat Raimund Poukar, the late Anton Proksch, Ludwig Reichhold, Dr. Viktor Reimann, the late Prof. Dr. Felix Romanik, Erwin Scharf, Dr. Paul Schärf, Dr. Peter Schramke, the late Kurt von Schuschnigg, the late Felix Slavik, Bruno Sokoll, Dr. Ludwig Soswinski, Dr. Josef Staribacher, Dr. Ludwig Steiner, Major Carl Szokoll, Edwin Tangl, Dr. Erich Thanner, Wilhelm Thurn und Taxis, Roman Weinstabl, Dr. Josef Windisch, the late Dr. Stefan Wirlandner, and the late Fritz Würthle.

NOTES

1. M. R. D. Foot, *Resistance: European Resistance to Nazism 1940-1945* (New York, 1977), gives an introduction into the techniques of underground activity.

2. "Emmanuel d'Astier and the Nature of the French Resistance," *Journal of Contemporary History* 8 (October 1973): 28.

INTRODUCTION

1

Austria, the Anschluss, and the Resistance

THE FIRST REPUBLIC, 1918-1938

The collapse of the Habsburg Empire and the foundation of the democratic Republic in November 1918, restricted to the German-speaking central core of the former Empire, mark the starting point of the wearisome road to the formation of the modern Austrian nation after 1945. The new state faced severe problems. The victorious Allied powers determined Austria's immediate postwar development by prohibiting inclusion of Austria into Germany — the Anschluss — in the 1919 Peace Treaty of Saint Germain. The most urgent task facing this residue of a once vast Empire, which inherited 22.3 percent of the inhabitants — 6,710,233 persons — and 32.4 percent of the factories of the Monarchy, was whether its infant coalition government could create a stable political and economic Republic.[1] Many Austrians considered themselves members of the German nation and were convinced of the impossibility of the independent existence of the new state and of the economic necessity of its incorporation into Germany. In fact, important segments of the population did not commit themselves to the idea of an independent Austria until 1945. Between them, all the major parties helped to undermine any national legitimacy that the Republic might otherwise have developed and, until the Nazi takeover in Germany in 1933, they all seemed to want the Anschluss.

The foreign powers imposed their rhythm on the process of Austria's emancipation. Dependent on extensive imports of coal and agricultural products, lacking strong export industries, and cut by the new frontiers from her former imperial markets, Austria alone could not overcome her antiquated economic and technological structures. The economic plight of the country during the disastrous inflation of the early twenties made the Austrian leaders anxious to steer away from their initial commitment to the

Anschluss. They insisted that Allied financial aid was vital for Austria's independence. In October 1922, Christian Social Federal Chancellor Msgr. Ignaz Seipel achieved this objective in the context of the League of Nations when he concluded an agreement with Great Britain, France, Italy, and Czechoslovakia for a loan of 650 million gold crowns.

The financial stabilization ensured political power to the Catholic interest, which held it until 1938. It marked a decisive point in the recovery of self-confidence by the traditional elites represented by the Christian Social Party (CSP). Their discovery that they could work the new Republican order in their own interests did not induce them to share power and wealth with its founders, the Social Democratic Workers' Party of Austria (SPÖ) and the trade unions. If anything, the departure of the SPÖ from the coalition government in 1920 had whetted the appetite of the Christian Social Party for further attacks on the Social Democrats. The Christian Social electoral victories in 1920 and 1923 reaffirmed the division of Austrian politics into three main political camps. The majority consisted of the Christian Socials and the much less numerous Greater-German nationalists, who constituted the opposition of the Social Democrats. Because no landslide victories occurred in Austrian politics, the two major parties, the CSP and the SPÖ, thus seemed assured of a permanent strength.

From 1920, the SPÖ, with its Austro-Marxist ideology, was condemned to permanent and radical opposition because the political system blocked the supposedly normal alternation of parties in government, thereby making the political scene immobile and encouraging the ruling CSP to abuse its power. The country's politics remained locked in a fortress of conservatism and clericalism in which one political camp played an exclusive role. The polarization generated a bitter struggle and a harsh political split between the interests of the rural areas and of political Catholicism, whom the Christian Socials represented, and the interests of the urban industrial classes, whose revolutionary spokesmen were the Social Democrats. The split became the central fact of political life until the Nazi takeover in 1938. The relative prosperity of the years 1925 to 1929 consolidated the position of the Christian Social Party at the expense of the Socialists. The latter were further alienated from the CSP-dominated government because the paramilitary Heimwehr—or Heimatschutz—organizations, which originated after 1919 as a defensive patriotic force, were developing into a militantly anti-Socialist movement with strong Fascist tendencies.

The great economic crisis and the rise of National Socialism in Germany in the early thirties decisively upset the highly unstable political equilibrium in Austria. These events reawakened German nationalism, resulting in large gains for the Austrian National Socialists at the municipal and provincial elections in April 1932. Only a strong and popular government could have mastered the grave problems and created an anti-Nazi block. However, because they were deeply hostile to Socialism and disillusioned with the workings of parliamentary institutions, the CSP leaders refused to endorse an alliance with the Social Democrats, who were still largely inspired by the rhetoric of revolutionary Marxism. In May, under impact of the sharp losses in electoral support for their party and its Greater-German allies, the Christian Socials set up a new coalition government headed by Engelbert Dollfuss.

The failure of the CSP and the SPÖ to cooperate strengthened the reactionary and semi-Fascist elements in Austrian society. The new cabinet no longer enjoyed a clear parliamentary majority and existed only because the opposition was divided. Dollfuss gradually imposed an authoritarian rule, under which the country's democratic institutions were repressed and political parties dissolved. This shift greatly favored the system's tendency to polarization and created a trilateral political struggle, with the National Socialist German Workers' Party (NSDAP) and the Social Democrats engaged in combative dialogue with the government. In this situation Dollfuss eliminated the parliamentary system in March 1933 and banned the NSDAP in June. This gloomy message to the antigovernment forces placed an almost intolerable strain on relations between the government and other political forces. In turn, it forced the Federal Chancellor to clash more bitterly than ever before in the Republic's history with the Social Democrats and National Socialists. Thus, in 1934, the opposition on both the left and the right formed large embattled encampments, in which the energies and rhetoric of activists were turned on the rapidly emerging national crisis.

In a series of bloody clashes with the Socialists, the SPÖ was smashed by the government security and armed forces in February 1934. About 300 people lost their lives. The brutal dragnet operations that the troops conducted through working class neighborhoods, the indiscriminate arrests of many suspects, and the later sentencing to death of nine officials of the SPÖ paramilitary unit, the Republican Schutzbund (SB), intensified the hostility to the regime. The Social Democrats, however, soon bounced back. They committed themselves to the underground struggle, trying to preserve a mass party network and a high level of semi-clandestine activity.

On July 25, 1934, the NSDAP attempted to overthrow the regime in an abortive putsch that brought about the Dollfuss assassination. The police shattered the NSDAP and destroyed its underground organization. Adolf Hitler publicly dissociated himself from the putsch, which clearly ran against his foreign policy objectives. He cut off the Nazi Party in Germany from its Austrian branch and prohibited any participation in Austrian affairs by former Austrian Nazi leaders.

The Austria of Dollfuss and his successor Kurt Schuschnigg was ruled in a new authoritarian institutional setting. The Fatherland Front became the only existing political movement in the country, replacing political parties. However, the regime was out of touch with industrial society; its public influence turned out to be minimal; its Christian-inspired corporative doctrine was not resilient enough to respond creatively to the demands of the time. In sum, while Austrian society was in ferment, ready to undergo social changes, the existing political and economic structures, retaining their paternalistic character, stood almost still. With no understanding of the needs of the working classes and with National Socialism gradually supplanting other kinds of Greater-German Anschluss ideology, the hard-pressed regime tried to turn the political and economic inertia to its advantage, citing the peril of Marxist-inspired Socialist revolution and the challenge of Nazism. It embraced the concept of the Austrian identity as a shield behind which to preserve the independence of the Republic and to maintain the authoritarian system.

The government endorsed a deflationary policy for running the Austrian economy—frugality and restrictive financing were its watchwords. It cut consumer purchasing power and retarded any development toward full employment. In 1933, the number of unemployed reached a staggering 557,000 persons.[2] These unimaginative policies, meant to appeal to its conservative constituency of small property owners, caused the regime to lose ground and also made it more difficult for it to maintain its legitimacy. By 1936 the most disturbing aspect of the situation was the regime's inability to overcome the serious domestic crisis. Clearly, Schuschnigg's peculiarly immobile government could not hope to influence developments unless it concluded an arrangement with some of its opponents. For Schuschnigg, the pressure of the militant conservatives, the influence of Mussolini, the rise of Hitler's Germany, and the memories of the gallows of 1934 made any attempt to renew the unity of action of 1918-20 with the Social Democrats almost impossible. His problems had grown because, in the meantime, the illegal NSDAP had reorganized and had chosen a more flexible policy line. Large segments of the middle classes had become increasingly ready to opt for National Socialism, so worried were they about the dismal economic prospects of the small state.

Having chosen to move toward the Greater-German right, Chancellor Schuschnigg sought to bring back the pro-Nazi nationalist elements to public life. His agreement of July 11, 1936, with Hitler was intended to pacify the Greater-German forces by attempting a reconciliation with the only outside power that could help his opponents at home. The agreement offered the nationalist opposition the opportunity to work as individuals within the nonparty state, whose very independence the opposition sought to undermine. The arrangement thus blunted Schuschnigg's ability to deal with the internal Nazi peril. By 1938 the regime had been repudiated by broad segments of the society, who had adopted the once-popular concept of Greater-German unity, now represented by Hitler. With its dwindling middle class support, the regime had to face alone Nazi Germany and her

Austrian supporters, whose increasingly organized defiance was rapidly worsening the domestic situation.

Schuschnigg made fatal mistakes. He pushed underground the Social Democratic movement that was ready to fight for Austria's independence and misjudged his temporary allies on the right. His errors led Schuschnigg to take a risky gamble. On March 9, 1938, he issued a call for a plebiscite to be held on March 13 to endorse a free and German, independent and social, Christian and united Austria.[3] The outlawed Socialists agreed to support the Chancellor, who expected to win a popular vote that would allow him to face the Nazi challenge. Taken by surprise, Hitler, Hermann Göring, and their aides exerted heavy pressure on Schuschnigg and under threats forced him to resign in the early evening hours of March 11. The next day German troops entered the country, enthusiastically acclaimed by cheering crowds. On March 13, Austria became "a province of the German Reich," soon to be parceled up into its constituent territorial units (Länder).[4]

THE OCCUPATION

From 1933 to 1938, the protracted conflict between Berlin and Vienna had created a curious atmosphere of ambiguity and considerable internal strain. When the regime collapsed under heavy Nazi pressure on March 11, outbreaks of popular enthusiasm and nationalist exultation attended the German occupation of the Republic. The Anschluss unleashed a surging feeling of All-German nationalism that represented one of the most curious, complex, and abrupt turnabouts of public opinion in modern European history.[5]

National Socialist propaganda touted the extension of the Reich's sovereignty into Austria as the fulfillment of Greater-German dreams. In effect, the Anschluss presented every Austrian with a dilemma. Should he declare his German nationality and erase his feeling of Austrian consciousness? Or should he assert his Austrian identity and abandon his German nationality?

Only in retrospect can one see that the Anschluss amounted to a dissolution of the country. This was not at all clear in March 1938 when Adolf Hitler, the charismatic embodiment of the All-German tradition, pretended to bind Austrian wounds and to set the country on its feet again—in union with the economically intimidating and politically dynamic German Reich. Hitler's successful deception was, undoubtedly, the main reason that he received an overwhelming mandate at the plebiscite on April 10; a good many young people and idealists assisted him in what they believed to be the construction of the Greater-German Reich. Even some important elements that once had supported the Austrian state had accepted the idea of Greater-German national unity as represented by National Socialism. Only a minority clung to pre-Anschluss concepts of Austrian patriotism.

THE GREATER-GERMAN IDEA AND ITS OPPONENTS

Resistance in Austria started largely as a protest against both the All-German dictatorship's supression of the Austrian identity and the National Socialists' totalitarian tendencies. It grew out of a violent disintegration, as traditional humanistic values fell apart under the combined pressures of the Greater-German movement and the National Socialist repression. The occupation of Austria was particularly unnerving. Suddenly, the country had to confront a totalitarian regime whose post-1933 political, economic, and social achievements and All-German nationalist ideology intoxicated many Austrians. Many unemployed, impoverished, and socially undermined members of the lower- and middle-income groups believed that the Anschluss would improve the precarious economic and political conditions created by the fall of the Empire in 1918. The younger generations in particular had confidence that an Austrian could participate more actively in German public life, economy, and culture, and do so both as a German and as an Austrian. Thus a good deal of continuity existed between the pre-Anschluss and post-1938 Greater-German ideologies. Yet, Hitler's resolve to assimilate Austria, and the German National Socialists' scorn of Austrian traditions, forcefully reminded the country that in fact the union brought a break with the past. The critics of the Anschluss and the opponents of National Socialism pointed to the particular national character of the Austrians as a real obstacle to any convincing integration into a cohesive All-German community. The tenacity with which some Austrians clung to their traditions, as well as to their moral and political convictions, provided the basis for the Resistance.

There arose a welter of Resistance groups, of varying political persuasion and sophistication, that were generally more susceptible to the claims of patriotism than of ideology. Moreover, Hitler's anti-Austrian policies of assimilation within the Reich, which Reich Commissioner Gauleiter Josef Bürckel implemented in Vienna, and the often insensitive conduct of the Reich German officials made it possible for Austrians to feel patriotic even in supporting the Reich's adversaries. From first to last, the Resistance in Austria was less ideologically oriented than movements elsewhere in occupied Europe.

THE DEFINITION OF THE RESISTANCE

The Resistance—like socialism, or democracy—cannot be identified for historical purposes in merely a conceptual form.[6] Yet without an operational definition, empirical evidence is little more than a mass of data that cannot be properly used and evaluated and whose chronological boundaries cannot be satisfactorily delineated. Moveover, the writing of comparative studies demands a definition.

Before and during World War II, the Resistance sprang up spontaneously throughout Europe as a reaction against the Fascist and National Socialist regimes of occupation. What was initially an individual, mostly political, moral, and national act of defiance developed into a series of organized actions. Those activities which initially involved passive resistance and protest — providing shelter and cover for resisters, disseminating rumors, scribbling slogans, and spreading handbills — became more defiant. Illegal publications, demonstrations, slow-downs, boycotts, strikes, acts of sabotage, the collecting and communicating of intelligence information, the maintenance of contacts with foreign countries, the concealing of weapons, recruiting, illegal networks, and guerrilla warfare — all became increasingly common. At a time of deep national crisis, ordinarily law-abiding citizens refused to accept the imposed law. As a potential revolutionary force, they developed into agencies of political mobilization and change whose existence suggested a political and ideological alternative to National Socialism.

Beyond its simple hierarchy of leadership, the Resistance had no elaborate social structures. Creators of their own networks, the chiefs enjoyed some prerogatives, as the clandestine life did not permit elections, large meetings, or assemblies. Within this diversified, heterogeneous, and fragmented body, a distinctive group consciousness and a sense of deep solidarity usually developed, through the presence of the same adversary and the occurrence of similar personal experiences. The Resistance was a composite movement made up of the multiple interactions of loosely connected local and national groups. Although politically and geographically disparate, the groups were personally highly integrated, and their individual members saw themselves deeply linked in sympathy and mutual support to their companions in other groups.

To find a more differentiated and descriptive definition, one must distinguish between opposition and resistance. A resister is not an inebriated individual arrested for offending the Führer or a person who had hailed Stalin in a fit of bad temper. Similarly, passive disobedience, or opposition unattached to tangible acts, has to be considered apart from the resistance activities. Opposition, then, is an attitude connoting a mental and affective disagreement with the regime. It may become illegal and it can evolve into a mass movement. Resistance — except in its final stage — remains fragmented and limited to groups engaged in individual or collective acts of protest. Opposition may eventually evolve into Resistance by becoming active, politically conscious, and organizationally structured. The Resistance, then, was any politically conscious, predominantly clandestine organized activity, perceived as hostile and declared as illegal by the National Socialist or Fascist ruling systems.[7]

THE NATURE OF THE AUSTRIAN RESISTANCE

Both the Resistance and National Socialism inaugurated and reflected a process that tore the Austrian historical structures asunder. Whereas National Socialism mobilized broad segments of the society, in particular the upwardly mobile strata of the politicized lower-income groups, and involved them in the daily functioning of the regime, the Resistance aimed at élites. Early commitment to organized defiance did not conform to any ready-made sociological pattern; class origin, professional qualifications, and provincial background do not provide easy clues. Personal rather than social character usually motivated people into becoming resisters. At the élite level, for the most part, the Resistance expressed the growing sense of national identity, of Austria's humanistic tradition and culture, which the oppressive nature of the system aroused.

The transitional pains and changes that accompanied the National Socialist takeover and the outbreak of the war forced segments of the population out of tradition-bound relationships and away from upper-class paternalism. Although by its nature the Resistance could not reach out beyond a narrow circle of support, it gathered in the most moral and politically self-conscious elements of Austrian society, who were convinced that the regime had to be disrupted and destroyed. As no legal opposition was permissible, the Resistance was driven to the fringes of society, where it remained powerless but dangerous nevertheless.

The multitude of groups of differing political hues provided a moral, political, and ideological alternative for those militants eager to bring down the government. Like any élite army unit, the movement needed a leadership, a self-discipline, and a trust that was born out of the free endorsement of certain ideological and political principles and out of the strict rules of behavior the activists applied to their own internal operations. For security reasons, militants were usually ignorant of the true identity of their fellow combatants. They deferred to both the instructions of their chiefs and to the voluntary consensus within the underground. The hierarchic character formed an integral part of the Resistance.

In Austria, as elsewhere in Europe, resistance to Hitler was the exception, accommodation the rule. Resistance was the monopoly of a tiny minority of people of conscience who spanned the political spectrum. The hardy activitists whom the National Socialist takeover outraged established the first conspiratorial groupings. Their development did not conform to that of the underground in other Nazi-occupied countries. In Austria, for instance, a resister was often compelled to fight against his own friends or relatives. The Austrian Resistance lacked the organizational context of the French, Czech, or Polish liberation movements. Austrians and Germans spoke the same language and belonged to the same ethnic group. Consequently, the occupation did not bring radical ethnic, political, and social changes. In Poland, and in the Czech lands, resistance was based on a wide-ranging feeling of national solidarity transcending the boundaries between those who joined the Resistance "and those who remained outside of its network."[8] In Austria the existence of a strong native National Socialist Party, of military conscription, and of a common tongue significantly limited the depth of popular solidarity with the Resistance and made much easier the task of the security forces. With its much smaller popular base, the Austrian underground formed a narrower, more loosely structured political network, existing largely apart from the majority of the population.

Other distinctive features were the underground's lack of a political hinterland abroad, its isolation, and the absence of firm political ties with the outside, where no official political exile organ existed. Unlike in other Nazi-occupied countries, especially in Western Europe, the Austrian groups operated predominantly on their own, and on a very modest scale. Only a few organizations maintained contacts with the outside. The Swiss radio newscasts and the British Broadcasting Corporation (BBC) played an important part in the political warfare by widely circulating war news in Austria itself. In the last stage of the war, the BBC became the vital link between the conspiracy at home and the Allies, helping to communicate instructions via coded messages. Similarly, after 1941, Radio Moscow broadcasts expressed Soviet policy by encouraging active resistance. Well into late 1944, the Austrian Resistance's objectives were undetermined and unaffected by overall Allied strategy. Without foreign directives and Allied assistance, the underground concentrated on recruitment, organization, clandestine propaganda, and information gathering. Unlike the French, Belgian, Dutch, and Norwegian Resistances, who received money, technical equipment, and supplies from the Allies, the Austrian Resistance could not effectively conduct its activities nor make full use of its intelligence gathering.

Austria's geographic position imposed certain limitations but also offered certain advantages. Long lines of communication to the outside from a landlocked country—with only two outlets, to neutral Switzerland and to Hungary—significantly hampered the establishment of ties with friends abroad. Isolated within the Reich, and out of the operational range of the early British aircraft, the country was unfit for guerrilla warfare until the Allied occupation of South Italy in 1943 and the spread of the Yugoslav guerrilla insurgency. Fortunately, the country's deep forests and mountain areas were suited to harboring the militants and deserters of the last war years. On August 8, 1944, to combat the guerrilla units, Heinrich Himmler ordered Southern Carinthia a special Battle Zone *(Bandenkampfgebiet).*[9] Large parties of Yugoslav partisans from Slovenia were operating in the region with some support from the local, mostly Slovene, population. Small arms and ammunition were more readily available throughout Austria than in the neighboring Protectorate of Bohemia and Moravia, no doubt because of the former existence of the paramilitary organizations and the readiness of individual soldiers to use their access to military supplies. Food and other rations were more abundant than in the occupied Eastern territories. However, the conversion of Austria to a war basis and the relentlessly imposed regimentation that touched every aspect of public activity made the lives of ordinary citizens extremely uncomfortable. They had to endure food rationing (instituted in the fall of 1939), labor conscription, military service, longer work hours, and intensified control and police supervision of public and private life; all of which generated a climate of fear, intimidation, and tension.

Faced with repression, and living in conditions of almost continuous uncertainty, the small cells of resisters had to consider security carefully. In particular, the police closely watched known Communists and former public figures. Senior Communist organizers were forced to become full-time resisters and to live underground permanently. To take care of the normal activities of life, activists wasted their energies on day-to-day routine. Living mostly in urban areas, they faced the complicated system of troublesome controls that required every citizen to carry identity papers, a labor booklet, and food ration coupons. Their every move involved personal risk and could be abruptly interrupted by police inspections of personal papers, travel documents, and parcels. Providing food, clothes, money, hideouts, false documents, and small arms to persons living underground often required the work of several individuals. The role of the resister was as much that of an administrator and provider as that of a combatant.[10] The emphasis throughout the early phase of the Resistance, then, was on organization, political program, moral uplift, appeals to the instincts of patriotism and humanitarianism, and, primarily, on mere survival.

The resistance movement tended to be pragmatic, with no far-reaching socio-ideological objectives or specific long-term economic political aspirations. Patriotic and democratic aims were drawn together under a vague, angry anti-Nazi and anti-German banner, where the carefully cultivated expectation of ultimate victory kept them. Apart from the clandestine Communist Party of Austria (KPÖ), the former political parties only rarely generated underground activity. Having been suppressed well before 1938, the political parties became in the minds of many the vehicles of democratic tradition. Not involved in the pro-Nazi policies, they retained their respectability. Unlike the action in the Reich in 1933, in Austria measures of repression hit the leaders of the conservative parties hardest, because since 1934 the Social Democratic Workers' Party had not maintained any position of power and thus had not posed any immediate threat to the regime.

Yet many of its former senior officials were arrested after the takeover and sent to Dachau concentration camp.

Deeply divided by the civil war of 1934, the members of the two largest parties, the Socialists and the Christian Socials, began to conduct themselves in the concentration camps as partners facing a mutual enemy. The common experience of the camps helped establish closer personal ties between the former adversaries, although in the underground their past differences still kept them politically separate. Indeed, until the very last months of the war, it is difficult to consider the politically divided and pluralistic Resistance as a homogeneous phenomenon. The two parties never completely retreated from their basic contentions that the specific anxieties and ambitions of their potential supporters could only be answered by the adoption of their own views. Yet a good measure of common sense, accumulated frustration, and resentment over the demise of the Republic and over the ruthless Nazi Greater-German policies of assimilation combined to make the former officials more appreciative of their shared purpose. The right and left were not as divisively separated during the closing war years when their leaders pursued practical goals, wanting neither a return to liberal capitalism nor a continuation of the promotion of Austro-Marxist tenets. In effect, the two parties played an all-important role in the seizure of power in Vienna and in the various Länder (provinces) during the spring of 1945.

At the outset, the part played by the non-Marxists in building up the resistance movement was large, although past political diversity still conditioned the objectives and nature of their networks. Its familiarity with clandestine life and its militant tradition enabled the KPÖ to devote its full energies to underground activities. Conversely, the Socialists did not initially respond to the pull of the past and did not switch to the underground. At this early date they preached rather a comfortable *attentisme,* causing grave doubts among some local militants who switched to Communist networks. Underlying divergencies at times rendered the process of national consensus-building delicate. The underground did not form a central organization based on broad cooperation among supporters of the main political tendencies until 1944-45.

REPRESSION

During the first stormy months of 1938, events unfolded with the somber inevitability of a classical drama. The end of the Republic came not in a grim battle but in a smooth transition. In fact, by the beginning of the spring, the National Socialist government was safely installed in power, under the emotional—if not ideological—support of enormous rallies in which huge masses shouted their approval of the "reunion" with the Reich. For some time, it appeared as though the country were in the midst of a

Greater-German dream. The pace of reunification intended to bring Austrians "home" to the Reich was shifted to one of total assimilation. The great economic and political expectations of the majority remained high throughout the country. Access to a vast German economic market made feasible full employment of Austrian labor. But the euphoria of some Austrians quickly dissipated when the Ostmark Act of April 1939 dissolved the country into seven Länder, called the Reichsgaue, directly subordinated to the Führer and to the Berlin central authorities. In 1939 the name "Austria" was blotted out of official terminology, to be replaced by the term "Ostmark." In 1942 even this concept was ordered into oblivion and a simple enumeration of the seven Alpine and Danubian Reichsgaue was substituted.[11]

While these changes were occurring, a spate of austerity measures was severely testing the benign mood of materialistic preoccupation and nationalist frenzy. Beneath the surface of an allegedly united Greater-German national community, segments of the former political movements, whether Communist, Socialist, Monarchist, Catholic, liberal, or Home Front (Heimatschutz), were deeply suspicious and scornful of the regime. Hitler's international successes, his continuing endorsement by large strata of the population, and the existence of a repressive security apparatus isolated these small opposition forces.

Allowing no legitimate channels for the expression of political disagreement, the National Socialists' first concern was to eliminate dissidence and to prevent the rise of an organized protest. The head of the Reich security forces, Reichsführer SS Heinrich Himmler, was the first high-ranking official to land at the Aspern airfield near Vienna in the early morning hours of March 12, 1938. In an immediate orderly transfer of power, he took direct control of the police and SS forces, which now operated independently of the Party and State authorities and received instructions directly from Berlin.[12] In the pre-March days the National Socialist agents had familiarized themselves with the operations of the Austrian police. The data the latter collected — particularly those on the Communist and Socialist underground — were soon useful in tracking down opponents of National Socialism. The Gestapo proceeded at once to organize its ruthless apparatus of political repression.[13] It became so effective in cutting off the underground cadres from their social constituency that from 1938 it made the preservation of group contacts appear as objectives in themselves for the resisters.

Charged with domestic political intelligence and ideological supervision, the Sicherheitsdienst's (SD) responsibilities in Austria included expanding its network of informers throughout the country to detect Resistance, planting its agents in underground organizations and supervising their reports, and gathering information on the foreign contacts of opponents and on their penetration into the ranks of the NSDAP and its affiliates. At the outset, the SD divided the hostile political opposition into the three main camps: (1) the left: Communists, Social Democrats, Marxist splinter groups; (2) the center: the People's Front, democrats, the so-called Geneva institutions and pacifists, Bible Students (Jehovah's Witnesses), bourgeois parties; (3) the right: Legitimists, Home-Front (Heimatschutz), Fatherland Front.[14]

During the initial round-up of political opponents in the wake of the Anschluss, the Gestapo detained, at least temporarily, nearly 20,000 persons. Vast numbers went through detention unreported, because the local Party, SA, and SS members carried out irregular arrests and scores of detainees were released within a short time.[15] Although initial repressive measures mainly affected former pro-Schuschnigg officials, they also encompassed some Social Democrats and Communists.[16] The first transport of 151 prominent public figures from the pre-1938 era left Vienna for Dachau concentration camp (KZ) on April 1.[17] On August 22, 1938, the Stapo-Leitstelle in Vienna held in custody 2,732 prisoners — 2,044 of them Jewish. Of this total, 663 (353 non-Jewish) were held in Viennese jails, 2,040 (313 non-Jewish) in Dachau KZ, 9 in Lichtenburg KZ, and 20 in the Stapo Branch at Wiener Neustadt.[18]

Immediately after the takeover, the Nazis dissolved all existing political and public associations. Opposition newspapers ceased publication, and those remaining became fervent supporters of the regime. Labor unions were reduced to one single organization, the German Labor Front (DAF), with no rights to bargain or strike. Purges swept out all anti-Nazis from public posts. The NSDAP assumed full control of public life. The takeover and the war brought the constitution of new courts as the National Socialist's major judicial weapons against its adversaries. On June 20, 1938, the provisions on high and state treason of the Reich Criminal Code went into effect, making political protest a severely punishable crime. With the outbreak of the war, the regime broadened the scope of the law and issued new decrees that imposed severe sentences on new criminal offenses, ranging from convictions for listening to foreign broadcasts and assisting war prisoners to undermining the morale of the armed forces, punishable by a mandatory death sentence.[19] To investigate and try political offenses, a system of special tribunals, supplementary to the regular Provincial Courts (LG), was introduced.[20]

Certain restrictions were imposed on the Gestapo operations. The Gestapo was required to hand a prisoner over for trial unless special permission for direct transfer to concentration camp was obtained from Berlin. Generally, the security organs attempted to separate the guilty from the innocent and to determine degrees of guilt. But techniques of interrogation included confinement in overcrowded or single cells, cross-examination, and evocation of fear for the fate of relatives. Severe interrogation involving the systematic use of physical violence was applied in serious cases. Initially, the Berlin headquarters had to approve it. In sessions often lasting all night, political suspects were trampled and stamped on and badly beaten with belts, rubber hoses, or sticks. In some cases, where the police were given a carte blanche to commit any excess they wanted, prisoners were mutilated, beaten to death, or hung for hours with their hands tied behind their backs. This brutal treatment usually took place in concentration camps *(Mauthausen)*.

Another often-used technique of interrogation was psychical pressure, during which a specialist subjected a prisoner to a lengthy interrogation. When the defendant denied involvement, the interrogator gave him or her a fairly accurate general answer that falsely implied that the Gestapo was thoroughly familiar with the facts and that there really was no need to undergo interrogation because the Gestapo had already learned everything. In many cases the Gestapo informer in their ranks had already revealed the names and activities of the suspects.[21]

The severe repression also included detention in the concentration camps. The Berlin headquarters of the Security Police (since September 1939, the Reichssicherheitshauptamt, RSHA) exercised the arbitrary authority to take summary actions against enemies of the regime by deporting them without formal accusation. With this special ruling, involving possible torture and indiscriminate executions (the so-called Special treatment, *Sonderbehandlung),* the arbitrary power of the security organs reached its height. As in other occupied countries, where tens of thousands of victims also underwent systematic torture under grim KZ conditions, the gruesome treatment of inmates had become institutionalized in a reign of terror against adversaries on both the left and right.[22]

NOTES

    1. According to the 1934 census, which also listed 48,251 Czechs, 3,615 Slovaks, 42,354 Croats, 31,703 Slovenes, and 18,076 Magyars. Vienna had 1,874,130 inhabitants. The 1910 census listed 28.6 million people, out of the total of 52 million, in the Austrian half of the Empire. Bundesamt für Statistik, *Statistisches Handbuch für den Bundesstaat Österreich* (Vienna, 1937) 17:7; Kurt W. Rothschild in Wilhelm Weber, ed., *Österreichs Wirtschaftsstruktur gestern-heute-morgen* (Berlin, 1961) 1:52-54, 262.

    2. Norbert Schausberger, *Der Griff nach Österreich. Der Anschluss* (Vienna, 1978), p. 468. See also Walter Goldinger, *Die Geschichte der Republik Österreich* (Vienna, 1962) p. 120.

    3. U.S., Department of State, *Documents on German Foreign Policy 1918-1945. From the Archives of the German Foreign Ministry,* Series D, I, 562-63.

    4. Ibid., pp. 591-95.

    5. See Radomír Luža, *Austro-German Relations in the Anschluss Era* (Princeton, 1975) pp. 42 ff. The Austrian Anschluss movement favored the preservation of the Austrian identity within the Reich.

    6. According to Henri Michel, the term "Resistance" was first used by General Charles de Gaulle in his broadcast from London on June 19, 1940. Michel, *European Resistance Movements 1939-1945. First International Conference on the History of the Resistance Movements Held at Liège-Bruxelles-Breendonk 14-17 September 1958* (Oxford, 1960), p. 1.

    7. For heuristic purposes, other students of Resistance formulated their own working definitions. See Christoph Klessman and Falk Pingel, eds., *Gegner des Nationalsozialismus.*

Wissenschaftler und Widerstandskämpfer auf der Suche nach historischer Wirklichkeit (Frankfurt a.M., 1980), passim; Martin Broszat, "Resistenz und Widerstand. Eine Zwischenbilanz der Forschungsprojekts," in *Bayern in der NS-Zeit*. Martin Broszat, et al. eds. (Munich, 1977-81) Vol. 4, *Herrschaft und Gesellschaft im Konflikt*, 1981, passim; Regine Büchel, *Der Deutsche Widerstand im Spiegel von Fachliteratur und Publizistik seit 1945* (Munich, 1975), pp. 50 ff.; Kuno Bludau, *Gestapo-geheim. Widerstand und Verfolgung in Duisburg 1933-1945* (Bonn-Bad Godesberg, 1973), pp. xvi-xviii; Hans-Josef Steinberg, *Widerstand und Verfolgung in Essen 1933-1945* (Hannover, 1969), pp. 15-16; Kurt Klotzbach, *Gegen den Nationalsozialismus. Widerstand und Verfolgung in Dortmund 1930-1945. Eine historisch-politische Studie* (Hannover, 1969), pp. 14-15; Friedrich Zipfel, "Die Bedeutung der Widerstandsforschung für die allgemeine zeitgeschichtliche Forschung," in Forschungsinstitut der Friedrich-Ebert-Stiftung, "Stand und Problematik der Erforschung des Widerstandes gegen den Nationalsozialismus," mimeographed (Bad Godesberg, 1965), pp. 3-4; Günter Plum, "Der Widerstand gegen den Nationalsozialismus als Gegenstand der zeitgeschichtlichen Forschung in Deutschland," ibid., pp. 22-25; Alban Vistel, *La nuit sans ombres* (Paris, 1970), pp. 13 ff., 29; Henri Michel in *European Resistance Movements*, pp. 1-2; Peter Hoffmann, *Widerstand-Staatsstreich-Attentat. Der Kampf der Opposition gegen Hitler* (Munich, 1969), pp. 10, 37; King, "Emmanuel d'Astier," *Journal of Contemporary History* (October, 1973): 25-31, 40-41.

For the Austrian authors, see Karl Stadler, *Österreich 1938-1945 im Spiegel der NS-Akten* (Vienna-Munich), 1966, p. 12; Dokumentationsarchiv des österreichischen Widerstandes, ed., *Widerstand und Verfolgung in Wien 1934-1945. Eine Dokumentation,* 3 vols. (Wien, 1975), 1: 10-11; Inge Brauneis, "Widerstand der Frauen in Österreich gegen den Nationalsozialismus 1938-45" (Ph.D. dissertation, University of Vienna, 1974), pp. 14-21; Walter Göhring, "Der illegale Kommunistische Jugendverband Österreichs" (Ph.D. dissertation, University of Vienna, 1971), pp. 433 ff.; Alfons Stillfried, *Die österreichische Widerstandsbewegung und ihr Rückhalt im Volk. Vortrag im grossen Musikvereinssaal gehalten am 17.6. 1946* (Vienna, n.d.), p. 3; Ernst Hanisch, "Politische Prozesse vor dem Sondergericht im Reichsgau Salzburg 1933-45" (Symposion "Justiz und Zeitgeschichte," 22.-23. Oktober 1976), pp. 7-8; Gerhard Botz in Dokumentationsarchiv des österreichischen Widerstandes, ed., *Widerstand und Verfolgung in Oberösterreich 1934-1945. Eine Dokumentation,* 2 vols. (Wien, 1982), 1:351 ff.

8. Jan Tomasz Gross, *Polish Society under German Occupation. The Generalgouvernement, 1939-1944* (Princeton, 1979), pp. 256, 283.

9. NA T 77, r. 748, 981977.

10. Foot, *Resistance,* pp. 95 ff.

11. Reich Minister and Head of the Reich Chancellery Hans Lammers, April 1, 1940. NA T 71, r. 7, 399978; Lammers to Martin Bormann, March 19, 25, and Bormann to Lammers, March 26, 1942, BA, R 43II/1358 ff.

12. The German police were divided into the Regular- *(Ordnungspolizei)* and Security Police. The latter was subdivided into the Secret State Police (Gestapo) and the Criminal Police. In Austria, Franz Josef Huber directed the Gestapo at its headquarters in Vienna. Five provincial offices *(Staatspolizeistellen)* were set up in Graz (Nosske), Innsbruck, (Dr. Harster), Klagenfurt (Dr. Weimann), Linz (Batz), and Salzburg (Rux). *Ostmark-Jahrbuch 1940:* 144-46.

13. Gestapo, Staatspolizeileitstelle in Vienna, DÖW 1848. Its headquarters in Vienna had an extensive field organization that operated at the provincial and city levels. The internal structure of its political divisions and subdivisions provide a close view of the broad scope both of the police operations and of the corresponding resistance actions. For instance, the key Fourth Department consisted of Section IV, Division 1a: Marxism; IV 1b: Reaction; Legitimists; Maligning; IV 1c: Foreign Labor; IV 2a: Parachute agents; IV 2b: Sabotage; IV 2c: Counterintelligence abroad; IV 3: Counterintelligence; IV 3a: Counterintelligence North; IV 3b: Counterintelligence South; Protection of Customs Border; Border Police; IV 4: Denominations; IV 4a: Jews; 4b: Catholics; IV 4c: Religious sects; IV 5: Special Service; IV 5a: Protective Service; IV 5b: Screening of Mail; IV 5c: Press, IV 6: Files, IV 6a: Protective

arrests; IV 6b: Political screening. Wolfgang Neugebauer in Verein für Geschichte der Stadt Wien, *Wien 1938* (Vienna, 1978), pp. 126-35 describes the security apparatus in Austria.

14. "Politische Gegnerformen," SD Wien 1938, DÖW 5120.

15. The postwar estimates of over 70,000 arrests appear exaggerated. *Rot-weiss-rot-Buch. Darstellungen, Dokumente und Nachweise zur Vorgeschichte der Okkupation Österreichs* (Vienna, 1946), 1:160. See "Gestapo, Staatspolizeileitstelle Wien, Tagesrapporte," September 2, December 1, 2, 1938, BA R 58/1080-1081.

16. Walter Wisshaupt gives a few names of the imprisoned Socialists in *Wir kommen wieder! Eine Geschichte der Revolutionären Sozialisten Österreichs 1934-1938* (Vienna, 1967), pp. 223-24.

17. For the list of the prisoners sent to Dachau, see DÖW 1792.

18. "Bericht an Gestapa Berlin," August 24, 1938, DÖW 8388.

19. See Friedrich Vogl, *Österreichs Eisenbahner im Widerstand* (Vienna, 1968), pp. 45-47, 231-43; Göhring, "Der Jugendverband," pp. 410 ff.

20. The People's Court (VGH) heard the most serious cases of illegal organizational activities, including those involving high treason, in Berlin or it sent its Senate to Vienna, Graz, or Klagenfurt. From June 1938 Special Senates (BS) at the OLG Vienna and in the provincial capitals heard less serious political cases as auxiliary courts of the VGH. *Die deutsche Justiz und der Nationalsozialismus. Quellen und Darstellungen zur Zeitgeschichte.* Vol. 16/I: Hermann Weinkauff, *Die deutsche Justiz und der Nationalsozialismus. Ein Überblick,* und Albrecht Wagner, *Die Umgestaltung der Gerichtsverfassung und des Verfahrens-und Richterrechts im nationalsozialistischen Staat* (Stuttgart, 1968); Vol. 3: Walter Wagner, *Der Volksgerichtshof im nationalsozialistischen Staat* (Stuttgart, 1974), pp. 442-59; Adelheid L. Rüter-Ehlermann and C. F. Rüter, eds., *Justiz und NS-Verbrechen. Sammlung deutscher Strafurteile wegen nationalsozialistischer Tötungsverbrechen 1945-1966,* vols. 1-11 (Amsterdam, 1968-1974). Not completed.

In November 1939 Special Courts (SG) at the Provincial Courts (LG) were established that dealt with minor cases. Maria Szecsi and Karl Stadler estimate that roughly 7,500 to 8,000 political cases were heard before the BS and about 9,000 cases before the SG. *Die NS-Justiz,* pp. 20-21. See also Bruno Frei, *Der kleine Widerstand* (Vienna, 1978), p. ii.

21. Oldřich Novák et al., eds., *KSČ proti nacismu. KSČ v dokumentech nacistických bezpečnostních a zpravodajských orgánů* (Prague, 1971). There was no basic difference between the Gestapo practices in Austria or in the Protectorate of Bohemia and Moravia.

22. Vogl, *Eisenbahner,* pp. 244-45. For a description of the concentration camps in Austria, see Gisela Rabitsch, "Konzentrationslager in Österreich 1938-1945," (Ph.D. dissertation, University of Vienna, 1967); Hans Maršalek, *Die Geschichte des Konzentrationslagers Mauthausen. Dokumentation* (Vienna, 1974).

Austrian Minister of Education Fred Sinowatz declared on March 12, 1973, that "16,493 [Austrian] resistance fighters were assassinated in the concentration camps and 9,687 fellow countrymen were killed in the Gestapo jails." [Austria], Bundesministerium für Unterricht und Kunst, ed., *März 1938-35 Jahre danach* (Vienna, 1973). See also Stadler, *Österreich,* pp. 344 ff.

2

The Labor Movement in the Authoritarian State

THE REVOLUTIONARY SOCIALISTS

On February 12, 1934, the largest political party, the SPÖ, went underground, its authority dissipated in the aftermath of the fiasco of its call for the general strike. Only in Linz, in the workers' quarters of Vienna and Upper Styria, and in a few Socialist strongholds did the Party's paramilitary wing, the Republican Schutzbund (SB), take up arms against the Dollfuss regime to press vainly for the restoration of parliamentary democracy.[1] After suffering a crushing defeat, a few of the SPÖ representatives, including the Party's most prominent leader, Otto Bauer, escaped to Brno in Czechoslovakia, where they established the Foreign Bureau of the Austrian Social Democrats (Auslandsbüro österreichischer Sozialdemokraten-ALÖS). In the view of its leaders, the main task of the ALÖS was assisting the underground party at home to mount an effective challenge to the traditional power elites that the Dollfuss government represented.[2]

As the old Social Democratic leaders were no longer able to inspire the rank and file, younger leaders formed an underground Party network. A direct heir to one of the most powerful Socialist movements in Europe, the illegal party—the Revolutionary Socialists (RS)—absorbed many former SPÖ members and embraced as its aims revolutionary dictatorship and furtherance of class struggle.[3] The Party's disintegration also encouraged the formation of small clandestine groupings who steered a radical course, mostly to the left of the RS. The most important of these groups was "Funke" ("Spark"), closely associated with the illegal German Social Democratic organization "Neu Beginnen" ("A New Beginning"), which influenced the RS with its belief in the superiority of a new elite organization of trained Marxists. Eventually, however, these groups joined the RS.[4]

Initially, the fundamental organizational and ideological changes at home were carried out under the active neutrality of the ALÖS. Internal and external unity was preserved and an effective RS illegal network and underground press were developed. However, the RS was hurt by the vigorous backlash and even some desertion to the Communists of those activists who were upset by the inability of the pre-February Socialist leadership to wage an efficient battle against the Dollfuss regime. The new course of the Socialist Resistance showed all the attributes that were to characterize the RS: the de facto abandonment of the pressure for parliamentary democracy; the adaptation of its organizational structure to a long, illegal struggle; the claim to speak for the working classes; and the conviction that a working-class movement could not opt out of reality through millenarian slogans. By 1937-38 the RS, with mass penetration but fuzzy ideology, possessed a strong clandestine organization and was making inroads in schools, factories, and free professions.

The RS was joined in the underground by the powerful clandestine Socialist Free Trade Unions (FTU). After 1936 the FTU's increased hold on politics was attributable not only to the growing Nazi threat to Austria's independence or to the weakening of the political executive, but also to their new outlook stressing carefully selected adherents. In the critical pre-Anschluss days of March 1938, Federal Chancellor Schuschnigg himself gave eloquent recognition to the Socialists' stake in Austria's destiny when he asked the labor movement for support. He thus legitimized the Socialists' long-term clandestine struggle and their claim to a share of power. Showing political foresight, the RS appealed to the working masses to uphold Austrian independence. The struggle for democratic freedoms thus merged with its defense of the Republic. But in the wake of the German armed intervention, the RS simply yielded to events. Once again, as in 1934, the Socialist organization was shattered. A handful of the RS leaders escaped abroad, while a few were arrested and sent to the concentration camps.[5]

THE COMMUNISTS

The Communist Party of Austria (KPÖ), which had been formed on November 3, 1918, amid the growing unrest that accompanied the disintegration of the Austro-Hungarian Empire, had remained for years ineffective. The divided labor movement engaged in internal struggles that ended with victory for the Social Democratic Workers' Party (SPÖ) in June 1919. Having lost to a powerful opponent, the KPÖ proved unable to send a single representative to parliament up to the end of the parliamentary regime.[6] But with the dawning of the Great Depression and the rise of National Socialism, conditions became generally more favorable for the Communists.

After the KPÖ was outlawed in May 1933, it went underground. The policy-making Party bodies moved to Czechoslovakia, Prague became the seat of the KPÖ Politburo and its Central Committee. The key position within Austria was entrusted to the clandestine Party Secretariat.[7] The disastrous Socialist uprising of February 1934 took the still feeble Communists by surprise, but provided the KPÖ with a great opportunity to become leader of the labor movement. With little hesitation, the KPÖ exploited the frustration, doubt, and despair of both the Socialist masses, disoriented by the sudden disappearance of their Party, and those of the radical segments alienated by the marked discrepancy between the revolutionary words and the cautious deeds of the confused SPÖ leadership.

The balance between the two parties changed with the influx of Socialist recruits into the KPÖ. Aided by the disarray of the Social Democrats, the well-disciplined KPÖ emerged almost overnight as a political force.[8] To left-wing militants, bewildered by the collapse of the Weimar Republic and by the overthrow of Austria's parliamentary system, Communism provided an ideology and a direction. In turn, the Communists now perceived a changed situation. They believed that the reunited labor movement headed by the KPÖ could achieve unity among the working classes. Its slogan, "labor unity of action", enabled the KPÖ to appeal to the industrial centers more effectively than had been the case in the past.

The SPÖ was seriously shaken by the February fiasco. Although still by far the dominant labor force in the country, the hard-pressed Socialists had to consider the views of those working people who favored an alliance with the KPÖ in a united front.[9] Acutely conscious both of the KPÖ's ultimate objectives and of the appeal of the united front's slogan to the workers, the RS decided early in 1936 to favor a joint action program that would combine the policies of the two parties.[10] The united front, however, never materialized. Persistent Communist efforts to penetrate and subvert Socialist cadres only strengthened the Socialists' deep-seated distrust and misgivings.

Since 1918 the KPÖ and SPÖ had espoused the Greater-German program. In 1936, however, the growing threat that the National Socialist policies posed to Austrian independence, and the European balance of power persuaded the Moscow Comintern to exert pressure upon the KPÖ to abandon its Greater-German line and to endorse the principles of Austrian national identity.[11] In the early spring of 1937, in a series of articles published in the Party organ *Weg und Ziel* that staggered and confounded many Party members, a Central Committee member, Alfred Klahr, formulated the thesis of an Austrian nation. He argued the existence of a specifically Austrian character and of a unique national culture. The KPÖ could endorse only such a development toward nationhood, which evolves in the direction of general historical progress, i.e., which reflects the interests of the world democratic movement and of the international class struggle of the proletariat. From this point of view our advocacy of the continuous free development of the Austrian people and of independent national evolution is unconditionally right. The destruction of Austrian independence . . . would not merely present a blow against the Austrian people themselves. It would not only make our struggle for reintroduction of democracy more difficult. . . . [But] the success of Hitler Fascism would also endanger the independence of other peoples in Central Europe and Europe, hasten the danger of war, and, ultimately, strengthen the prestige of Hitler in Germany. . . . The Hitlerite conquest of Austria would, moreover, bring about national oppression by German Fascism. National oppression is possible even when the oppressor speaks the same language.[12]

Ernst Fischer, another Communist leader and a former Social Democrat, subscribed to the same ideas in the next issues of the journal. The new policy was again underlined at the national conference of the Union of Communist Youth of Austria (KJV) in 1937, when Party head Johann Koplenig declared the struggle for Austrian independence a "struggle for political as well as national freedom."[13] Finally, the Party Conference in Prague in August 1937 adopted this decisive alteration of the Party line.[14] But the abrupt about-face completely surprised the rank-and-file members. Consequently, the new policy encountered strong opposition within the cadres of the illegal Party. Nevertheless, although the issue remained troublesome up to the post-Anschluss period, it never seriously threatened the unity of the Party.[15]

The KPÖ's endorsing of the concept of the Austrian national identity sought to undercut the SPÖ's Greater-German proclivities. It also rendered the KPÖ respectable to traditional patriotic elements and won supporters for the embattled idea of a united front. By applying pressure on the Schuschnigg government to defend the Republic and by creating a climate of resistance, it helped mobilize the country against a National Socialist takeover.

On the eve of the Anschluss, the Party's clandestine structure was fairly strong. Within a few months of the February Uprising, membership had shot up from 3,000 to 16,000.[16] Unlike the RS, the clandestine KPÖ cadres had been attempting since 1933 to infiltrate the NSDAP and its affiliates.[17] Having thus successfully prepared, the KPÖ was able to exploit the turmoil convulsing the country in 1937-38. Yet in the final days of the Austrian Republic it fully supported the Schuschnigg government, preferring it to Nazi rule.

NOTES

1. Founded in 1923, the SB had 80,000 members in 1932. Only some 10,000 members participated in the February street fighting. Estimates of its dead varied between 196 and 270 persons. Nine members were executed. Dokumentationsarchiv des österreichischen Widerstandes, ed., *Widerstand in Wien,* 1:486-88, 504-5; Kurt Peball, *Die Kämpfe in Wien im Februar 1934* (Vienna, 1974), passim.

2. Otto Bauer, *Arbeiter Zeitung,* February 25, 1934, in Wisshaupt, *Wir kommen,* pp. 14-15.

3. For more information, see Otto Bauer, *Die illegale Partei* (Paris, 1939); Joseph Buttinger, *Am Beispiel Österreichs. Ein geschichtlicher Beitrag zur Krise der sozialistischen Bewegung* (Vienna, 1972 ed.); Wisshaupt, *Wir kommen;* Otto Leichter, *Zwischen zwei Diktaturen. Österreichs Revolutionäre Sozialisten 1934-1938* (Vienna, 1968); Charles A. Gulick, *Austria from Habsburg to Hitler,* 2 vols. (Berkeley and Los Angeles, 1948); DÖW ed., *Widerstand in Wien,* 1:15-22; Franz West, *Die Linke im Ständestaat Österreich. Revolutionäre Sozialisten und Kommunisten 1934-1938* (Vienna, 1978); Wolfgang Neugebauer, *Bauvolk der kommenden Welt. Geschichte der sozialistischen Jugendbewegung in Österreich* (Vienna, 1975), pp. 292 ff.

4. Wisshaupt, *Wir kommen,* pp. 18-19, 34, 102; Karl R. Stadler, *Opfer verlorener Zeiten. Geschichte der Schutzbund-Emigration 1934* (Vienna, 1974), pp. 33, 78; Buttinger, *Am Beispiel,* passim; Bauer, *Die illegale Partei,* passim. See Walter Schmitthenner and Hans Buchheim, eds., *Der Deutsche Widerstand gegen Hitler* (Cologne-Berlin, 1966), pp. 200-9.

5. Gestapo, "Österreichertransport nach Dachau," Wien, April 1, 1938, DÖW 1792; Wisshaupt, *Wir kommen,* pp. 223-24.

6. Julius Braunthal, *Geschichte der Internationale* (Hannover, 1963), 2:159-62; Hans Hautmann, *Die verlorene Räterepublik. Am Beispiel der Kommunistischen Partei Deutschösterreichs* (Vienna, 1971), passim; Gulick, *Austria,* 1, passim. At the 1923 election, 1,311,000 and 22,000 votes were cast for the SPÖ and KPÖ respectively. The figures for the last national election in 1930 were 1,516,913 were 1,516,913 and 10,626 votes. Braunthal, *Geschichte,* 2:339; DÖW, ed., *Widerstand Wien,* 1:213; *Rot-weiss-rot-Buch,* p. 28.

7. "Gestapo, Staatspolizeileitstelle Wien," March 30, 1938, DÖW 4111/2, 6704a.

8. Stadler, *Opfer,* pp. 69-76; Neugebauer, *Bauvolk,* pp. 308 ff; Wisshaupt, *Wir kommen,* pp. 38 ff, 56-57, 101-2, 125 ff; Arnold Reisberg, *Februar 1934. Hintergründe und Folgen* (Vienna, 1974), passim; West, *Die Linke,* passim; "Gestapo, Staatspolizeistelle Linz, Verhalten kommunistischer und marxistischer Kreise," December 30, 1940, DÖW 1449.

9. Göhring, "Der Jugendverband," p. 1; DÖW, ed., *Widerstand Wien,* 1:307-36.

10. Wisshaupt, *Wir kommen,* pp. 139-45. See also Stadler, *Opfer,* pp. 69-76; Leichter, *Zwischen zwei Diktaturen,* pp. 150, 178 ff, 268 ff; Buttinger, *Am Beispiel,* pp. 295-323; West, *Die Linke,* pp. 102 ff, 107 ff, 141-51.

11. The promoter of the new KP policy of Austrian independence, Georgi Dimitrov, the Comintern secretary, apparently forced the issue after the conclusion of the July 12, 1936 Agreement between Hitler and Schuschnigg. As late as July 11, the KPÖ Politbureau still maintained the old thesis that the "Austrian people consider themselves to be a part of the German nation with which they would merge." Karl Vogelmann, "Die Propaganda der österreichischen Emigration in der Sowjetunion für einen selbständigen österreichischen Nationalstaat (1938-1945)" (Ph.D. dissertation, University of Vienna, 1973), pp. 23-34; West, *Die Linke,* pp. 202, 249 ff.

12. Alfred Klahr, "Zur nationalen Frage in Österreich," *Weg und Ziel* 2, No. 4 (April 1937).

13. Franz Marek, "Diskussionen über die nationale Frage," in Historische Kommission beim ZK der KPÖ, ed., *Aus der Vergangenheit der KPÖ. Aufzeichnungen und Erinnerungen zur Geschichte der Partei* (Vienna, 1961), p. 26; West, *Die Linke,* pp. 254-60.

14. Johann Koplenig and Erwin Zucker-Schilling, in [KPÖ], *Die Kommunisten im Kampf*

für die Unabhängigkeit Österreichs. Sammelband (Vienna, 1955), pp. 5-7. Wolfgang Neugebauer stated that even after 1938 the KJV's organ "Der Soldatenrat" failed to display any distinct pro-Austrian tendency. (Symposion, "Anchluss 1938," March 14-15, 1978), DÖW.

15. Franz Marek, "Diskussionen," *Aus der Vergangenheit,* pp. 25-26; Franz Marek, "Im Kampf gegen den deutschen Faschismus," *Weg und Ziel* (December 1954): 868-69. See also Fritz Keller, "KPÖ und nationale Frage," *Österreichische Zeitschrift für Politikwissenschaft,* 6 (1977): 183-91.

16. Ústav marxismu-leninismu, *Komunistická Internacionála,* p. 350.

17. "Gestapo, Staatspolizeileitstelle Wien," March 21, 1938, DÖW 9414.

In the immediate wake of the Republic's collapse, the underground movement adhered to the polarized traditions embedded in Austria's political culture. The various clandestine groups acted independently and the lines remained clearly drawn between the main clandestine components, the Socialist- and Communist-oriented networks, and the traditional groups that drew membership largely from former adherents of the post-1933 regime. It was a rare case, indeed, when somebody directly entered a conspiratorial organization without having earlier participated in one of the political movements. Among the non-Marxist formations, most group members lacked experience outside their political worlds. The fragmented character of the groups themselves made for a loose structure among the traditional segments of the underground, who generally prided themselves on their own patriotic pro-Austrian views. Because the KPÖ and SPÖ had not been involved in the Dollfuss-Schuschnigg regime and had fiercely opposed National Socialism, they retained their prestige throughout the Anschluss era. The outlawing of the former in 1933 and the going underground of the latter in 1934 immunized them against attacks questioning their integrity.

Gradually the National Socialist presence became more real for the former adversaries, the Socialists and the Christian Socials, than their past confrontation. The National Socialist regime turned out to be the most effective integrating factor in Austrian politics. It compelled the conservative and Socialist resisters to close the breach between them and to end the former bitter and nearly equal division of the country between left and right. Similarly, the higher and lower echelons of the SPÖ and CSP were undergoing a transformation. Beneath the surface of the Resistance, broad agreement emerged that the fearful division and mutual isolation in which over six-and-a-half million Austrians had lived since 1918 could not continue, that it must stop when Austria should be free again.

It would be a grave distortion to treat the Resistance as unified from its inception; both the chronological framework of and the differences between the various elements must be considered. Thus Part One focuses on the non-Marxist Resistance groups, who in their initial period were often as much separated from each other as from the left-wing camp. Since each of the main formations was organizationally unique and manifested its own historical pattern of development, I describe each separately. In addition, a short chapter deals with the Roman Catholic Church because of the central role, acknowledged by the Nazi authorities, that this institution played in Austrian life.

3

The Legitimist Resistance

The abrupt collapse of Schuschnigg's authoritarian regime in March 1938 demonstrated the growing irrelevance of the Austrian right, composed of the Fatherland Front (VF), the exmilitants of the dissolved paramilitary Home Front (HS), and the Legitimist movement. Although claiming to be the official political movement of the authoritarian system, the VF remained very much peripheral. Gathering hundreds of thousands of people, whose adherence was very often compulsory, the VF served merely to frighten members of the prohibited political parties into unwilling support of the government. With nothing to back it, the VF disintegrated almost overnight when the Gestapo took many of its prominent leaders into custody.[1]

In contrast to the VF and the HS, the less numerous Legitimists had lost none of their zeal. Attempting to transcend party or political tendencies, Austrian Legitimism supported what it considered to be the Habsburg family's legitimate claim to the throne. Two of its main concerns were to identify the elements of continuity in Austrian and Central European history and the ideas and forces that had contributed to Habsburg leadership in the creation of a strong Austrian state. The Legitimists regarded the reintroduction of monarchical institutions as the best guarantee of peace and social progress. The Legitimist circles were above all concerned to gain recognition from the Western Powers for an independent Austria as the future core of a larger federation of smaller nations in the Danubian area. Hence, they rallied around the son of the late Emperor Charles, Otto Habsburg, who resided in exile in Steenockerzeel, Belgium; and their attachment to the Habsburg dynasty became more insistent as National Socialism displayed more disregard for the separate Austrian identity.[2] The Legitimists' political opportunity was of course not of their own making. The international situation created it, as did Otto Habsburg, who bravely pleaded for opposition to National Socialism and armed resistance to the occupation of the Republic in a protest published in Paris on March 15, 1938.[3]

The active core of the Legitimists was composed of the nobility, former World War I officers, and some Catholic clergy.[4] There was a good deal of ideological and personal continuity in their clandestine work. Three days after the Legitimist academic fraternity, the "Corps der Ottonen," dissolved itself in March 1938, fifty members decided to go underground.[5] Its senior (president), Willi Klein, reported the decision to Otto Habsburg, who charged the Corps with the overall direction of clandestine work in the homeland. After Klein emigrated to Paris, the newly elected senior, Hauptmann Karl Burian, formed a Legitimist Central Committee. Mg. Josef Wotypka, a pharmacist's assistant, became Burian's deputy. Rochus Kozak, an auto mechanic, was charged with organizational affairs; the teacher Julius Kretschmer with propaganda; the historian Ludwig Krausz-Wienner with ideological problems; a landowner, Dr.-Ing. Josef Krinninger, became the courier.[6]

The Central Committee was in contact with the other Legitimist organizations (the Hebra and Zemljak groups) and was amply supplied with necessary funds from abroad. It communicated with Habsburg through the former Greek Consul in Vienna, Michael Georg Koimzoglu, and Krinninger provided additional contacts via Habsburg's confidants in Switzerland and Czechoslovakia. He also met Habsburg in France on September 21, 1938. The former Ottonen member, Dr. Othmar Slavik, now living in Solothurn, Switzerland, arranged a meeting for Burian with a Polish intelligence service member in Vienna on August 27. Burian supplied the Poles with information on the German mobilization plans, but his contact man, Josef Materna, a former HS member and a former imperial officer, betrayed him to the Abwehr in Vienna. On October 13, 1938, Burian was arrested while leaving the coffeehouse where Materna had just handed him some military documents. The remaining activists were rounded up in October.[7]

Independently, in May 1938, the Legitimist writer Wilhelm von Hebra flung himself into action by grouping militants from the pre-1938 patriotic conservative organizations. The network expanded even beyond Monarchist circles and was divided into several branches. Hebra himself was in touch with both the French and British intelligence services through the former Austrian press attaché in Paris Dr. Martin Fuchs and former ambassador in London Dr. Georg Franckenstein. A few British citizens took part in the operations. An Englishman, John Lennox, traveled secretly to Vienna to assist the group and help them make necessary financial arrangements by locating persons who intended to leave for England. These emigrants were to leave their money in Austria, in exchange for the equivalent sum in British currency to be handed to them after their arrival in England.

Some cells also engaged in propaganda work. During the night of July 25, the anniversary of the assassination of Chancellor Dollfuss in 1934, the head of one of the cells, Josef Eder, a tailor, and three supporters scattered approximately 1,000 leaflets commemorating Dollfuss in the streets of Vienna.[8] During the September 1938 crisis, the Eder circuit duplicated broadsheets, written by Hebra, calling upon the railwaymen to prevent the outbreak of the war through passive resistance. The circle around a wine cellar keeper, Franz Zeller, distributed tracts signed "Östfrei" ("Austria Free!") emphasizing that "Austria is not a part of the German Reich" but a land "conquered by cunning, by lie and by force. We, the Austrians . . . differ from the other Germans. . . . We form a nation: the Austrian nation. . . . We want to win our independence."[9]

Extensive recruiting, preparation for acts of sabotage on the railroads, the establishment of liaison abroad, and propaganda activities drew the attention of the Gestapo, which successfully implanted its informants in the network. On March 21, 1939, an Englishwoman, Gabrielle Vawdrey-Church, a courier between Vienna and Fuchs in Paris and Franckenstein in London, was taken into custody.[10] On March 23, the leadership was arrested.[11] However, soon after, an organizer left England for Hungary, and from Budapest reestablished contact with the battered remnants in Austria. This line of communication with Vienna existed until the end of 1944.[12]

Pressed by the Gestapo, which apparently fed the same informers into their ranks, the Legitimists faced a struggle for survival. On November 9, 1938, the police seized the adherents of one of the more important Vienna-based Monarchist groupings, that headed by Dr. Wilhelm Zemljak.[13] Zemljak, who had contemplated cooperation between the main political tendencies, had approached former Social Democrats and suggested a formation of a politically broad "Austrian People's Front," espousing an independent democratic Austria. Motivated by strong patriotism, Zemljak drafted a People's Front program and propagated it among his sympathizers. The Front was not to be a political party, but an all-embracing new political alliance. It

> opposes brown as much as red Bolshevism; it attacks the traitor Hitler as much as the traitor Stalin; . . . it wants to preserve peace and condemns any form of imperialism. It favors a close cooperation of all European states on the basis of equality. . . . The Social Democrat should remain Social Democrat; the Legitimist, the Christian Social, the Heimwehr should remain what they were but now [united] in the struggle for a new Austria . . . one needs to establish a united people. . . . The economic program of the 'Volksfront' is Socialist. Austria can be reconstituted again only within the framework of a well organized planned economy.[14]

Another significant Monarchist organization, grouped around Johann Müller, was active in Vienna and in the other provinces.[15] As in most of the Legitimist groups, its members had usually been deeply engaged in Legitimist activities before 1938. Müller, a former head of the Arbeiterkammer (Chamber of Labor) in Graz, consulted, after his release from prison in August 1938, his Christian trade unionist friend Franz Waschnigg and they decided to form a clandestine nucleus in consultation with Otto Habsburg. Undoubtedly, the intensification of the Czechoslovak crisis in the late summer of 1938 also sharpened their resolve. In the spring of 1939, Waschnigg left Vienna to join Habsburg. He took up residence in Dijon, which became a liaison center with the Monarchist Resistance at home.[16] Müller established another link via Budapest, which he visited repeatedly to hold talks with Waschnigg and Count Geza Palffy, the Hungarian confidant of Habsburg, and with other Legitimists. Here he collected considerable funds to cover the expenses at home.[17]

To disguise his work, Müller purchased a perfume shop in Vienna at the end of November 1938. The store, with its large warehouse facilities, became the headquarters for the network. Eventually, Müller had cells of five to ten adherents at work throughout the country, all organized under provincial commands. In addition, special sections carried out various missions in the post, telegraph, and railway sectors.[18] Müller's organization was mainly concerned with transmitting situation reports and intelligence material abroad. By mid-1939, the organizers had set up a courier service via Styria and Hungary; they had also established escape routes and constructed several radio transmitters.

By 1939 other groups had become closely associated with the Müller network. In Vienna, in the spring of 1938, a handful of patriotic students emerged whose core was composed of the former members of the Monarchist student associations, the Catholic-Austrian Landsmannschaften: Dr. Erich Thanner, Alexander Auer, a law student, Geza von Mukarovski, a university student, and Dr. Friedrich Heer. During their visit to Switzerland and France, Mukarovski and Auer established contacts with Habsburg, Dr. Fuchs, and Dr. Ernst Hoor from the Austrian Exile Committee in Paris. The Paris committee advised that the home movement maintain, temporarily at least, a lower-than-usual profile because of the wave of arrests. It believed that any premature rise in activities would only unleash Nazi reprisals and thus seriously endanger the nascent network. The home leadership around Müller generally shared this prudent outlook. Adjusting rapidly to the new situation, Müller's network sought to widen contacts with outside groups, among them the Social Democratic grouping around Felix Slavik, an RS militant, trade unionist, and senior SPÖ official seeking introduction to the Christian-oriented underground. Slavik approached the network through Jakob Fried, canon at St. Stephen's Cathedral, who was also in touch with Müller.[19]

The activists of the Thanner Catholic Legitimist network met regularly at the home of Hedwig Zuleger-Prankl and Louise-Marie Mayer, a Jewish writer, who introduced her friends to various medical, theatrical, and artistic circles. Because of the grave international crisis, Thanner and Auer traveled to Brussels and Paris in June 1939 to receive fresh directives from Otto Habsburg and Waschnigg. Instructed to merge their group with Müller's network, they established contacts in July but wisely continued to work as a separate network. Soon after, Thanner left for Linz, where he integrated the local Legitimist youth groupings into the Müller movement. The new Linz organization engaged primarily in propaganda. Similarly, Thanner's network forged contacts with the military circle around Baron Gaupp and Baron Nikolaus Maasburg.[20]

Müller's achievements reinforced his claim to central leadership. His broad-based movement flourished: he gained access to a Communist group; to the Austrian Freedom Movement of Roman Scholz through Adolf Woboril, a Christian unionist; to a peasant circle in Upper Austria through Johann, the brother of Franz Waschnigg; and to a former Heimwehr grouping. However, the broad base of his movement also left it vulnerable to Gestapo informers.[21] On August 6, 1939, Josef Alge, a weaving-mill owner from Lustenau in Vorarlberg, approached Müller. Presenting himself as Waschnigg's associate who ran a courier line to Switzerland, Alge handed Müller a cipher-code to be used in written correspondence and a request from the Legitimist center in exile to prepare a detailed situation report. Müller was to forward coded reports to Waschnigg through Alge, who owned another mill in Switzerland and was thus able to move in and out of the country inconspicuously with a special border permit. In mid-October Alge went to Vienna to see Müller again and told him of funds that Count Palffy held in Budapest.

Since the late summer, the networks of Müller and Mayer-Thanner had been under Gestapo surveillance. In the wake of the attempt to assassinate Hitler in the Old Beer Hall in Munich, a wave of arrests enveloped Vienna. Among those apprehended on November 9, were Müller and his associates. Altogether, ninety-eight people were rounded up, but some were released after a short time. Meanwhile Mukarovski relayed the information about the breakup of the organization to the West, where the Allied radio and press widely publicized the news. In prison the Gestapo commissar Toifl showed Müller the original copies of the two coded letters Müller had forwarded to Alge whom, it materialized, the police had picked up earlier for currency transgressions. He had agreed to act as an agent. Using various pretensions, he had penetrated the movement in Switzerland and served as a courier to Austria.[22] When the trials took place in 1943 and 1944, no one was sentenced to death, but since Mayer was a Jew, she was transported to a concentration camp in the East.[23]

Although the widespread arrests scattered Müller's groups, some

LIBRARY
COLBY-SAWYER COLLEGE
NEW LONDON, N.H. 03257

96785

surviving sections remained active. To renew communications with countries abroad, one of the remaining members, Dr. Georg Zimmer-Lehmann, asked the Chancellor of the Swedish Consulate General in Vienna, Gösta Edeling, for help in establishing contacts with the British and United States embassies in Stockholm. In September 1941 Edeling was handed a list to be forwarded to the Allied ambassadors of twelve reliable Austrians, who included Baron Maasburg, Dr.-Ing Ludwig Strobl, a former member of the Schuschnigg cabinet, and Friedrich F. G. Kleinwaechter. The list reportedly reached the desk of British Foreign Secretary Anthony Eden.[24]

The rest of the Viennese network limped through to the spring of 1941, all the time extending communication to other circles, some of which were politically naive. The Viennese chief of the Müller organization, a former teacher, Karl Polly, founded a group called the "Austrian Workers' Party" at a meeting in a Viennese restaurant on January 29, 1940. The objective of his fertile imagination was the creation of democratic people's monarchies in Bavaria, Rhineland, Austria, Czechoslovakia, Hungary, and parts of Poland, where the native rulers would be subject to the overall authority of Emperor Otto Habsburg. Their twenty-point program placed a high priority on social justice. The social-oriented "Volksmonarchie" ("People's monarchy"), which would implement progressive social legislation, would be based on the British parliamentary system, but would expressly exclude the National Socialist and Communist parties. The relatively harmless group received propaganda material from the Hungarian Legitimists and through a police official, Franz Kirchweger, penetrated the Viennese police.[25]

Similar activism was displayed by a larger group headed by Leopold Mahr, a clerk, in Vienna in 1938-39. Its followers were mostly retired persons, among whom women predominated. Each adherent received a membership card and paid a monthly fee of RM 1. Similar donations were collected to support the families of the imprisoned Legitimists. In the main, they engaged in recruitment. The group was broken up on April 22, 1940. Eighty-three persons were indicted, but the Gestapo failed to find any clue linking Mahr and the liquidated Central Committee.[26]

For many Monarchists who refused to repress their ideas, clandestine activity was the only alternative. In 1938, Dr. Roland Kary served as intermediary between the Central Committee and the militant circle around the former Legitimist Kaisertreue Volkspartei (People's Party Faithful to the Emperor—KV) represented by Leopold Eichinger, a janitor, and Leopold Hof, a gardener. From these discussions emerged the so-called "Illegal Austrian Front Faithful to the Emperor" (IÖKF) whose unifying concern was to defend the idea of Austrian independence.[27] Most of the eighty or so activists (including many elderly housewives and maids) in the IÖKF were recruited from among the Kaisertreue Party rank and file. From May 1940 to September 1942 the IÖKF distributed in Vienna alone, in thirty-one separate actions, between 70,000 and 80,000 leaflets. On August 16, 1942, some 6,000 leaflets were strewn in the vicinity of the Prater Amusement Park and in the wooded areas of the Viennese suburbs.[28] Hof and Eichinger also published an underground bulletin. In September and November 1942, the Gestapo smashed the movement.

Far into the war, other Legitimist activists demonstrated their opposition individually or in small circles. Anticipating early in 1941 that Germany would be defeated, Eduard Schramm, an undertaker, formed an underground section at the German Red Cross that explored possible actions against the Nazis.[29] National patriotism was the dominant theme of Legitimist propaganda, and the proselytizing was often associated with a burning hatred of Germany. Thus siblings Franz (an inspector in the City of Vienna administration) and Marie Schönfeld railed at the NSDAP in their violently slanderous circulars that were mailed to the local party bosses and strewn in the streets. The Gestapo followed the action from May 1942 and caught the culprits a year later.[30]

Undoubtedly, Habsburg's followers perceived him as a living symbol of the distinctive Austrian identity. His early attempts to counter the occupation excited and molded the early Legitimist groups and helped shape the process of national identification by presenting one visible Austrian alternative. By persistently urging that alternative in their underground publications, the Legitimists undermined the façade of political uniformity that Nazi propaganda strove to create.[31] Their publications also motivated others to resist.

THE PRO-HABSBURG
CATHOLIC-CONSERVATIVE CAMP

The Legitimist appeal transcended its own ranks because the Habsburg cause provided a rallying point for the politically disenchanted. During the early phase of the war, Catholics, with or without Monarchist sympathies, participated in Legitimist networks. Hitherto at odds over commitment to the republican regime, they were both actively involved in keeping resistance alive and in giving its supporters a sense of identity and purpose. More important, both Legitimists and Catholics upheld the continuation of the Austrian state, thereby providing an integrating ideology that conferred legitimacy on a great variety of conservative clandestine groups and their programs.

When the storm over Austria broke in March 1938, the Catholic youth movement was prepared.[32] In Tyrol, Rudolf Ottyk and Franz Rainer, the leaders of the former youth associations, combined their fifty or so young companions into a fighting group, "Freedom Austria." In the early, heady days its members pledged their full support to resurrecting the Austrian state, and saw the need to mount direct actions. Each member received an assignment to assemble a circle of sympathizers. At the outset, the clandestine youth formation developed without difficulty even while disregarding the basic safety rules of conspiracy. On the anniversary of Chancellor Dollfuss's assassination, it called for an open-air assembly in the forest near Matrei. In the course of outings and excursions, oaths were taken, membership cards given, experiences shared, and common objectives discussed. Soon a small printing press was set up, and broadsheets were distributed providing information on the times of the Paris anti-Nazi broadcasts. Most of the participants were caught in October 1938 because a Gestapo agent-provocateur had penetrated the group. Those arrested were eventually released with a warning in March 1939.[33]

Another organization headed by Kreszenzia Hell, the wife of an unskilled worker, joined Franz Rainer's group after his release from detention. As time went by, Rainer and Ottyk grew more political and in March 1939 formed a new network known as the "Kampffront" ("Battle Front") in Innsbruck. They expected a war between the Reich and the Western powers and assumed that several German army units would join the invading Allied armies in an anti-Nazi uprising. Their efforts centered on preparations for the overthrow of the regime. The network reached out to Bavaria, and attempts were made to establish contact with the French authorities. In July and August 1939 the Gestapo, which had infiltrated the group, arrested over sixty followers.[34]

After this latest blow, the movement held together only through its firm belief that a favorable shift in the course of events was inevitable. Courageous individuals also maintained the cause. In June 1939, Dr. Karl Wanner, a lawyer with a staunchly patriotic First World War record, was released from prison in Klagenfurt where, as a former senior Heimatschutz (HS) official, he had been detained since the takeover. He settled in Vienna, where he reassembled former Heimwehr and Legitimist followers into a secret force. Wanner's contacts included the former Italian Vice-Consul in Vienna, Vistallo Taxis and associates of the Italian Crown Prince Umberto. As the embryo of a future organization, Wanner and his confidant Ing. Karl Karasek, a builder and onetime member of the Styrian HS, established cells in Vienna and Upper Austria.[35] The Viennese circle met weekly as an informal circle ("Stammtischrunde").[36] It anticipated a military and political collapse of the Reich and nursed ambitions that the restored Austro-Hungarian Empire, which would include South Tyrol and Southern Germany, would save Austria from complete ruin. Disseminating foreign broadcast news items and rumors became its primary propaganda activity.

In the winter of 1941-42, Wanner arranged contacts with a large Legitimist network in Klagenfurt, "the Anti-Fascist Freedom Movement of Austria" (AFÖ). Many of the AFÖ's more conservative adherents had been associated with the Home Front (HS) and had undoubtedly known Wanner as a senior HS official. Its chiefs were former member of the Carinthian Diet and Fatherland Front secretary Karl Krumpl and a Catholic priest from Klagenfurt, Dr. Anton Granig.[37] They were ready to incorporate new followers by absorbing smaller local groups with Socialist, Christian Social, and HS tendencies. The AFÖ also included a Slovene group and worked closely with its cells in Tyrol and Styria. It infiltrated the Air Force unit stationed in Klagenfurt and in July 1941 undertook a large propaganda action in that town, scribbling the signs of the hammer and scythe and the slogans "Long Live Austria!" and "Austria, Awake!" on walls. In March 1942 thousands of leaflets were distributed throughout Carinthia calling for an end to all divisions among the local population: "Carinthians! Stand up in the struggle against the messengers of Prussian imperialism! It does not matter whether you are Socialists, Catholics, or Communists. What matters is our homeland, Austria."[38] The action served to uphold popular morale and to sustain the Resistance's self-confidence.

In that same month, March 1942, the Wanner network joined the AFÖ. In Vienna and Eisenstadt, the Franciscan monks served as couriers between the two movements. A printing machine was installed in the monastery to produce clandestine publications. Eventually, the Provincial of the Franciscan Ostmark Province, Dr. Eduard Steinwender, and the rector of the Franciscan residence in Eisenstadt, Guardian DDDr. Wilhelm Pieller, were executed because they had provided financial assistance, shelter, and small arms to the AFÖ.[39] Large segments of the group were liquidated on February 8, 1943. The arrest of an AFÖ courier led to the group's collapse, and enabled the Gestapo to dismantle the network in the summer of 1943.[40] Krumpl, who served in the Army in Tunisia, was arrested, brought to Vienna, and with Granig, Steinwender, Pieller and four co-defendants sentenced to death. Executed on March 22, 1945, his last words were, "For Austria!"[41]

The chances of survival as a separate body were small for any activist group. Particularly after the arrests of Burian and Müller, the Legitimists lacked a domestic center to guide and coordinate their widely scattered units. An external center was also wanting, because after Otto Habsburg moved to the USA in 1940, his contacts with Austria were sporadic.[42] The invasion of the Soviet Union, with its manpower demands on the Wehrmacht, disrupted what remained of the illegal cadres because their members were drafted into the armed forces. Eventually, the remnants of the Legitimist constituency became virtually indistinguishable from the conservative-Catholic underground. Prince Willy Thurn und Taxis established a group ("Prinz Eugen") in Vienna after his release from the Wehrmacht in 1941. He maintained links with the representative of the Czech Resistance Zdeněk Bořek-Dohalský in Prague, and with Carl Goerdeler in the Reich. In 1944, Thurn und Taxis's friends joined the central network 05 through Baron Maasburg and Dr. Franz Sobek.[43]

In the last years of the war, the Legitimists faded back into the nonparty patriotic All-Austrian networks. A variegated movement that had coalesced around a strong leader and a compelling cause, by the winter of 1942 had neither. Nevertheless, the Legitimist tradition lingered. As late as May 1943, a cohort of seventeen Hitler Youth (HJ) members was seized in Drosendorf in Lower Austria. They had formed a clandestine circle, "Freischar Ostmark," which had called for the restoration of the Danubian Monarchy under Otto Habsburg and for the removal of the Germans from Austria.[44]

THE COMMON CAUSE

The change in Austria's status in 1938 and in the international situation in 1939 infused fresh vigor into the waning support for an Austrian monarchy. In the early Anschluss era, Legitimist opposition to the reunion with the Reich, supplemented by national pride and anti-Nazi and anti-Prussian sentiments, converted many conservatives, Christian trade unionists, and Catholics into supporters of the monarchy. The Habsburg tradition that symbolized the Greater Austrian idea became the pole for pro-Austrian and anti-German feelings.

In 1939-40 those members of the underground cognizant of the West European situation perceived that the questions of an independent Austria and of the Danubian or Central European Federation evoked the possibility of a Habsburg restoration among some influential policy-makers in France, Great Britain, and the United States.[45] In consequence, monarchical convictions within the Resistance flourished, gaining more distinction than ever before.[46] The Nazis too acknowledged this special status by tending to regard all their conservative and right-wing opponents as Monarchists.[47] Indeed, an SD report from Graz stressed that "above all, the clericals and Legitimists must be viewed today as our truly active opponents."[48] However, in the early summer of 1940 during the euphoria over the German victory on the Western front, resistance seemed almost futile. The result was a general slowdown in subversive activities.

Catholicism and Austrianism rather than monarchism served as the major link between the many groups of the traditionalist network. Anti-German, anti-Nazi, and patriotic Austrian objectives motivated the most important non-Communist movements of the early Resistance. Both Legitimists and non-Legitimists directed their energy, largely infused with deep patriotic zeal, into a common political channel. Relying on the Catholics for support, the Legitimists did not overemphasize the Habsburg restoration to the detriment of other issues.[49] In their turn, many Catholic non-Legitimist resisters, apparently eyeing the Habsburg restoration with growing acceptance, joined Legitimist networks.

Essentially, the Legitimists were low-income people, but they also numbered some wealthy and upper-class persons. All had accepted Otto Habsburg's authority. His anti-Hitler record appealed to many conservatives, and his stay in the centers of the Western powers boosted his prestige. On his side, he assiduously cultivated extensive relations with the homeland from 1938 to 1940.[50] In common with some Catholic and conservative Austrians, the Legitimists shared the apprehension that inactivity or indifference would further weaken the national will to defend Austria. In addition, they believed that the reasons for the weakness and final collapse of the small states in East Central Europe were identical. In their eyes, the renewed interest in the Habsburg Federation was the logical response to shifts in the distribution of power within Europe. Their stance certainly projected them into an Austrian-wide movement that stood out as a strong political irritant to the Nazi regime. For most Legitimists, political propaganda and intelligence-gathering constituted the only possible action.[51] More often than not, because they underestimated the competency of the security forces, the networks operated in a rather amateurish, bumbling, and indiscreet way. As a consequence, they were vulnerable to the informers that the Gestapo implanted.

Politically, Legitimism functioned on two distinct levels in the Resistance. On the organizational level, it operated under the direction of Habsburg, whose restoration supplied the movement's unifying impetus. Ideologically, it embodied, in opposition to National Socialism, the alternative of an Austrian commonwealth with which the Monarchy had historically been identified. Ultimately, however, the Legitimists, who barely survived the stunning blows that the Gestapo inflicted, were largely dismantled by 1943. The small cells that escaped elimination joined the active ranks of the Resistance in the final stage of the war. The thrust of the Red Army westward and the shift in European public opinion to the left deprived them of their former international base in the West. In the end, the Habsburg cause turned out to be not only hopeless but also a political embarrassment to its former protagonists.

NOTES

1. A good many resisters were former Fatherland Front (VF) recruits and not a few had belonged to the Heimatschutz groups. "Politische Gegnerformen," SD-Wien, 1938, DÖW 5120; "Meldungen aus dem Reich," RSHA, December 1938, NA T 175. For the VF, see Irmgard Bernthaler, *Die Vaterländische Front. Geschichte und Organisation* (Vienna, 1971); Verein für Geschichte der Stadt Wien, *Wien 1938:* 18-38.

2. For some time, the Nazi judicial authorities sought the proper criteria to justify proceedings against the Legitimists. On September 20, 1941, the Oberreichsanwalt (Reich General Attorney) indicated to the RMdJ that he intended to put the "Ostmark Legitimists" on trial on the same political charge for which more than one hundred Bavarian Monarchists were tried in January 1940. Wagner, *Der Volksgerichtshof,* pp. 442-43.

3. After the fall of the Habsburg Empire, a host of small Legitimist groups sprang up, but they enjoyed no practical significance. In 1930 Otto Habsburg charged former Austro-Hungarian ambassador Dr. Friedrich von Wiesner with the unification of the Monarchist movement in Austria. In 1931 Wiesner founded an umbrella organization, "Iron Ring," which gathered together more than twenty-five Monarchist associations and had some 30,000 registered members in 1935. Only in the Schuschnigg era did Legitimism become a political factor. Its program aspired to reestablish the Habsburg dynasty in an independent Christian-

German Austria. The monarchy would be strongly socially oriented, based on a corporatively organized national community. The Legitimists categorically rejected the union of Austria and Germany. AS, "Oberreichsanwalt beim VGH, 12J 97/40," July 29, 1940, DÖW 6914; "Meldungen aus dem Reich," RSHA, December 1938, NA, T 175; Emilio Vasari, *Dr. Otto Habsburg oder die Leidenschaft für Politik* (Vienna-Munich, 1972), pp. 113-17, 196-213.

4. "Meldungen aus dem Reich," RSHA, December 1938, NA, T 175.

5. On March 11, Otto Habsburg had requested his Paris aide, Georg Bittner, to return to Vienna to establish the first links with his followers. Interview with Otto Habsburg.

6. For Burian, see Molden, *Der Ruf*, pp. 59-61. A tailor's son, Burian became an active officer who finished World War I as First Lieutenant. He had been frequently unemployed before he joined the Austrian Army in 1936. After 1938 when the Wehrmacht took over, he was promoted to Hauptmann and attached to the Reserve-Army Inspection in Vienna. Krinninger had visited Otto Habsburg in 1928 and in July 1938. U, VGH, 8J 324/39g-5H 110/43, DÖW 4150/b/1.

7. Interview with J. Kretschmer; NA, T 84, roll 13, 39800, 39807, 40069-073. See also Julius Kretschmer in Franz Danimann, ed., *Finis Austriae. Österreich Marz 1938* (Vienna, 1978), pp. 219 ff. NA, T 84, r. 13; a report by Mg. Wotypka, May 28, 1948, DÖW 2494; report by J. Kretschmer, OM, No. 68; Stadler, *Österreich*, p. 103. Burian was executed in March 1944. The Gestapo found much incriminating material against Burian in the files of the Polish General Staff in Warsaw after the defeat of Poland. Krinninger died in the Mauthausen KZ.

8. DÖW 4131.

9. AS, VGH, 8J 475/39, April 5, 1940, DÖW 4399/1.

10. NA T 84, r. 15, 43190-91.

11. More than thirty people were seized in Vienna in March and April 1939. Hebra was executed on February 18, 1944, and Lennox was sentenced to death. The network allegedly included several hundred members. DÖW 4131, 4399/1, 4, 8389; OM, "Hebra," No. 80; Molden, *Der Ruf*, pp. 61-63. For the informer, see OM, No. 68, and *Die Presse*, September 20, 1950.

12. "Ereignisse um eine Widerstandsgruppe," DÖW 8389.

13. AS, VGH, 8J 375/40, December 17, 1940, DÖW 4292.

14. Ibid. The extensive economic program was critical of capitalism.

15. J. Müller, "Bericht," September 8, 1945, DÖW 8389; U, VGH, 8J 376/43, 8J 393/43, DÖW 3299/1; AS, VGH, 8J 376/40, March 9, 1941, DÖW 3218/1; Molden *Der Ruf*, pp. 85-90.

A member of the CSP since 1918, Müller had worked at the Christian trade union center from 1921 to 1936. His visit to Habsburg in 1935 impressed him enough to join the Habsburg cause. AS, VGH, March 9, 1941, DÖW 3218a.

16. Interview with Dr. Otto Habsburg; Vasari, *Dr. Otto Habsburg*, pp. 223-25; DÖW 3218a.

17. Working since June 1939 as a salesman, Müller was able to travel abroad. In the summer of 1939 he received, from England, RM 50,000. Interview with Dr. Thanner; DÖW 3299/1; Molden, *Der Ruf*, pp. 87-88. Palffy arranged the printing of leaflets in Hungary and their transportation to Austria. He saw Habsburg in Belgium several times. Vasari, *Dr. Habsburg*, p. 242.

18. Müller's second-in-command was Alfred Gruber, a former secretary of the Association of the Christian Members of the Austrian Armed Forces. Each of the provincial branches had its Landesleiter, such as Karl Polly for Lower Austria and Franz Gaiser for Styria. The network abroad appointed Stefan Lechner from Innsbruck for Tyrol. DÖW 3299/1, 8389.

19. Fried and Slavik had met regularly since the summer of 1939. They were seized on November 2, 1939, in connection with the downfall of the Müller group. 8J 376/40, VGH, DÖW 3218/1. Sentenced by the VGH in 1943 to two years in prison, they were released and became active again. Fried was a link to the Catholic Church. OM, No. 70, May 28, 1955. Slavik was elected Mayor of Vienna in the 1960s.

20. Maasburg emerged as a resourceful and brave resister of exceptional character who commanded great respect. Seven times arrested, once temporarily assigned to the Salzburg

Abwehrstelle, he, nevertheless, performed liaison services abroad. He set up a courier base in his Slovene hometown, Maribor, contacted the Yugoslav Royal Intelligence, and later communicated with the Tito Partisan forces. In 1938 Maasburg visisted Otto Habsburg in Belgium and Otto's brother Felix in Zürich and supplied them with situation reports and other clandestine materials. In the fall of 1938 he carried abroad reports prepared by Thanner and Mayer to be broadcast by Radio Liberty in Paris. Wolfgang Kudrnofsky, *Vom Dritten Reich zum Dritten Mann. Helmut Qualtingers Welt der vierziger Jahre* (Vienna, 1973), pp. 37-61, 113-27; Molden, *Der Ruf,* pp. 89-90.

 21. J. Müller, "Bericht," DÖW 8389.

 22. Ibid; "Bericht über die Tätigkeit der Gruppe Mayer-Thanner," OM, Mappe IX; DÖW 3299/1, 5732c; Molden, *Der Ruf,* pp. 89-91. Müller and Thanner were each sentenced to fifteen years in the penitentiary; others received lighter sentences. In general, the courts dealt openhandedly with the Legitimists. Thus, the Fifth Senate of the VGH expressly stated in November, 1943, that "one cannot attach to the illegal Legitimist organizations in the former Austrian Länder that importance which has been given to the Austrian Communist movement because in most of the cases the Legitimists formed splinter groups without any connections or with only a very loose connection with one another." U, VGH, 8J 476/39- 5H 127/43, DÖW 4131.

 23. "Bericht über die Tätigkeit der Gruppe Mayer-Thanner," OM, Mappe IX. Mayer knew what awaited her. Before she left, she smuggled a note to Thanner: "I know that death is awaiting me. Please, let everybody know that I have been proud to be able to die for Austria and that my last gasp of breath would still belong to our young Emperor. Louise-Marie."

 24. "Bericht Dr. Zimmer-Lehmann," March 17, 1949, OM, No. 4.

 25. Eleven were reportedly arrested in May 1940. In 1943 the VGH sentenced Polly and Zach to twelve years' imprisonment. Before 1938, most of the members had been active in the pro-Schuschnigg movements. U, VGH, 8J 317/41-5H 135/43, DÖW 4267/2, 5427; DÖW, ed. *Widerstand Wien,* 3:140-41.

 26. "Oberstaatsanwalt LG Wien," 8J 458/40, August 17, 1940; DÖW 4890; interview with J. Kretschmer.

 27. "Bericht über die Tätigkeit der Gruppe Mayer-Thanner," OM; Molden, *Der Ruf,* p. 62; interview with J. Kretschmer. Hof and Eichinger became leader and deputy leader, respectively, of the IÖKF. AS, VGH, 8J 70/43, September 16, 1943, DÖW 4175, 9504, 10122, 10127, 10184; "Tagesrapport Gestapo," January 12-13, 1939, NA, T 84, r. 16, 43462.

 28. The slogans read: "Hitler's Work: War, Hunger, and People's Slavery," "Out with the Hitler regime!", "Against the Brown Tyranny!", "Front and Homeland: You Are Fighting For a Fool." Hof was sentenced to death. U, 8J 70/43; 8J 75/43, VGH; 8 OJs, 111, 112/44, OLG Wien, DÖW 7558; DÖW, ed., *Widerstand Wien,* 3:144; "Tagesrapport" Gestapo, 1942, DÖW 5733/c; DÖW 4176 a,b. The underground press was largely financed out of membership fees and donations. DÖW 4175.

 29. Schramm joined the NSDAP after 1938 and was arrested in October 1941. AS, VGH, 8J 228/43, DÖW 4283; DÖW, ed., *Widerstand Wien,* 3:149.

 30. The two were executed in 1944. AS, VGH, October 13, 1943, DÖW 4282; DÖW, ed., *Widerstand Wien,* 3:125-27.

 31. Throughout the war, the clandestine press was the prime instrument of the Resistance in France, Poland, and other occupied countries. For Austria, see Herbert Exenberger, "Die illegale Presse in Österreich 1938-1945." Typewritten. (Vienna, 1979).

 32. The young people had adhered to the various post-1933 government-sponsored associations. DÖW 4144.

 33. Ibid., DÖW 4143, 4143/I, 15643.

 34. DÖW 1094, 3400, 4862, 7952, 8019; "Gedächtnissprotokoll," July 1, 1946, DÖW 1542; AS, VGH, July 29, 1940, DÖW 6914, 8036; NA, T 84, r. 14, 40775.

 35. DÖW 2062. Karasek allegedly succeeded in transmitting the production plan of the Saurer-Works to the Allies. "Tätigkeitsbericht," January 9, 1946, DÖW 8389.

36. Tagesrapport Gestapo," DÖW 5734/a; AS, VGH, June 9, 1944, DÖW 2062; U, VGH, 5H 11/44, DÖW 4858.

37. Krumpl had been detained in protective custody after the Anschluss and was released in 1941. In prison he had met Wanner.

38. At the outset, the Gestapo regarded the action as Communist-inspired. U, OLG Wien, 7 OJa 612/43, DÖW 9226; AS, VGH, January 31, 1944, DÖW 4173.

39. "Tagesrapport Gestapo," DÖW 8475, 9226.

40. Interview with Hans Leinkauf; DÖW 9226. Some of the Wanner network's cells continued their work even after Wanner's downfall. DÖW 8389.

41. Rot-weiss-rot Buch, p. 144; DÖW 8389.

42. After 1942, Habsburg communicated via Lisbon and Budapest. Interview with Otto Habsburg.

43. Interview with Prince Willy Thurn und Taxis; Molden, Der Ruf, p. 244. See below. Other clandestine formations sprang up in various regions. In 1943 Legitimists—some of them members of the NSDAP or its former supporters—headed by Wilhelm Ritter von Fritsch were arrested in Graz. They were associated with two Austrian noncommissioned officers, one of whom, Feldwebel Kurt Grabenhofer, would command the armored train used against the Tito forces in the fall of 1943. Before his arrest, Grabenhofer planned to join the Partisans. AS, 7J 72/44 VGH, May 25, 1944; U, 5H 52/44-7J 27/44, DÖW 10998.

44. "Tagesrapport Gestapo," DÖW 5734/c.

45. Helene Maimann, Politik im Wartesaal. Österreichische Exilpolitik in Gross Britannien 1938-1945 (Vienna, 1975), pp. 92-99, 171-75; Franz Goldner Die österreichische Emigration 1938 bis 1945 (Vienna-Munich, 1972), pp. 41-42, 58-60, 64-68, 87-89, 100-7; Vasari, Dr. Otto Habsburg, pp. 227-42, 256-57, 303-4; Fritz Fellner, "Die aussenpolitische und völkerrechtliche Situation Österreichs 1938. Österreichs Wiederherstellung als Kriegsziel der Alliierten," in Österreich. Die Zweite Republik, Kurt Skalnik and Erika Weinzierl, eds. (Vienna-Graz, 1972), 1:62-65.

46. The ummation report of the Vienna SD for early 1938 indicated that, "the adversary is . . . still strongly impressed and relatively quiet." This summation applied to Marxist—as much as to democratic—and right-wing opponents. "The Legitimists are still very much stupefied and have abandoned their fight as completely hopeless." DÖW 5120. In contrast, the SD December 1938 report recorded that "further developments in the course of 1938 showed that in Austria the reactionary circles and, in particular, Legitimism rather quickly recovered their self-assurance and initiated active opposition." The report bitterly complained about the clandestine intelligence activities, about the support given Habsburg by influential circles in Paris, and about his communication with Hungarian groups whose influence reached members of the Budapest cabinet. BA R 58/1094.

47. Interviews with H. Leinkauf and J. Eidlitz; see also Kudrnofsky, Vom Dritten Reich, p. 42.

48. T 84, r. 14, 40700-701. On October 15, 1939, sixty people laid flowers at Chancellor Dollfuss' burial place. Ibid., 41022.

49. The Legitimist or conservative label has always tended to be ambiguous. Professor Stadler correctly stressed that it was impossible to draw a sharp line dividing the Catholics and the Legitimists. Österreich 1938-1945, pp. 241 ff.

50. The Nazis viewed any participation in the Habsburg movement abroad as grounds for heavy punishment. Thus on June 9, 1942, the VGH sentenced to death the nephew of former Austrian Prime Minister Count Stürgkh, who had emigrated to Paris in the fall of 1938. 8J 257/41-2H 19/42, Wagner, Der Volksgerichtshof, pp. 443-44. Hitler himself was informed of the verdict.

51. The importance of the Legitimist underground might have been somewhat exaggerated in police reports. Because it included Catholics, the movement became, on the surface, more impressive than it might have been.

4

The Non-Marxist
Youth Movement

Traditionally, Austrian and German youth had been highly organized in diverse groups and movements. The differences between the movements were especially pronounced between the pro-Marxists and the less politically conscious. In general, the labor movement tended to exercise close control, to limit the independence of its youth sections, and to deny any special political role to its youth. On the other end of the political spectrum, religious and bündisch (fraternal youth group) affiliations satisfied the organizational needs of the middle-class young.[1] Although the Catholic and bündisch organizations barred party politics, the anti-Socialist attitude of the Austrian Church and the principles of the bündisch youth obviously considerably compromised the professed nonpartisanship. Lack of ideology and abstention from party engagement made these youths' involvement in the Resistance more direct and immediate than that of the working-class youths, who had usually enlisted in a labor youth organization before they were recruited for the Resistance.[2]

Following the defeat in 1918, many predominantly middle-class young people gathered in closely bound groups (Bünde). Lacking any clearly delineated doctrine or program, these groups vaguely perceived their purpose as the preservation of existing moral principles. They promoted a spirit of close comradeship through regulations that required abstaining from alcohol and tabacco and the wearing of distinctive costumes, and through social activities such as hiking and folk-singing. After the Nazi takeover, the bündisch youth militants became largely irrelevant. The HJ became the sole youth movement. Systematically and methodically, the National Socialist regime destroyed the bündisch heritage of the German and Austrian youth. Those groups that survived in Nazi Austria pondered that national community which they could best serve. But the disparate, tentative, and sporadic efforts of thinly scattered small circles of militants remained on the periphery of effective resistance. The pathetic political inadequacy of the bündisch formations and of their individual efforts were telling indictments of their lack of democratic self-consciousness. And yet in that harsh world, their innocent zeal, aflame with deep affection for their homeland and for the old simple virtues, nurtured their idealism.

Before Hitler's march into Austria, the youthful bündisch activists had confidently predicted that any Nazi aggression would not go unopposed. In the first March days of 1938 in Vienna, the student militants aroused support for armed resistance to uphold Austria's independence.[3] These students came mainly from the middle school (gymnasium) milieu and from the Schuschnigg regime youth organization (Österreichisches Jungvolk— JV) forming the core of the bündisch association the Grey Free Corps. This nucleus, led by former leaders of the bündisch youth, numbered fewer than one thousand students, mostly ranging from 10 to 18 years of age.[4] On March 11, the Viennese cell "Helmuth Wenger" mobilized and armed its members and close friends from the JV and several Catholic youth associations. Altogether about 250 armed young men, ready to fight, gathered in their alarm center and in various school buildings in Vienna. They refused to follow Schuschnigg's instructions to disperse and continued their vigil until the next day.

Amidst the public joy and exuberance of the first hours of the Anschluss, the restive groups—a fringe phenomenon, to be sure—decided to disperse but to keep their arms.[5] Their embittered leaders later acted as catalysts among segments of the opposition, creating cracks in what appeared to be overwhelming support for National Socialism by the youth of Austria. One of the Corps leaders, twenty-year-old Otto Molden, formed a clandestine Free Corps Leaders' Group and in July met in the Vorarlberg Alps with the adherents of the Innsbruck Free Corps who had just been released from prison.[6] The Tyrolian group had already engaged in various propaganda acts such as removing swastika flags from parked cars during the night and distributing leaflets in the streets of Innsbruck. It had also transmitted information on the Austrian Church to the Vatican. The youthful participants of the July meeting gathered in the City Parish Office in Innsbruck and prepared a leaflet displaying a poem that criticized the Nazi policy of abandoning South Tyrol; 4,000 copies were strewn in the streets during the night, causing alarm among the authorities.[7]

Taking a long view of the situation, a group of Free Corps gymnasium students met regularly in Vienna in the late spring for training and indoctrination with the intent of eventually becoming the cadres of the future Austrian political leadership.[8] But eventually, faced with the threat of imprisonment, most young activists abandoned clandestine activities and volunteered for the Army, where they sought shelter against the Gestapo. Because of these circumstances, the bulk of the organizational work fell to the youngest members. Their political training, activist tradition, and willingness to take risks despite numerous house searches by the police helped the core of the group to survive, and to surface in the early fall of 1940 during the bündisch youth demonstrations at the Don Cossacks concert in Vienna. After the concert, the Gestapo apprehended Fritz Molden, Otto's younger brother, and more than 100 other young people, and expelled them from the schools.[9]

After 1938 the student members of the grouping "Helmuth Wenger," headed by eighteen-year-old Johann Eidlitz, insulated themselves from the attention of the Gestapo. The military draft of Eidlitz and many of his followers in the summer of 1939 and the spring of 1940 also quelled activity. After Eidlitz was discharged from the Wehrmacht in 1941, he revitalized the conservative network as the "Austrian Fighting Association" ("Österreichischer Kampfbund"), and new organizers set up cells in Vienna.[10]

Those bündisch-oriented animators of the Catholic parochial youth associations, who in March 1938 had joined the chorus of discontent in Vienna, founded youth activist circles in several parishes soon after. The central group of Catholic youngsters was the "Frei-Jungdeutschland" ("Free Young Germany"), set up by Alfred Ellinger in April 1938.[11] Its adherents poked fun at the regime. They painted a large white crooked cross, the symbol of the Schuschnigg system, and the slogan "Long Live Austria" at one of Vienna's main squares, the Schwarzenberg Square, superinscribed the name "Dollfuss Street" over the signs of the recently constructed Vienna Forest Road (Höhenstrasse), and distributed various tracts. An informer helped the Gestapo to round up the leading members in June.[12] Nevertheless, Vienna continued as a focal point for the clandestine activities of the parochial Catholic youth organizations in 1940-41.

On December 12, 1939, a captured deserter, Leopold Buliczek, revealed during interrogation that he had belonged to the "Österreichische Bewegung" ("Austrian Movement") in Vienna. Largely made up of former Catholic Jungvolk (JV) followers, many of whom were only 15 to 18 years of age, the movement sought to regain Austrian independence. Its program contained a curious mélange of claims and assertions but failed to retain a measure of common sense. "Austria has been at all times a guardian of the Reich, of the West, of Christianity. Only through her own independence can she fulfill her mission, and serve the All-German ideas. . . . Naturally, we are enemies of Bolshevism and National Socialism, and we oppose Judaism with all its laws and elements."[13] They subordinated their strong Greater-German impulses to the need for the preservation of the Austrian state and its distinct culture and mentality. Their aspirations also revealed loyalty to the principles of the post-1933 authoritarian regime.

The thirty-member group, consisting of two circles, was differentiated both socially and culturally. The original cell around Friedrich Theiss, a law student with an authoritarian temperament, was mainly conditioned by memories of the strong Catholic tradition of the Seipel Gymnasium in Meidling and by experiences of the Schuschnigg regime. The members of the other cell were recruited by the eighteen-year-old Christian Social accountant Camillo Heger who joined the Movement in the fall of 1938.[14] Heger and his associates, who were linked with the Catholic working youth movement, advocated a more militant stance than that of Theiss' circle.[15]

The issue of full independence gave birth to other anti-Nazi activities among the young. During 1940, Otto Haan enlisted ten students in a circle to reestablish the JV, and he urged sympathizers to "fight together under one flag and one leadership against our sworn enemy, Adolf Hitler, and his Nazi band of murderers." Haan was negotiating with another cell of parish youth in October 1940 when the police rounded up the young people.[16] In another development, four eighth-grade students from the gymnasium in Vienna III headed by Josef Landgraf listened to foreign, mostly British, broadcasts, and spread their contents in leaflets and handbills.[17] Landgraf was arrested in September 1941, and with his colleague Anton Brunner sentenced to death by the VGH in August 1942.[18] When the chairman of the VGH's Senate inquired whether Landgraf held that, "Fiat pax et pereat Germania," the defendant spontaneously replied: "No, I don't hold this opinion, but I have always believed that, 'Fiat pax et pereat Hitler.' "[19] In 1943 the Gestapo liquidated another Catholic-bündisch group, "The League of Young Catholic Germans." The League, modeled on the Teutonic Knights Order, claimed to be the vanguard of a twentieth-century Counter-Reformation movement to defend Christianity.[20]

The pockets of bündisch resistance also included former adherents of the socially progressive "Neuland-Bund," a central Catholic youth federation, who before 1938 had joined the illegal HJ and promoted the Anschluss. Although the Anschluss originally evoked their approval, they soon began to regard the Nazi leadership with misgivings and distaste. Many, such as the law student Paul Flach and chaplain Johann Nebenführ, believed the Church teachings and National Socialism compatible when they first joined the Neuland and the illegal HJ. National Socialism attracted them for national, not for ideological, reasons. But soon after March 1938, the persecution of the Catholic Church turned them into opponents of the regime.

In 1940 Flach assembled a bündisch-oriented network in Innsbruck. In August 1940 in Wachau his group (Horde) merged with Nebenführ's circle in Hollabrunn, Lower Austria. Joined by other bündisch cells, they formed a "Youth Order" that followed the aims of the dissolved "Neuland-Bund." Flach distributed mimeographed letters, urging his followers and potential sympathizers to prepare for active participation in the impending cultural struggle between the Church and Nazism. Further indoctrination was carried out within small circles of gymnasium students, whose resentment at the prohibition of the parochial and other Catholic associations generated anti-Nazi feelings and Catholic fervor. Because everything associated with Nazism had become morally tainted, the circles, called "hordes," were to serve as elite schools to train the Catholic cadres for the decisive battle between National Socialism and Catholicism that would follow the Nazi victory.[21]

The observer who examines the Catholic- and Bündisch-oriented youth movements glimpses a cluster of small groups who yearned for spiritual renewal. As their members grew disillusioned with the Nazi Reich, they turned, in high expectation, toward a vision of a future Austria where Christian values would be restored. They displayed a curious proclivity for patently extravagent objectives. Because their activities were unmodified by experience, the groups did not secure tangible results. They lacked a durable political foundation and thus faded away or were easily liquidated. However, solitary militants among them reappeared in 1944-45 to take part in underground organizations of moderate and conservative coloration.

NOTES

1. For more information, see Radomir Luza, *History of the International Socialist Youth Movement* (Leyden 1970), pp. 15-56; Neugebauer, *Bauvolk*, passim; Gulick, *Austria*, 1:583-643; Werner Helwig, *Die blaue Blume des Wandervögels. Vom Aufstieg, Glanz und Sinn einer Jugendbewegung* (Gütersloh, 1960); Walter Z. Laqueur, *Young Germany; A History of the German Youth Movement* (New York, 1962); Gestapo, Wien, Report to the "Oberstaatsanwalt beim LG Wien, April 9, 1943" DÖW 7928/a.

2. The writer bases this observation on the data which he possesses on many hundreds of resisters. In 1927 the German youth movement had over four million members in ninety-six organizations.

3. The Grey Free Corps was constituted in 1936. Otto Molden, *Der Ruf des Gewissens. Der österreichische Freiheitskampf 1938-1945* (Vienna-Munich, 1958), pp. 55-56; Report Otto Molden, Privatarchiv Otto Molden (OM), Institut für Zeitgeschichte, University of Vienna.

4. After the takeover in Germany in 1933 and in Austria in 1938, the National Socialists liquidated the existing youth associations.

5. "Bericht Otto Molden" and "Bericht Johannes Eidlitz," OM; Molden, *Der Ruf*, pp. 57-58; interview with Hofrat Dr. Hubert Jurasek.

6. Fritz Molden, *Fepolinski & Waschlapski auf dem berstenden Stern* (Vienna, 1976), pp. 110-12.

7. Molden, pp. 110-12.

8. DÖW 6346.

9. "Bericht Otto Molden," OM; Molden, *Der Ruf*, pp. 57-58. The Cossack songs extolling their heroes encouraged a feeling of bündisch solidarity. The Gestapo warned in its ordinance of January 3, 1938, that the concerts of the Don Cossacks and of other Russian emigré groups were being used by the bündisch youth as occasions for demonstrating their views.

10. "Bericht Johannes Eidlitz," OM; interview with J. Eidlitz; Molden, *Der Ruf*, pp. 109, 244.

11. "Staatsanwaltschaft Wien I an Oberreichsanwalt beim VGH," DÖW 11488. The report listed the names of thirty-four students and fourteen other students from another group. The

group had contacts with the circle around O. Molden and the student grouping *Stahlhelm*. Most of the activists had belonged to youth associations during the Schuschnigg regime. See Gestapo reports to the "Staatsanwaltschaft Wien I," December 1, 2, 1938; "Gestapo, Vernehmung," August 30, 1938; "Lagebericht Wien. Beschluss," May 20, 1940. DÖW 11482. The authorities tended to be lenient toward the students at this early stage.

12. The group acted under the name "Iron" ("Eisen"). Interview with A. Ellinger, H. Jurasek, and Msgr. Dr. Alfred Kostelecky; Molden, *Der Ruf*, p. 58; F. Molden, *Fepolinski*, p. 159; "AS beim LG Wien," June 10, 1939, DÖW 5138. The activists favored the establishment of a South German monarchy. "Staatsanwalt Wien, LG Wien Anklage gegen Johann Ellinger," June 10, 1939, DÖW 5138.

13. "Urteil des SG II beim LG Wien," December 17, 1941, DÖW 4381/1; "Gestapo Wien, Tagesrapport," February 8-9, 1940, NA T 84, r. 15, 42469.

14. Interview with Dr. Windisch; "Staatspolizeileitstelle Wien, Tagesrapport," July 15-17, 1939, NA, T 84, r. 15, 42997.

15. On March 11-12, 1938, they were prepared to face the National Socialists. When the Schuschnigg government, to avoid civil war, refused to distribute firearms, the militants swore allegiance to the Republic and dispersed in bitterness. Interview with Dr. Windisch.

16. "Gestapo Wien, Tagesrapport No. 9 vom 19-21. Oktober 1940," DÖW 5731; DÖW, ed., *Widerstand Wien*, 3:114-15.

17. "Abschriften aus dem Tagebuch des Pg. Egon Arthur Schmidt, Reichshauptstellenleiter." Schmidt was charged by Josef Goebbels to attend the VGH trials in Austria as political observer. His important diary covers the period between July 27, 1942, and March-April 1943. DÖW 897; DÖW, ed., *Widerstand Wien*, 2:440-43.

18. "U, VGH," 8J 521/41q-2H 98/42, DÖW 2542. Landgraf was pardoned.

19. DÖW 897, 2542.

20. A German student of theology recuperating in a military hospital in Vienna, Lieutenant Otto Fuchs, was its head. "Gestapo Wien, Tagesberichte" No. 9, October 29-31, 1943; DÖW, ed., *Widerstand Wien*, 3:117-18.

21. Flach was arrested in February and Nebenführ in March 1943; both were sentenced to 18 months in prison. According to the Gestapo reports, the group spread to Munich and Bayreuth. "Tagesrapport," DÖW 5734b; DÖW 7928/a; "Bericht Dr. Paul Flach," Innsbruck, DÖW 2000. For "Neuland-Bund," see Viktor Reimann, *Innitzer. Kardinal zwischen Hitler und Rom* (Vienna-Munich, 1967), pp. 69-73. The police encountered difficulties in dealing with the bündisch youth because of the absence of legal grounds for persecution. Eventually, its prohibition was based on Himmler's ordinance of June 20, 1939. For the text of which, see DÖW 7928/a.

5

The Traditionalists

Although many different impulses activated the Catholic or conservative underground, its conception of its leading role within the Austrian political tradition was the primary motivation. Traditionalist groups drew members from the former HS and CSP followers, hard hit by the Anschluss. The emergence and strength of the organizations were, however, largely due to the pervasive influence and exceptional quality of their founders, whose policy was to destroy the Nazi regime from without, through war or economic collapse, rather than from within. However, the Resistance chiefs saw that if they were to contribute toward the Nazi defeat they would have to present their political argument for Austrian independence.

THE THREE CHIEFS: SCHOLZ, KASTELIC, LEDERER

As the founder of probably the most important non-Communist network in the early phase of the Resistance, the Augustinian canon Roman Karl Scholz demonstrated an intuitive understanding of Austrian political realities.[1] He created, in league with his friend Dr. Viktor Reimann, the "Austrian Freedom Movement" (ÖFB) in the fall of 1938. A gifted and complex person with a strong moral message, Scholz found attractive the impulsive and aggressive lifestyle of a resister driven by a sense of personal mission and deep ideological and religious motivation.[2] Self-confident and authoritative, he displayed a mixture of sound pragmatism and recklessness. Rejecting the world of the slums, this high-minded, exalted, and snobbish cleric made it clear not only that he regarded himself as a superior man, but that he acted for an elite.

From the outset, Scholz, as the uncontested chief, emphasized recruitment, operational code, and ideological persuasion. He realized that direct action would not succeed against the effective security machinery. He disapproved of the resisters' engaging in special military training because he believed that the Wehrmacht would eventually call the men into military service. He believed that the organizational framework of political cadres was inappropriate for organizing the masses. The number of activists had to remain small because of the danger of detection. His accent was on the elitist character of the movement, composed, in theory, of groups of hundreds subdivided into subgroups of thirty and then again into cells of three men. There was also a special women's group.

To Scholz what mattered most was indoctrination, a political response to what was undoubtedly a political challenge. He was determined to promote ideas that the people would accept and that would thus enable him both to indict the Nazi regime and to inspire his followers. To this effect in schooling sessions and lectures to small circles, he used the writings of Hermann Rauschning and Thomas Mann, which he had smuggled from Switzerland.[3]

The Resistance soon became a romantic adventure. Every member took a solemn oath and pledged unconditional obedience to obey the security rules and to make all possible personal sacrifices.[4] Scholz set the membership fee at one percent of personal income. Since many followers had to report for military duty, they received a small stamp-sized identity card to be used for identification should the Allies capture them.[5]

Never comprising more than two hundred people,[6] the movement attracted a number of free-floating circles of activists driven by idealism, patriotism, or the Catholic faith. Through twenty-year-old Gerhard Fischer-Ledenice — steadfast, imperturable, prudent, down-to-earth — some twenty to thirty young men joined the ÖFB in the summer of 1939.[7] Some followers came from amongst Scholz's students who established a separate Klosterneuburg cell with the theology student Hanns George Heintschel-Heinegg as its leader. The large apartment of Heintschel-Heinegg's parents in Prinz Eugen Street soon became the contact house where Scholz and his senior aides Dr. Johann Zimmerl and Fischer-Ledenice held their evening schooling sessions. Gradually Heintschel-Heinegg took over the indoctrination. This independent young Christian showed great depth and range of thought, an outlook high and moral, and a mind penetrating and acute. Through his visits to Innsbruck, he kept a network in Tyrol afloat. His international connections reached to the Protectorate of Bohemia and Moravia, Switzerland, and France. He possessed a rare knack for collecting the funds badly needed by the organization. In contrast to most attending the schooling sessions, who found it difficult to engage in violent acts, the State Theater (Burgtheater) actor Otto Hartmann, who had joined the network toward the end of 1939, was intent on developing specially trained action units.

The blending of these various elements made the ÖFB a heterogeneous movement. Scholz, his deputy Zimmerl, Fischer-Ledenice, Heintschel-

Heinegg, Hartmann, and the leader of the women's group Luise Kanitz formed the Executive Committee, which met every week. Scholz's initial plan was to build up his organization so that he could establish contacts abroad, above all in London, to enlist support there for the Austrian cause. He had gained access to Conservative Party circles during his first visit to London in the summer of 1938. The outbreak of the war cut short his second journey, in August 1939, but his ties with England were not cut completely. He was able in the fall of 1939 and in the first weeks of 1940 to dash off, in English, seven situation reports, including lists of political prisoners, and information about the situation in the Austrian Church and the mood of the clergy.[8]

The war accelerated the buildup of his network.[9] In addition to its routine tasks of recruiting adherents, establishing contacts, and providing guidance, the ÖFB began to communicate with the public through tracts and flysheets distributed in and around Vienna.[10] In Zimmerl, who joined the ÖFB in the winter of 1939-40, the movement gained a born leader, a fighting man of integrity who was forward-looking, imaginative, and firmly committed to direct action. A convinced traditionalist with a Monarchist outlook, he attracted and held an admiring and devoted following among what was a congregation of the elite.[11] Under Zimmerl's growing influence, the ÖFB shifted markedly toward a more hard-line policy. This shift also enabled the aggressive Hartmann to insinuate himself into a position of confidence with Scholz. In addition, the daring German campaigns in Norway and France, which had increased the ÖFB's already deep sense of embattled isolation, strengthened the position of the militants around Hartmann who criticized the movement for being indecisive and inactive.

Determined to establish liaison with Allied diplomats and to get the ÖFB's cards accepted as evidence of the status of the Austrian Resistance, Scholz and Hartmann dispatched Rudolf Strasser, a Hungarian citizen, to Budapest in April 1940. Strasser approached a secretary "Dupont" at the French Legation, who eventually gave him the password "Dupont-Engerau" to facilitate further contacts with the French authorities. In the early summer, Strasser sounded out the Soviet and American representatives in Bratislava in Slovakia.[12] While his network was making steady headway, Scholz continually emphasized its political rather than military nature. He believed that the Resistance could be of inestimable value to the hard-pressed Austrians when the Reich collapsed. To consolidate moderate and conservative forces and to coordinate their activities, he contacted the two other major Viennese networks of Dr. Jakob Kastelic and Dr. Karl Lederer. He expected his movement to gain further strength from the proposed discussions.

Kastelic, though not an exciting personality, was an ambitious and friendly man who combined political acumen with a genuine, almost instinctive, yearning to serve his country. His devout Catholicism and fiery patriotism could not completely conceal the pragmatic politician who understood the nature and exercise of power.[13] In the fall of 1938 Kastelic, aided by the Social Democratic journalist Johann Schwendenwein and the writer Dr. Karl Rössel-Majdan, initiated the Great-Austrian Freedom Movement (GÖFB).[14] To gain a broader political base for his movement, he established a relationship with the associates of Albert Sever, an old Viennese Socialist official, and of Karl Seitz, a former Socialist Mayor of Vienna. Eventually the leadership included Oskar Broucard as secretary, Rudolf Schalleck, Lieutenant-Colonel (ret.) Dr. Johann Blumenthal, the link to the former Austrian officers' corps and Heimwehr circles, and finally Heinrich Hock, who was charged with propaganda.

Kastelic felt that Austria and the other successor states of the Austro-Hungarian Empire had been stagnating for the previous two decades. Expecting the ultimate defeat of Nazi Germany, he argued that it was time for the networks to work together in Austria's self-interest. His aim was to offer his cadres political and moral training, so that when the war was over and the Germans defeated, the underground would take charge of the country. In his view, a monarchy, preferably under the Habsburgs, would then unite the former territories of the Habsburg Monarchy and South Germany.[15]

In 1939-40 Blumenthal approached other former Austrian officers about the possible course of the military operations that would accompany the Nazi's final defeat at the Western front. The theme of the talks, at which other leaders participated, was the creation of a military group. Lieutenant-Colonel (ret.) Rudolf Puchinger was picked as the future commander of the City of Vienna. Early in 1940, Rössel-Majdan was enlisted for military service at the Western front, where he made contacts with some fellow officers. He devised plans to divide the German armed forces by opening a breach at the front to aid the expected French offensive. During his leave in Vienna, in April, he discussed his plan and the possible repercussions of the German collapse in Austria with Puchinger and others.[16] The network successfully expanded from its base in Vienna and Lower Austria to Upper Austria in the winter of 1940. Encouraged by Kastelic and Blumenthal, Dr. Florian Rath, a Cistercian priest at the monastery at Wilhering, directed the group in Upper Austria and assembled a body of followers in Linz and surrounding areas. The core revolved around five Cistercian priests from Wilhering.[17]

Unperturbed by the German military successes and foreseeing a lengthly conflict, Kastelic was reluctant to engage in premature direct actions. He preferred a loose underground structure, although he felt that he could dispense neither with the membership fees he charged nor the membership cards he issued — both very dangerous devices, running counter to the basic rules of conspiracy. He made preparations for collecting arms and ammunition and for securing equipment for an underground press; he also sought links with the outside. Under these circumstances scope for practical political engagement was narrow. Some of his companions, wanting to stir up Austrian sentiment by an increase in illegal publications, disagreed with Kastelic, whose activities were largely confined to planning.

Disturbed by what they considered a lack of combativeness, the students Ernst Haller, Peter Schramke, and Herbert Christian endeavored to engage GÖFB support for cooperation with the Scholz movement, which enjoyed a reputation for activism. In the spring of 1940, the students met Fischer-Ledenice and joined the ÖFB to secure cooperation between the two movements. Schramke then arranged for Günther Loch, the representative of the GÖFB, to meet Fischer-Ledenice.[18] There ensued a series of high-level talks attended by the representatives of the two networks, at which they agreed to hold regular meetings, exchange information, and plan joint operations. At this juncture, the ÖFB was about to plunge into a series of violent undertakings with whatever strength it could muster.[19] Its plans called for a wide-reaching propaganda campaign and for small diversionary operations. Strangely, the two movements seemed to be setting course for militancy at a time, the early summer of 1940, when Great Britain's situation was critical and the Reich was reaching the zenith of its power.

Although each movement was to retain its organizational structure, they had achieved definite progress toward unification. However, while opting for possible consolidation, the ÖFB and GÖFB could not ignore the existence of the third major network, Dr. Karl Lederer's "Austrian Freedom Movement" (ÖF). Possessed of an impulsive temper and somewhat blunt, Lederer, a lank, blond giant, shared the formative experiences of the conservative and Catholic members of the underground. The 1934 he had become a VF member and had joined the paramilitary OS two years leter. His work was dominated by one overriding concern—love for Austria. His ideas were Catholic and patriotic, stressing the creative possibilities of free men liberated from the restraints of class and prejudice. His generous idealism concerned itself with laying the foundations of a democratic Austria. In February 1939, he was dismissed from the *Finanzprokuratur* because of his mixed Jewish origin.[20] In the Greater-German chorus of the time, his traditionalist view, a passionate defense of the unregarded Austrian identity, was a dissonant voice. Unlike that of Kastelic or Scholz, Lederer's vision never passed beyond the Austrian frontier. He doggedly pursued his ambitions within the narrow context of Austria proper, never venturing into the international or federalist Central European arena.

As the other Resistance chiefs had done, he had early dissociated the political from the military struggle. In common with Scholz and Kastelic, he assumed that eventually the Reich would face economic collapse or military defeat. All three were convinced that at the final stage of the conflict the existence of a national, underground-controlled, mass movement would guarantee Austria's integrity. In the meantime, all believed that a period of indoctrination and propaganda should precede any attempt at direct action. Consequently, they stressed organizational and political, not military, issues. Lederer with his two principal aides, Rudolf Wallner and Dipl.-Ing. Alfred Miegl, sustained the main burden of running the clandestine press.[21] In 1939 he began to issue, at irregular intervals, a typewritten underground paper.[22] Tendentious coverage of the progress of the war and stories about Nazi corruption preempted the pages. Moreover, Lederer requested every member to spread rumors to strain the nerves of the population and to help undermine public confidence in the regime.

The search for an effective organizational structure involved the ÖF leadership in the establishment of a number of clandestine branches. Between the fall of 1939 and the winter of 1940, Lederer set up two military cells under former Austrian officers who were to train special combat teams. In 1940, with its enrollment increasing, the network emerged as a major organization, whose influence was concentrated in Vienna and whose active following numbered more than 200 people from all social groups and classes.[23]

From the outset, Lederer wanted to cooperate with other networks. In the spring of 1939 he had met Scholz, and in conversations, they had attempted to establish a basis for cooperation between or even fusion of their groups. Allegedly, the two chiefs even discussed the possible membership of a future Austrian cabinet. Apparently, however, Scholz broke off the talks. He met Lederer again in March 1940. By nature a tense and stern man to whom close collaboration came hard, Lederer possibly could not muster the tact necessary for negotiation where prestige was an issue.[24] In 1940, personal differences notwithstanding, the networks moved once more toward unity in a series of high-level talks between Lederer and Kastelic and their companions, the last of which took place in Kastelic's apartment in April.[25] In principle, the two networks agreed to merge and to downgrade the future importance of armed activities in favor of intensified political propaganda. Significantly, they gave priority to the creation of a loose organization instead of one with a central command. Similarly, the ÖFB and GÖFB arranged to close their divided ranks. In April the three networks finally agreed to coordinate their actions while keeping their organizations separate. No joint center was formed, doubtless for reasons that included both prestige and security. They also took care to avoid any large scale coup de main actions.[26]

Suddenly on Sunday, July 22, 1940, the networks were dealt a devastating blow. A wave of arrests began at the very time the ÖFB reluctantly accepted the demand of its militant section for direct action, despite the course of prudence the networks had agreed on earlier. Mainly on Hartmann's insistence, the ÖFB was about to begin a new phase of activity—but ruin followed. The Gestapo seized all the major operators and in the following weeks and months rounded up 121 civilian resisters and twenty-two former officers. They had also ascertained the identities of an additional 300 less-involved activists, but these were not arrested because of the overcrowded conditions of the prisons.[27]

The police had learned about the clandestine activity on June 17, 1940, when Hartmann approached the Gestapo and supplied it with detailed information. The police instructed Hartmann to act as an informer and agent provocateur. Promised safety, the defector voluntarily gave ample evidence on the movements and named his accomplices.[28] Hartmann's betrayal, which was attributed to his emotional instability and greed, completely wrecked two years of clandestine work.[29]

After having survived numerous German prisons, their courage and faith unmodified, the captives were tried before the VGH in Vienna between December 1943 and March 1944.[30] Fischer-Ledenice, Scholz, Heintschel-Heinegg, Zimmerl, Kühmayer, Christian, Loch, Kastelic, Lederer, Wallner, and Miegl were sentenced to death.[31] On the evening of March 2, 1944, the first day of the ÖF trial, Lederer told a companion that his case was clearly hopeless.

> Well then, tomorrow, Harry, is the last day. I will not come back to my cell because the verdict can only be the death sentence. Nevertheless, I would do the same thing for Austria again even if I had known my end before. . . Send my greetings to my mother, to all those among us who would live to see freedom . . . in a new, free Austria. And now I have to go to sleep to be fresh and hearty tomorrow. Lebe wohl![32]

On May 10, 1944, at 6:00 P.M., Lederer, Scholz, Zimmerl, Miegl, and Wallner were executed. Scholz's last words were: "For Christ and Austria!"[33] His farewell letter to his fellow priests at the monastery shows self-control:

> What I have been through was a purgatory. What is now ahead of me is not far away from hell. It would be difficult to bear it without God's mercy. . . . Thus I hope to take it all, unbroken until now. . . . I also know for what I die: for everything that is great and good and noble; and also largely for God's Word.[34]

On his way to the executioner's stand on August 2, Kastelic "voiced one single word in front of our cell . . . Lebt wohl!"[35]

OTHER MOVEMENTS

The principal targets of the purge after the takeover in 1938 were the conservative elements, especially former officials of the Schuschnigg regime. Unlike the Communists, they had no time to go underground. Nevertheless, in the fall of 1938 Dr.-Ing. Otto Kühnel managed to assemble some graduates of the Viennese Institute for World Trade (Hochschule für Welthandel) who had been forced to retire or removed from the Federal Service. Among them was the group's chief, former professor at the Institute, Dr. Karl Meithner.[36] This Catholic-oriented grouping, although small in number, assisted political prisoners and their families and established a continuing relationship with the district committee of the Communist Party in Vienna-Ottakring headed by Paul Antl and Leopold Gelany.[37] The nucleus fell, however, in 1940.[38] Another member, Max Gererstorfer, took over the network, which extended its activity to Croatia and Belgium, and made contacts with important groups around Major Alfons Stillfried in the *Auslandsbriefprüfstelle* (Office of Censorship of Foreign Letters), Dr. Hans Dorrek, Dr. Karl Gruber, and Dr. Alfred Migsch.[39] In the end, these ties laid the foundations for the unified Resistance in the latter stage of the war.

Another Home-Front-inspired organization arose in Graz even before the Anschluss. Perceiving the Nazi evil, Anselm Grand and his friends discussed the formation of a group around the Schuschnigg paramilitary *Frontmiliz* in the winter of 1937-38. After the Nazi takeover, they stored arms belonging to the *Frontmiliz* and went underground. The organization spread to other provinces, getting in touch with HS companions. Despite his close association with right-wing groups, Grand also cooperated with the Communists and Socialists and attempted in July 1938 to devise with them and the Legitimists a joint plan of action.[40] However, in August 1938, when a Communist contact-man was caught, Grand abandoned the plan.

More significant than his attempts to cooperate with the left was Grand's decision to establish contact-points in neighboring Yugoslavia. One of the original members, Dr. Fritz Holl, assisted by a wide circle of Yugoslav relatives and friends, settled in Yugoslavia, where he quickly made the necessary arrangements, supported by the tacit agreement of the Yugoslav authorities.[41] At Zagreb, the group also had constant contact with the intelligence officers at the French Consulate. However, on September 28, 1938, Grand and a few associates were detained and sent to Dachau KZ. Unaware of the nature of their illegal activities, the Gestapo eventually released them. When the Yugoslavs detained Holl for his anti-German activities at the beginning of 1939, the Graz journalist Dr. Wolfgang Mayer-Gutenau took over the Zagreb connection. In the meantime, the Styrian circuit distributed tracts and participated in other diversive activities, such as spreading nails on roads. These developments increased the concern of Nazi security organs, who then planted an informer, Mayer-Gutenau's former fiancée Maria. She offered to transmit important documents to her former fiancé. Although warned by his French contacts of the possibility of betrayal, Mayer-Gutenau went to the border meeting place, where the German police who awaited him opened fire, wounding him and killing his two companions. The Gestapo then destroyed the network.[42]

The small core of Schuschnigg faithful followers ardently proclaimed their allegiance to Austrian independence. In Salzburg between May and August 27, 1940, former Jungvolk (JV) district secretary Johann Graber published seventeen issues of a clandestine tract, "Hör zu! Kampfblatt der Heimatfront." A corporal in the Wehrmacht, Graber produced the pamphlet in his office at the headquarters of the Deputy General Command of the XVIII Army District in Salzburg. Lieutenant Otto Horst, a former RS militant, helped him.[43] Graber in turn asked his companions from the JV and former Catholic associations for financial help and for assistance in distributing the tracts.[44] It was not difficult to trace the culprit, as Graber directed his appeal to former Schuschnigg officials.[45] In August and September 1940 the remaining members of the Salzburg group were caught.[46]

THE EARLY PHASE

If many had entered the Resistance still naïve, they emerged tempered by their experiences, yet neither shattered nor cynical.[47] Essentially, the non-Marxist groups were no more than a diverse and diffuse collection of men and women sharing various patriotic, mostly traditionalist, feelings. They hailed from a wide range of political persuasions, from right-wing Catholics to former Social Democrats. But their goals remained largely restricted to the homeland, where they became the vocal champions of liberal principles, without possessing, however, much understanding of the structural implications of social and economic reforms. For many of them, the Austrian idea was an ideological and moral concept, and their democratic demands were little more than a vague extension of their patriotism. Nevertheless, their demands for Austria's independence and for democratic pluralism allowed them to develop a coherent political line.

As the belief central to the Resistance, the Austrian idea helped make the Resistance politically exclusive. Yet the traditionalist motivation was truly mixed. Along with their anti-German sentiments went their awareness of the depreciation of human dignity within the Nazi regime, where vituperative contempt for Austrian traditions, racism, and violence were the political and moral criteria. These ideological and psychological factors seemed to play a larger role in the cultivation of patriotism than did the frustrated social ambitions and economic hardships generated by the Nazi takeover. A deep insecurity and a gnawing sense of the transitory character of the present conditions may also have led the activists to transfer patriotic legitimacy to the Resistance and to turn to it for political guidance. They thus spurned a situation that constantly reminded them of their lost prestige and status, and turned to the clandestine organizations that met their demand for reassurance.

The traditionalists never developed a proper organizational structure for common action. Surrounded by the Greater-German enthusiasm of the majority of the population, and lacking the popular support that the Czech, Polish, and Yugoslav movements drew on, they could undertake few effective actions. The general weakness of the inexperienced, overly confident Austrian underground was mirrored in the conspiracy's amateurish disregard for security and confidentiality and was compounded by the decisiveness of the formidable Nazi security organs that continually penetrated its ranks. As in the other occupied countries during the early phase of the war, the first resisters grossly underestimated the Gestapo and SD skills. Enthusiasm, optimism, and idealism could never combat professional competence and adequate planning. Surprised by the Nazi military successes of 1940 and almost crippled by the military draft and the wave of arrests in 1939 and 1940, the networks squandered their energies in building clandestine organizations that achieved few tangible results—beyond spreading the news from foreign broadcasts through whispering campaigns and tracts, providing information, recruiting, establishing contacts, and voicing protests. Although from a variety of backgrounds, the early activists lacked political experience and conspiratorial skill. In the past, some had opposed the democratic Republic and had aligned themselves with the Schuschnigg regime. A few who had defended the freedom of the individual could be termed liberal democrats. However, most seemed to alter their political behavior once they joined the underground. They usually abandoned their earlier rigidity and adopted a broader political outlook as more appropriate to the new conditions.

Preoccupied as the resisters were with the German presence and with their own function as the conscience of the Austrian people, they hardly noted that their highly regarded Austrian humanitarian traditions found no active support among the populace. But they knew that without at least silent and passive popular support and without a favorable international situation, they could never act effectively.[48] In the precarious conditions of the first two war years, had the Resistance networks even formed a broad well-organized coalition, they could not have been successful. With only personal affinities and shared moral values on which to build, the initial non-Marxist underground structures consisted of a variety of cells of friends and acquaintances and of table societies inexperienced in conspiratorial tactics. More important, the Resistance's poor public impact had less to do with its own inadequacies than with the regime's chain of diplomatic and military successes and with its policy of full employment. Popular espousal of Nazi hegemonic expansion in Europe also weakened the Resistance's appeal. Consequently, the non-Communist underground was easily crushed in 1940, before it had time to mature.

NOTES

1. U, VGH, February 23, 1944, DÖW 3399; AS, VGH, 8J 95/41g, DÖW 4145; Molden, *Der Ruf,* pp. 70-84.

2. Interviews with Hans Christian, Dr. Herbert Crammer, Alois Hradil, Dr. Viktor Reimann, Dr. Peter Schramke.

Born in northern Moravia, Scholz grew up in a fervent Greater-German atmosphere. He entered the Klosterneuburg monastery as a novice in 1930 and became a professor there in 1939. He joined an illegal Nazi cell in 1934. Initially committed to the All-German tradition, he decided in 1938 to call his network "German Freedom Movement," and seek the union of Austria and Bavaria. Embittered both by the outbreak of the war in September 1939 and by what he viewed as the Germans' unjust treatment of the Austrians, Scholz restricted the aims of the movement to Austria proper and selected a new name, the "Austrian Freedom Movement." DÖW 3399; Christine Klusacek, *Die österreichische Freiheitsbewegung. Gruppe Roman Karl Scholz* (Vienna, 1968), pp. 12, 53.

3. DÖW 3399, 4145. Scholz also stressed the discussion of Hitler's *Mein Kampf* and Alfred Rosenberg's, *Mythos des 20. Jahrhunderts.*

4. DÖW 4145.

5. The English text read: "The bearer of this certificate is a member of the 'Österreichische Freiheitsbewegung' (Austrian Resistance Movement). He is recommended to the Allied authorities for special treatment and use. Vienna 1940." Signed "The President of the Executive Committee." Molden, *Der Ruf,* p. 72; Klusacek, *Die Freiheitsbewegung,* p. 13.

6. Rudolf Strasser, December 6, 1950, OM, No. 47. Molden calculated the membership at about 400 people, *Der Ruf,* p. 73. The Gestapo estimated over one hundred. DÖW 3399.

7. Dr. Rüdiger von Engerth, OM, No. 30; R. Strasser, OM, No. 47.

8. Ibid.

9. A few cells performed some acts of violence, inflicting slight damages to mail boxes and public telephone booths. R. Strasser, OM, No. 47.

10. For the text of the slogans, see DÖW 414 b, e; 4145.

11. DÖW 3399; Dr. R. Engerth, OM, No. 30.

12. R. Strasser, OM, No. 47; DÖW 4145.

13. O. Molden stated that many people viewed Kastelic, a friend of Schuschnigg, as "the most important political brain of the Austrian Resistance in its first phase," *Der Ruf,* p. 77. See also DÖW 399.

14. On the night of July 27, 1939, Dr. Rössel-Majdan damaged the memorial to the Nazi participants of the July 1934 Putsch. "Tagesrapport Gestapo Wien," DÖW 5732 a.

15. The final Gestapo report, DÖW 3043 b; Dr. Rössell-Majdan, OM, No. 76; AS, May 15, 1944, GSAW, O Js 276/44, DÖW 6824; AS, May 15, 1944, GSAW, O Js 239/44, DÖW 6776; U, OLG, 80 Js 238/44, DÖW 1557; 6776.

16. Dr. Rössel-Majdan, OM, No. 67.

17. The Gestapo liquidated the group in the late fall of 1940. AS, September 16, 1943, VGH, DÖW 4294; Harry Slapnicka, *Oberösterreich als es "Oberdonau" hiess (1938-1945)* (Linz, 1978), p. 262.

18. Loch, a journalist who had escaped from Germany to Czechoslovakia in 1934, settled in Austria in 1935 and since 1938 had lived in Vienna under the alias Dr. Wilhelm. DÖW 2142/2; AS, VGH, October 27, 1943, DÖW 2114/1; interview with Dr. P. Schramke.

19. DÖW 2142/2, 3399. Apparently there were internal disagreements within the ÖFB about Hartmann's hardline policy. Scholz himself favored restraint and tried to steer a middle course, arguing the advantages of a cadre organization and the priority of the propaganda struggle: "We have to prepare our organization for the X day, for the moment of the collapse

which is bound to come. Then we must be the first to surface in the streets." Interview with Alois Hradil.

20. Dr. E. Roeder, OM, No. 72; Dr. Rössel-Majdan, OM, No. 67; Molden, *Der Ruf,* pp. 76-77; AS, September 27, 1941, DÖW 3353; interview with Dr. Herbert Crammer; "Schlussbericht, Geheime Staatspolizei, Staatspolizeileitstelle Wien," January 30, 1941, DÖW 3043c.

21. Lederer, aided by Wallner, drew up formal bylaws for his organization and prepared the draft of its program "What We Want," DÖW 3043c. The membership fee amounted to one percent of monthly income. The oath was similar to that of the Scholz movement. Every member was assigned a number, a very unwise practice sooner or later bound to get the activists into serious trouble.

22. The tracts advised the readers to withdraw their savings from the banks and to buy objects of value, and to give as little as possible to the Nazi-organized Winter-Aid collections. In all, eighteen issues were published. Miegl fell into police hands on May 30, 1940, when he handed a copy of the pamphlet to a recruit at his workplace. DÖW 3353.

23. DÖW 3041, 3353. Almost half of this group was women.

24. DÖW 3353, 3399, 4145.

25. AS, GSAW Wien, O Js 239/44, DÖW 6776. For the last meeting, see Dr. Rössel-Majdan, OM, No. 67.

26. Ibid.; Dr. P. Schramke's report, DÖW 2142/2.

27. "Tagesrapport," Gestapo Wien, February 12-13, 1941, DÖW 5732a; "Schlussbericht, Gestapo Wien," January 30, 1941, DÖW 3043 b, c.

28. "Schlussbericht Gestapo Wien," December 17, 1940, DÖW 3043. After May 1945 Hartmann, under a cover name, joined the Innsbruck police. He was discovered and arrested in July 1946. Trial against Hartmann, DÖW 6825; Klusacek, *Die Freiheitsbewegung,* pp. 39-44; R. Engerth, OM, No. 30.

29. Ignaz Kühmayer, *Auferstehung* (Vienna, 1947), p. 75. Scholz indicated to his companion, Kühmayer, when they accidentally met in prison, that he did not believe that Hartmann had acted as an informer from the beginning. Others have shared this opinion. Klusacek, *Die Freiheitsbewegung,* p. 21.

30. While in prison, Scholz wrote his novel *Goneril,* his drama "Männer" ("Men"), set in Peru at the time of the Spanish conquest, a collection of poems, and worked on another manuscript dealing with political issues. See also DÖW 9255. Heintschel-Heinegg composed a cycle of thirty poems in prison *(Vermächtniss,* Vienna, 1947). Klusacek, *Die Freiheitsbewegung,* pp. 23-27; Molden, *Der Ruf,* pp. 80, 83.

31. Eventually, the sentences on Christian and Kühmayer were commuted to long imprisonment. Nine other defendants died in prison. In all, ninety-four men and thirty-three women from the three networks spent a total of 362 years in jail. Molden, *Der Ruf,* p. 79; DÖW 2172, 2256, 2628, 3043a-c; interview with Hans Christian.

32. Dr. E. Roeder, OM, No. 72. Even under duress, Lederer reportedly had not been made to talk. Molden, *Der Ruf,* p. 83. Similarly, Scholz and Kastelic admirably acquitted themselves during the interrogations. Klusacek, *Die Freiheitsbewegung,* p. 54.

33. Molden, *Der Ruf,* p. 81. Zimmerl's last call was: "Long Live Free Austria!" *Rot-weiss-rot-Buch,* p. 162.

34. Dated February 15, 1944. Klusacek, *Die Freiheitsbewegung,* pp. 71-72.

35. Kühmayer, *Auferstehung,* p. 155; DÖW 399. On May 10, Heintschel-Heinegg stood beside Scholz at the execution wall when a clerk announced: "Heintschel, you stay back. A cable has just arrived according to which you ought not to be executed." In effect, his parents had succeeded in staying his execution until December 5. Kühmayer, p. 165; Klusacek, *Die Freiheitsbewegung,* pp. 31-34.

36. Felix Romanik and Johann Wollinger, *Der Anteil der Akademikerschaft am österreichischen Freiheitskampf* (Vienna, n.d.), pp. 52 ff; Molden, *Der Ruf,* pp. 93-94; DÖW ed., *Widerstand Wien,* 3:111-13. The membership list included many Schuschnigg supporters.

37. DÖW, ed., *Widerstand Wien*, 2:176-77; DÖW 879. Antl was sentenced to death on September 10, 1942, and Gelany received an eight-year jail sentence in 1943.

38. DÖW, ed., *Widerstand Wien*, 3:111-13.

39. Romanik, *Der Anteil*, pp. 35, 53-55; Molden, *Der Ruf*, p. 94. Dorrek was drafted into the Wehrmacht and sent to Greece where he joined the Partisans. The British brought him to Rome, where he worked with the British Intelligence Service. His successor as head of the Viennese group, a medical student Gustav Ziegler, was executed in the spring of 1944. Drafted into the Army, Gererstorfer fell near Schwechat on April 6, 1945.

40. Interview with Anselm Grand; "Tätigkeitsbericht," DÖW 8377; Anselm Grand, "Entstehung der Widerstandsbewegung," OM, No. 28/III. See also Anselm J. Grand, *"Turm A ohne Neuigkeit," Erleben und Bekenntniss eines Österreichers* (Vienna-Leipzig, 1946), passim.

41. Grand stated that Prime Minister Milan Stojadinović, Slovenian Minister Msgr. Dr. Antun Korošec, and Archbishop of Zagreb Alojz Stepinac received Holl. OM, No. 28/III.

42. Mayer-Gutenau and two followers were sentenced to death in 1941. See also Molden, *Der Ruf*, p. 19. Holl escaped to a Croatian monastery in April 1941 but was captured in 1942 and died in a concentration camp in 1945. DÖW 8377.

43. The two were sentenced to death on December 2, 1943, VGH, 8J 97/41g-6H 171/43, DÖW 413a; AS, VGH, 8J 97/41g, September 29, 1943, DÖW 4257.

44. AS, VGH, 8J 472/40, DÖW 7350/2; U, VGH, 6H 205/43-8J 472/40, DÖW 4275.

45. In his somewhat awkward appeal, Graber sought to castigate National Socialist policies. "The leading positions in our state and economy have been occupied by Prussian Nazis as if we, the Austrians, were too stupid to be able to run our economy. . . . Dollfuss is the first great hero-victim of Austria [in her struggle] against Nazism. . . . If all our German brothers and sisters were united against our number one enemy, Nazism . . . then any repetition of the Nazi episode will be impossible forever." DÖW 7350/2.

46. Another clandestine organization run by Friedrich Leinböck-Winter in Vienna in 1941 aimed to create a South German federation including Austria, Czechoslovakia, and Hungary. It spread to Norway through the work of Austrian airmen and young Norwegians. In all, thirty-one members were tried in November 1942, and six were sentenced to death. "Feldgericht im Luftgau Norwegen," K St. L. 1031/42. DÖW 9206/a.

47. For instance, Arthur Preis, a student, succeeded in escaping from jail in Vienna on January 21, 1941. Without personal documents and shabbily clad in a self-made civilian suit, Preis boarded an express train in Vienna for Berlin and jumped off while it was crossing the Reich Protectorate of Bohemia and Moravia. He struggled through to his grandfather's small factory in Bystřice near Holešov. He joined a Partisan band of escaped English, French, and Dutch prisoners of war in the Slovakian mountains. Molden, *Der Ruf*, pp. 73-74.

48. The Nazi argument presented a dilemma for every Austrian: the preservation of Austrian independence was possible only at the cost of destroying the Reich and—in the process—laying waste the home country.

6

Jehovah's Witnesses

Among the chief sufferers from the constraints of the regime was the society called Jehovah's Witnesses, which carried out its mission through the Watchtower Bible and Tract Society in the United States and through the International Bible Students Association (Internationale Vereinigung Ernster Bibelforscher, IBV) in the Reich and Austria.[1] The Nazis outlawed the Society because as ministers of Jehovah's Kingdom, Jehovah's Witnesses owed allegiance to no government, state, or nation; they participated in no wars, honored no flag, and refused to be drafted, to bear arms, or to use the Hitler salute. They would not vote, recognize racial laws, nor take any oath to the Führer. As active Bible students and ministers, all members devoted some time to distributing literature advertising the advent of the Heavenly Kingdom and to teaching their message. In their view, Satan controlled Hitler and the National Socialists.[2]

The regime worried about the IBV for three reasons. The first was that the Society had links with western Europe and the United States. The second was the autocratic nature of the Witnesses and their fanatical hostility to National Socialism. The third was the refusal of the members to be conscripted into military service or to work in armament industries. On August 17, 1938, a new law stipulated that any refusal or abetment to refuse to do military service was punishable by death or, in less serious cases, by imprisonment.[3] The law made conviction of the Wittnesses virtually automatic, since they believed that enlistment into the armed forces was opposed to Jehovah's command, "Thou shalt not kill."[4]

Despite the ban, the strongly hierarchical, theocratically oriented movement, directed by its American president, set up a well-structured network. In Austria, the Land Servant (Landesdiener) represented the Society, which divided the country into two zones (Vienna with its surrounding areas and the rest of the country), made up of local groups headed by local servants (Ortsdiener). Special agents were responsible for smuggling the *Watchtower* magazine and other literature from Switzerland and Slovakia and for producing illegal pamphlets. Up to 1940, 14,389 books and booklets were distributed.[5]

The members met in clandestine circles to hold home Bible talks. The duplication and distribution of their literature, study of the Bible, communication of their beliefs, aggressive missionary work, and assistance to members in need naturally encouraged disloyalty to the Nazi government. In consequence, the regime regarded their acts as advocating or inciting subversion against the state and threatening its institutions. On their part, a great many Witnesses preferred to suffer imprisonment or even death rather than to renounce their faith. They were thrown into concentration camps, jailed, maimed, shot, and hanged. Of this beleaguered activist sect, which had 417 ministers in 1938,[6] 131 members died at the hands of the Nazis and twenty-five were executed,[7] a staggering figure, indeed, for a tiny association of conscientious objectors, most of humble origin, belonging to low-income groups.[8] Relatively more IBV adherents were jailed than were the members of any other organization in the Reich.[9] The Society faced problems that were much tougher than those confronting other clandestine groups. Their fierce loyalty to their exclusive Messianic mission placed the Witnesses at a distinct disadvantage because of the semi-overt nature of their actions.

After March 1938 the Land Servant August Kraft in Vienna led the IBV. After his arrest in May 1939, Ernst Bojanowski and Peter Gölles took over.[10] The international crisis of the late summer of 1939 confronted the Witnesses with a perilous choice between their faith and the law of the country. A different breed of opponent, the Witnesses displayed a quiet determination to die for their principles. For instance, in the small community of St. Martin near Pörtschach in Carinthia, twelve of a congregation of twenty-four members lost their lives and only four, mostly women, stayed in the locality throughout the war.[11]

The fight against the IBV in Austria presented the security forces with legal difficulties because, unlike in Germany, membership in the Society was not punishable and only the police, not the courts, could prosecute members.[12] Although the military courts' handling of objectors' cases was usually fair because officials generally tried to persuade the defendants to save their lives by complying with the law, Witnesses, on being released from the RKG, were often rearrested and then sent to concentration camps.[13] The first death sentences on the Witnesses were passed as early as the late fall of 1939.[14] From then on executions were common.[15] From the first quarter of 1939, the SD had reported scattered IBV activity.[16] Constant harassment and repression of IBV congregations intensified with the coming of the war.

In October 1939 the Gestapo initiated a chain of arrests in Vienna and Tulln, which spread to Krems and St. Pölten.[17] By November 19, 1939, seventeen Witnesses had been seized in the Land of Salzburg.[18] By December 11, thirty-six had been arrested. The Land leader in Graz, Josef Schön, who was responsible for distributing propaganda material, was jailed on February 6, 1940. On June 12, 1940, the RSHA ordered into protective custody all IBV members and confiscated the Society's literature. Gölles and his aides were apprehended in Vienna. The arrests and confiscations of propaganda material continued in Vienna during July; by the end of that month, thirty-five members had been jailed, four indicted, and six more let go.[19] In Tyrol, a group of thirteen who had smuggled literature, held Bible Meetings, and collected contributions, was seized in June 1940. They had been supplied with IBV literature from Switzerland through Land Servant Bojanowski and, after his arrest in 1939, from Vienna. Another group was arrested in Vorarlberg, but it had no contact with the Innsbruck congregation.[20] A seventeen-member group, seized in Upper Austria in June and August 1940, received jail sentences ranging from six months to three years, after declaring before the court that they could comply with the laws of the Reich only insofar as the laws did not oppose Jehovah's commands. In dutifully following God's command "Thou shalt not kill," the men refused to take up arms in any service and the women refused to work in armament plants.[21] Despite all persecution, the dedicated militant sect continually reminded the Gestapo of its existence. On July 12, 1941, the head of the Vienna Gestapo, SS-Oberführer Franz Josef Huber, found an IBV brochure in his private mailbox.[22]

The attacks on the Society ebbed in 1942 but continued to the end of the war because the activist sect never abandoned its proselytizing.[23] Throughout all their trials and tribulations, the members courageously upheld their beliefs.[24] Their total devotion to their prophetic faith and its unique vision enabled most Witnesses to renounce the worries, troubles, and sorrows of the "dying old world," and to accept their sentences as their freely chosen fate.[25]

NOTES

1. The sect, in which every member is a minister, was organized in New York in the 1870s. It promotes Bible teaching, and preaches a special world-wide message that the Heavenly Kingdom is approaching, but that Satan still challenges God. At an ultimate battle at Armageddon, Jehovah (God) will destroy Satan and restore paradise. Jehovah's Witnesses will alone survive the battle.

2. For more information, see Friedrich Zipfel, *Kirchenkampf in Deutschland 1933-1945. Religionsverfolgung and Selbstbehauptung der Kirchen in der nationalsozialistischen Zeit* (Berlin, 1965), pp. 174-203; Michael H. Kater, "Die Ernsten Bibelforscher im Dritten Reich," *Vierteljahrshefte für Zeitgeschichte* 17 (April 1969):181-218; Gestapo, "Schlussbericht," Innsbruck, June 26, 1940, DÖW 8024; DÖW, ed., *Widerstand Wien*, 3:161-88; John Conway, *The Nazi Persecution of the Churches 1933-1945* (London, 1968), pp. 195-99; Anthony A. Hoekema, *The Four Major Cults* (Grand Rapids, Mich.), 1963, pp. 223-371.

3. Zipfel, *Kirchenkampf*, p. 198.

4. The Witnesses were good citizens who never resorted to violence, and who accepted the civil law, paid taxes, and worked hard. Himmler expressed his high esteem for the exemplary moral qualities of the Witnesses in a letter to Ernst Kaltenbrunner, head of the RSHA, July 21, 1944. Ibid., pp. 200-201.

5. DÖW, ed., *Widerstand Wien*, 3:171; DÖW 8024.

6. Marley Cole, *Jehovah's Witnesses. The New World Society* (New York, 1955), p. 221. There were 19,268 members in Germany. From 1933 to 1945 some 10,000 German Witnesses were arrested and about 4,000 to 5,000 of them died in the concentration camps and jails; Kater, "Die Ernsten Bibelforscher," p. 180. Zipfel's figures differ: Of 6,034 members in Germany, 5,911 were jailed between 1933 and 1945, and over 2,000 of them were killed. Zipfel, *Kirchenkampf*, p. 176.

7. DÖW 1902. This is an incomplete list.

8. Kater, "Die Ernsten Bibelforscher," p. 182; Zipfel, *Kirchenkampf*, pp. 177-79.

9. Szecsi and Stadler, *Die NS-Justiz*, pp. 91-92.

10. DÖW 8024; DÖW, ed., *Widerstand Wien*, 3:164-71. Another IBV leader, Ludwig Cyranek, was sentenced to death on March 18, 1941. Ibid., pp. 170-71.

11. A report on Michael H. Kater's interview with Franz Wohlfahrt on February 11, 1967. DÖW 8825.

12. "Stimmungsbericht des SD, SS-Oberabschnitt Donau," February 14, 1940, T 84.

13. Vogl, ed., *Eisenbahner*, p. 85.

14. DÖW 8825; NA, T 84, r. 14, 41500; DÖW, ed., *Widerstand Wien*, 3:172.

15. For a few cases, see ibid., pp. 181-84.

16. SD reports 1939, NA, T 175, r. 10, 2511681 ff.

17. NA, T 84, r. 16, 43433, 43532-33, 43588, 43703, 43739, 43753, 43781. See also DÖW, ed., *Widerstand Wien*, 3:167-68.

18. "Inlandslagebericht. SD-Leitabschnitt Wien," November 19, 1939, NA, T 84, r. 14, 40756. On December 2, 1939, the SD reported increased IBV activity in the industrial areas of Upper Styria. In early December three draftees deserted to Switzerland because they refused "for religious reasons" to fight for Germany. "Meldungen aus dem Reich," RSHA, December 4, 1939, NA, T 175, r. 258, 750379.

19. "Gestapo, Staatspolizeileitstelle Wien. Tagesrapporte," October 1939-August 1940, NA, T 84, r. 15, 42107-111, 42213-14, 42224, 42257, 42272, 42291, 42355.

20. "Gestapo, Schlussbericht," Innsbruck, June 26, 1940, and "U, SG beim LG Innsbruck, KLs 46/40," August 28, 1940. There were a few arrests in Styria in 1940. DÖW 12260, 12262, 12265.

21. "U, LG Linz, 6 Vr 866/40," DÖW 9336; 14598. For more information on Upper Austria, see DÖW, ed., *Widerstand in Oberösterreich*, 2:200-210.

22. DÖW, ed., *Widerstand Wien*, 3:174-76.

23. U, VGH, October 4, 1943, DÖW 4128. On October 4, 1943, the VGH sentenced Helene Delacher from Innsbruck to death because she had handed IBV brochures to her Italian fiancé. Because of her IBV ties, Delacher had already received an eight-month jail sentence in 1940.

24. DÖW, ed., *Widerstand Wien*, 3:176 ff.

25. Another sect, Seventh-day Adventism, played a much smaller role. DÖW, ed., *Widerstand Wien*, 3:186-88. For other sects and religious communities, see DÖW, ed., *Widerstand Wien*, 3:189-93.

7

The Persecution
of the Catholic Church

Because approximately 90 percent of the population belonged to the Roman Catholic Church, the National Socialists considered it a most dangerous rival.[1] Like the Communist organization, the Catholic Church sought to guide the individual in every facet of life. Gradually the Nazi policies deeply disturbed the Austrian Church, but initially its bishops tread warily, anxious as they were to find a *modus vivendi* with the new regime and to buy religious freedom at an acceptable price. All appeared well when on March 18, 1938 the bishops issued a declaration urging the faithful to endorse the Anschluss. Their endorsement was meant as a gesture to Adolf Hitler who, in a personal audience on March 15, had led Viennese Archbishop Cardinal Theodor Innitzer to understand that he would seek an accommodation with the Church in Austria.[2] During the spring and summer of 1938, in prolonged negotiations with Reich Commissioner Josef Bürckel, the highest political authority in the country, the episcopate sought assurances from the government that it would maintain Church prerogatives and property and allow it freedom of communication.

However, the Church was soon rudely awakened. While still negotiating, the authorities carried out basic reforms separating church from state. In July they declared the Austrian Concordat void. They introduced obligatory civil marriage, expropriated or confiscated various Church properties, restricted Church influence in education, closing 1,417 Catholic schools and educational institutions, and reduced its social activities. Eventually, they dissolved over 6,000 Church associations, endowments, relief funds, and foundations, and the NSDAP took over the Catholic press.[3] Because of the continuing antichurch actions, the bishops broke off negotiations. In a letter of September 28, 1938, they listed their grievances and asked the Führer for redress.[4]

The struggle between the regime and the Church grew almost daily more bitter. The Catholic youths' large prochurch demonstration at St. Stephen's Cathedral on October 7, 1938, prompted an attack on the archiepiscopal palace by young Nazi supporters the next day.[5] As one of the most abused institutions in the country, the Church automatically became a symbol of opposition for anti-Nazis. Communicating through Bavaria, the bishops used their international connections to send clandestine reports on persecution to the Vatican. Msgr. Josef Neuhäusler, political adviser to the Archbishop of Munich, Cardinal Michael Faulhaber, and his close friend Dr. Josef Müller, a young lawyer from Munich, served as intermediaries between the Austrian hierarchy and the Vatican officials, Secretary of State Cardinal Eugenio Pacelli and his confidant Reverend Robert Leiber, S.J. The communication worked fast; information given in the afternoon to Neuhäusler by the Bishop of Innsbruck, Paulus Rusch, was turned over to Müller, who transferred it to Rome to be broadcast by Radio Vatican the next morning.[6]

Despite such activities, the Church was not swept up in political crusades to become a center of opposition to the Nazi state. It had always held and taught certain moral principles as having absolute value, understanding its mission as seeing that the faithful be taught to follow these norms. The emphasis in Catholic doctrine on belief in a God who ultimately transcends the affairs of this world was incompatible with political action. The Church, therefore, could not become engaged in open resistance against a secular power, but it could distill and spread an ideology that contradicted the basic Nazi tenets of racist fundamentalism and that menaced the stability of the system.[7] In effect, the regime could neither tolerate nor silence an institution whose arguments raised issues of ethics differing radically from its own. The bitter church-state conflict, initiated by the state's repressive measures, soon became an antagonism of principles. Despite the continuing argument, the Church had not been directly involved in politically motivated activity nor had it openly criticized the Nazi state. The Church could have coexisted with National Socialism had not the regime called for total commitment.

Against this political background, the Church emerged as the only legally existing ideological opponent. In practice, indeed, there was no overt resistance from the Church, which traditionally preached loyalty to the established authority and supported the war effort. There existed only the personal, often spontaneous, acts of resistance of some of its members acting independently. However, pastoral practice and observance of Church tenets elicited government acts of repression.

Because the simmering dispute constantly threatened to erupt into sharp confrontation, the security agencies closely watched for any transformation of the underlying religious-ideological ferment into political activity. They never failed to seize any opportunity to denounce the Church and the clergy as gravely compromising the efforts of the authorities, and to arrest, evict, transfer, fine, or expel any churchmen whom they suspected of extra-religious activity. In their turn, the bishops accused the National Socialists of repressing the Church's rights.[8] The controversy provoked the opposition of those Catholics who felt threatened or victimized because of their faith. The silent, largely passive but broad popular support of the Church during the antichurch campaign drew attention to the regime's repressive nature, undermining the consensus on which the National Socialists had built their policies. Undoubtedly, it also assured the few Catholic resisters of the moral value of their acts.[9]

In response to the constant pressure and the trimming of its social and educational activities, the Austrian Church stressed pastoral duties of its priests. The SD situation reports indicated that the regime viewed the Church as one of its most implacable adversaries, possessing considerable moral influence and power of attraction. The regime considered the Church's readiness to preach Christian humanism as a subtle subversion of Nazi values. Harsh treatment of the deeply distrusted clergy pushed aside the early theme of reconciliation, on the grounds that the Church by its very existence was undermining state authority and was offering a base for effective opposition to a sympathetic public.

Throughout the war, the security organs focused on the clergy's work among youth and on their appeal to the faithful. Minute administrative supervision of daily routine and petty interference at church services imposed increasingly narrow limits on church life. Officials sought to curb public observance of religious holidays, publication of parish newsletters, religious instruction, and attendance at the church services. Time and again they took to task and punished individual priests who had allegedly engaged in religious propaganda.[10] In January and again in August 1940, the RSHA complained that the public mood was unsatisfactory in those parts of the Ostmark where the influence of the clergy was the strongest.[11]

In the second half of 1939, the head of the "Sicherheitspolizei und der SD" Reinhard Heydrich grew particularly disturbed over the Jesuit Order's increased activity in Austria. Supported by the RMdI, he asked Reich Minister Hans Lammers, head of the Reich Chancellery, for Hitler's approval to dissolve the Jesuit Order in the Ostmark, alleging that the Order served as the driving force behind the clergy. However, the Führer prudently refused to heed the recommendation, preferring not to exacerbate still further the poor church-state relations.[12]

A favorable international situation enabled the Nazi leadership to intensify its drive against the churches. Between the takeover in 1938 and 1940, the authorities persisted in curbing and suppressing the nonreligious activities of the Church. Professor Erika Weinzierl-Fischer has stated the main design of the campaign: first, the systematic elimination of the Church from public life; second, the political and moral vilification of the clergy.[13] The new regulations and arbitrary administrative measures confined the

Church to purely religious activities.[14] The final goal was to be the liquidation of the Church at an appropriate future time because of its allegedly treasonable attitude during the war.[15]

In the wake of his victory on the Western front in 1940, and in the midst of the widespread optimism that the Reich could surmount any internal divisiveness, the Führer stressed ideological commitment in his quest for internal uniformity. He drew a sharp line between the regime and its ideological opponents. In Austria, chief among the rivalries that Hitler had in mind was the smoldering ideological, cultural, and political conflict between the regime and the Church. In January 1941, in a swift turn of events, Hitler and Martin Bormann abruptly ordered a major series of confiscations of monasteries, nunneries, and other church properties and evictions of monastic communities, in particular in the province of Salzburg (the monasteries of St. Peter and Michelbeuern), in Upper Austria (the monasteries of Hohenfurth [Vyšší Brod], Kremsmünster, Schlögl, St. Florian, Wilhering), and in Vienna (the monastery of Klosterneuburg and the convent of St. Gabriel). In Salzburg the Archiepiscopal Diocesan Teachers' Training College and the Archiepiscopal Theological Seminary were closed.[16] Ultimately the unsettling and corrosive effect of the church and state conflict disturbed the Führer when the Eastern front became one of the epicenters of the war. In the late summer of 1941, he suspended further confiscations of church property throughout the Reich.[17] An offhand attitude toward the churches then lasted until the end of the war. However, at a local level the Party occasionally bowed to the wishes of the anticlerical elements.[18]

The Church had carefully shunned all political ties. Its advocating of Gospel values contributed to its persistently strong religious influence. Catholics remained overwhelmingly devoted to their bishops, and there was no visible attrition of loyalties among veterans and active soldiers. In the latter part of the war, even NSDAP members took part in religious life. In June 1943, the SD reported that throughout Upper Austria the attendance at the Corpus Christi Day processions was much heavier than in 1942. In the provincial capital Linz, where the participation was "frightfully heavy," the participants seemed to use the occasion to show their disaffection with the Party. In the past, such disaffection had usually been well hidden under a surface show of compliance. The SD was particularly incensed over the religious inclinations of the NSDAP members, whose participation at the processions it singled out as an overt display of a decline in ideological dedication. In the countryside, the capacity of Church to mold the faithful and to engage in religious celebrations and functions remained uncontested to the great chagrin of the Party authorities.[19]

A number of priests and members of the religious orders worked in the Resistance.[20] Karl Roman Scholz, Dr. Heinrich Maier, Hanns Heintschel v.

Heinegg, the Provincial of the Franciscans, Dr. Eduard Steinwender, P. Dr. Wilhelm Pieller, and Dr. Anton Granig were executed because of their prominent roles in the underground. The Abbot of Wilhering, Dr. Bernhard Burgstaller, died in prison in 1941. The death sentence on Ignaz Kühmayer was commuted to a long prison term. Matthias Spanlang was crucified in Buchenwald KZ on June 5, 1940 because he had offered religious assistance to a fellow prisoner. Johann Gruber was tortured to death in 1943. Josef Pontiller, a Benedictine who left for Hungary in 1938, was sentenced to death on December 15, 1944, because of his letter to a Benedictine abbot in Hungary. The Tyrolian priest Otto Neururer was kept hanging by his feet until he expired on May 30, 1940, because he had offered religious instruction to non-Catholics in Buchenwald. His obituary notice announced that he had succumbed "after much suffering" and added that "his death will never be forgotten." Dr. Karl Lampert, the Provicar of the Apostolic Administration Innsbruck-Feldkirch, was jailed because of the obituary. Denounced in the prison by an informer who claimed Lampert had attempted to convert him to Catholicism, he was executed in July 1944. In 1944 the same punishment was inflicted on P. Johann Steinmayr, S.J., a member of the Flora Innsbruck group. In 1942 the Gestapo lured from Spain to France, where he was arrested, P. Jakob Grapp from Tyrol, who had vigorously condemned the regime and had left Austria in winter 1938. A parish priest from Styria, Heinrich Dalla Rosa, went to his death in January 1945 because he had voiced doubts about the final victory. A nurse, Sister Restituta (Helena Kafka), was executed in 1943 because she had distributed a few copies of two antiregime pamphlets. P. Johann Schwingshackl, S.J., from Upper Austria was executed in February 1945 because of his correspondence with a soldier arrested in Norway. August Wörndl suffered a similar fate in June 1944.[21]

A handful of fervent Catholics, dedicated to the observance of the moral code, refused to take a military oath and rejected military service on the grounds of Christian conscience. A Pallottiner from Feldkirch, P. Franz Reinisch, went knowingly to death on August 21, 1942, citing his repudiation of the Nazi government. Some other Catholic conscientious objectors also voluntarily chose death.[22]

It was not easy for churchmen, habituated to civic compliance in exchange for the preservation of their privileged position, to engage in clandestine work. Tradition militated against their using the Church as an underground forum, and they had to reconcile the contradictory loyalties that their opposition to political authority demanded. Moreover, the conspiracy demanded skills and experience that as members of the Church community they understandably lacked. Through their individual commitment, the resisters sought to promote not power for the Church, but moral obligation and human dignity. Because of these circumstances, the Nazis destroyed the community of some 8,000 priests and members of the religious orders in Austria. In all, 15 priests were executed, 724 were jailed, 110 were sent to concentration camps where 20 died, 208 were evicted or expelled from the country, and more than 1,500 were forbidden to teach or preach.[23]

There were, to be sure, exceptions. Fear, natural indolence, and an instinct for self-preservation in the harsh realities of war life tended to erode moral standards; ethical impulses were often submerged in the daily routine of administration tasks. But in times of stress, the deepened solidarity of the Catholic community around the clergy provided the social basis for the continued vitality of the Church. The war heightened emotional needs, and many believers drew from the Church a strong sense of belonging and affection that gave them enhanced stability. The Church seemed to foresee what Hitler had helped to create and to which he could not himself adjust: a changed Austria whose population wanted, above all, to avoid economic and social turmoil that would disrupt their lives.

THE CARDINAL AND THE JEWS[24]

The Church hierarchy in the Reich saw that the modus vivendi of 1941 was clearly an emergency solution that could not endure once the regime emerged victorious from the war. Since 1933—in Austria since 1938—it had had no desire to precipitate a confrontation. The forced coexistence did not, however, bridge the disagreements in basic objectives. The divisions came to light with the sharpening anti-Semitism of the regime, which prompted the Church leaders to dissociate the Church from the extremist anti-Jewish course. To be sure, the Vatican itself extended assistance, chiefly to the converts, but devoted relatively little time to the plight of the non-Catholic Jews.[25]

From the start, Cardinal Innitzer took a firm attitude against anti-Semitism, a slippery question in a city where a large Jewish minority formed a high percentage in certain professions and in a country where many churchmen still regarded Christianity and Judaism as opposing movements. Innitzer had given his official blessing to the voluntary semilegal action, headed by the Jesuit Georg Bichlmair, in support of the convert Jews. Countess Emanuela Kielmansegg, using the cover name "K." directed a staff of ten aides who provided needy Jews with moral and material assistance.[26] The Cardinal, who took final responsibility for the Bichlmair action, contributed a monthly subsidy of RM 3,000 out of his private funds. Such charitable measures helped to alleviate material distress, but even more important for boosting the morale of the Jewish Catholic community was assistance in providing emigration visas and transportation.[27] On November 10, 1939, the Gestapo arrested Father Bichlmair and in December expelled him to Upper Silesia.

To make the welfare-aid more secure, Innitzer, in 1940, officially established a welfare agency that operated under his patronage and protection as the "Archiepiscopal Relief Agency for non-Aryan Catholics," and he charged the German-born Father Ludger Born, S. J., with its administration. Sister Verena from the *Caritas Socialis* replaced Countess Kielmansegg. The Cardinal provided an office for the Agency in his own palace. Because the Nazis strictly controlled his own resources, he pleaded with the Vatican for financial aid, appealed for cash to his friends, and collected private donations to cover the average monthly payments of RM 7,000.[28] The Agency handled between forty and fifty cases of emigration daily until the fall of 1941, when the regime stopped the emigration.[29] When the mass transportation to the East started, the Agency sought to stay in contact with its protégés in Poland and in the concentration camp in Terezín. It also supplied them with food parcels, sending, in 1944 alone, 7,277 parcels.[30] Eight of the twenty-three Agency's female helpers perished in concentration camps.[31]

On September 18, 1941, one day before the police issued the ordinance ordering Jews to wear the yellow star of David, the Cardinal's office instructed his parish clergy that "all Christians, including non-Aryan Christians, can participate at the church services, as has been the case in the past."[32] The Church was to remain a community of all.

NOTES

1. The narrative in this chapter draws on my article, "Nazi Control of the Austrian Catholic Church, 1939-1941," *Catholic Historical Review* 63 (October 1977): 537-72.

The much weaker Evangelical Church enjoyed more favorable treatment than the Catholic Church because initially in many cases its ministers welcomed the nationalist spirit of National Socialsim. During the Anschluss period, five ministers were imprisoned and nine expelled from the country or forbidden to be active in their provinces. Twenty-nine church buildings were confiscated and 102 associations were disbanded. The Swedish Mission administered assistance to the Evangelical Jews until 1941. For more information, see Erika Weinzierl, "Christen und Juden nach der NS-Machtergreifung," in *Anschluss 1938. Protokoll des Symposiums in Wien am 14. und 15. März 1978*, ed. Rudolf Neck and Adam Wandruszka (Vienna, 1981), pp. 192 ff; DÖW, ed., *Widerstand Wien*, 3:150-60; Gustav Reingrabner, *Protestanten in Österreich. Geschichte und Dokumentation* (Vienna, 1981), pp. 270-71. The Old Catholics played no role in the Resistance, DÖW, ed., *Widerstand Wien,* 3:189.

2. Viktor Reimann, *Innitzer: Kardinal zwischen Hitler und Rom* (Vienna-Munich, 1967), pp. 99-101. See also Weinzierl, "Christen und Juden," pp. 176 ff.

3. Jakob Fried, *Nationalsozialismus und die katholische Kirche in Österreich* (Vienna, 1947), pp. 43, 49, 52, 59, 72, 86.

4. "Denkschrift," Sept. 28, 1938, BA, R 43 II/178. Bürckel's reply dismissing the charges as unsubstantiated reached the bishops in March 1939. Bürckel to Innitzer, March 20, ibid.

5. Reimann, *Innitzer,* pp. 187-98; *Neue Freie Presse,* October 13, 14, 1938. For auxiliary bishop Dr. Jakob Weinbacher's testimony, see *Wiener Tageszeitung,* October 15, 1947.

6. Harold C. Deutsch, *The Conspiracy Against Hitler in the Twilight War* (Minneapolis, 1968), pp. 112-13, 122-23.

7. Karl Rudolf correctly stated that, "in the fulfillment of its mission the Church was simply bound to come to an implacable opposition to the regime." Thus, the observance of the Church's teachings developed spontaneously into opposition. *Aufbau im Widerstand. Ein*

Seelsorgebericht aus Österreich 1938-1945 (Salzburg, 1947), p. 12. P. Josef Otto Pinzenöhler, who spent over four years in Nazi jails, indicated that while the "Church as such was not engaged in the Resistance, its self-assertion clearly presented an act of opposition." Interview, April 25, 1974. See also Katholische Sozialakademie Österreichs, "Kirche und Widerstand Österreichs im Dritten Reich," *Österreichische Zeitgeschichte 6* (Wien 1969), p. 12.

8. On July 1, 1941, the Austrian bishops lodged a strong protest with the RMdJ. BA, R 43 II/1271. The former regularly attended the episcopal conferences of the German bishops held annually at Fulda. In their pastoral letters, all bishops sharply condemned the regime's anti-church measures. Eventually, the situation of the Church in Austria grew worse than in Germany. See Heinz Boberach, ed., *Berichte des SD und der Gestapo über Kirchen und Kirchenvolk in Deutschland, 1934-1944* (Mainz, 1971), passim; Johannes Neuhäusler, *Kreuz und Hakenkreuz. Der Kampf des Nationalsozialismus gegen die katholische Kirche und der kirchliche Widerstand,* 2 vols. (Munich, 1946), passim.

9. I concur with Heinz Boberach that "the reports of the SD and Gestapo corroborate the existence of a religious-oriented popular opposition giving moral support to the active resistance of individuals." Boberach, ed., *Berichte,* p. xlii. See also Richard Berczeller and Norbert Leser, . . . *mit Österreich verbunden. Burgenlandschicksal 1918-1945* (Vienna-Munich, 1975), p. 200; Ernst Wolf, "Zum Verhältnis der politischen und moralischen Motive in der deutschen Widerstandsbewegung," in Walter Schmitthenner and Hans Buchheim, eds., *Der deutsche Widerstand,* pp. 245-46.

10. See the reports for 1939-40 by the "SD-Leitabschnitt Wien," and the "Inspekteur der Sicherheitspolizei und des SD in Wien," NA, Miscelleneous German Records Collections, T 84, rolls 13-14, and "Meldungen aus dem Reich," and their forerunners, "Berichte zur innenpolitischen Lage," October 1939-July 1944; NSDAP, Schutzstaffel Records of the Reich Leader of the SS and Chief of the German Police," NA, T 175, r. 10, 258-59. See also "Geheime Staatspolizei. Staatspolizeileitstelle Wien, Tagesrapporte," September 1938-September 1940, NA, T 84, r. 13-16; "Tagesberichte der Gestapo. Staatspolizeileitstelle Wien," Sept. 14, 1940-August 31, 1943, DÖW, 5731-5732 a-d, 5733 a-f, 5734 a-d, 8475-8477, and for 1944, 8478-8479; "Gestapo Berichte," 1940-43 (from the "Zentralarchiv" at Potsdam, GDR), DÖW 1444-1455; "Meldungen aus dem Reichsgau Oberdonau, 1943, SD-Abschnitt Linz," NA, NSDAP, T 81, r. 6

11. "Meldungen aus dem Reich," RSHA, January 22, 1940, in Boberach, ed., *Berichte,* p. 393, and August 22, 1940, NA, T 175, r. 259, 752150 ff.

In his report of August 10, 1940, to RMdJ, Dr. Franz Gürtner, the GSAW in Graz, complained of the anti-regime propaganda of "the two strongest enemies of National Socialism, political Catholicism and Communism." Both groups drew the public's attention to the high cost of living, high food prices, and food shortages. They also complained about food rationing, lack of proper housing, and time blackouts. BA, R 22/3365.

12. "Meldungen aus dem Reich," December 18, 1939; Heydrich to Lammers, May 3, 1940; Lammers to Heydrich, June 6, 1940, in Boberach, ed., *Berichte,* pp. 384-85.

13. "Österreichs Katholiken und der Nationalsozialismus," *Wort und Wahrheit* 17 (1963):518-20; DÖW, ed., *Widerstand Wien, 3:9-46.*

14. Up to the collapse of the Third Reich, 120 churches and chapels, 26 large monasteries, and 188 church establishments were closed. Fried, *Nationalsozialismus,* pp. 71, 87; DÖW, ed., *Widerstand Wien,* 3:9 ff; Neuhäusler, *Kreuz,* 1:153-55, 351-57; Stadler, *Österreich,* pp. 97 ff; *Die Furche* (Vienna), March 2, 1946.

15. Henry Picker, et al. eds., *Hitlers Tischgespräche im Führerhauptquartier 1941-1942* (Stuttgart, 1965), pp. 154-55, 436-39; Bormann's circular to the Gauleiters, June 9, 1941, in Zipfel, *Kirchenkampf in Deutschland 1933-1945,* pp. 211 ff.

16. See the Austrian bishops' letter of protest to RMdI Dr. Wilhelm Frick, July 1, 1941, BA, R 43 II/1271. For Upper Austria, see Rudolf Zinnhobler in DÖW, ed., *Widerstand in Oberösterreich,* 2:29-35.

17. Conway, *Persecution,* pp. 279, 285-86, 442; Fried, *Nationalsozialismus,* p. 199. Hitler also called off the secret practice of mercy killing. For its continuing use in Vienna after 1942, see the Volksgericht trial in Vienna. Staatliches Archivlager Göttingen, No. 317.

18. A crowd of young Nazis interrupted Cardinal Innitzer's service at St. Stephen's Cathedral on the evening of December 8, 1941. On December 17, 1942, the City of Vienna prohibited religious instruction of pupils in its reformatory institutions. Fried, *Nationalsozialismus,* pp. 202 ff. For other disturbances in Vienna, see DÖW, ed., *Widerstand Wien,* 3:44-45.

19. For 1942-43, see the SD reports from Upper Austria, and "Weltanschauliche Lageberichte" of the "Gauleitung Niederdonau," in Stadler, *Österreich,* pp. 384-389.

20. The German reports gave a wide range of reasons for the arrests: listening to foreign broadcasts; charging sermons with emotional language; offering shelter to deserters and refugees; collecting financial contributions; violating the rules regulating religious instruction; notification of church services and bell ringing; gathering youth and other church groups; celebrating church holidays; propagandizing among the youth; distributing religious literature; assisting the Jews; and spreading hostile rumors. DÖW, ed., *Widerstand Wien,* 3:46-80. It was prohibited to commemorate the religious nature of Christmas and to sing Christmas carols in the Viennese kindergartens. Ibid., p. 154.

21. For the clergy, see Benedicta M. Kempner, *Priester vor Hitlers Tribunalen* (Munich, 1966), passim; DÖW, ed., *Widerstand Wien,* 3:46 ff; Weinzierl-Fischer, "Katholiken," pp. 522-23; Fried, *Nationalsozialismus,* passim; P. Gaudentius Walser, *Carl Lampert. Ein Leben für Christus und die Kirche, 1894-1944* (Dornbirn, 1964); Johann M. Lenz, *Christus in Dachau oder Christus der Sieger. Ein religiöses Volksbuch und ein Kirchengeschichtliches Zeugnis* (Vienna, 1957); Hans Rieger, *Verurteilt zum Tod. Dokumentarbericht. Seelsorge im Gefängnis des Wiener Landgerichts 1942-1944* (Wuppertal, 1967); Kühmayer, *Auferstehung;* Heinrich Zeder, *Judas sucht einen Bruder. Schicksale aus dem Freiheitskampf Österreichs* (Vienna, 1947); Johann Holzner et al., *Zeugen des Widerstandes* (Innsbruck, 1977); Berczeller and Leser, . . . *mit Österreich verbunden,* pp. 200, 205, 278-96; Helmut Tschol, *Pfarrer Otto Neururer, Priester und Blutzeuge* (Innsbruck, 1965); Gerhard Wanner, *Kirche und Nationalsozialismus in Vorarlberg* (Dornbirn, 1972); Rudolf Zinnhobler, ed., *Das Bistum Linz im Dritten Reich* (Linz, 1979); Neuhäusler, *Kreuz,* 1:351 ff; DÖW 4709, 5734d 6904, 8388, 9858, 13358. For the SD and Gestapo reports, see above note 10.

22. DÖW 2442, 4711, 5297c; Heinrich Kreuzberg, *Franz Reinisch: Ein Martyrer unserer Zeit* (Limburg, 1953). Another conscientious objector who voluntarily died in 1942 was a simple peasant, Franz Jägerstätter. Gordon C. Zahn, *In Solitary Witness: The Life and Death of Franz Jägerstätter* (New York, 1964); DÖW 1539. Zahn noted that only seven Catholics had refused to be drafted into military service. Six were executed, of whom three were Austrians, Reinisch, Jägerstätter, and Josef Mayr-Nusser, an official of Catholic Action. The other three were Germans who had spent much of their lives in Austria. *German Catholics and Hitler's Wars* (London, 1963), pp. 54-55.

23. Fried, *Nationalsozialismus,* pp. 71, 86-87. For Upper Austria, see Rudolf Zinnhobler in DÖW, ed., *Widerstand in Oberösterreich,* 2:13-24. Zinnhobler gives data on ninety-nine priests and members of male orders who were arrested in Upper Austria in 1938-45. Sixteen died in jail or in concentration camps. See also Johann Mittendorfer, "Oberösterreichische Priester in Gefängnissen und Konzentrationslagern zur Zeit des Nationalsozialismus (1938-1945)," *72. Jahresbericht des Bischöflichen Gymnasiums und Diözesanseminars am Kollegium Petrinum. Schuljahr 1975/76* (Linz), pp. 77-102; *73. Jahresbericht 1976/77,* pp. 39-104.

24. This portion appears in my article, "Nazi Control of the Austrian Catholic Church, 1939-1941," *The Catholic Historical Review* 63 (October 1977): 564-67, and is reprinted here with permission of the editor. Some footnotes were shortened or changed.

25. Secrétairerie d'État de Sa Sainteté, *Actes et documents du Saint Siège relatifs à la Seconde guerre mondiale,* Vol. 6: *Le Saint Siège et les victimes de la guerre, mars 1939-décembre 1940* (Vatican City, 1972), passim. See also Friedrich Muckermann, *Im Kampf zwischen zwei Epochen. Lebenserinnerungen* (Mainz, 1973), pp. 482-83.

26. For the Jewish relief action in Vienna, see DÖW 16538; Reimann, *Innitzer,* pp. 249-65; Molden, *Der Ruf,* pp. 68-70; OM, VIII, No. 76 and No. 77; interview with Father Ludger Born, S.J.; G. Metzler, *Heimführen werd ich euch von überall her. Aufzeichnungen am Rande des Zeitgeschehens* (Vienna, 1959). Metzler was one of Father Born's full-time aides.

27. Bichlmair's organization supported homes for the aged; provided medical care and legal help; contributed welfare payments to those without basic income or old-age benefits (between December 1940 and June 1941, it gave RM 30,717 to 1,742 Jews); helped to set up a special private school for Christian and nondenominational Jewish children; and distributed food and clothing. "Der erste Arbeitsbericht der Erzbischöflichen Hilfsstelle für nichtarische Katholiken," in Reimann, *Innitzer,* p. 254.

28. The financial assistance paid in 1943 amounted to RM 74,942.81. Ibid., p. 258. Innitzer wrote for help to the archbishops of New York, Chicago, Philadelphia, New Orleans, and Boston and to the Catholic Bureau for Immigration in Washington. Archiepiscopal Archives in Vienna, ibid., pp. 256-57.

29. *Actes et documents du Saint Siège,* 6:11, 15, 351 ff. In Vienna the Society of Friends primarily served the needs of the nondenominational Jews, and the Swedish Mission in Stockholm provided care for the Evangelical Jews until 1941. At the end of 1941, there were 3,836 Catholic Jews in Vienna. Reimann, *Innitzer,* pp. 251, 254; Molden, *Der Ruf,* pp. 69-70; DÖW, ed., *Widerstand Wien,* 3:150-51.

30. Reimann, *Innitzer,* pp. 260-64. Many Jews were brought to the Cardinal for personal audiences through a rear entrance in his palace.

31. DÖW 16538.

32. Reimann, *Innitzer,* pp. 264-65; Metzler, *Heimführen,* passim. For Innitzer's September 1941 letter on the pastoral work among the Catholic Jews, see "Meldungen aus dem Reich," RSHA, November 24-26, 1941, in Boberach, ed., *Berichte,* p. 599; Reimann, *Innitzer,* p. 264. The Conference of the Austrian bishops discussed the assistance to the converted Jews in the autumn of 1941. Weinzierl-Fischer, "Katholiken," pp. 426-27. As late as April 3, 1944, Innitzer interceded with Gauleiter Baldur von Schirach in favor of the members of mixed marriages who were to be removed from their apartments, DÖW, ed., *Widerstand Wien,* 3:71-72.

PART TWO
The Left-Wing Democratic Alternative

8

The Socialists

In the early morning hours of March 11, 1938, the last Revolutionary Socialist (RS) conference endorsed its Central Committee's direction to all members prohibiting clandestine work for the next three months. The newly established exile RS central organ in Paris (Auslandsvertretung der öster-reichischen Sozialisten, AVÖS) heartily endorsed the decision to dissolve its home underground network immediately.[1] Knowing that the powerful Nazi security organs possessed the names of 5,000 illegal RS cadres, the RS leadership opted for prudent restraint. In its view, those activists who had attracted Nazi attention should cease illegal work. In the future, an entirely new personnel alignment was to be created: small cells instead of a centrally directed organization were to undertake clandestine operations.[2]

In fact, the former RS and SPÖ adherents turned away both organiza-tionally and functionally from their pre-1938 underground structures. They responded almost instinctively to the new situation by forming small infor-mal circles of Party notables. Avoiding clandestine work, a few Party friends would meet privately to exchange opinions.[3] With a few exceptions, no clandestine Party cells or groups were formed. This insulated system of personal political communication kept the Party subculture alive through-out Austria within a network of separate noninterlocking, informal circles. Both the SPÖ and RS, who anticipated that any internal changes would be mainly influenced by external events, believed that the possible costs in human life and suffering from clandestine activity outweighed any im-mediate benefits.[4]

After assuming power in Austria, the National Socialist regime stressed its Socialist character with gestures designed to appease the former Socialist rank and file. The workers were repeatedly reassured that the new regime would expand the economy to relieve social grievances and to cut unemployment. To win over the former Socialist Party members, the new rulers reinstated many Socialists ousted for participating in the February 1934 uprising.[5] Although few of these Socialists were likely to shift allegiance to the Nazis, it was not in their immediate interest to oppose openly the regime that was projecting vigorous, energetic, social concern. The Anschluss thus drastically changed the operational environment of the RS and SPÖ.

After some initial vacillation, the RS and SP cadres drew together. The activists seemed disinclined to engage in any covert activity, preferring to demand more favorable social and economic arrangements and more efficient protection of the workers' interests. Many experienced and disciplined former trade unionists succeeded in preserving their roles at the factory level. Because the Nazis lacked their own trained cadres, they were unable in their official unified labor movement (Deutsche Arbeitsfront, DAF) to develop an effective organization. As a result, the Social Democratic trade unionists took positions within the DAF in the factories and municipal enterprises in Vienna and Lower Austria. Retaining their Social Democratic traditions, they sought to work within the system, thus discouraging any open worker opposition. They supported the new productive goals and accepted the tactical necessity of endorsing all the "voluntary" donations enacted by the regime. Compliance with the regime's instructions did not adversely affect their prestige in the factories. With their peculiar combination of loyalty and guile, the Socialist workers could still indulge in criticism of many economic and social measures. The Viennese Gestapo complained that the workers expressed considerable concern over the calling of Austrians for work in the Reich and over food shortages. Furthermore, the Socialist workers spread rumors unfavorable to the regime and never missed an opportunity to highlight the differences between the Austrians and the Germans. The Gestapo reports added that such discussions had been taking place during breakfast or lunch hours or at times when the workers were unsupervised. They pointed out that whenever former Social Democrats were jailed, almost immediately their friends collected donations to support family members.[6]

Because the material conditions of life could not keep pace with early expectations, the initial public enthusiasm for the Anschluss soon subsided. The unsettling effects of a hasty transition started to erode the workers' confidence in the new economic policies. With their wages frozen, the steady rise in prices hurt the workers. The regime also enforced a stricter work discipline and strengthened work norms. Within a few months, the workers experienced reduced real earnings. Between March 1938 and the end of 1940, prices of food and everyday commodities in Austria rose by more than 50 percent and were often 30 percent higher than in Berlin. Prices of vegetables shot up by 200 percent. In addition to the wage ceiling, the new tax on wages, the war-surtax, and the new rates of assessment further reduced real wages and lowered the workers' purchasing power.[7] Not a few workers were unable to purchase their food rations when rationing was introduced after the outbreak of the war.

The authorities by 1939 had little to boast about with regard to real wages; indeed the Gestapo reports grudgingly agreed with the flood of workers' complaints. In their evaluations, they viewed the deterioration in living standards as perhaps the most important cause of the workers' mounting dissatisfaction, in itself a source of propaganda for the underground Socialists and Communists. The reports tended to blame the regime, criticizing the NSDAP's disparaging attitude toward the workers. Initially faced with what the head of the Linz Gestapo called an "enthusiastic" reception by the workers, "arrogant, tactless" Party members and officials has successfully discouraged the workers, including former Socialists, from seeking support in the NSDAP. He described the treatment the Party meted out to the workers as "impudent." As a consequence, an opposition emerged that presented a "favorable jumping-off point for the internal enemy," assisting him to undermine the regime.[8]

The Munich crisis of September 1938 coincided with the peak of the first tide of growing disenchantment that swept across disgruntled segments of the Austrian working class.[9] Particularly in September, general uneasiness and restlessness became evident, and the anti-Nazi whisper propaganda increased. Open acts of defiance and of contempt toward Party officials (such as at the Steyr Works), a wave of "sickness" among the workers,[10] and more frequent listening to foreign broadcasts underscored the security organs' suspicion that they might be facing an organized protest action.

Apparently overestimating the strength of a spontaneous antiwar protest, the head of the Sicherheitspolizei SS-Gruppenführer Reinhard Heydrich instructed the Viennese Gestapo headquarters on September 27 to "take into protective custody all former leading SPÖ and KPÖ officials," whenever they might be suspected of having engaged in activities hostile to the Reich. As a result, the Gestapo offices in Graz, Linz, Klagenfurt, and Salzburg rounded up 42, 47, 51, and 11 persons, respectively. The Vienna Gestapo did not think the moment appropriate to arrest anybody.[11] The next preventive measures were taken before the outbreak of war on August 22 and 31, 1939, when over 300 former SPÖ and KPÖ officials were arrested, many of whom were sent to KZ Buchenwald.[12]

THE RS, KPÖ, AND AUSTRIAN INDEPENDENCE

Although the exile RS and KPÖ representatives had signed joint proclamations assailing Nazi imperialism on the occasions of the plebiscite of April 10, 1938, the Munich crisis of September 19, and Czechoslovakia's dismemberment of March 1939, deep political differences threatened the March 1936 Agreement in which the two movements had established a

Community of Action.[13] As each party sought to build its own political power base, they constantly promoted existing party policies. In this light, the RS statement of August 3, 1939, on mutual relations was designed to prevent political alliances and to protect RS interests at home, where the RS and KPÖ rapprochement represented to the Communists merely a temporary tactical maneuver. Only in exile were the two parties allowed to communicate with each other. In the RS view, they should maintain friendly contacts with the KPÖ, but no Socialist militants should participate in joint activities nor sign any joint declarations. To minimize the danger to its domestic position, where KP participation could damage Socialist prospects, the AVÖS abandoned the 1936 agreement because, "naturally within Austria there was no ground anymore for maintaining the original form of cooperation. . . . Today as a rule there are no organizational contacts between the RS and KP in the homeland."[14]

From the outset, the KPÖ and the RS disagreed on how to defeat the National Socialists. The KPÖ, stressing national unity as an all-important interim phase of the revolutionary process, wished to collaborate closely with anti-Nazi forces of all political shades. For their part, the RS leaders abroad reasserted their own doctrinal and political purity. In a bold but unreal All-German perspective, they advocated a revolutionary transformation by the workers of the existing social order in Germany and Austria.[15] For the Socialists, their Greater-German view represented nothing new; their original doctrinal premises had always been, after all, Greater-German.[16]

In the Socialist strategy of the All-German revolution, then, the Austrian right to self-determination came to have mostly tactical significance, remaining an issue with which, up to the fall of 1943, they were fundamentally uneasy.[17] They regarded an independent Austrian state as a transient form that would hamper the class struggle of the proletariat and deflect their Socialist revolution. All this was rather surprising in a party that had once developed a bold program of national autonomy for the nationalities in the Habsburg Empire. After the Anschluss, they could hardly base a popular anti-Nazi movement on the Greater-German vision. Since the growth in opposition and resistance was primarily related to the rise of Austrian patriotism, the leadership of the left-wing Resistance naturally devolved to those who most acknowledged the national sentiments—the Communists.

In the early Anschluss era (1938-40), after the RS's abrupt withdrawal from clandestine activities, many Socialist militants shifted their allegiance to the KPÖ-inspired groups that filled the organizational and political vacuum on the Austrian left. Thus in many instances, the KPÖ emerged as a substitute for the Socialist Resistance. The new Communist networks were conceived as the elite core of a mass-oriented political party. In this way, Austria had the unique experience of a labor resistance movement conducted by many individual Socialists—but neither by the SPÖ nor the RS

—who provided the backbone for the clandestine work ultimately directed by carefully selected Communist cadres.

Only after the Moscow Declaration in 1943 did the Socialist line turn gradually from the Greater-German idea to the concept of a separate Austria. Paradoxically, the very underestimation of the national susceptibilities reflected the opinion of large segements of the Austrian population still reluctant to endorse Austrian national identity. Thus, in the final stage of the war, the Socialist Party could preserve the solid foundation it had erected before 1938 and ultimately emerge as a mass movement with broad popular bases. This development shifted the balance from the RS to the moderate and more pragmatic pre-1934 Social Democratic elements who gained heavily as the original RS strength faded, drained by the assimilation of some of their cadres in the Communist underground. The absence of a strong, cohesive Socialist Resistance that would almost certainly have been suppressed with considerable loss of life among moderate Party leaders thus contributed to the postwar creation of a unified Socialist movement.[18]

THE FIRST STEPS

The RS and SPÖ cadres were largely unsympathetic to the patriotic implications of the anti-German resistance during the early occupation. However, as the Resistance gradually became the vehicle of Austrian self-consciousness, an emotional attachment to Austria suggested the possibility of a modernized and socially advanced society. This dynamic vision eventually brought the Socialists and the non-Communist Resistance together.[19]

The RS lost some of their senior officials during the wave of arrests in March 1938 and some to flight abroad, which partly explains why RS groupings were remarkably few until the winter of 1944 when the moderate reformist SPÖ veteran leaders, above all, Dr. Adolf Schärf, former secretary of the SPÖ Parliamentary Club, provided a medium for the Socialist movement. Nevertheless, several important circles did emerge. Almost immediately after the occupation, Roman Felleis, Franz Fleck, Franz Hackenberg, Stefan Wirlandner, and Otto Probst formed a loose RS nucleus centered in Vienna but with branches throughout Styria (Fritz Matzler, Andreas Stampler), Carinthia (Ferdinand Wedenig, Anton Falle), and Salzburg. In 1938 Henrich Widmayer, who built a network in Lower Austria from the local branches of his farm laborer's trade union, worked an escape route via the Thaya Valley to Czechoslovakia. Another organization, the "Storfer" group, managed to weld former SB members, Socialists and Communists, into a single organization carrying out extensive propaganda. The later nuclei around former RS officials Felix Slavik, Ludwig Kostroun, Dr. Alfred Migsch, and Franz Pfeffer conducted some activities on a limited scale.[20] Naturally, it was a severe loss when Slavik was arrested on November 8, 1939, after he had established the first contacts with the

Christian Social-Legitimist network in an attempt to find common political ground with the Christian unionists.[21]

These isolated circles were not tied together within a central organization. They discontinued their communications with the leadership in exile.[22] Often the cells existed under a cover. For instance, a functionary of the RS youth, Franz Gawlik gathered reliable youths in the German League against Alcoholism which had officially replaced numerous, mostly Socialist-inspired, abstinence associations. Although the opportunities for serious clandestine work were few, the cell survived the war to form the nucleus of the Socialist Party youth movement in Vienna in April 1945.[23]

Yet another early concern of the Socialists was aid to the families of imprisoned Socialist activists. In 1934 the RS had established a secret circle exclusively concerned with the welfare of the victims of the underground struggle. Initially, the Socialist Workers' Assistance (Sozialistische Arbeiterhilfe, SAH) was separated from the underground network the better to protect its relief work from possible police disruption. Two women, first Wilhelmine Moik, then Frederike Nödl, ran the circle. After the Nazi takeover, the SAH acted as the main clandestine link between the AVÖS and the central leadership of the RS. It offered financial assistance to the families of arrested Socialist officials in Vienna, Salzburg, Styria, and Carinthia. The expenses were covered by funds left over from before 1938 by a wealthy American, later the wife of RS chairman Josef Buttinger, Muriel M. Gardiner, a medical student who had been living in Vienna for years. Individuals emigrating abroad also provided money by leaving their funds in the country in exchange for foreign currency from Socialists abroad.

The SAH operated quietly, running a courier service to Prague until its members were seized in July and August 1938.[24] A key RS Vienna functionary who turned out to be a Gestapo informer, Hans Pav, betrayed them.[25] Pav was one of the most successful of the informers whom the Nazis developed into their most effective instrument for infiltrating and then controlling a number of underground cells. Another was Eduard Korbel, a teacher, former SPÖ and SB member, and Austrian police informer, who reported systematically, if inaccurately, up to 1941 on the echelons of the RS cells in Vienna. Among those he denounced were a few youth circles.[26]

Apparently Pav also informed on another SAH circle consisting mainly of women — all trusted RS veterans, Helene Potetz, Ida Fürnberg, Rudolfine Muhr, Frieda Weinlich, Marie Pokorny, Karoline Proksch, Hermine Hromada—who also provided financial support to the incarcerated militants.[27] As Fürnberg and Weinlich, who resided in Prague, could travel across the borders, the circle had become involved in liaison with the RS branches in Brno and Prague in Czechoslovakia, and with the AVÖS in Paris, where it had moved from Prague. It had enjoyed the support of the RS leadership abroad, receiving funds, instructions, and political guidance. However, in the summer of 1939, the police rounded up the activists in Vienna and Prague.[28]

Other circles banded together around individual RS or SPÖ organizers. In Carinthia near Radenthein a young worker set up a cell of ten called "Freedom Movement," which worked in the Drau and Möhl valleys from summer 1938 until November 1939; it recruited Communist as well as Catholic followers whom the struggle against the Nazis, rather than tradition or ideology, had led to the Socialist movement.[29] In another development, the Gestapo seized, in October 1938, some former trade union Socialist officials because of their connections to Viktor Stein, a former Socialist member of parliament. Stein had collected and made available information about the situation in Vienna to the Czechoslovak Social Democratic daily in Carlsbad, *Volkswille.*[30]

Dismantled by its own leaders after 1938, the RS only limped through to the end of the war. Almost exclusively concerned with retaining the morale and loyalty of its adherents, the RS accomplished little. A mood of anxious concern about the political future pervaded the leaders, who deliberately avoided any organized conspiratorial work. They considered it important to remain apart from any other clandestine groups so as to save their own groups from possible foundering, and to make politically astute use of them after the Nazi defeat.

NOTES

1. Buttinger, *Am Beispiel,* pp. 542 ff; Wisshaupt, *Wir kommen,* pp. 222-23. The ALÖS residing in Brno was dissolved. The new center — AVÖS — set up in Paris in April 1938 predominantly consisted of the members of the RS Central Committee who had fled abroad after the Anschluss. RS-Korrespondenz, June 18, 1938. DÖW 3057 B/21. In October 1938, the Paris center called on the RS militants at home to stop illegal activity because it was useless. Muriel Gardiner-Joseph Buttinger, *Damit wir nicht vergessen. Unsere Jahre 1934-1947 in Wien, Paris und New York* (Vienna, 1978), p. 122.

2. Buttinger, *Am Beispiel,* p. 244; Stadler, *Österreich,* pp. 74-75. The RS organ in Paris gave an explanation of the necessary accommodation to the changed conditions: "The experience from Germany has taught a lesson: all those old organizations that continued their old activities have been destroyed. . . . New ones have to be built up without any connections to the old forms. The promoters of new organizational structures can be chiefly those individuals who are not burdened by any links to the past illegal work. . . . At present, no journals, tracts, regular bulletins or brochures can be published." *Der sozialistische Kampf,* July 2, 1938.

3. Szecsi-Stadler called the loose informal Socialist meetings "Gesinnungsgemeinschaften" *Die NS-Justiz,* p. 50. The Salzburg Socialist Josef Kaut noted that "apart from illegal groups there has been . . . contact among socialist friends, an often only loose fraternal relationship based on . . . mutual confidence. . . . Time and again, the Socialists gathered in small group-ings to exchange information and to ponder the future perspectives." *Der steinige Weg. Geschichte der sozialistischen Arbeiterbewegung im Lande Salzburg* (Vienna, 1961), p. 148. The Croatian SPÖ member of parliament Fritz Robak recalled after the war that such contacts involv-ed "A fleeting greeting . . . some encouraging news about the situation; that was all." Franz Danimann, ed., *Finis Austriae. Österreich, März 1938* (Vienna, 1978), p. 100.

4. According to former SPÖ member of the government Karl Maisel, "Parole war: ab-zuwarten" (" 'Bide one's time' was the watchword"). Interview with Karl Maisel.

5. Luža, *Austro-German Relations,* pp. 151 ff; Stadler, *Österreich,* pp. 72-73.

6. "Geheime Staatspolizei, Staatspolizeileitstelle Wien," December 23, 1940, to the RSHA, and "Staatspolizeistelle Linz" to the RSHA, December 30, 1940. DÖW 1449. The Gestapo

viewed the Comunists' and Socialists' oral propaganda in the factories and at open food markets as far more dangerous than the distribution of illegal tracts.

7. Gestapo Wien, December 23, 1940, DÖW 1449. For example, the price of 1 kg pork increased from RM 2.13-2.40 in March 1938 to RM 3.60-4.00 at the end of 1940; of 1 kg margarine from 1.76 to 1.96; of one egg from 0.05-0.07 to 0.11-0.13.

8. "Geheime Staatspolizei, Staatspolizeistelle Linz," to the RSHA, December 30, 1940, DÖW 1449.

9. "Gestapo, Staatspolizeistelle Salzburg to Sicherheitspolizei, Berlin," October 10, 1938, DÖW 4209. At Erzberg in Styria during the first half of August, the workmen at the huge iron ore mines held a strike that threatened to engulf other Styrian enterprises. Helmut Fiereder, "Die Reichswerke 'Hermann Göring' in Österreich. Zur Gründungsgeschichte der Vereinigten Österreichischen Eisen-und Stahlwerke (VÖEST)" (Ph.D. dissertation, University of Salzburg, 1979), p. 110.

10. DÖW 1576.

11. "Lagebericht über Österreich, Sicherheitspolizei, Berlin," October 23, 1938, DÖW 4236. The Innsbruck Gestapo carried out the arrests before the order was issued. The Viennese Gestapo prepared a list of eighty high- and middle-rank officials and 150 suspects to be arrested at a future time. Franz J. Huber to "Geheime Staatspolizeiamt (Gestapa), Berlin," September 30, 1938, DÖW 1576. The Salzburg Gestapo seized only former KPÖ officials. DÖW 4209.

12. The names of the SPÖ senior officials were recorded in the so-called "A-1 Kartei," which consisted of a list of former leading Austrian public figures who were to be sent to concentration camps at a time when vital Reich security interests would be at stake. On August 22 and on the following days, seventy-four Communists and forty-seven RS were rounded up in Vienna and Wiener Neustadt. "Gestapo Wien to SS-Oberführer Müller, Gestapa Berlin," August 24, September 3, 1939, DÖW 1580; DÖW 1590; Stadler, *Österreich,* p. 74.

13. "Ein Aufruf der Österreichs," DÖW 4074/76; RS-Korrespondenz No. 4, September 21, 1938.

14. RS-Korrespondenz, August 3, 1939, DÖW 3057 B/21.

15. "In contrast to the RS' conception, the KPÖ has formed its entire policy on the hope of reconstructing an independent Austria. Its propaganda uses the Schuschnigg resistance formula 'Rot-weiss-rot bis in den Tod.' The KPÖ abroad strives to form on the basis of Austrian independence a political alliance reaching from the Communists to the extreme right (Legitimists). . . . The weakness of the Communist argument is best seen in their senseless attempt to view Austria as an individual nation and to proclaim the struggle of the Austrians against the Hitler dictatorship as a struggle for national liberation." RS-Korrespondenz, June 18, 1938, DÖW 3057 B/21. After August 1939 the KP position on Austrian independence became more cautious and the term disappeared from the KPÖ vocabulary until the summer of 1942. Reinhard Bollmus, "Österreichs Unabhängigkeit im Widerstand," *Zeitgeschichte* 4 (November 1976): 56 ff.

16. Otto Leichter, *Otto Bauer, Tragödie oder Triumph* (Vienna, 1970), pp. 146-48; Buttinger, *Am Beispiel,* p. 555; DÖW, ed., *Widerstand Wien,* 2:31-33, 37-40; Helene Maimann, *Politik im Wartesaal. Österreichische Exilpolitik in Grossbritannien 1938 bis 1945* (Vienna, 1975), passim; Friedrich Weber, "Die linken Sozialisten 1945-1948" (Ph.D. dissertation, University of Salzburg, 1977), pp. 63-65; Otto Leichter, "Für ein unabhängiges Österreich. Eine Denkschrift aus dem Jahr 1939," *Die Zukunft,* nos. 1-2 (1973):29-34; Karl Renner, *Österreich von der Ersten zur Zweiten Republik* (Vienna, 1953), pp. 200-204; Karl Renner, "Die Gründung der Republik Deutsch-Österreich, der Anschluss und die Sudetendeutschen. Dokumente eines Kampfes ums Recht, herausgegeben, eingeleitet und erläutert von Dr. Karl Renner," Vienna, 1938, DÖW 6946.

17. Leichter, "Für ein unabhängiges Österreich," *Die Zukunft,* pp. 29-34; the memoranda by Oscar Pollak, July 1942, and by Karl Czernetz, August 1942 in Maimann, *Politik,* pp. 302 ff.

In the fall of 1941, a special message from former Socialist mayor of Vienna, Karl Seitz, to the RS in London argued for Austrian independence. Maimann, *Politik,* p. 309. In general, the RS underground favored the Greater-German course. Usually indictments against the RS did not charge them of attempting to separate Austria from the Reich ("Die Losreissung der Alpen-und Donaugaue vom Reich"). As late as September 1944, the Carinthian RS still considered the Austrians as a branch of the German nation, publicly renouncing their view only in March 1945. DÖW 857. The Socialist leader Dr. Adolf Schärf abandoned his Greater-German perspective in 1943, *Österreichs Erneuerung 1945-1955* (Vienna, 1960), pp. 23-25.

18. See also Stadler, *Österreich,* pp. 183-90.

19. The Gestapo reports treated the Socialists under the headline "Marxists."

20. Molden, *Der Ruf,* pp. 135-36; Stadler, *Österreich,* pp. 76-77; interview with Frieda Nödl. See also Herbert Steiner in Verein für die Geschichte der Stadt Wien, *Wien 1938* (Vienna, 1978), pp. 143-44. Probst, Slavik, Migsch, Kostroun, Widmayer, Wedenig, Stampler, and Falle held important positions within the SPÖ after 1945.

21. AS, VGH, March 9, 1941, DÖW 3299; Molden, *Der Ruf,* pp. 87-91; F. Slavik Bericht, OM, 73.

22. Buttinger, *Am Beispiel,* p. 548.

23. "Gedächtnissprotokoll der Befragung von Landtagsabgeordneten Franz Gawlik durch Dr. Wolfgang Neugebauer," October 6, 1967, DÖW.

24. Interview with F. Nödl; AS, VGH, 6J 518/38-1H 18/39, April 1, 1939; Gardiner-Buttinger, *Damit wir nicht vergessen,* pp. 73-115.

25. Buttinger, *Am Beispiel,* pp. 546-48; interview with F. Nödl; Erwin Scharf, secretary of the CC of the KPÖ, in Danimann, ed., *Finis Austriae,* pp. 224-25. M. Gardiner was in contact with the Czechoslovak Embassy, which supplied dozens of Czechoslovak passports to the RS leaders. She left the country in June 1938. Gardiner-Buttinger, *Damit wir nicht vergessen,* pp. 122-24. For Pav, see DÖW 17136.

26. Interview with Dr. Josef Staribacher, Federal Minister of Trade; Dr. Staribacher's files; reports by "Edi," DÖW 7596.

27. U, OLG, O Js 24/40, DÖW 7656.

28. On her release in 1940, Muhr formed a small nucleus that distributed food parcels to arrested RS adherents. Interview with R. Muhr; Josef Hindels, *Österreichs Gewerkschaften im Widerstand 1934-1945* (Vienna, 1976), p. 298.

29. Stadler, *Österreich,* p. 185; DÖW 12300.

30. NA, T 84, r. 13, 39853, 39864, 39879, 39886; DÖW 4503, 8724.

9

Between Austria and Germany: The Revolutionary Socialists of Austria (RSÖ)

A sense of involvement in the struggle against National Socialism developed in a number of Socialists long before 1938. A few had volunteered to take over clandestine assignments after the Weimar Republic collapsed in 1933 when the SPD presidium moved to exile in Prague (the SOPADE). To organize the chains of contacts with the undergound in the Reich and to get information on the situation there, SOPADE set up outposts along the Czechoslovak-German border. The twenty-seven-year-old librarian, Waldemar von Knoeringen, an SPD official who had escaped from Munich to Austria and then to Czechoslovakia, was responsible for liaison with the resistance in Bavaria. Under his guidance, the underground deemphasized its initial intent to win over the masses. The assignments of the newly organized groups, which carefully selected individuals, were everywhere alike: to maintain their existence on a strictly selective basis as a stepping-stone for the formation of a large underground at a time of crisis; to collect political, military and economic intelligence; and to pass on well-informed situation reports to their center in Czechoslovakia. The groups existed apart from each other but retained direct links with the exile center.

Knoeringen drew close to the revolutionary New Beginning group that split from the SPD.[1] In 1933-34 he developed useful contacts with Tyrol and Vienna,[2] but the bloody events of February 1934 in Austria seriously threatened to cut the SOPADE communication lines with Germany that ran across Austria. As a consequence, Knoeringen had to increase his recruitment drive. In 1935-37 he had cells at work in Wörgl, Häring, Innsbruck, Salzburg, and Vienna. In 1937, thirteen cadre groups operated in Bavaria and Austria, having emerged from the original mass resistance decimated by the Gestapo in 1933-34. He used his base in Wörgl near the Tyrolian-Bavarian border as an important communication point. From Wörgl his aides Alois Brunner, a railwayman, and his wife Josefine maintained the lines between the Prague center and the networks headed in Munich by the former chairman of the Association of Socialist Students at the University of Munich Dipl.-Volkswirt, Hermann Frieb, and in Augsburg by the electrician Josef Wager. Because her husband's past political involvement in the SPÖ made him a security risk, Josefine Brunner acted as principal courier and underwent special training in the use of secret ink and microfilms in Prague in the summer of 1937. After the Nazi takeover, the Brunners passed information to Knoeringen on the number and movements of the German troops, the construction of military barracks and industrial plants, and the mood of the population.

Another close association of Knoeringen in Wörgl was the former head of the local Schutzbund, Johannes Lenk. After Lenk's release from jail in 1936, he became Knoeringen's contact man with the bases in Austria and Germany. The model recruit, however, was Dr. Otto Johann Haas, a high school teacher in Vienna.[3] Knoeringen encountered Haas in 1934, and their personal contact soon grew into a close political association. A pragmatic idealist, always armed with facts, and a patient and modest man, Haas became the chief of the Viennese section. He set up safehouses and dead boxes and transmitted reports and letters to and from the Bavarian sections in Rosenheim, Nördlingen, Landshut, Regensburg, and Munich. Ultimately, Haas and the Austrian network were placed in charge of communications between Prague and the Reich, microfilming and transporting reports, Party directives, and propaganda materials.[4] In Vienna, Haas contacted Hauptmann Walter Wach, an officer of the Wehrmacht, who provided information about the German armament industry and the armed forces. Haas met Wach regularly until the early fall of 1941, when Wach left for the Russian front.[5] In May 1939, the Wehrmacht drafted Haas and eventually transferred him to the Air Force Weather Service Bureau in Bratislava, the capital of Slovakia. Although the locus of clandestine work shifted to Paris and Zurich after the Anschluss, Haas remained in touch with the exile leadership even after Knoeringen had been forced to move to Paris prior to the occupation of Prague in March 1939.[6]

While the center was safely settling in Paris, Frieb and Haas were setting up the main structure of the operations in Germany and Austria.[7] Lucie Vargas-Morin, a Paris University lecturer, who replaced Lenk as courier, transported directives from Paris, urging the German and Austrian networks to explore the possibilities for continuing their work should armed hostilities break out. The network was to exploit through political propaganda any opportunities the war might provide for expanding the revolutionary forces in Germany. The followers were requested not to engage in direct actions and to "act only if a revolutionary situation developed."[8] By the winter of 1938-39 the organization was working efficiently and smoothly. Since 1935 not a single member had been arrested, despite the network's claim to number 170 adherents.[9] But the coming of the war cut off the direct lines to Knoeringen.[10] Deprived of the moderating influence of the exile center, the home sections gradually became restive, advocating more extensive actions and interpreting the regime's difficulties as signs of its impending disintegration.

In this atmosphere, Haas feared Gestapo penetration of the increasingly militant Salzburg and Bavarian sections. He believed that Socialist Resistance should be coextensive with politics. For an established political intelligence organization, Haas identified two critical tasks: first, vigorous political-ideological training of section chiefs to prepare, direct, and harmonize political warfare activities; second, adaptation to the operational requirements and techniques of illegal struggle. Even during the unfavorable international developments after the collapse of France, Haas still believed that the Reich would lose the war, and that in the ensuing chaos, his organization should be ready to maneuver for key political positions. Consequently, he began to press for a special intelligence branch. He had his way at a meeting in Vienna in September 1940 attended by Frieb and the two key figures of the Vienna group, Rudolf Polak, a mechanic, and Eduard Göth, a high school teacher.[11] The group charged Johann Eberl and his wife Erna, both old friends of Haas, with the administration of the new intelligence branch. The Eberls controlled a wide network in Vienna and Lower and Western Austria that collected data on the mood of the population.

Since 1936 and indeed even earlier, the Vienna section composed of Haas's Socialist companions had been engaged in clandestine activity: arranging safe mail boxes and false addresses, transmitting political situation reports, supplying political literature, providing shelters and home photo-laboratories, and arranging communication systems and courier lines to other sections. The work intensified in 1940-41 when Göth activated his cells in Lower Austria, particularly along the main railroad line from Vienna to Salzburg. As activity mounted, cooperation grew among the various sections. Haas's reputation for integrity and honesty enabled him to develop a well-integrated team of operators, who helped him pool military, political, and economic data and prepare news and commentaries for release to his network.

Until the early spring of 1940 Knoeringen remained in touch with Haas, always encouraging the militants to join the revolutionary forces who would take a prominent part in the destruction of Nazi dictatorship. The revolutionary situation, Knoeringen maintained, would make any Allied military intervention in Central and Eastern Europe unlikely, provided the great powers continued to pull in divergent directions. Knoeringen, who expected the United States to remain neutral and the Soviet Union to support the revolution, believed that Germany could survive without any dealings with the Allied powers, the Soviets, or the Americans. The main tasks of the

German revolution as he saw them were the destruction of German imperialism and the defense of the future revolutionary German state. Local leaders, too, as they grew in confidence became more active. Late in 1939 the head of the Salzburg section Anton Graf, a locksmith, made contact with a newly established RS organization in Salzburg, composed largely of personnel from the Reich Railways and Salzburg Railway and Street Car Company. The railwaymen Engelbert Weiss, Alfred Reska, Karl Seywald, and the traffic inspector August Gruber formed the local RS leadership. They improved the communication line with Switzerland where former SPÖ member of Parliament Anton Linder from Vorarlberg was their liaison man. The same contacts reached to Upper Austria.[12] Assistance also came from the railwaymen on the Linz-Salzburg main line as well as from those working on the secondary lines.[13] In all, they enrolled around one hundred RS members from other branches of the Reich Railways, and used part of the membership fee to assist the families of arrested companions or to support the activists.

Frieb visited Weiss, Reska, and Gruber early in 1940 and called upon the Salzburg activists to supply him with reports on the workers' attitude to the regime, the go-slow campaign in the factories, the quality of products, the military use of railways, the troop transports, and their destination. Unfortunately, Frieb did not consider security precautions and requested the Salzburg RS to contact the chiefs of the sections in Vienna, Wörgl, and Augsburg directly. He boasted about Haas's alleged ties to Comintern agents in Hungary and to SOPADE and about contacts with the Soviet Trade Mission. Despite the earlier Nazi military success in Poland, the participants anticipated Nazi military defeat in the West. Deeply concerned with the political future of Germany after the collapse of Nazism, they resolved to acquire more small arms for their network.

The Salzburg RS group contributed a political impulse along Socialist lines. Graf's group and the RS group easily found a common ground in the summer of 1940, and the expanded movement named itself the "Revolutionary Socialists of Austria" (RSÖ). However, the association between the Salzburg activists, the German sections around Frieb, who was drafted into the Army on August 1, 1941, and Wager was operationally unsound, because the network failed to devise adequate security checks. Informed by Frieb, Haas also voiced his misgivings. He had favored retaining a cadre organization rather than assembling a large following. In the end, however, Haas reluctantly agreed to make contact with the Salzburg branch. In July and November 1941, the main activists outlined their plan to establish a string of new bases. Reliable operators were to work not only the railroad line from Vienna to Salzburg but also the region stretching from Southern Germany to the Ruhr Valley. Haas expected the railway workers to serve as couriers but opposed any closer contact. For security reasons, he was unhappy with the growing involvement of the militant Salzburg group;

neither did he favor the establishment of direct communications between the Salzburg and Tyrolian sections, an arrangement Frieb and Wager apparently approved of.

Haas's prudent approach was shared by the former trade union officials in Vienna, by Richard Freund, last chairman of the Socialist Free Trade Union of the Railway Workers, and by Andreas Thaler and Karl Dlouhy, who had played prominent roles in the illegal Free Trade Union movement before 1938. In his talk with Haas, Thaler reproached the Salzburg RSÖ for its radicalism and lack of caution.[14] Soon after the formation of the Salzburg group, Reska informed his former trade union boss Freund and requested advice. When Freund saw Reska and Weiss in Salzburg in the summer or fall of 1939, he informed them that he was reluctant to run risks and form clandestine cells, but preferred instead to assure the presence of an effective leadership for the decisive moments of the liberation.

During his second visit to Salzburg in the fall of 1940, Freund met RS militants, including Frieb, who called on "all the revolutionary Socialist groups in former Austria to set up an unified organization which would be closely connected with the Bavarian groups of similar political stance."[15] Without minimizing the ideological distance that separated the RSÖ from the KPÖ, Frieb endorsed the principle of a community of action with the Communists. He suggested that consultations with the Communists proceed at a national level and was anxious for his Salzburg friends to establish direct links with Haas, who could formulate proposals for mutual cooperation through his Communist contact in Budapest. Freund, for his part, in assessing the current situation, outlined an alternative plan. He left no doubt as to his rejection of any alliance with the Communists, who, in his view, would want to assume a leading role in any left-wing coalition. He vigorously reaffirmed his opposition to any intensification of clandestine activities, which would only enable the Gestapo to penetrate the Socialist ranks and to liquidate the old cadres. For the time being, he and his friends were determined not to create an underground Party network in Vienna.

The Communists' and the Socialists' mutual distrust of closer links continued unabated over the whole country, with the exception of Salzburg, where the RSÖ extended a helping hand to the local KPÖ elements. In 1940, the RSÖ initiated interparty negotiations at the regional level to form a mutual alliance that would heal the political split. The numerous discussions between the RSÖ delegation and its communist counterpart ultimately broke down in 1941. The main reason for the failure was reportedly not political and ideological divergencies, but differences concerning the functions the officials would hold in the unified organization.[16] The end result was, nevertheless, fatal. As the Gestapo had caught up with the Salzburg Communist network, it also learnt about the RSÖ.[17] Poorly trained for illegal work, and inadequately prepared with safety measures, the determined

Salzburg and Bavarian activists had pursued their missions in the hope that the war would be short. Not realizing the value of cut-outs and safe houses, they became an easy target for Gestapo destruction.[18]

While the RSÖ were fighting, they belittled security demands—only the struggle mattered. As the armed conflict intensified, the militant elements, such as Frieb, Wager, Reska, and Weiss, intensified their work, ignoring the urgent advice of Knoeringen, Haas, and Freund. As they sought to step up their activities, they broke away from their early commitment to a realistic course of action. Since small arms were in critically short supply, the activists began to collect and store them. They planned to set up five-man raiding parties to carry out carefully selected attacks on lines of communication, local NSDAP headquarters, and informers.[19] In 1941 and 1942 they prepared to engage in railway sabotage on the strategically important Brenner line.[20] These individual gestures were quixotic indeed, planned at a time when the Nazi presence must have looked permanent to the population. As affirmations of political faith, they certainly were not significant enough to weaken the regime. However, as an astute observer commented, "the aspirations and motivations of the Resistance were, in a sense, always more important than its concrete achievements because it was in these that the Resistance had its precise identity."[21]

After having penetrated the KP ranks, the Gestapo closed in on the KPÖ in Salzburg in early 1942. Under torture, several functionaries revealed their contacts with the RSÖ. The resulting arrests decimated the entire RSÖ network.[22] The Gestapo shattered the Salzburg network first. In April the Brunners, Frieb, Wager, and four other adherents from the Augsburg section were caught. The Vienna group followed in June and August. The roundup continued till December 1942, with arrest following arrest. Finally, Freund, Dlouhy, and Thaler fell into Gestapo hands in 1943.[23] All in all, some 200 Socialists were brought to trial, twelve were sentenced to death, and twelve died in prison.

The trial against Haas, Göth, Frieb, Wager, Gruber, Brunner, and Graf took place before the VGH in 1943; all were sent to their death. A few days after he had received his death sentence, Haas wrote to his sister (December 19, 1943): "I have taken the sentence composedly and my bearing is steady. Eventually, I could not have expected anything else. . . . For whoever dies or has to die, dying is not so terrible."[24] Wager, in his last letter smuggled from his death cell in Munich-Stadelheim, revealed his steadfastness: "Be strong; the victory belongs to us, and when we die, it will not have been in vain. Let us bury the hatred; our goal is much higher. Our sacrifice reflects a historical necessity."[25] They went to their death with faith, integrity, and fortitude.

The RSÖ was an ambiguous phenomenon. It neither espoused the revolutionary policies of the AVÖS and its refusal to identify the Socialist cause with the Austrian Resistance, nor did it espouse the mass-oriented activism of the KPÖ. Knoeringen and Haas managed to rally the politically disenchanted Socialist militants. In their reluctance to engage in mass clandestine propaganda and in their concern about the practical implications of their work, their movement rivaled other democratic movements. Their early rally to the underground embodied an activist idealism, a vision of a better society, and a rebellion against political oppression.

For a number of German and Austrian Socialist militants, the central concern was not a sense of national purpose nor championship of Greater-German nor Austrian nationalism but a devotion to moral and humanistic purpose in life. In their minds, the expected social and economic changes were irretrievably tied to the coming of the All-German revolution, merging Germany and Austria.[26] The distinguishing feature of the movement, however, was the capacity of Haas, Knoeringen, and their associates to sustain the political effect of their ideology through an elaborate clandestine structure dedicated to collecting intelligence. Apparently, Haas had been able to build a liaison system with the British Intelligence in London and to camouflage his data collection by intensive political propaganda.[27] He was instrumental in channeling the anti-Nazi Socialist spirit into a wide array of tangible political and intelligence activities.[28]

The similarities of the German and Austrian activists suggest that they shared many views. Their common Socialist experience minimized any Austrian patriotic tendency. The highly skilled workers and lower supervisory personnel forming the core of the RSÖ in Salzburg were representative of the labor community.[29] Involved in daily relations with fellow workers and sharing a background of common experience, they were apt to be aware of co-workers' grievances and feelings. They did not engage in any spectacular acts but showed determination in constituting a force-in-being, ready for the future. The most important figures were former trade union and party officials retaining links with the rank-and-file. Most of the followers were between thirty and fifty years of age, and included many who had participated in the underground against the Schuschnigg regime and had been active in party politics before 1934.

The merging trade unionists and Socialists within the RSÖ obviously manifested a quest for wider contacts, just as their interest in illegal work sought to identify resistance with the respectability of Austrian Socialism. Both the trade unionist and political segments of the Socialist movement mounted clandestine activities that promoted solidarity among an array of leftist groupings. The lessons of the RSÖ for the future of Socialist politics lay not in ideology but in action, in the more pragmatic search of the RS for a new political role in which moral commitment and practical achievement emerged as the primary Socialist objectives. In effect, the RSÖ was less an extension of the revolutionary Marxist tradition than a response to national emergency by segments of the traditional Socialist constituency.

NOTES

1. The movement became associated with the Austrian RS. See also R. Harris Smith, *OSS. The Secret History of America's First Central Intelligence Agency* (Berkeley, 1972), pp. 208-9, 218-19; Lewis J. Edinger, *German Exile Politics. The Social Democratic Executive Committee in the Nazi Era* (Berkeley, 1956), pp. 97, 164.

2. For accounts of the Austro-German RSÖ network, see "Gestapo, Staatspolizeistelle Innsbruck, Ergänzung zum Schlussbericht vom 30. Juli 1942," December 8, 1942, DÖW 3217; AS, VGH, 7J 649/42, January 27, 1943, DÖW 398; AS, VGH, 7J 366/43, September 6, 1943, DÖW 2040/a II, 3337; U, VGH, 7J 421/42g-6H 63/43, DÖW 3217/2; DÖW 485, 3383; U, OLG Wien, 60Js 444/43, December 15, 1943, DÖW 1788, AS, O Js 444/43, August 12, 1943, DÖW 233; U, VGH, 7J 649/42-6H 24/43, DÖW 10969; U, OLG Wien, 70Js 560/43, January 18, 1944, DÖW 200; AS, VGH, 7J 404/43, October 26, 1943, DÖW 4119; "Gestapo, Staatspolizeileitstelle Wien, Tagesberichte," DÖW 5734/c; "Bruno Sokoll, 1938-1945. Erinnerungen," DÖW 7141; "Kurzbericht über die illegale Tätigkeit der südbayerischen und österreichischen Gruppen der SPD," DÖW 2673; interviews with Dr. Paul Schärf, Bruno Sokoll; Szecsi-Stadler, *NS-Justiz,* pp. 60-65; DÖW, ed., *Widerstand Wien,* 2:63 ff; Eugen Nerdinger, ed., *Flamme unter Asche* (Augsburg, 1979); Heike Bretschneider, *Der Widerstand gegen den Nationalsozialismus in München 1933 bis 1945* (München, 1968), pp. 113-20; Gerhard Hetzer in Martin Broszat, et al., eds., *Bayern in der NS-Zeit, Vol. 3: Herrschaft und Gesellschaft im Konflikt.* Teil B, 192-205.

3. Interview with B. Sokoll; DÖW 3217. Haas' father, a Socialist district councillor in Vienna, died in 1923. Otto had to take odd jobs to continue his studies. Later, his mother represented the SPÖ in the City Council.

4. During his stay in Prague as Knoeringen's guest in the summer of 1937, Haas underwent training in clandestine communication techniques. DÖW 2040/a/II.

5. Ibid.

6. DÖW 3217.

7. DÖW 7596.

8. DÖW 2673.

9. Haas and Frieb financed their work from funds collected from Jewish emigrants who received the corresponding sum in foreign currency abroad. DÖW 3217.

10. Backed by the British Labour Party, Knoeringen and his German Social Democratic friends were charged with the "Broadcast of the German Revolution" transmitted to Germany. *Der Kochel-Brief,* December 1963; Michael Balfour, *Propaganda in War 1939-1945. Organizations, Policies, and Publics in Britain and Germany* (London, 1979), p. 466.

11. Polak and his wife had been involved in the underground from 1934 and served as couriers to the Salzburg and Tyrol sections. When arrested, Polak hanged himself in his prison cell on October 12, 1942. Another high school teacher, Josef Sommerauer, was responsible for photo-technical work, microfilms, and book bindings. The books were used to smuggle reports and propaganda material on microfilms hidden in bindings. *Der Kochel-Brief,* December 1963.

12. Stadler, *Österreich,* p. 366.

13. Vogl, *Eisenbahner,* pp. 177, 179, 182.

14. Stadler, *Österreich,* p. 367.

15. DÖW 4119.

16. DÖW 9798; Vogl, *Eisenbahner,* p. 176.

17. DÖW 2673.

18. A cut-out is the making of contact between two persons without their knowing each other.

19. In 1942 the Gestapo seized forty-eight revolvers and pistols, as well as munition and explosives from Frieb and eight pistols from Wager. DÖW 1448.

20. DÖW 2673, 6345/b.

96   REVOLUTIONARY SOCIALISTS OF AUSTRIA

21. King, "Emmanuel d'Astier," *Journal of Contemporary History,* 8 (1973):31.

22. For the German side of the RSÖ, see Nerdinger, ed., *Flamme,* passim. For the numerous adherents of the Salzburg RSÖ, see Vogl, *Eisenbahner,* pp. 182 ff, 191.

23. By June 1942, Haas knew that his arrest was imminent but he made no attempt to run away. He probably did not want to incriminate his relatives and friends. Paul Schärf, *Otto Haas. Ein revolutionärer Sozialist gegen das Dritte Reich* (Vienna, 1967), p. 16.

24. Ibid., pp. 21-22.

25. *Der Kochel-Brief,* December 1963. Alois Brunner wrote from his Stadelheim cell in his last letter to his imprisoned wife: "Tell it to all others: 'We were faithful till death.' "

26. DÖW 233; Schärf, *Haas,* pp. 18-19.

27. In 1943 Haas's sister reportedly mentioned to some close friends the possibility of the British taking Haas in exchange for a German agent caught by the British. At the end of 1943 some Swiss officials were approached in Vienna in this matter. Interview with Dr. Paul Schärf.

28. The Innsbruck Gestapo viewed the intelligence-gathering as the RSÖ's main objective. "The intelligence was divided into two phases. One part was used for training purposes. . . . The second part originating from various bases moved . . . right up [to Haas]. . . . We believe that the data gathered by Michel [Haas] were forwarded for evaluation either to the headquarters of the illegal SPD or, what is more likely, to the enemy's intelligence service." December 8, 1942, "Ergänzung zum Schlussbericht vom 30. Juli 1942." Schärf, *Haas,* p. 27.

29. Vogl, *Eisenbahner,* pp. 182 ff; OLG Wien, 7 OJs 411/42, May 5, 1943, DÖW 9798.

PART THREE
The KPÖ in the Resistance: The Communist Cadres and the Socialist Rank and File

10

The Beginning

THE CLANDESTINE STRUCTURE OF THE KPÖ

On the night of March 11-12, 1938, senior KPÖ officials assembled in Prague drafted a resounding answer to the Nazi occupation of Austria. In its proclamation, the Party advocated continuing its policy of national unity designed to acquire it political respectability in an anti-Nazi struggle that would unite the Austrian patriotic forces. "On March 11 the last liberation war of the Austrian people started. . . . Through her own power and with the assistance of the world peace front, a free, independent Austria will be reborn."[1] The commitment to Austrian identity and to the struggle against Nazi domination played a dominant part in the KP efforts to occupy the left wing of the political spectrum vacated by the RS. Through the Resistance, the KPÖ sought to restore the Party's fortunes.

In August 1938 the Central Committee (CC) laid down for itself in its main political directive the task of conducting

(a) the struggle against foreign rule and for self-determination and self-government of the Austrian people;
(b) the struggle for the people's democratic rights;
(c) the struggle against the economic plunder of the country;
(d) the struggle against the war policy of German Fascism;
(e) the struggle against cultural barbarism and antisemitism.[2]

The KPÖ emerged from the Schuschnigg era experienced in underground operations, but impeded by its clandestine organizational structure. The illegal KPÖ still resembled a political party more than a resistance movement. Its structure was that of a Leninist-Stalinist cadre organization, centralized and disciplined. Almost inevitably, a tendency ensued to view the clandestine movement largely as a political instrument for disseminating Party propaganda. To alleviate this difficulty, the KPÖ opted for a new approach. In the late spring of 1938, the CC abroad ordered the reorganization of the command structure and prohibited any contacts and horizontal alignments among the local cells. Instructions were to be channeled through loose vertical lines of communications. Activists were forbidden to communicate with each other. When local branches needed to get into touch with the home center, special passwords or coded messages were arranged. Another set of directives instructed Party veterans and Jews to withdraw from politics to secure safety. Party officials were not to be remunerated for their services; and the underground cells were to remain small.[3]

To keep in touch with the public, Party members adopted the Trojan horse tactic and penetrated the ranks of the NSDAP, HJ, SA, DAF, or other Nazi organizations and formed cells in large industrial and municipal enterprises, above all in city transportation, and in electricity and gas works.[4] VGH files and Gestapo reports reveal that Communist militants joined Nazi organizations to disorient the Nazi followers or to assist the Communist underground. In the factories the Party's major task was social propaganda and agitation. The rise in consumer prices, higher taxes, German interference, strict work discipline, and new regulations and restrictions created resentment and ill feeling among disgruntled elements of the working classes. The Communists busily agitated for social benefits as the initial public confidence in the regime gave way to doubts about its ability to boost material conditions. The Party tried to secure the workers' cooperation on nonpolitical, bread-and-butter issues. Clearly, open persuasion could not be successfully combined with clandestine actions, which entailed risks disproportionate to their effectiveness. The emphasis on clandestine propaganda among the industrial workers made secrecy and security practically impossible, since it was obviously hard to guard closely the Communist-run sections when they engaged in semi-public actions. The weight of evidence tells of the usually short-lived factory cells whose members labored hard and risked their lives for leaflet and clandestine press operations.

Production, distribution, and circulation of propaganda material had been the responsibility of a separate branch, the so-called central Literature-apparatus (Lit-ap) in Vienna. Theoretically, for security reasons, this service operated independently of the main organizations. In practice, however, the division of the duties overlapped, presenting a serious threat to the entire Party network. The central Lit-ap, after its downfall at the end of 1939, was never completely rebuilt. Its demise undoubtedly increased the influence that the district and local literature cells (Literaturstellen) and the smaller KP groups exercised over propaganda work, especially the production and distribution of written material. The distributing and even the reading of an underground Communist tract was punishable by long imprisonment or sometimes even by death.

Helmut Konrad has identified two main types of underground publications: (1) those directed to the non-Communist public, among whom the Party sought supporters and allies; (2) those addressed to the Party rank and file. The large number of clandestine papers and tracts testified to the authorities the existence of the home resistance and threatened to instill insecurity and doubt in the public mind.[6] The tracts were a complementary weapon to the forbidden (since September 2, 1939) foreign broadcasts: for what they lacked in immediacy and reliability, they made up in psychological impact. The illegal press did not confine itself to passive reporting but served to mobilize supporters and to guard the Party line against possible political deviation. However, as tracts were readily available, the Gestapo carefully followed up every lead by tracing the names of local Communists in the police files or by infiltrating the groups. Although the propaganda apparatus, which usually operated separately, had designed strict rules to secure the safety of its contacts with the network, the Gestapo often quickly fractured the Lit-ap lines, which left the associated main Communist network, usually operating without a proper cut-out system, dangerously exposed.[7]

Throughout its existence, the KPÖ maintained close relations with the Comintern and the Soviet Communist Party. The KPÖ's chairman, a worker, Johann Koplenig, who enjoyed Stalin's confidence, never strayed from the Comintern line. In September 1938 the KP moved the CC from Prague to Paris and in 1939 to Moscow. From the outset, the Party kept its own organizational apparatus, but the KP exile center appointed each of the major operators in charge of the clandestine apparatus at home. Through its handpicked organizers, directives, and printed material smuggled into Austria, the center and the Kremlin assured the continuation of their control and prevented the formation of any independent homegrown Communist leadership.[8]

In the aftermath of Munich, the KPÖ had to streamline its chains of command, and its operative practices. Recognizing the need to strengthen its links to Austria, in August the exile center set up a new liaison station in Maribor, Yugoslavia, for work in Styria and Carinthia. It also created a base in Zurich to run contacts to Austria and to supply the central Lit-ap in Vienna with propaganda material.[9] Within the country, a new structure was established. The party's primary task was to be political and not the gathering of intelligence nor the engaging in direct action. The home leadership was built up in Vienna around a Landesleiter who headed the Landesleitung (Central Command) for Austria. As the principal source of authority at home, he directed the organization. However, the exile center remained the true source of authority responsible for policy decisions. The two centers, at home and abroad, were never seriously at odds with each other.

In large factories, public utilities, and smaller communities, underground representatives of the workers headed the local cells. These representatives were connected vertically by contact men to the district chiefs who served as liaison agents to the regional representative (Kreisleiter). He, in turn, was in touch through his liaison men with the Viennese or Provincial Directorate serving as the operation command for Vienna and the remaining part of the country.[10] The Viennese and Provincial Directorates were directly subordinated to the Central Command. The Provincial Directorate existed sporadically, and the underground apparatus in the more remote provinces of Styria and Carinthia was run from Yugoslavia. Thus, a small number of reliable Communist operators were the network's leading spirits while the rank-and-file members consisted mainly of former Social Democrats.

At the factory level, the workers' underground representatives strenuously tried to enroll new followers. They collected membership fees that supported the clandestine work and prepared reports on the situation in their workshops or factories. The district chiefs usually handed the membership fees to the Kreisleiter and collected propaganda literature from him to be distributed among the local sections. A number of the districts produced their own tracts. The usefulness of the political activities varied, but the existing structure imperiled its members by attracting too much attention.

By the spring of 1939, after the downfall of three successive central commands, it was evident that the clumsy organizational structure badly required an overhaul. To render political subversion a safer activity, the factory sections were incorporated, in the summer of 1939, into three branches, each serving one sector: municipal enterprises, metal manufacturing, and the remaining industrial sectors. A special organizer, providing liaison to the Kreisleiter, headed each branch.[11] Up to the last phase of the war, the factory and local cells formed the core of the Communist underground, separated into provincial networks composed of groups that never exceeded a few hundred militants.[12] Even this size permitted Gestapo penetration by double agents, usually Communist veterans who had broken down during police interrogation. In general, Communist chiefs had an average life expectancy of less than one year.

THE FIRST CENTRAL NETWORKS

Under the direction of CC member Wilhelm Frank, a twenty-eight-year old locksmith, who as the chief organizer played a key role, the KPÖ built a centralized underground with strong roots in Vienna. In July 1938, after he had established the sections in Vienna and arranged contacts via Czechoslovakia and Zurich with the Party center abroad, Frank handed the direction of the network over to Karl Zwifelhofer and made his way to Czechoslovakia. Frank's early role was important; but being already well known to the Austrian police, he could hardly have carried on his activity for long.[13]

His successor, Zwifehofer, a Viennese locksmith, became a Communist in 1920 and was active in the Communist Youth Union (KJV). From 1930 to 1933, he lived in the Soviet Union, returning then to Vienna where he went underground. In 1936, he took part in the Spanish Civil War as a member of the KP contingent. In Paris, he was appointed head of the KPÖ network in his homeland. He returned to Vienna illegally in June 1938 to secure control of the reconstructed KPÖ.[14] Zwifelhofer was responsible for the Party for too short a period to be able to get a firm hold on the organization. He was recalled to Paris in September, apparently in connection with the sharpening international crisis, because the Comintern, readjusting itself for the possibility of war, needed experienced Party bureaucrats.

Before his departure on September 20 or 22, Zwifelhofer introduced as his successor Bruno Dubber, who had just arrived from Prague.[15] With his panache, mind-boggling energy, and brashness, Dubber had established a reputation as a tireless and idealistic Party official. Born in Hamburg in 1920, he worked as a lathe operator and in 1926 joined the Communist youth movement, where he rose rapidly to high-level functions. He lived in the Soviet Union from 1932 to 1934, after which he moved to Austria to take over the KJV leadership. By 1935, when he was forced to escape to Czechoslovakia, he was already known as an accomplished youth leader, always drawn to action.[16] A wide-ranging organizer, Dubber made increased use of the lines with Zurich and Prague for smuggling propaganda material. He intensified contacts with the activists, set up new safe houses, attached the cells in Styria, added Upper and Lower Austria to his command, and formed the central nucleus in Vienna, where dozens of clandestine cells had sprung up.

The growth of Communist activity made the Nazis anxious to identify their opponents. In the late summer of 1938, they put under surveillance some prominent Communists in Vienna, among them the head of the Viennese network, Gebietsleiter Josef Csarmann.[17] On November 14, the Gestapo captured Dubber and his courier in a coffeehouse. His enthusiasm still running high, Dubber sent out propaganda and schooling instructions for his young adherents from his prison cell, even though he had been badly mauled during the interrogations.[18] Csarmann fell into police hands the next day, and another forty-one militants were rounded up in the second half of November and in December, among them two messengers from Switzerland and the heads of the railway, student, and telegraph sections.[19] The decapitation of the central command eliminated almost without trace the first central leadership. However, the Party network still remained a vigorous force in the country.

The KPÖ's capacity for suffering was certainly high at all times. In Vienna and Lower Austria alone in the period from the Nazi takeover to the end of 1938, 890 individuals were arrested under suspicion of Communist activities. Many enrolled members appear to have been swept into the Communist ranks because of their hostility to the regime; they were not tried to the movement by political affinity. With the exception of those in the highest Party echelons, the typical adherent was usually either a former Socialist activist, who had joined the Communist underground as the only alternative to his own politically inactive movement, or a fighter who had divested himself of the prudent Socialist policies to join a militant anti-Nazi movement.[20]

Most Communist activity consisted of showing the flag and of demonstrating its presence by written propaganda. In 1938, the Viennese Gestapo seized 127 pamphlets, 1,005 brochures, 1,000 copies of the CC resolutions, and 5,000 leaflets.[21] The KPÖ staked its claim to leadership on its power bastion in Vienna, where it concentrated on selected industrial areas and on operating the factory cells. The City Directorate (Stadtleitung) exercised control in Vienna, which was divided into several circles that functioned as command centers of the districts. These, in turn, organized themselves around a system of subdistricts and local cells.[22] In the late spring of 1938, the City Directorate founded local cells in the South Circle (Kreis), comprising the populous districts of Landstrasse, Simmering, and Favoriten.[23] It also assigned Party officials to important factories and to enterprises with substantial numbers of workers. Close attention was given to Floridsdorf, an important industrial suburb on the left bank of the Danube, where, time and again, scores of Party officials were rounded up.[24]

Another development was politically of great importance to the KPÖ. From the ranks of the youth, activists emerged who quickly assumed the initiative in organizing the clandestine network of the Communist Youth Union (KJV).[25] Dubber was the first KP leader to construct a solid youth underground at a national level. Despite its Communist tag, the KJV attracted the politically literate Socialist youth. Because a large number of militants were called up for military service or could not be recruited, the responsibilities of youthful outfits increased.[26]

Largely unknown to Gestapo, which was armed only with lists of Party membership from the pre-1938 era, the youth movement provided the natural infrastructure for the Party underground. The KVJ soon expanded into a country-wide organization of working-class youth. Under Dubber's inspiration, the KJV instructions reflected the Party's commitment to Austrian statehood. They called for unity of action with other anti-Fascist forces and urged the young activists to join the HJ and other regime youth and sport associations so as to subvert the system from the inside.[27] Simultaneously, the system of three-man cells was extended. Formed into blocks and subdistricts, the cells were placed under the authority of district and regional chiefs. In the second half of 1940, the City of Vienna was divided into four KJV regions (Gebiete).[28] Each region was composed of five to six districts and operated its own literature apparatus.

With Dubber's arrest, the first centrally organized youth network was badly shaken, but it did not disintegrate. It was revitalized in 1939-40. The Party's new precautionary measures were partly responsible for the limited number of casualties; in the fall, the Party instructed each of its networks to build a parallel apparatus to alleviate any troubles the network might experience in the case of its downfall. It required the operators to engage an alternate occupant for every position in the organization. Furthermore, it recommended the enrollment of women as second-in-command.[29] However, as KJV organizational work entailed great exposure to the security organs, the arrests of the youth cadres became frequent. The Gestapo caught up with some of the KJV sections in 1938 and 1939.[30] In November 1938, it broke up a student outfit. Associated closely with the KPÖ and inspired by the traditions of the revolutionary student movement, the radical students had established cells linked with Csarmann and Dubber;[31] entangled in the KP central network that was under Gestapo surveillance, they were picked up by the police.[32]

THE STYRIAN CONNECTION

During the difficult period of initial readjustment to the Anschluss, the KPÖ worked intensely in Vienna. In the provinces, adjustment to the changed situation was slow. In May 1938, a directive issued from Vienna called on August Pirker in Graz, Styria, to reorganize the Party apparatus in that area. Pirker, a twenty-eight-year old boiler-maker, was a graduate of the Lenin Political School in Moscow, which he had attended in 1935-36. In 1937 he was instructed to return unobtrusively to Graz and to establish a cover.[33] After the Anschluss, his task as the new regional chief was to recreate the Party network. Severing connections with Vienna, he communicated directly with the exile CC through its branch in Maribor, Yugoslavia, situated near the Austrian border. He placed the underground in Styria and Carinthia under the control of the KP station in Zagreb, Yugoslavia, which also supplied Party literature. After Pirker's departure from Vienna, Zwifelhofer was put in charge of the KPÖ Yugoslav section. He constantly briefed Pirker and the various KPÖ and KJV messengers from Styria and Carinthia who came to see him in Maribor.[34]

The havoc that the Nazi takeover wrought among the Party followers made Pirker abandon the existing pre-1938 clandestine structure, that of Party local, district, and regional sections. Instead, he organized a network of three-man cells, with each cell responsible for its own political indoctrination. The persevering efforts put into recruiting workers were rewarded with considerable success. Pirker infiltrated the largest Graz armament plant, the Steyr-Daimler-Puch Works, through a net of factory cells at each of its departments. Working at a fast pace, Pirker assembled many groupings throughout Styria. He kept in touch with Anton Buchalka, the chief organizer of a large network in the Upper Styrian industrial basin, and worked closely with the KJV operators in and around Graz.[35] He established contacts with the KPÖ representatives in Yugoslavia during his journeys in November 1938 and February 1939. They urged him to construct a unified national coalition integrating Catholic and Socialist activists, but nothing came of that suggestion. Suddenly, on February 14, Pirker was apprehended in Graz, and a number of arrests from January to March 1939 devastated the network. In all, of fifty suspects, twenty-three were charged with high treason. Later Pirker's trusted aide was unmasked as a double agent: having fallen into Gestapo hands at the end of September, he had changed sides. Through him the Nazis had broken into the network and had waited patiently before closing in.[36]

Among the young Communist militants in Upper Styria, the Anschluss lent urgency to the rebuilding of the illegal KJV structures in the industrial areas around Knittelfeld, Leoben, and Bruck an der Mur. In the second half of March 1938, the Viennese KJV requested the head of the KJV Knittelfeld district, Alois Lew, to resurrect support for underground work.[37] The activities gained impetus with the appearance of former KJV provincial chief Friedrich Pietzka, an electro-mechanic, and his fiancée Hermine Sagmeister, a teacher. They successfully restructured the pre-1938 KJV underground in Upper Styria, Klagenfurt, and Villach. The group was linked with Pirker in Graz, and in the summer of 1938 it communicated with Zwifelhofer in Vienna. In April 1939, Sagmeister met Zwifelhofer in Yugoslavia. In May and June, 1939 disaster struck the KJV when forty-three activists were captured.[38] The disruption of the wide-ranging group was felt throughout its recruiting area in Upper Styria.

For a while, Communist influence among youths remained limited, but the Communists were not easily intimidated into disbanding their organization. In the summer of 1938, Anton Buchalka, a twenty-six-year-old electro-technician, had created a cell in the large Böhler Works in Kapfenberg. His militant Socialist past brought him close to the KPÖ. In his community, he wielded enough political reputation for the Nazis to pick him for one of the celebrated free journeys into the Reich in 1938. In the early summer of 1939, a senior KPÖ official from Vienna responsible for the work in the southern provinces, Wilhelm Wehofer, contacted him.[39] Greatly encouraged by his talks with this experienced operator, the combative Buchalka committed himself to founding a network of small nuclei embracing all of Upper Styria.

Because of his Socialist background, Buchalka was not on any KP membership list known to the police, and it therefore took some time for the
Gestapo to catch up with him.[40]

In August 1939, the conclusion of the Molotov-Ribbentrop Non-
aggression Pact greatly confused the KPÖ. The Party believed the situation
demanded greater intensification of its propaganda, as numerous supporters ceased their activities. Upon Wehofer's urging, Buchalka set up a
printing works, where in the fall of 1939 he produced four pamphlets.[41]
Although highly laudatory of the Soviet Union in general and of its fight
against "the Finnish imperialists," the statements showed sensitivity
toward the patriotic aspirations of Austrians and appealed to the working
class to end the war and to wage a struggle against Hitler. Undoubtedly, the
easily traceable mass propaganda imperiled the resisters; it annoyed the
Graz Gestapo, who soon found those responsible when its informer provided copies of Buchalka's tracts. Losses were heavy. Buchalka was seized
on January 30, 1940. Some 250 persons joined him behind bars by October
1940.[42] The Graz Gestapo reported in December that although chiefs of the
network were without exception old-time Communists, its followers by contrast were largely former Socialist activists.[43]

Because of the major character of the organization, the Nazi authorities
launched a thorough investigation into the causes of the resisters' discontent, and found their disaffection related to social grievances. First, the
resisters railed against the DAF for treating them as second-class citizens
because of their former Marxist views. Second, contrary to all its promises,
the regime had not overly concerned itself with their declining standard of
living. In general, the difference between higher prices and low wages remained a serious cause of trouble.[44]

Pressure was also brought to bear on the KP underground in other provinces. The provincial center in Carinthia rashly built in the fall of 1938 was
caught in the Gestapo sweep. In Linz, Sepp Teufel, a former CC KPÖ
member, used his skills to set up a cell, which was penetrated in the fall of
1944.[45] For the KPÖ, as for the rest of the Resistance, mere survival was the
priority. They could not insulate the movement from the adverse pressures
of the overall European conflict. But there was no real gloom in the
underground, because nobody had expected instant success.

THE SECOND LEADERSHIP, 1939

In the period following Dubber's arrest, the growing volume of news and
rumor once again disturbed the Gestapo. The introduction on January 1,
1939, of the higher rates of income tax prevailing in the Reich increased the
tax burden of wage earners and upset the low-income groups. The growing
unrest was reflected both in the escalating number of Communist leaflets

circulating in Vienna during January and in sporadic, small acts of sabotage at the Siemens-Schuckert Works in Vienna-Leopoldau. On February 18, an attempt was made to burn the exhibition, "Bolshevism without its Mask," at the Vienna Northwestern Railroad Station hall.[46] The effect of clandestine propaganda on popular morale was difficult to gauge, but the tracts stung the regime into counteraction.

The temporary leadership vacuum involved no abandonment of the resistance posture in Dubber's area of work.[47] A large number of Communist-run cells remained in Vienna and its environs, their nature and importance varying almost from section to section. Through hard work, a former SPÖ member, Johann Schöber, a street-car conductor and chief organizer of the Vienna Street Car System section, maintained the dynamic momentum of the initial progress. Throughout 1939, he welded the KP cells into an extensive network, with some 150 members particularly active in the Socialist stronghold of Ottakring.[48]

The police described Josef Wipplinger, the cofounder of the Vienna network, as one of those personalities who exercised a direct and formative influence on the effort to recreate an active Party underground in 1939. He maintained communication lines with the Party CC in Paris and assumed responsibility for the delivery of the clandestine press from abroad and for its production at home. His task required his undertaking several journeys to Yugoslavia to hold talks with the KP representatives.[49]

In the spring of 1939, the situation in Vienna appeared confused, and the CC in exile strove to reforge the bonds with the home network. In the early spring, Wilhelm Frank returned to Vienna. He soon contacted Schöber to survey the remaining forces. At the same time, two full-time CC instructors, Anton Reisinger and Josef Angermann, returned from France to settle under various covers in Austria.[50] Within a month, Frank met a number of organizers to whom he emphasized ideological training, and he directed the cells to conduct lectures on various ideological themes. The stress on indoctrination reflected the KP concern with the political loyalty of its members, but it betrayed a dangerous neglect of basic clandestine rules requiring complete discretion and a minimum of mutual contacts. Within a few months, Frank left for Switzerland, but not before he had introduced Ludwig Schmidt, whom the CC in Paris dispatched as its chief representative to Austria.[51] The KP leadership in Paris desired to keep in steady touch with the homeland and to handle the problem of coordination and reorganization. In fact, the CC never relinquished its guidance of the Party underground.

Schmidt laid a solid foundation in Vienna and the provinces.[52] With the conclusion of the Nazi-Soviet Pact, the KPÖ found itself face to face with a political issue that urgently needed explanation. The Party felt that the new Moscow line describing the war as a conflict between two imperialist blocks, for which British and French capitalist governments were mainly responsible, called for an increased circulation of Party literature. Schmidt helped to assemble a special editorial board to draft texts; he organized the pick-up and control of tracts by special delivery channels, the collection of new material, the selection of political themes, and the monitoring of Radio Moscow.[53] The Nazis observed the KP work with considerable unease because they feared its psychological impact upon the population.

The growing volume of propaganda actions, the improved techniques of production, and the unified character of the operations in the summer and fall of 1939 convinced the Gestapo that a centrally run organization had conceived the campaigns. Wipplinger and other known KP activists were immediately put under surveillance. The result was fatal. On December 9, 1939, Schmidt was picked up in the street near his safe house in Vienna. His security precautions were poor, and the Gestapo found in his house incriminating materials, including his notes, cover identity, and a list of foreign addresses.[54] The KP central Lit-ap had been liquidated four days earlier. Thus the propaganda activity had endangered the entire network. When the interrogators discovered the close connections between the Lit-ap and the activists under surveillance, they picked up a further thirty-five suspects. Between December 5 and December 19, the Gestapo seized 119 persons. Schöber and others were caught between January and March 1940.[55]

No substantial differences between the Austrian and other Communist clandestine movements in Europe existed. Their range of activity was small: the KPÖ regular networks did not carry out diversions, acts of sabotage, or gather intelligence.[56] However, notwithstanding the many setbacks and shortcomings, it would be unfair to state that the KPÖ achievements were minimal. Even though the slogans scribbled on the cities' pavements and walks, the proclamations issued, the leaflets posted, and the paper circulated had no more to offer the common people than vague exhortations, they were much feared by the authorities, if one takes the Gestapo reports at their word. No doubt, the Communists were partly fulfilling the necessary function of adversary in the Nazi system, which could be relied upon to exaggerate the effectiveness of the Communist Resistance.

Nevertheless the regime did single out the Communist clandestine press for special attention, and the security organs made special efforts to scrutinize its impact closely. Although the number of copies of confiscated Communist "hate literature" publications declined from 513 to 347 between 1937 and 1939 within the old Reich, its volume increased in Austria and the Protectorate of Bohemia and Moravia in the last quarter of 1939. In Austria, the number of seized copies of publications had a general declining tendency, with periodic ups and downs; it peaked in November 1938, and was up again in May, July, and August 1939. In January 1940 it reached its nadir, where it remained until July 1940.[57]

In the atmosphere of fear, suspicion, and natural caution, which the arrests engendered within the underground, it became more difficult to restock the clandestine cadres with replacements. No one in a position of authority in the underground felt secure. Yet, the underground continued to grow, involving in its labyrinthine structure dozens of old and new cells with different spheres of activity. Each cell served as a constant reminder that the attaining of Austria's independence and the defeat of National Socialism still remained a strong enough vision for a few to risk their lives.

NOTES

1. The proclamation adopted the Schuschnigg slogan, "Red-White-Red till death ensues!" See the Central Committee of the KPÖ in *Die Kommunistische Partei zur nationalen Frage Österreichs, 1937-1945* (Vienna, 1945), pp. 9-10; Wolfgang Neugebauer, Symposium, "Anschluss 1938," 14.-15. März 1978; Exenberger, Die illegale Presse in Österreich, p. 8; Eva Priester in *Volksstimme,* March 10, 1978. Helene Maimann indicates that the concept of Austrian independence was not included in any official KP statements between August 1939 and October 1942. On October 22, 1942, Moscow radio announced the formation of the "Austrian Freedom Front" within the country calling "for a free, independent Austria." Reinhard Bollmus, "Österreichs Unabhängigkeit im Widerstreit," *Zeitgeschichte,* 4, November 1976, 56 ff; Wilfried Aichinger, "Sowjetische Österreichpolitik 1943-1945" (Ph.D. dissertation, University of Vienna, 1977), pp. 46-49. However, Helmut Konrad notes that illegal KP publications, except *Die Rote Fahne,* endorsed an independent Republic. Similarly, the Nazi courts always considered that the Communists had attempted to tear Austria away from the Reich. *Widerstand an Donau und Moldau. KPÖ and KSČ zur Zeit des Hitler-Stalin-Paktes* (Vienna, 1978), pp. 144-54. Ernst Schwager, "Die österreichische Emigration in Frankreich in der Zeit vom 'Anschluss' Österreichs an das Deutsche Reich im März 1938 bis zum Kriegsende 1945" (Ph.D. dissertation, University of Vienna, 1979), pp. 280-85, supports Konrad's view.

2. *Die Kommunistische Partei zur nationalen Frage,* p. 5; DÖW, ed., *Widerstand Wien,* 2:97.

3. Leopold Hornik, the CC KPÖ representative in Paris, to Karl Zwifelhofer in June 1938, OM, AS, VGH, 7J 278/42, July 7, 1942. The Gestapo seized the lists of Communists prepared by the Schuschnigg regime. Hermann Mitteräcker, *Kampf und Opfer für Österreich. Ein Beitrag zur Geschichte des österreichischen Widerstandes 1938 bis 1945* (Vienna, 1963), p. 19.

4. Gestapo, Vienna, to Gestapa, Berlin, March 30, 1938, DÖW 4111/2; Gestapo, Vienna, January 3, 1939, DÖW 4111/1; SD, Vienna, "Politische Gegnerformen," 1938, DÖW 5120; Gestapo, Vienna, to Josef Bürckel, March 21, 1938, DÖW 9414.

5. See also Wilhelm Wienert, "Grundlagen und Praxis des Widerstandkampfes der österreichischen Arbeiterklasse gegen den Nationalsozialismus (1938-1945)" (Ph.D. dissertation, University of Vienna, 1976), pp. 120-23.

6. Konrad, *Widerstand,* pp. 61 ff, 239 ff. For the clandestine press, see Foot, *Resistance: European Resistance,* p. 60; Gross, *Polish Society,* pp. 250 ff; Exenberger, Die illegale Presse, pp. 7-31; Konrad, *Widerstand,* pp. 61 ff. During the occupation in Vienna alone, the KPÖ produced or distributed the central party organ "Die Rote Fahne," "Weg und Ziel," "Hammer und Sichel," "Die Rote Front," "Revolution," "Jung-Österreich," "Die Rote Jugend," "Tribunal," "Das Signal," "KPÖ-Nachrichten," "Mitteilungen der KPÖ," and others. Ibid., pp. 61-73; Exenberger, Die illegale Presse, pp. 7-28, DÖW, ed., *Widerstand Wien,* 2:230-65, 300-8.

7. The cut-out system divided the line of communication into separate compartments. It was, of course, difficult for a political organization to maintain the strict rules of security that usually worked well for a small intelligence circuit. The identities of the members of the KP groups had to be kept secret, and the militants referred to themselves by pseudonyms.

8. This was apparently the Comintern policy followed by other Communist parties, such as the KSČ, who had been traditionally closely associated with the KPÖ. Michael Genner offers some glimpses on the role of KP Central Secretary Friedl Fürnberg in the selection of the officials sent to Austria, *Mein Vater Laurenz Genner. Ein Sozialist im Dorf* (Vienna, 1979), pp. 161, 178, 192-94. For the Comintern aid to the KPÖ, see Arnold Reisberg, "Chronik zur Geschichte der Kommunistischen Partei Österreichs 1935-1939," p. 33. Manuscript, 1976. DÖW.

9. RSHA report, December 1938, BA R 58/1094. The KPÖ organ *Die Rote Fahne* (The Red Flag), printed in Paris under the editorship of Alfred Klahr, was smuggled to Vienna from Zürich. DÖW 1573. After the outbreak of war, the paper was moved to Belgium. After the invasion of Belgium in May 1940, the editorial board moved back to France. *Volksstimme,* August 15, 1948.

10. In fact, because of the shortage of competent members able to act as liaison agents, the contacts between the factory cells and the district leaders were often direct and failed to use cut-outs. These careless arrangements usually enabled the Gestapo to roll up complete chains of command and members of cells.

11. U, OLG, Wien, OJs 215/40, AS, GSAW, OJs 159/40, June 9, 1941, IfZ.

12. Predictably, the KPÖ was an urban phenomenon with its strongholds situated in Vienna and the industrial areas of Lower Austria, Styria, and Salzburg.

13. Frank was apparently working in the Comintern apparatus. In 1940 he went to Belgrade and Istanbul. In 1944 he organized the Austrian Battalion in Yugoslavia where he fell during armed action. Margarete Schütte-Lihotzky, DÖW 13338.

14. Mitteräcker, *Kampf,* pp. 16 ff; DÖW, ed., *Widerstand Wien,* 2:99; AS, VGH, 7J 278/42, July 7, 1942, OM-XIV.

15. AS, VGH, 7J 278/42, OM, XIV.

16. For Dubber, see AS, VGH, February 17, 1941, 7J 70/40, DÖW 1364; U, VGH, 7J 91/41-2H 131/40, DÖW 353; OJs 54/41; Herbert Steiner, "Bruno Dubber," in Historische Kommission beim ZK der KPÖ, ed., *Aus der Vergangenheit der KPÖ* (Vienna, 1961), pp. 105-13; Mitteräcker, *Kampf,* pp. 24-25; Willi Weinert, "Bruno Dubber—zum 70. Geburtstag," *Weg und Ziel,* no. 12 (1980): 451-54.

17. Gestapo Vienna, "Lagebericht," December 1938, DÖW 1577; DÖW, ed., *Widerstand Wien,* 3:92, 214.

18. For the KJV, see below, pp. 127 ff. Dubber demanded that the KJV devote its attention to the regime "youth associations, such as the HJ, BdM. . . . Our youth members and all anti-Fascist youth should get involved and fight in these organizations." He called for the formation of a "unified Communist-Socialist youth movement." Dubber behaved bravely in prison. In a letter to the VGH, he bitterly complained about his maltreatment by the Gestapo agents and eloquently defended his point of view: "Neither . . . abuse nor . . . sweet talk could have caused me to plead guilty before the Viennese state police because I have no confessions to make. I don't feel guilty of committing any crime. To be a Communist and take an active part in the KPD . . . presents no reason for me to make confessions. . . . "DÖW 1364-65. Dubber received a life sentence. Poisoned by the Nazis, he died in prison in 1944.

19. U, OLG Wien, OJs 97/40, DÖW 353, 7707.

20. See "Lagebericht," Gestapo Wien, January 3, 1939, DÖW 4111.

21. DÖW 4111. Direct action was almost nonexistent: the Gestapo listed only seven acts of sabotage in Vienna and Lower Austria.

22. For the vast Communist underground in Vienna, see DÖW, ed., *Widerstand Wien,* 2:128-208.

23. The early network of the South Circle was smashed during the second wave of arrests in the fall of 1939. AS, GSA, OJs 215/40, Wien, June 9, 1941, DÖW 3017/5; OJs 159/40, June 9, 1941; "Schlussbericht," Gestapo Wien, November 14, 1939, DÖW 7756.

24. In April and May 1938 the KPÖ established a district network in Floridsdorf. The City Directorate concentrated its propaganda upon the factories and City enterprises in this former

SPÖ domain. Six successive district leaders—rounded up between May 1939 and June 1941—each had an SPÖ and trade union background. A circle of factory cells complemented the district organization, DÖW, 170, 822, 1541, 1782, 1959, 3302, 3373, 3386, 4398, 4934, 10961.

25. See Göhring, "Der Jugendverband;" DÖW, ed., *Widerstand Wien*, 2:265-308. The 1939 RSHA report called the KJV "the most important organization" of the illegal KPÖ. DÖW 1451.

26. Göhring, "Der Jugendverband," pp. 256-60.

27. The directives were printed in the 1938 special issue of the KJV organ, "Jung-Österreich." The issue was disguised as a Nazi pamphlet published by the NSDAP Publishing Office in Munich and Berlin. DÖW 4063/1.

28. DÖW 10961; AS, OLG, OJs 37/41, May 8, 1941.

29. Göhring, "Der Jugendverband," pp. 262-64.

30. AS, OLG, OJs 172/39, January 31, 1940, DÖW 7430, and AS, VGH, 7J 547/39, December 5, 1939. See also GSAW, OJs 144/39, February 9, 1940, DÖW 685; Karl Flanner, *Widerstand im Gebiet von Wiener Neustadt 1938-1945* (Vienna, 1973), pp. 49-56.

31. Marie Tidl, *Die Roten Studenten. Dokumente und Erinnerungen 1938-1945* (Vienna, 1976), p. 6. For the infiltration of the NSDAP, see ibid., pp. 48-54.

32. Ibid., pp. 56 ff; AS OJs 165/40, September 25, 1940, DÖW 1976; DÖW, ed., *Widerstand Wien*, 2:214.

33. U, VGH, 7J 268/39-1H 66/29, IfZ. Apparently, Pirker had direct contacts with the Comintern.

34. AS, VGH, 7J 548/39, February 8, 1939, DÖW 7434.

35. OLG, OJs 97/39, July 1, 1939, IfZ. The effectiveness of Pirker's network highly impressed the Gestapo. "Bericht, Gestapo Graz," January 31, 1939, DÖW 1571.

36. DÖW 1571; "Bericht, Gestapo Graz," October 31, 1938, DÖW 1446; 682. Pirker was sentenced to twelve years' imprisonment. In 1943, he was drafted into the Special Punishment Battalion 999 and sent to Greece, where he joined the Greek ELAS Partisan units. See his report of December 28, 1969, DÖW 5889.

37. The Knittelfeld district embraced the industrial centers of Judenburg and Fohnsdorf. In the town alone, four KJV cells were at work.

38. "Vermerk, RSHA," Berlin, August 26, 1939, DÖW 1580. See also DÖW 179, 2669, 7433-34; interview with Dr. Herbert Steiner.

39. Wehofer was seized in Vienna on December 12, 1939, having been under surveillance by the Gestapo who had shadowed him to Styria. DÖW 3297.

40. The group included cells in the Böhler Works, Kapfenberg, Bruck a.d. Mur, Leoben, Donawitz, Eisenerz, and Vordernberg.

41. U, VGH, 6J 103/40g-2H 115/40, DÖW 7889. For the impact of the Non-Aggression Pact, see DÖW 3297; Konrad, *Widerstand*, pp. 123-35.

42. RSHA, Frebruary 20, 1940, DÖW 1453, 2505. Buchalka was sentenced to death on February 12, 1941. DÖW 67, 7889.

43. "Gestapo Graz to RSHA," December 10, 1940, DÖW 2505. Some smaller cells not directly involved in the Buchalka network remained operative.

44. DÖW 2506. The sample of fifty-four convicted activists shows that all—except one—were industrial workers. Less than 20 percent (at least ten of them) belonged to the HJ or NSDAP. Most had started out in the SPÖ before 1934. In the Kapfenberg youth group, two out of nine adherents were Communists and the rest belonged to the HJ.

45. Some seventy activists were rounded up. Teufel did not return alive. Mitteräcker, *Kampf*, p. 19; Magdalene Koch, "Der Widerstand der Kommunistischen Partei Österreichs gegen Hitler von 1938 bis 1945." Ph.D. dissertation, University of Vienna, 1964, p. 186; Franz Marek, "Im Kampf gegen den deutschen Faschismus," *Weg und Ziel* (December 1954):876, 881.

46. "Lagebericht, Gestapo Wien." January-March 1939, DÖW 1578. The Gestapo

reported a KJV action in Vienna-Simmering on January 24, 1939, and voiced surprise that the chief organizer was an SA man.

47. The KPÖ was intensely aware of the need to alter its poor security practices and called for the decentralization of its work. *Die Rote Fahne*, No. 1, February 1939, DÖW 4237.

48. DÖW 897; AS, VGH, 7J 44/42, May 26, 1942, IfZ; U, OLG Wien, 60Js 288/42, IfZ.

49. AS, VGH, 6J 144/41g, August 26, 1941, DÖW 3347. Wipplinger, an insurance agent and a former SPÖ activist, had been under Gestapo surveillance since the summer of 1939. His numerous contacts multiplied the number of KP resisters the Gestapo was able to track down. Through Wipplinger's meetings with the CC delegate Ludwig Schmidt, the police had apparently found out the identity and whereabouts of the latter. Gestapo Vienna to VGH, May 24, 1940, 70Js 181/40.

50. As a veteran CC member, Reisinger had to leave Austria after the Anschluss. He was caught in 1940 and executed in 1943. Angermann fled the country for France in 1936. He was arrested in Austria after 1940, sent to Dachau KZ, drafted into the Army, and moved to Russia, where he went over to the Red Army. In 1943 he parachuted behind the German front line. He was caught in Vienna in June 1943, while preparing to assassinate the Viennese Gauleiter Baldur von Schirach. See below. "Gestapo Bericht," June 18-21, 1943, DÖW 5734c; Kommunistische Partei Österreichs, ed., *Unsterbliche Opfer. Gefallen im Kampf der Kommunistischen Partei für Österreichs Freiheit* (Vienna [1946], pp. 23-24, 87; Marek, "Im Kampf," *Weg und Ziel* (December 1954): 876; [KPÖ], *Die Kommunisten im Kampf für die Unabhängigkeit Österreichs. Sammelband* (Vienna, 1955), pp. 124, 136.

51. VGH, 7J, 44/42, May 26, 1942, OM, XIV. Since 1933 Schmidt had been a full-time KP-organizer. Gestapo Wien, May 24, 1940, 70Js 181/40.

52. Before the invasion of Poland, the Vienna Gestapo became nervous over left-wing activities and arrested seventy-four Communists and forty-seven RS in Vienna and Wiener Neustadt on August 22 and on the following days. It confiscated several printing presses and typewriters. Gestapo Wien to RSHA, September 14, 1939, DÖW 1590.

53. The international Communist movement was mechanically devoted to Lenin's views on the importance of the party and its organization, and considered working-class support of its policies as one of its most important aims. The dedication to mass propaganda was to cost the KPÖ dear as arrests were made in batches of tens and hundreds.

54. 70Js 181/40; U, OLG Wien, OJs 35/41. Schmidt was executed on January 14, 1943, DÖW 3313/II.

55. In all, the police took into custody 206 individuals and the courts instituted legal proceedings against 166 Communist suspects. Four printing presses, a large amount of paper, stencils, and other materials were confiscated. DÖW 8489/9; DÖW, ed., *Widerstand Wien*, 2:93-94; 70Js 181/40; "Bericht," RSHA, February 20, 1940, DÖW 1453.

56. Konrad points out that in its organ, "Weg und Ziel," No. 4, 1940, the KPÖ expressly rejected any armed action, boycott, or act of sabotage as harmful in the present circumstances. Not all Party members followed this instruction. This stance changed abruptly with the outbreak of the war between the Soviet Union and Germany. *Widerstand Wien*, 2:176-77. The Comintern instructions to the KSČ followed the same line in opposing direct actions: Oldřich Janeček, ed., "Depeše mezi Prahou a Moskvou 1939-1941," *Příspěvky k dějinám KSČ*, no. 3 (1967): 402, 422.

57. RSHA, February 20, 1940, DÖW 1453, 2505.

11

In Full Swing

THE THIRD LEADERSHIP

In the spring of 1940, the survival of Communist cells depended on the performance of local chiefs. The strength of the Viennese underground owed much to a few personalities who united the fragmented groups. Although signs of strains were evident in their relationships, their hostility toward the regime bound them together. The Party bounced back and gradually three principal centers emerged, based on cells in the large industrial plans and the huge municipal enterprises and utilities. One group under Mathias Pista, a city official, controlled the work in Floridsdorf.[1] A second under Gustav Kiesel, a compositor, and Leopold Tomasek, embraced Ottakring and the City Streetcar organization led by Rudolf Sturm. A third network, headed by Rudolf Fischer, worked mainly in Favoriten. The three networks maintained an uneasy alliance while each tried to dominate the Provisional City Directorate.[2]

The Moscow center carefully watched the development of the Party underground. Its full-time members, Zwifelhofer and Erwin Puschmann, traveled on the Communist lines in Yugoslavia, Switzerland, Rumania, Bulgaria, and Slovakia, transmitting instructions to the cadres, supervising their work, and controlling the selection of trusted aides for assignments. They played a crucial part in organizing the KPÖ. Their work reflected the Moscow center's preoccupation with the situation in Austria. At their Christmas 1939 meeting in Split, Yugoslavia, Puschmann, Franz Honner, and Frank, all CC members, decided to restructure their contacts with the homeland. They looked for assistance to Turkey, where a Communist cell had been established by Herbert Eichholzer within the Austrian and German community in Istanbul in 1938. It centered on the exiled Univ-Prof.

Josef Dobretsberger, former minister of social affairs, and architect Professor Dr.-Ing. Clemens Holzmeister, whom the Turkish government had invited to draft plans for the construction of a number of public buildings.

The KPÖ acquired as couriers to Austria three architects, Ines Victoria Maier,[3] Eichholzer,[4] and Margarete Schütte,[5] who made their way separately back to Austria in 1940. There they contacted the KP networks. In Graz, Eichholzer had no trouble contacting the theater director Karl Drews, Josef Neuhold, Gertrude Heinzel, an insurance agent and fiancée of Drews, and Dr. Franz Weiss, an official at the Styrian Provincial Governor's office.[6] Gradually, they established a broad alignment of cells in Graz, and in the Styrian towns of Judenburg, Mürzzuschlag, Voitsberg (which became a district seat with six cells and 170-180 adherents), Frohnleiten, Fohnsdorf, and Übelbach. When Eichholzer volunteered to join the Wehrmacht, Drews acted as his deputy. Heinzel, a member of the NSDAP since 1935, was responsible for the underground literature shop that produced tracts disseminating the new Comintern policy. The texts also included some useful information brought by couriers from Moscow via Turkey.[7]

In a separate action in Graz, a teacher, Richard Zach, prepared in October 1940 a typewritten tract on the anniversary of the outbreak of the Bolshevik Revolution. Some 100 to 150 copies were strewn near the industrial plants in and around Graz. In the fall of 1940 Zach circulated the copies of his paper "Der Rote Stosstrupp." In all, four issues came out before Elfriede Neuhold and her father, both of whom had encouraged Zach, were apprehended in February 1941.[8] The organization was connected through Maier to the KP Provincial Directorate (Provinzkommission, Proko) in Vienna.[9]

The arrival of trained cadres helped the buildup of the Party underground. In the fall of 1940 Puschmann moved from Bratislava to Vienna and assumed control of the KP underground, which the Proko and the Vienna Directorate had run until then.[10] Originally a locksmith, Puschmann had occupied a variety of posts in the KPÖ apparatus since 1926, serving with distinction. Upon his arrival in Austria, Puschmann resolved to solve the factional polemics within the Vienna network.[11] He disciplined the Tomasek-Kiesel group by ousting its leaders from the Party and by dissolving the Vienna Directorate.[12] The reconstituted Provisional Directorate was led by Fischer, Fritzsche, and Pista. Puschmann designated Karl Hodac, who had joined the KPÖ in 1939, as head of the Vienna City organization. He also put Hodac in charge of the underground press.[13] Otto Vostarek, head of the Circle II, and Alois Houdek provided Hodac with a line to the Vienna Czech Communist group, which since 1940 had attracted Gestapo attention by a series of acts of sabotage.[14]

In discussions with Party officials in December and January, Puschmann consolidated his hold in the Vienna networks. In a reshuffle of responsibilities, he outlined his administrative plans. A central committee, subordinated to the Moscow center, was to become the home central command. The clandestine organization was divided into regional, district, and local subsidaries. The Vienna City Directorate was broken into four regions. Each region comprised three or more rayons, each rayon consisting of three or more factory groups, each responsible for three factory cells.[15] By mid-January 1941, Puschmann successfully controlled the Viennese networks and had buttressed Moscow's hold on the apparatus. He was about to leave for Bratislava when the Gestapo suddenly arrested him on January 22.[16] His capture started a nine-month wave of police raids and arrests that shattered the centrally run movement,[17] destroyed the leadership,[18] and cut the Party's direct contact with Moscow. A total of 589 suspects were interrogated and 536 of them were incarcerated. Sixteen mineograph works and 18,500 sheets of paper were confiscated.[19]

In October 1940, previous to these events, Puschmann had arranged with the KSČ for Zwifelhofer to move to Prague.[20] The Czech Communist officials Eduard Urx and Jarmila Taussig successfully helped the KPÖ to transmit its messages to Koplenig in Moscow. In turn, Koplenig confirmed Zwifelhofer's appointment as the KPÖ emissary in Prague and requested Puschmann to leave Austria. The communication line between Prague and Vienna was run by Puschmann's chief assistant "Ossi." On February 8, "Ossi" informed Zwifelhofer of Puschmann's jailing and of the breakup of the Provisional Party Directorate. Soon thereafter, in the night of February 12-13, the KSČ Central Committee in Prague was wrecked. Zwifelhofer found himself under arrest on March 26, 1941.[21] Under heavy pressure, he broke down, talked, and did much damage. At his trial in Vienna before the VGH on November 16, 1942, Zwifelhofer asserted in his concluding plea:

> I consider it madness what the Soviet Union has attempted to achieve in its foreign policy. . . . Twice homesickness brought me back to Vienna. . . . I traveled to Russia in 1940. I was badly shaken by what I saw and heard there. If I hadn't got away from Moscow, I would have fallen a victim of that frightful terror. It was much worse than one could describe.[22]

The downfall of the Party networks was brought about by the deliberate betrayal to the Gestapo by its agents "Ossi" and his girl friend "Sonja," who, as old-time KP officials, had deeply penetrated the KP Central Command.[23] Apparently, "Ossi" was mainly responsible for the Party's heavy casualties since 1938. In fact, a part of the KP activities had been Gestapo-controlled and the Nazi deception scheme continued to work until the end of 1942. Tough men of fierce loyalties and courage, some KP leaders had disregarded elementary prudence by sharing with couriers information that concerned other underground lines, the real identities of clandestine operators, and secret missions. Overconfidence, indiscretions, and lack of security throughout the central network were among the causes of ruin.

Yet the battle continued.[24] The Viennese organization broke up to escape complete annihilation. The mood of its remaining cadres remained one of defiance. Feeling insecure, Hodac handed over his position as the City chief to Friedrich Fass, but retained control of the underground press. He closely cooperated with Hedwig Urach, a pre-1938 member of the Central Committee who lived in a hideout after her clandestine return from Belgium in the fall of 1940. She carried out her assignments in Vienna as a member of the Provisional Party Command and as a close aide to Puschmann. She fell into the Gestapo's clutches on June 17, 1941, knowing well that she had been betrayed.[25] This time, Hodac, who had outmaneuvered the police for the previous two years, and his associates, all former SPÖ members, were not allowed to escape. They were picked up in June and July and executed in 1942.[26]

By this time, the outbreak of the German-Soviet war had changed the political perspective. In a swift reversal of its political line, the Comintern called for the formation of a broad national front. Considering the Communists its most dangerous enemy, the regime decided to crush them without mercy. According to the RMdJ directives issued at the outset of the Russion campaign, the VGH was instructed to render death verdicts in all trials involving charges of Communist activity. Even those persons, Communists or non-Communists, who contributed to the Red Relief (RH) were sentenced to death, because the RH was regarded as a Communist organization. The OLG, which handled less serious political cases, followed a more moderate course, delivering death verdicts only in those political cases where the defendant committed an act that went beyond mere KP membership or payment of KP membership fees. The merciless retribution was accompanied by an equally severe restriction of acts of clemency. The RMdJ recommended remittance of the death penalty by an act of pardon only in a very few cases.

This harsh indiscriminate conduct of the Reich judicial bureaucracy was quietly challenged in two provinces in the Reich—Lower Austria and Salzburg. Gauleiters Dr. Hugo Jury and Dr. Gustav Scheel intervened in numerous cases at the Reich Ministry of Justice and at the Führer's Office, appealing for clemency and arguing that the regime had not had sufficient time to demonstrate its social achievements and was thus unable to win the full confidence of the working people. In cases where the defendants acted because of false idealism, the two Gauleiters believed that an act of pardon was appropriate. Up to May 1943, Scheel intervened in twenty-three cases, appealing for clemency in ten. Generally the Führer's Office tended to endorse the Gauleiter's view or at least abstained from taking a position. Although in the early stages of the war the Gauleiters' challenges were usually futile, by 1943 the ministerial bureaucracy had become increasingly alarmed that Scheel was able to prevail in three cases and to win suspension of the final decision in four other cases. Ultimately, in 1943, Scheel requested that in all cases the RMdJ take no decision without his consent.[27]

Whereas the Reich judicial authorities appeared oblivious to the political impact of their ruthless practice in the hundreds of political cases before the courts after June 22, 1941, some Nazi leaders in Austria questioned the judicial bureaucracy's manipulation of the VGH. No doubt, they took an interest not because the defendants were deprived of a fair trial, but because the unfair sentences caused uneasiness among their constituents even though the press scarcely reported political trials. In effect, the specific situation of Austria, where the resistance intensified in 1941, posed political problems for the regime. The Gestapo experienced delays in handling new cases because of a shortage of trained police officers. Since there were not enough detention places, thousands of suspects could not be taken into custody.[28] In special circumstances, such as at the Reich Railways, the Gestapo did not pick up some suspects because their arrests could have jeopardized the performance of an enterprise considered vital to the war effort.[29]

THE PROVINCES

Through all these events in 1940-41 the Proko held firm, although the security organs struck hard blows at individual groups in the provinces. During the Schuschnigg regime, the Austrian Länder had been drawn into the KP central Viennese orbit by the important Proko that supervised the chronically unstable operations outside of Vienna. The Proko consisted mainly of its chief and a handful of couriers linking him with the provinces. From the beginning of 1940 it was run by Fritzsche, who worked hard rebuilding an integrated network. Fritzsche, who had collected intelligence for the Soviet Union, pressed for expanding the clandestine press.[30] Basing itself in Vienna, the Proko divided the country into provinces; and Frizsche and other militants visited the local groups and cells, incorporating them into the KP central network. Unfortunately, efforts to centralize Communist resistance made it much easier for the security organs to infiltrate it.

At the outset of 1940, an old-time KP official, Johann Ebner, reconstructed the KP network in and around St. Pölten. His colleague August Steindl, a railwayman, formed several cells at the Reich Railways. The bulk of the resisters consisted of former Social Democrats and Socialist trade unionists.[31] The network's growth and importance were reflected by the establishing in the fall of a Provincial Command for Lower Austria in St. Pölten. Ebner was designated as provincial chief and Franz Schmaldienst as head of the St. Pölten district. Steindl was entrusted with the running of the communication lines. In the summer the risky rail transportation from Vienna of the clandestine publications, *Die Rote Fahne* and *Weg und Ziel,* was discontinued. Instead, the St. Pölten network received a mimeographed machine for which Fritzsche's financée Stephanie Engler supplied stencils she had typed in Vienna.[32] Steindl himself worked with enthusiasm on the publication of tracts, drew up sabotage plans, and still had time to run the Red Relief.

Gradually, the network gained a foothold in Krems and Waidhofen an der Ybbs, in the St. Pölten City Streetcar system, in the local bus branch of the Reich Post Office, and in the main industrial plants in the area. The cells at the Reich Railways expanded, involving over 160 railwaymen. They linked up with the Communist-run network within the Reich Railways in Vienna, extending to the main Viennese railroad stations and the huge Railway Workshops in Simmering and Floridsdorf, Vienna. The Gestapo broke up the network in December 1941 and the arrests continued until the late spring of 1942.[33]

The avalanche of arrests originating in Vienna in January 1941 left no part of the network untroubled and intact. In St. Pölten, Krems, and Waidhofen, 217 persons were apprehended and the number of suspects reached 340, which included fourteen members of the Wehrmacht, by the end of 1941.[34] After the capture of Ebner and his aides in January and March, the parallel apparatus under Leopold Leeb, and other former Socialists, whom Ebner had selected, began to reorganize the network.[35] Because of the organization's downfall, the need for relief aid was urgent. In the period from June to October, before the new cell was destroyed, Leeb collected RM 1,000. The arrests continued throughout 1941. In the fall of 1941 another section with thirty-eight railwaymen was destroyed.[36]

Comparable but earlier gains were reported from Salzburg. In the summer of 1938, a former KJV official, Franz Ofner, a barber, had created an active nucleus. By the spring of 1940, Ofner had substantially extended his network. Six local circles were set up in the city of Salzburg; other nuclei spread to Hallein, and three local and two KJV cells started in Salzburg and Hallein. Ofner also headed a Lit-ap, arranging the publication of "The KPÖ Political Training Letter" and the "Information Bulletin" reporting international news. The Viennese Lit-ap provided an extensive program of political education, forwarding copies of the KP organs *Die Rote Fahne* and *Weg und Ziel.*

In early 1940, Ofner established direct communications with Fritzsche, who had come to Salzburg as early as February 1940.[37] In July, Fritzsche and Ofner faced the serious problem of devising a new organizational framework for the expanding network. As a result, a Provincial Command, with Ofner as its political head, was created to supervise the work in the Salzburg province composed of the Salzburg City Region and several subregions.[38] Eventually, the Communist-dominated organization, mainly composed of former Social Democrats made contact with the local RS network (Reska-Weiss) to coordinate their efforts. But after a few meetings, each stressed its independence and went its separate way. The drive to knit the separate KP sections into one network embraced the adjoining areas of Upper Austria, where there were cells in Braunau, Mattighofen, Ebensee, Bad Ischl, and Goisern.[39]

When the chief operators were apprehended at the beginning of 1941, an RS member from Ebensee, Josef Kasberger, replaced them until his own arrest in March 1942. In all probability "Ossi," who received some information through Friedrich Schwager, betrayed the Salzburg center.[40] In January 1942 and in the following months, the Gestapo attacked the network in and around Salzburg. No circuit escaped police investigation, as they were all interconnected at the provincial level; arrests ran over two hundred.[41]

Drastic alterations occurred in the movement in Styria when the Puschmann network collapsed. In 1942, the VGH sentenced to death Eichholzer, Drews, Neuhold, Weiss, and twenty-five members of the KP district leadership in Voitsberg and Fohnsdorf along with local organizers.[42] Over 250 suspects were interrogated and scores were arrested throughout 1941.[43] The police also trapped the Mürzzuschlag group, including a large number of railwaymen whom Engler served from Vienna. The arrests involved the RH cells, including some railwaymen collecting contributions for the families of the political prisoners incarcerated since 1939.[44]

In Burgenland—partitioned between Styria and Lower Austria in 1938—the victims of the Proko's downfall totaled more than one hundred militants. In the fall of 1938, the Proko requested former SPÖ member Johann Wallner, a textile worker in Pinkafeld in southern Burgenland, to organize a clandestine organization. The Viennese KP followed a calculated policy of opening up its ranks to the workers, artisans, and small farmers of this economically underdeveloped area. Wallner succeeded in enlisting the energy and devotion of scores of former Socialist activists. The repression launched in February 1941 after the capture of Fritzsche, his successor Pawlin, and the Proko's liaison agents to Burgenland, enveloped Wallner and 106 activists.[45] At the VGH session in Graz in August 1942, Wallner and ten militants were sentenced to death. The Gestapo rounded up still another cell, which in August 1941 claimed to be preparing for a joint action with Soviet parachutists who were expected to be dropped into the area. The resisters received short shrift: they were executed.[46]

At least in part, the Resistance in Burgenland was the almost inevitable effect of the social grievances that spurred radical segments of the working population to antiregime antagonism. The authorities were sensitive to the necessity of remedying some of the glaring abuses.[47] The constant disaffection was reflected in the continued existence of KP cells in the southern area of Burgenland. In September 1941 the Gestapo discovered one such nucleus, which mirrored a rural and small town social background: out of six members only one was a skilled worker.[48] Another line ran to Zurndorf, Gols, and Frauenkirchen in the northeastern part of the province.[49] Other cells in the adjoining part of Lower Austria were no more fortunate. On February 8, 1941, the Gestapo tracked down another Proko member, Margarete Jost, a commercial clerk, who was busy handling the underground in the Baden area and along the Southern Railway line. She had collected the remaining contacts of a largely SPÖ-oriented workers circle around Friedrich Gaubmann that had been destroyed in July 1940. Her arrest involved some fifty persons.[50]

The separate development of the underground in Carinthia reflected both its distance from Vienna and its proximity to Yugoslavia. The Proko apparently avoided direct contact because Carinthia did not belong to its target area. However, the Party center had managed to keep safe houses in Carinthia and lost few opportunities to gain contacts in the province.[51] Up to the outbreak of the war, the Party activists' main job had been propaganda.[52] When the war broke out in 1939, a number of the Slovenes escaped to Yugoslavia to avoid being drafted into the Wehrmacht. After Schmidt's capture in Vienna, the Nazis picked up eighty resisters. Headed by Kilian Schauss, a baker's aide who had returned from the Soviet Union in February 1938, the KP Provincial center in Klagenfurt was severely shaken by the Gestapo in 1940. Schauss was executed.[53] In 1941 the invasion of neighboring Yugoslavia and the opening of the Eastern front created a guerilla insurgency against the Germans that swept through Carniola and Lower Carinthia. By September, small detachments of Yugoslav Partisans swarmed over the occupied Yugoslav territory, attacked German police and armed forces and engaged in raids and sabotage in the borderland, at times penetrating Austrian territory.[54]

At the western end of the country in Vorarlberg, the underground had limited contact with Vienna and the other provinces. The great distance to Vienna complicated the conspiratorial work. In the period from 1938 to 1940 a Communist group, the AKO (Activist Fighting Organization), was run from Switzerland. Its core in Dornbirn was broken up in the late spring of 1940.[55] Communist activity in the region was never strong and ebbed in the forties.

In the wake of the downfall of so many KP groups, the scattered remnants went out of action. However, they stirred to life again when they learned that two Party officials, dispatched by the Moscow center, had arrived in Vienna.

NOTES

1. See above, pp. 111-12.
2. The attempt of the Kiesel-Tomasek faction to dominate the Provisional City Directorate elicited strong opposition from within the KPÖ underground because these leaders criticized

the new Soviet policy of August 1939. Some Party officials made no secret of their unease over the senior Party officials sent from abroad to occupy leading positions in Austria and over Soviet foreign policy after the conclusion of the Nazi-Soviet Pact. The main conflict emerged in a dispute between the Kiesel faction and Erwin Puschmann's orthodox pro-Moscow group. AS, VGH, July 7, 1942, OM, XIV; AS, VGH, 7J 213/42, June 16, 1942, DÖW 164, and VGH, 288/42, July 27, 1942, VGH, 7J 113/42, May 26, 1942, OM, XIV. Each circle comprised between 400 and 600 activists. By December 1940 Circle I was collecting between RM 300 and 400 a month, the other Circles between RM 80 and 100, DÖW 164.

3. Maier, a citizen of Chile, was recruited by Eichholzer. She went to Vienna in May 1940 where she was apprehended in 1941. AS, VGH, 7J 257/41, May 4, 1942.

4. A noted architect, Dipl.-Ing. Eichholzer had joined the SPÖ in 1926. He went into exile in Paris in March 1938. There he met the senior Communist official Erwin Zucker-Schilling. In November he arrived in Istanbul, where he became Holzmeister's aide. He was then a liaison man between Moscow and the KPÖ foreign apparatus (Puschmann, Frank, Reisinger, and others) until his return to Graz at the end of April 1940. He applied for permission to return home through his brother, a noted National Socialist lawyer in Graz. The Gestapo assured him that he would not be persecuted. On his way to Graz, he met Puschmann in Bucharest and Belgrade. In Zagreb, Frank thoroughly briefed him and assigned him the tasks of setting up a communication system between Klagenfurt and Zagreb and of building a cell in Graz. Maier, who had returned earlier, arranged contact for Eichholzer with the Communist officials in Vienna and with Puschmann, who now lived in Bratislava, Slovakia. AS, VGH, 7J 257/41, May 4, 1942, IfZ.

5. Schütte worked in Moscow between 1930 and 1937. In 1938 she moved to Istanbul and joined the KPÖ the following year. In 1940, the KPÖ instructed her to make a trip to Austria to transmit messages, and to collect reports on the situation in the country. Interview with M. Schütte, December 1, 3, 1965 in DÖW 2569, 6188, 13338; Margarete Schütte-Lihotzky, "Erlebnisse 1940-1945," manuscript, DÖW, passim; Tidl, *Die Roten Studenten,* pp. 34-40. Schütte left Istanbul for Zagreb in December 1940 where the architect Julius Kornweitz, an official of the Communist technical apparatus for Southeast Europe, briefed her and gave her the coded address of a safe house in Vienna.

6. The organizers were former SPÖ members. DÖW 671, 897; U, OLG, 70Js 201/42, DÖW 7143.

7. DÖW 671.

8. U, RKG, St PL (HLS) III 75/42. DÖW 3638.

9. DÖW 671.

10. Direct responsibility for the operation of the KP organizations outside of Vienna was vested in the Proko linking them with the Center Command around Puschmann.

11. Janeček, ed., "Depeše," *Příspěvky* (1967):426-433.

12. AS, VGH, 7J 275/42, July 7, 1942, DÖW 151, 660; AS, VGH 7J 252/42, OM, XIV.

13. The Moscow center and the KPÖ kept the crude arguments supporting the post-1939 policy in the forefront of their propaganda effort. In contrast to past practice, the manuscripts of the papers were now centrally prepared, mostly by Puschmann and his editorial staff; the production and distribution were entrusted to the individual circles. AS, VGH, 7J 171/42, July 8, 1942, 7J 213/42, June 16, 1942, 7J 288/42, July 27, 1940.

14. VGH, 7J 288/42, July 27, 1942.

15. VGH, 7J 252/42, July 20, 1942, OM, XIV.

16. DÖW 6188, 13338. Accompanied by his aide, "Ossi," he had held numerous meetings with Schütte briefing her on the situation before her planned departure for Istanbul on January 23. She was arrested with Puschmann at the coffeehouse Viktoria. Ibid.

17. The RSHA situation report of August 13, 1941, compared the activities of the various Communist parties in Europe before and after the attack on the Soviet Union. The KPD work in the Reich was viewed as insignificant whereas the KPÖ's actions increased in number. In Denmark, Holland, Belgium, France, and Yugoslavia 193, 420, 341, 596, and 813

Communists, respectively, were apprehended after the invasion. As for the KSČ, after June 22, 1941, the scope of its work widened, although it had always been broad. According to the SD report form Prague on July 1, 1941, 5,796 Communists were arrested in the Protectorate up to May 31, 1941. In July 1941 alone, 510 Communists were taken into custody. Alena Hájková, *Strana v odboji* (Prague, 1975), pp. 243, 249. The figures for Austria would not be significantly lower. In Vienna and Lower Austria, the Gestapo seized 742, 1132, 837, and 1507 Communists from 1938 through 1941. "Tagung der . . . Referenten der Ostmark bei der Staatspolizeistelle Wien," March 28, 1944, DÖW 5080.

18. Besides the KP foreign apparatus operators—Puschmann, Zwifelhofer, Reisinger, Maier, and Schütte—many leading Viennese organizers fell into police hands. DÖW 897, 1541, 7533. The Gestapo also dealt the Proko a hard blow. Fritzsche, his successor Theodor Pawlin, and his courier Stefanie Engler were apprehended, as were the principal messengers. "Tagesrapport, Gestapo," Wien, DÖW 5732 a, 7533. Schütte recieved a fifteen-year sentence mainly because her husband was employed at the Turkish Ministry of Education and the Nazis did not want to hurt the German position in Turkey by executing her. Schütte-Lihotzky, "Erlebnisse," passim. DÖW.

19. "Tagesberichte, Gestapo," Wien, October 27-28, 1941, DÖW 5732 f; 7533.

20. The KPÖ and KSČ had traditionally enjoyed close mutual contact; the Czechoslovak Communists played the role of senior partner.

21. VGH, 7J 278/42, OM XIV. The direct liaison line with Moscow went not only via the KSČ clandestine transmitter but apparently also through the Prague Soviet Consulate. The transmitter and its operators were seized in Prague in early February. Hájková, *Strana,* pp. 241-42; *Hlas revoluce* (Prague, July 20, 1974); Janeček, ed., "Depeše," *Příspěvky,* 425 ff.

22. DÖW 897. Zwifelhofer received the death sentence. In his diary, the Nazi observer of the Austrian political trials Schmidt characterized Zwifelhofer as "highly intelligent and witty." Zwifelhofer's three brothers served in the Wehrmacht. See also Mitteräcker, *Kampf,* p. 36. To save his life, Zwifelhofer allegedly worked as an informer, sharing his prison cell with various political suspects in Vienna. In 1945 he vanished. Tidl, *Die Roten Studenten,* p. 61.

23. For "Ossi" (Kurt Koppel, also "Hans Glaser") and his girl friend "Sonja" (Gretl Kahane), see Tidl, *Die Roten Studenten,* pp. 34-40; Mitteräcker, *Kampf,* pp. 35-36; DÖW 2569, 2616/1, 6188; *Mahnruf,* March 1958; Brauneis, "Widerstand der Frauen," pp. 98-99, 174, 213. Arrested by the Gestapo in 1938 as a KJV member, Kahane changed sides. Reportedly of Jewish origin and an old KP member and Spanish Civil War veteran, "Ossi" had served as one of the couriers of the KPÖ central apparatus. He traveled abroad where he held contacts with the KP center. The two had infiltrated both the KPÖ and KJV. Only in the spring of 1942 did the news spread in prison that "Ossi" was the Gestapo informer.

24. Puschmann reported to Zwifelhofer in 1940-41 that the KPÖ membership amounted to some 20,000 paying members. 7J 278/42, OM, XIV.

25. Mitteräcker, *Kampf,* pp. 19, 33, 36; DÖW 25, 13338; AS, VGH, 7J 95/42, May 29, 1942, IfZ; 7J 213/42, OM, XIV; DÖW 3585, 4159. Urach's execution was announced to the public.

26. DÖW 897.

27. RMdJ, June 4, 1943, DÖW 4933.

28. "Lagebericht," GSAW to State Secretary Dr. Hans Schlegelberger, March 29, 1942, BA R 22/3368.

29. Ibid., "Der Oberreichsanwalt beim VGH to the RMdJ, October 3, 1942, DÖW 4934.

30. Fritzsche had been a full-time KP operator since 1934. All his family members were militant National Socialists, and his four brothers were recruited into the SS. AS, VGH, 7J 288/42, July 27, 1942, 7J 112/42, June 5, 1942, DÖW 155; DÖW 897, 13338. He was sentenced to death.

31. DÖW 27.

32. DÖW 197, 199, 503, 1913, 3355; Vogl, *Eisenbahner,* pp. 121-243; U, VGH, 6H 543, DÖW 1828.

33. "Tagesberichte, Gestapo Wien," DÖW 1448c, 5732g, 5733a, c; "Gestapo, Berichte," DÖW 1455. A group of over seventy railwaymen—Socialists, Communists, Christian Socials —was sent to Mauthausen KZ where it arrived on July 14, 1942. A detachment of SS guards surrounded the leader Mathias Nagel and five militants, all naked, handcuffed, and chained, and ordered their dogs to attack the prisoners. At the end of a harrowing twenty minutes of dreadful torture, the inmates were herded into a bunker. Two days later, they were shot. Vogl, *Eisenbahner*, pp. 91-92, 114-15; "Gestapo, Berichte," DÖW 1455.

34. "Gestapo, Berichte," DÖW 1455, 1488d, 5733a. Ebner, Schmaldienst, Steindl, and eight others from the original leadership group were sentenced to death. DÖW 422/I-II. The St. Pölten organization was the largest clandestine network of railwaymen in Austria. The next strongest were in Knittelfeld and Salzburg.

35. AS, VGH, 6J 18/42g; Vogl, *Eisenbahner*, pp. 123-25. Three main organizers were put to death. An important factor preventing complete breakdown was the formation of the so-called parallel apparatuses. When possible, the KPÖ formed parallel groups as a reserve to be activated should the Gestapo crack down on the active network. The Comintern had used this method for a long time. See also DÖW, ed., *Widerstand Wien*, 2:338.

36. "Gestapo, Berichte," DÖW 1448 a-d; AS, VGH, 6J 41/42g, May 12, 1942, DÖW 3370; 6J 43/42, May 11, 1942. See also VGH trials, DÖW 9574-9611.

37. U, VGH, 7J 405/42 - 2H 266/42, IfZ.

38. DÖW 484, 897, 1383, 6577, 8671.

39. U, OLG, 7 OJs 218/41, DÖW 8243; AS, VGH, 7J 543/41, December 10, 1941, DÖW 1381; OLG, OJs 22/42, June 18, 1942, DÖW 1152; Brauneis, "Widerstand der Frauen," pp. 81-82; DÖW, ed., *Widerstand in Oberösterreich*, 1:184-86, 226 ff.

40. AS, VGH, 7J 440/42, September 8, 1942. Friedrich Schwager, a mechanic and former Socialist, had undergone political schooling in the Soviet Union after 1934. He returned under an alias to Austria, where he was caught in 1936. From his residence in Upper Austria, he came to Vienna in 1940. He acted as liaison man between Vienna and Salzburg. Schwager was captured on March 4, 1941, but escaped in the night of July 11, 1942. After September he was active in Vienna, where he was caught on November 21. Sentenced to death, he was reluctantly recognized by the Nazis as a "man of extraordinary and keen intelligence." DÖW 897, 6928; DÖW, ed., *Widerstand Wien*, 2:115-16; "Tagesrapport, Gestapo," Wien, DÖW 5733 f.

41. DÖW 897, 9356, 9616, 9622, 14653; "Berichte, Gestapo," 1942, DÖW 1448 b; Vogl, *Eisenbaehner*, pp. 186 ff.

42. DÖW 897. The execution of three KP activists on September 30, 1942, was made public. The district chief, Albin Kaiser, was an old-time KP veteran; the other two belonged to the SPÖ, as had many of their followers. DÖW 412, 811.

43. DÖW 9720-29, 9741-42, 9744, 9802-06.

44. DÖW 7786-87, 7897.

45. AS, GSAW, 7 OJs 176/42, October 30, 1942, DÖW 1288; OJs 377/42, DÖW 1320; 155, 897. For a thorough survey of the resistance, opposition, and persecution in the province, see DÖW, ed., *Widerstand und Verfolgung in Burgenland 1934-1945. Eine Dokumentation* (Vienna, 1979), pp. 166 ff.

46. DÖW 897. See also Norbert Leser in Richard Berczeller and Norbert Leser, . . . *mit Österreich verbunden*, p. 291.

47. DÖW 897.

48. AS, GSAW, OJs 371/42, October 30, 1942, DÖW 679, 1273, 13121.

49. DÖW 155; "Tagesberichte, Gestapo," Wien, DÖW 5734 b, 11491; DÖW, ed., *Widerstand im Burgenland*, pp. 183 ff.

50. U, 6J 22/41g - 2H 41/41, IfZ; DÖW 55, 897, 1828.

51. Göhring, "Der Jugendverband," p. 280.

52. "RSHA - Bericht SD-Abschnittes Klagenfurt," November 9, 1939, DÖW 4237, 891.

53. DÖW 693, 14670, 15676; Mitteräcker, *Kampf*, p. 32.

54. "Berichte, Gestapo," DÖW 1448 a.

55. U, 7 OJs 141/41, OLG Wien, DÖW 8197.

12

The Battle

THE MOSCOW EMISSARIES: LEO GABLER
AND JULIUS KORNWEITZ

The January 1941 crackdown by the Gestapo intended to stifle the disaffection at the factory level that had been caused by the growing disparity between fixed wages and rising prices, the economic inequalities between the Reich and Austria, and German economic exploitation of the Austrian economy. The regime was well aware of its limited active support among some segments of the working population. Haunted by the events of November 1918, the authorities tried to combat the war's disruptive consequences both by alleviating justified grievances and by displaying police power. In February, the Viennese Reichsstatthalter and Gauleiter Baldur von Schirach submitted to the Führer the Ostmark Gauleiters' joint economic program for the equalization of the German and Austrian economies.[1] Such a step, they believed, would help ease the tensions in the factories that Communist propaganda had skillfully exploited by designing its statements to alienate the fewest possible segments of society.

The KPÖ's public aim was not to establish Socialism but to restore the Republic.[2] In its view, the precondition for its final success was the voluntary self-elimination of the RS-SPÖ—the political force most favored by tradition in areas of massive labor concentration—and the intensive enlistment of the former Socialist activists whom the RS had left without a political base. In the initial post-March 1938 period, the narrow core of old-time KP operators strenuously attempted to draw the Socialist cadres into resistance movements that the Communists would direct. The Socialist and non-Communist presence was one of the causes for the intensive indoctrination that all the successive home centers from Frank to Puschmann relentlessly pursued. To ensure its overall control, the Moscow center exercised persistently strict and systematic control over the underground. It relied to a large extent on its own militants, carefully placed in posts of command. The KPÖ believed that eventually the Socialist rank and file within the Communist-dominated Resistance could be persuaded of the advantages of working-class unity and that the SPÖ would be denied a mass base in the postwar era. There was still another reason for the Party's policy. Because its activists were generally known to the Austrian police, they could hardly have been used for clandestine work. There was, thus, no real alternative to the incorporation of Socialist and nonparty supporters into the Communist underground.

The Gestapo arrests throughout 1941 almost wrecked the cadres in the factories, in the Vienna municipal enterprises (streetcar system,[3] gas, electricity, and water works), and among the railwaymen.[4] Even while the arrests swept out in ever-widening circles, the new Moscow emissary was on his way to Vienna. In January 1941, Koplenig requested former KJV chairman Leo Gabler to return to Vienna to help Puschman and to take charge of the party's ideological training as chief instructor.[5] His task was eased by the publication of a special letter addressed to KPÖ members by Koplenig, who formulated the propaganda line for the Party at home. At the end of February, Gabler left Moscow. At the beginning of March he met Kornweitz in Zagreb, where the latter informed him of the capture of Puschmann and his aides. The two officials agreed that they both had now to rebuild the underground. They decided to create an effective clandestine movement that would embrace all the opponents of National Socialism. The news of the invasion of Soviet Russia found Gabler in Maribor, Slovenia, where he was working on his line to Vienna, which he reached via Carinthia in the first days of August. Kornweitz arrived two weeks later.

Gabler's assignment bristled with difficulties. He was unaware that his own security was already hopelessly compromised because "Ossi" had reported his presence to the Gestapo.[6] Unfortunately, many cells were already dispersed or crushed, and many of Gabler's past associates were near ruin, as was the central network to which he had been summoned. But the Party's disarray did not deter him. His experience had taught him tenacity and perseverance. After an impoverished boyhood, he had become a bag-maker before being drawn to politics. In his political career, Gabler showed himself determined, vain, gregarious, and unencumbered by self-doubt. He possessed a sharp incisive mind, and behind his bright smile and cheerful mien was a tenacious operator, clawing and pushing his way past any obstacle.

Gabler helped develop a new momentum, and concentrated on circulating *Die Rote Fahne* and on uniting various groups. He was lucky enough to have two first-class contact persons working under him, his old KJV comrade Friedrich Hedrich, an electro-mechanic, and Leopoldine Kovarik, a postal employee. Gabler gave the Party a more popular image. He forged useful contacts with the Viennese Czech group, and with the Steyr Works' nucleus and other cells, but mainly he patiently organized with Kornweitz a wide-ranging group of activists. Although he soon found out that the police had been shadowing him and suspected that "Ossi" was the traitor, he remained active. On October 20, a police detachment arrested him at his cover address. After more than one year of torture and hunger, he was transferred to Mauthausen KZ, sentenced to death, and executed in Vienna on June 7, 1944. Kornweitz survived a little longer. Living on the edge of disaster, he forwarded the concept of a KPÖ Central Committee to direct the work at home. Seized on April 25, 1942, he was killed in Mauthausen in 1944.[7] The loss of these two brave men was especially troubling to the KPÖ, which regarded political action as a special obligation and responsibility. Their loss severely restricted the Party's activities and greatly reduced its organizational strength.

THE COMMUNIST YOUTH (KJV)

The KPÖ had always given special attention to its youthful followers. The result was accelerated growth of the KJV. But from 1939 to 1941, restiveness in the KJV ranks led to renewed demands for central direction. Despite the danger involved in forming a single center that the Gestapo could more easily penetrate, the young Communists modeled their organizational structure on the centralized pattern.[8] During the spring and summer of 1941, the KJV expanded into a city-wide organization headed by its own Directorate, consisting of Elfriede Hartmann, a student, Alfred Fenz, an electrical engineer, Friedrich Mastny, a commercial clerk, and Walter Kämpf, a chemist. They separately infiltrated the NSDAP. Fenz joined the SA in March 1938, and another KJV organizer, Franz Reingruber, an electro-mechanic, entered the HJ, where he reached a high rank and was put in charge of the schooling of the HJ-Unterführer. By identifying themselves with the ambitions and grievances of young people within the HJ and NSDAP, young Communists sought to broaden their political base.[9]

To recapture lost terrain in the provinces, the Directorate strengthened its contacts with the cells in St. Pölten ("Ossi" was one of the liaison agents), Stockerau, Wiener Neustadt, Brunn am Gebirge, Ebergassing, Maria-Lanzendorf, Salzburg, and Steyr. More important, it tried to influence young Austrian soldiers within the Wehrmacht. For that purpose, it established a separate line. In the early summer Reingruber prepared a letter addressed to soldiers at the front, condemning the war and calling on the soldiers to stop fighting. Alfred Rabofsky and Christian Broda drafted several letters directed at the soldiers' views and worries. Some 3,000 copies were distributed among soldiers on leave, at the military hospitals, and at the front. In August, Kovarik herself, assisted by Gabler, wrote a letter demanding that the soldiers, "cease the mass murders. Our enemy is not the Red Army. Our enemy stands in our own country: the German and capitalist lust for power. Refuse to die for the profit of the wealthy capitalists! Fraternize the people from around the world whom capitalism oppresses! . . . this is the road to peace![10] To intensify the campaign, the group embarked in 1941 on the publication of several thousands of copies of a more regular tract in the form of a chain letter, "Der Soldatenrat," appealing to the soldiers to defect to the Red Army and to engage in passive resistance. The pamphlet was distributed along the KJV lines as far as Salzburg and Upper Austria and showed that written propaganda could move inside the country and reach Wehrmacht soldiers with reasonable ease. "Ossi," and Kahane supplied the Gestapo with copies. The fourth and last issue was published in April 1942. The organization also took upon itself the production and distribution of its organ, "Die Rote Jugend."[11]

The KJV outpouring of energy was impressive.[12] There was no overlapping of organizational ties across the cells, and the senior KP organizer, Anton Gajda, provided the link to the KPÖ network. He was charged with the political supervision of the activists while the operational responsibility remained in Mastny's hands.[13] In the fall of 1941 Mastny prepared a handbill for the anniversary of the foundation of the Austrian Republic in November 1918. On November 11, the public found hundreds of these handbills scattered on some of the busiest streets of Wiener Neustadt and near the entrance gates to the larger factories. A growing number of daring individuals were ready to engage in direct actions and to resort to sabotage. Mastny, Kämpf, and Fenz were generally overoptimistic about the effects of individual acts of industrial sabotage. They fabricated small fire bombs and self-inflammatory fire-iron plates devised by the resourceful Kämpf, who supervised a special sabotage team set up in December 1941.[14] The sabotage material was widely distributed, but not much use was made of it. Sabotage actions against several railroad yards and other targets failed or achieved negligible results.[15]

The authorities soon became aware of the potential threat of industrial sabotage, which could inflict as much material damage as it could psychological harm,[16] and they crushed the youthful resisters before they could start their actions. Their roundup started in May and continued until the spring of 1943, wiping out the network's entire leadership.[17] Tiny pockets of survivors floundered about helplessly after 1943. But the performance of the Communist youths had been remarkable. This segment of the radical Austrian youth, which included a sprinkling of nonparty and Catholic followers, had possessed such staying power that the Nazis required almost five years of intense and often brutal repression to put it out of circulation.[18]

THE UPSURGE OF VIOLENCE, 1940-41

The early achievements of the Resistance were understandably insignificant in sabotage work and in direct action. Much industrial sabotage remained undetected, and diversionary actions were almost nonexistent. However, two groups from the RS and KPÖ in Vienna actually engaged in direct action. In the fall of 1938, hardliners around the KP militants Ing. Edgard Diasek, Franz Nakowitz, and MUDr. Erich Halbkram carried out arson and sabotage. The group secretly manufactured explosives and time and fire bombs. In a separate development, Alois Houdek and Alois Valach started, out of Vienna's youthful RS and Communist Czech minority, a group that collected propaganda for the Czech Resistance in Prague.[19] In 1940, Houdek demanded direct action so the Czechs merged with the Nakowitz-Diasek circuit.

The security organs reported that from the start of the war the extent of sabotage work in Austria had become much larger than in the old Reich.[20] The Gestapo in Vienna estimated that by September 1941 forty acts of arson had cost RM 100,000. On August 31 and September 1, 1940, seventeen fires were set in grain warehouses in four Viennese districts. On October 14, a charge went off at the Michael Gate at the Hofburg in the center of Vienna. There were six later bombing incidents in the inner City prior to July 18, 1941. The group's industrial and military sabotage made their achievements more impressive: they allegedly damaged the Brevillier and Urban factory and a hangar at Essling airport, and set on fire some armored vehicles stored in Floridsdorf.[21] Tipped off by "Ossi," the KPÖ command's liaison man to the group, the Gestapo rounded up the suspects in September and October. Heinrich Himmler ordered twenty executed without trial at Mauthausen KZ on November 6, 1941.[22] The group's militarily unimpressive but psychologically important exploits in the second largest city of the Reich had acquired political significance through their effects on the authorities.

Industrial sabotage also consisted in damaging special machines, going slow on repairs, reducing output, and failing to follow production instructions. It was a task requiring highly skilled operators to ensure that no one person could be held responsible. Several circles were involved in the action. Particularly effective were Eduard Rabofsky's group at the Saurer Car Works in Vienna and the subcontractors who supplied special machine tools. The group slowed down production and ultimately damaged gears in over 100 military caterpillar vehicles by substituting a slightly different milling tool. As a student, Rabofsky had been active in the KJV. After 1938, he made contact with Hedrich and other functionaries. He was arrested in November 1941, but the Gestapo failed to discover his involvement in the sabotage exploits.[23] Arthur Jäger, a former Socialist, organized similar tasks at the Fross-Büssing automobile factory in Vienna.[24] Leopold Weinfurter, head of the KP cell at Brown Boveri Works, and Rudolf Kleckner established a nucleus that slowed down submarine engine production. The cell remained active until the end of the war—despite the earlier arrest of its chief organizers.[25] Early in 1942, the Gestapo broke up a KJV circle in Himberg near the southern suburbs in Vienna. Its chief, Leopold Müller, who had earlier started a KP cell at the Ostmark Works in Vienna, was collecting material for the production of small iron-fire plates.[26]

The unrest among the Austrian workers seems to have increased after the Nazi invasion of the Soviet Union. The number of arrests for serious political offenses in Austria exceeded that in Germany. In the first seven months of 1942 the VGH handled eighty-seven political cases from Austria alone, but only ninety-four cases from the ten times more populous Germany—certainly a tribute to the Austrian spirit of independence.[27] British, Soviet, Swiss, and other foreign radio station broadcasts helped the mood of the Resistance. In particular, Radio Moscow and the newly established (November 19, 1942) "Radio Free Austria" in Moscow pushed the new Soviet political line of Austrian independence.[28] The authorities were anxious to prevent foreign news about the war spreading through the country. Their most disturbing problem was the unnerving effect that foreign radio propaganda was having on Austrian morale.

During the summer of 1941, manifestations of violence arose in other parts of the country, partly due, no doubt, to the outbreak of the Eastern campaign. In the period between June 17 and November 13, over 200 individual acts of sabotage were detected at numerous railroad yards in Styria and Carinthia. The targets were mostly military trains carrying war material and personnel on the main line. In Carinthia they included the Italian troop transports. The railway saboteurs usually damaged air brakes, put sand stones or coke into the axle bearings, or set fire to freight cars. On August 22, they put glimmering cotton waste into a car loaded with ammunition in the Selzthal freight yard. The explosion was prevented at the last moment.

With sabotage work on the increase, the Gestapo raided the networks. Sixty-two Socialist and Communist railwaymen were apprehended, among them three local organizers from Bruck a.d.Mur, Leoben, and St. Veit/Glan. The police complained that, for the most part, the suspects were members of the SA.[29] In Eisenerz a predominantly mine workers' sabotage team stored stolen explosives. It planned to cut the vital line between Leoben and Linz to delay iron ore traffic to the Hermann Göring Works in Linz. Its fourteen members were seized in October 1941. Their leader, a former hardline Socialist, Martin Michelli, had impressed the VGH with his "extraordinary intelligence."[30] Undoubtedly, the scope of the sabotage exploits focused the attention of the security machinery on the Communist underground. The Gestapo tightened its stranglehold on the Party's top echelon in the winter of 1941-42 when, at last, the Soviets had succeeded in stopping the German attack.[31]

NOTES

1. Luža, *Austro-German Relations*, pp. 202-7.

2. The KPÖ propaganda stubbornly continued to stress the categories of Stalinism. The sudden change in Comintern policy after August 23, 1939, was swiftly endorsed although not without some reluctance. Although the KPÖ attacked the Social Democratic parties as agencies of the bourgeoisie, denounced Anglo-French imperialism, and welcomed the Soviet occupation of the Baltic states, the Party steadfastly condemned Nazi imperialism and called for "the liberation of Austria from Prussian subjugation" (the KPÖ letter to Josef V. Stalin, "Die Rote Fahne," spring 1940). The Communist fight against Hitler for Austrian independence remained relatively unaffected by the new line. In general, the pompous verbosity of the Communist press declined after the invasion of the Soviet Union in 1941. Konrad, *Widerstand,* pp. 97 ff; Exenberger, Die illegale Presse, pp. 15-27.

3. Traditionally, the City of Vienna Streetcar system had served as a KP bastion. The organization started as relief action cells for the families of incarcerated colleagues. Members were requested to contribute regularly (usually between RM 0.50 and 1.50 per month). For many participants, the assistance was less a reflection of their political beliefs than an expression of traditional solidarity with the unemployed and needy. The regime viewed such gestures as an important factor in helping the KPÖ to organize politically the rank and file who might otherwise have been too frightened to become involved in the underground.

4. Some of the cells formed mainly relief-oriented nuclei, and many Socialist workers were sentenced to death or long terms of imprisonment merely because they had contributed to the Red Relief. There even existed a KP-oriented relief circle in the NSDAP-owned enterprise, the Eher Publishing House. DÖW 420, 897; DÖW, ed., *Widerstand Wien,* 2:311-401.

5. The Soviet textbook, *A History of the Communist Party of the Soviet Union,* served as his main reference. Born in Vienna, Gabler joined the KJV in 1922 and became its secretary in 1931. A CC member and KJV chairman, Galber went to the USSR in November 1937 to attend the Party University. He was elected to the Executive Committee of the Communist Youth International at its Sixth Congress. When Koplenig arrived in Moscow in the winter of 1939, Gabler became his trusted aide. A cheerful young man, he was easy with chit-chat and small pleasantries and was popular with women.

6. DÖW 28; AS, VGH, 6(7) J 518/43, February 16, 1944, DÖW 7363.

7. "Tagesbericht," Gestapo Wien, DÖW 5733c; AS, VGH, 7J 343/42, July 7, 1943, IfZ; M. Schütte in DÖW 13338. On April 29 the Party organized a large leaflet campaign in the Viennese factories. DÖW 5733c. This action, taking place in the wake of Kornweitz's arrest, demonstrated that some segments of the network remained intact.

8. AS, OLG Wien, OJs 322/43, June 17, 1943, IfZ; VGH, 7J 297/43, 299/43, August 4, 1943. DÖW 239, 1560, 4628; Göhring, "Der Jugendverband," pp. 267-75; Tidl, *Die Studenten,* pp. 116-54; Szecsi-Stadler, *Die NS-Justiz,* pp. 85-87.

9. DÖW 75, 239, 897.

10. AS, VGH, 7 J 299/43, DÖW 28, 239; Tidl, *Die Studenten,* p. 143.

11. Tidl, *Die Studenten,* pp. 34-41, 145-48; DÖW 28, 4063/4.

12. Tidl, *Die Studenten,* pp. 123, 169-170; Romanik, *Der Anteil,*p. 17; DÖW 239; Molden, *Der Ruf,* p. 94. The authorities regarded the KJV as "successful and therefore dangerous." In particular, they were apprehensive of its subversive work within the Nazi organizations. DÖW 897.

13. "Berichte, Gestapo," Wien, DÖW 5733 d; DÖW, ed., *Widerstand Wien,* 2:222.

14. The Wiener Neustadt group obtained fire-iron plates from Kämpf. These hardliners fell in May 1942. Flanner, *Widerstand,* pp. 125-42; DÖW 897, 1560.
15. DÖW 28, 879; Tidl, *Die Studenten,* p. 149.
16. DÖW 75, 1560, 3367. The VGH files contain data on KJV fabrication of sabotage material. It appears that Gabler refused to endorse sabotage and preferred to maintain the primary political character of the KJV with its emphasis on factory strikes, on recruiting foreign labor, and distributing underground publications. DÖW 7363. He reflected the opinion of the KJV majority. Göhring, "Der Jugendverband," p. 429.
17. DÖW 5733c; Göhring, "Der Jugendverband," p. 275; Mitteräcker, *Kampf,* p. 80; Gestapo Wien, "Tagesbericht," DÖW 5733c. For more information on the KJV, see Göhring, "Der Jugendverband," passim; DÖW, ed., *Widerstand Wien,* 2:265 ff; Mitteräcker, *Kampf,* pp. 70 ff; Tidl, *Die Studenten,* passim; Brauneis, "Widerstand der Frauen," pp. 161 ff; Franz Danimann, "Aus Überzeugung!", *Mahnruf* (March 1958). Herbert Steiner published moving extracts from the correspondence of those awaiting death. *Zum Tode verurteilt. Österreicher gegen Hitler. Eine Dokumentation* (Vienna, 1964), pp. 100 ff.

Göhring's estimate of the number of KJV followers apprehended since 1938 amounted to more than 2,350 persons whom he could identify. In all, fifty-two were given the death penalty. "Der Jugendverband," pp. 418-20. The age and social distribution of this sample of fifty-two militants seems characteristic of the KJV. DÖW 897, 5733c; DÖW, ed., *Widerstand Wien,* 2:260 ff. Most of the youths were born in the 1920s in working-class or low-income families in metropolitan Vienna. They were largely blue- and white-collar workers, with a strong sprinkling of students. However, none of the four leaders was a worker. Moreover, the KJV was one of the few resistance movements where women achieved positions of responsibility.

18. From the shattered KJV remnants a new organization, the "Illegal group KJV Wien 44," emerged in Vienna in mid-1944. In April 1945 these eighty youthful activists fought during the battle for Vienna. DÖW 1120; Brauneis, "Widerstand der Frauen," pp. 175-78; Göhring, "Der Jugendverband," pp. 327-36; Tidl, *Die Studenten,* pp. 235-38.
19. The group became known as the "Czech Section of the KPÖ." Houdek maintained contact with the Czech Resistance as well as with Dr. Haas. DÖW 5796.
20. "Tätigkeit der Kommunisten in Deutschland und in den von Deutschland besetzen Gebieten nach Beginn des Krieges mit der Sowjetunion," RSHA, DÖW 1444; "Gestapo, Berichte," DÖW 1448, 1455. For the Vienna Czech group, see DÖW, ed., *Widerstand Wien,* 3:338-43; Brauneis, "Widerstand der Frauen," pp. 209-15; interview with Antonia Brůha and DÖW 5796; DÖW 897, 3827, 4873; Karl M. Brousek, *Wien und seine Tschechen. Integration und Assimilation einer Minderheit im 20. Jahrhundert* (Vienna, 1980), p. 96.
21. Mitteräcker, *Kampf,* pp. 65-66, lists the Gestapo reports on twenty acts of sabotage carried out in Greater-Vienna and its suburbs between June 1940 and January 1941.
22. *Völkischer Beobachter,* November 10, 1941. The group formed a relatively homogeneous team, despite differences in nationality (fourteen were Protectorate citizens, Czechs), numbering 100 persons. A. Brůha stated to this writer that originally about twenty-five to thirty women were activists. Brauneis, "Widerstand der Frauen," p. 210. The preliminary Gestapo report listed seventy members of the Czech section. DÖW 4935. See also DÖW, ed., *Widerstand Wien,* 3:338-42; "Berichte, Gestapo," DÖW 1448, 1455, 4873.
23. *Volksstimme,* April 6, 1975; Tidl, *Die Studenten,* passim; DÖW, ed., *Widerstand Wien,* 2:372; Mitteräcker, *Kampf,* pp. 43-46. For other sabotage activities in Vienna, see ibid., p. 49; DÖW, ed., *Widerstand Wien,* 3:496-503; for strikes and work stoppages, ibid., 2, 401-6.
24. Mitteräcker, *Kampf,* p. 47; DÖW, ed., *Widerstand Wien,* 2:379 ff. Jäger was one of the KP's eight district officials in six large Viennese factories and enterprises, all former SPÖ members and workers, who were sentenced to death. DÖW 897.
25. Mitteräcker, *Kampf,* pp. 47-49.
26. "Tagung," March 28, 1944, DÖW 5080; DÖW, ed., *Widerstand Wien,* 2:205-6; "Tagesbericht," Gestapo Wien, DÖW 5733 d. The Ostmark-Works' cell, comprising twenty followers, was smashed on July 22, 1942.

27. DÖW 897.

28. Vogelmann, "Die Propaganda," pp. 56, 103; Aichinger, "Sowjetische Österreichpolitik," p. 46.

29. Twenty-one Styrian and seven Carinthian railwaymen from St. Veit/Glan paid for their work with their lives. DÖW 897, 1444; 1448 a; Vogl, *Eisenbahner,* pp. 145 ff. A sample of thirty railwaymen seized in Styria reveals a mixed group of workers and civil servants, mostly former Socialists.

30. DÖW 897, 3312, 3398.

31. In Hainburg, close to the Slovakian border, one of the better organized networks was dismantled between January and April 1942. Seven of twenty-six arrested members received death sentences. Fourteen were prewar SPÖ adherents, and eight followers were long-time Communists. DÖW 897, 7532.

13

The Defeat

THE CENTRAL COMMITTEE IN VIENNA AND LOWER AUSTRIA

No major letup occurred in the Communist Resistance after the arrest of Gabler. The Party's never-tiring propaganda, countless underground meetings, Radio Moscow and BBC broadcasts, and the successes of the Red Army revived the KPÖ fortunes. Remarkable activism and devotion permitted the Party to sustain casualties unacceptable to democratic forces and enabled it to act as spokesman for the militant segment of the working classes. However, in the final analysis, it was the Soviet-Nazi conflict that nourished fresh political expectations and helped reinforce a distinctive view of the Austrian future. The Party firmly kept to its original strategy of seeking support primarily among the urban wage-earners.

Faced with the Moscow center's increasing commitment to immediate action, Kornweitz and Gabler switched their organizational efforts in the summer of 1941 from the regular cadres, which Nazi informers time and again deeply infiltrated, to the tough, alert, but comparatively amateur KJV recruits. While the youths were carrying on clandestine actions, the remaining Party organizers pressed for a reorganization of the underground structures.

After the destruction of its directing personnel in 1941, the Party regrouped around a new action group, undoubtedly set up earlier as a parallel organization for just such a contingency. It took a few months for the reconstituted center, the Central Committee of the KPÖ, to coalesce around the remnants of the Vienna network.[1] The Committee met weekly, chaired alternatively by each of its five chief organizers.[2] To patch up the crippled cells in Vienna, they divided the city into three sectors, set up a new

City Directorate in April 1942, and enlisted persons untainted by former ties with the KP, whom they instructed to function as liaison men.[3] In places, the old network remained intact, and a few regional chiefs still operated, although without direct lines to the new City Directorate.[4] Having established its priorities, the Committee rebuilt a central Lit-ap, which circulated pamphlets and leaflets before the Gestapo liquidated it in July 1942.[5] Their aggressive appeals disclosed the dangerous anger among the largely closed world of the Communist and Socialist activists.

Workers, Peasants, and Soldiers! Make an end to Hitler's bandits.
. . . Sabotage Hitler's war machinery! Organize the resistance against the Fascist system of repression! Close your ranks and set up fighting committees in the factories![6]

The new leaders committed themselves to direct actions, believing in an early Soviet victory. Neustadtl even started special sabotage teams.

The Committee followed security rules more strictly than before. The five CC members communicated with the sectors through cut-outs and couriers. A string of branches, each of which appealed to a special interest group, complemented the Committee. A nucleus around Dr. Adalbert von Springer, an officer and military staff physician in Vienna, started in the fall of 1941. Springer, a former supporter first of the SPÖ and then of the NSDAP not only wrote three pamphlets, but also collected useful information. First Gajda and Däninger, then from June 1942 the more combative Jirak, arranged contents with Springer.[7] The Schutzpolizei-cell under Däninger and Hauptwachtmeister Hermann Schneider started in the summer of 1941.[8]

Much larger was the City of Vienna firefighters' section. Hauptwachtmeister of the City Fire Police and a member of the KP City Directorate, Hermann Plackholm was apprehended during the roundup of the City Directorate on February 2, 1943. During the interrogations, the Gestapo found enough incriminating material to arrest forty-eight more firefighters.[9] This seemed to be quite a lucky coup for the police, who had rather accidentally discovered the group.[10]

The Gestapo was privy to the Central Committee line almost from the outset. As early as May 21, it had informed the Oberreichsanwalt during his visit to Vienna that it had penetrated the new KP home center.[11] It was then easy for the policy to apprehend Neustadtl and Gajda at a clandestine street rendezvous on July 13, 1942, and Jirak and Däninger the next day. The disaster was closely connected with the KJV roundup in May, which apparently enabled the police to travel directly along the KJV lines to the Committee.[12] Possibly carelessness, ineffective security safeguards, poor compartmentalization of the varied activities, unnecessary horizontal communications, and insufficient insulation of courier lines and cells hastened the downfall. Very likely, "Ossi" or another Gestapo informer was involved.[13]

The regime responded to the intensification of the war in the winter of 1941-42 by exercising continuous pressure on the resistance within the labor force,[14] where the Communists often concealed their efforts under the cover of Red Relief or the special Solidarity Fund. The KPÖ provided the organizational framework and initiative for relief of imprisoned workers' families, skillfully manipulating social concern into political propaganda.[15] But before the factory cells could accomplish much, the Gestapo struck again.[16] One of the largest cells was discovered at the Siemens-Schuckert Works in Leopoldau near Vienna in 1942 when more than 100 workers were rounded up. Fourteen ringleaders, all old-time Socialists, were executed after a series of VGH trials in Vienna in 1943.[17]

Numerically smaller was a cell the worker Josef Postl built in 1939-40 at the Wiener Neustadt Locomotive Works. Situated in the all-important industrial belt, it closely cooperated with the Viennese leadership. The militants set up a printing shop and issued handbills and leaflets. After the start of the Russian invasion, the cell intensified its propaganda campaign, calling upon the Austrian people to "rise to fight for freedom," assailing "the Prussian military dictatorship's oppression of other nations," and urging the workers to "follow the KP directives! Go slow, strike, engage in sabotage activities!" The texts advocated the nationalization of capital and the partition of large estates among the peasantry.[18] Neustadtl and Gajda did meet Postl on June 28, 1942, and confirmed him as the KP chief for the Wiener Neustadt district. Unfortunately, before the year was over, Postl and his two main aides fell into police hands.

Another mixed Socialist-Communist circle under the worker Alois Czipek spread to Burgenland from the industrial basin around Wiener Neustadt, where it had built up its nucleus at the Locomotive Works.[19] Besides the usual relief actions, the sections circulated leaflets or painted anti-Nazi slogans on walls. In a series of raids between November and February 1943, the Gestapo smashed the organization:[20] seven militants went to their death and eighteen workers received heavy jail sentences.[21]

The KP's emphasis on clandestine factory propaganda was deliberate. In the Marxist view, industry concentrates a mass of working people in one place, uniting them in their common economic interests. This unity allows workers to form associations to defend those interests, and simultaneously to develop a political consciousness. The KPÖ realized that the success of its activities largely depended on its ability to expand its struggle for immediate social aims into a political struggle against the regime. Consequently, a tiny number of cadres were able to mobilize large numbers of former Socialists.

This many-sided, dialectical linkage of socioeconomic with political-national problems in the underground necessitated an ideological and political bond fusing the many factory cells and local groups. The clandestine press thus became a prerequisite "for ideological and tactical unity" of the Party, as it was through clandestine publications that "a harmonious Party nucleus capable of uniting" the various cells "into a single organization could be set up."[22] The mass propaganda action, which every successive Communist center implemented, ate like acid into its own networks, ultimately causing their destruction. Notwithstanding the frightful losses, by 1941-42 copies of the clandestine press made almost a routine appearance every night in the working-class quarters of Vienna.

Under more favorable conditions, the underground in other European countries followed the same course of action. Thus, the French Communists published 316 clandestine issues of their organ *L'Humanité* and helped to print *Die Rote Fahne* in 1943. The French underground press produced 1,106 publications. In 1943 alone, the Vichy police confiscated 540,000 copies of underground papers. In Poland, 1,500 clandestine papers were published during the war.[23]

IN THE PROVINCES

On July 8, 1942, the Gestapo captured a Soviet parachutist, the Austrian-born Hugo Börner, who had come to Vienna on an intelligence mission from East Prussia, where he had been dropped in the night of May 16-17.[24] Börner first headed for Innsbruck in Tyrol, where he found shelter with Josef Werndl, a house painter and an old-line SPÖ adherent, and Andreas Obernauer, a railway conductor, who ran a railwaymen's cell.[25] On June 17 Werndl drove Börner to Vienna, where Börner made further contacts. These, however, went awry because the Gestapo learned on June 22 from one of its undercover agents that a Soviet operator had arrived in the city for a KP rendezvous.[26] Meanwhile, in Innsbruck, the Gestapo caught up with Werndl and Obernauer, who had run into serious trouble for yet another reason. Werndl maintained contact with the Tyrolian section of the large Robert Uhrig Communist organization in Berlin, but no joint action had started before the Uhrig network collapsed in the first days of February.[27] Subjected to brutal torture in the Innsbruck jail, Werndl committed suicide on July 17.[28] The Werndl grouping, originally set up in 1940 to provide relief to an imprisoned colleague, was picked up only in 1943.[29] Another circle was at work from 1940 to 1942 in eastern Tyrol and western Salzburg, and the Gestapo, which was on its trail, pulled in eight persons in April 1942.[30]

There had always been much indigenous Communist agitation in Styria, where the Marxist Resistance had grown out of the powerful industrial and labor strongholds. In 1942 the Russian campaign encouraged the Styrian militants to increase activities. But the security forces' sweep of the Styrian Socialist-Communist cells between June and August 1942 squashed them. The Central Workshop of the Reich Railways in Knittelfeld had been a center of opposition since before 1938. Several sections under Heinrich Gärtner, who committed suicide after his capture on July 7, operated there. Some seventy activists were caught in the dragnet, and at the VGH trials at Graz in February 1942, eight received death penalties.[31] In a parallel effort, Gendarmerie-Hauptwachtmeister Franz Hiebler from St. Oswald near Graz collected resisters in the spring of 1942.[32] After his downfall in August the Gestapo estimated that approximately 250 persons had been at work in Kapfenberg, Graz, Mürzzuschlag, Weiz, Judenburg, Bruck a.d.Mur. Hiebler's downfall signalled the final demise of the Graz-centered KP underground that had taken over the Party regional organization in 1940 when Neuhold was caught.[33] The network ceased in August 1942 but some sections limped on until 1943, when they broke asunder.[34] The Nazi retaliation hit even the less incriminated followers. Throughout February and March 1943, in a vast program of intimidation, the OLG meted out two- to fifteen-year penitentiary terms to 164 persons in twenty-seven cells, among them miners, craftsmen, and farmers.[35]

The police sweep in 1942 did not ignore another traditional bastion of the labor movement, the largest Austrian motor car factory at Steyr. Since the spring of 1940, a nucleus of young workers had operated a network that centered on cells at the Steyr factory and the Nibelungen Works in St. Valentin.[36] The Communist sector of the organization, based on the three-man cell system, kept contact with the center in Vienna. The group was smashed in September 1942 and six leaders received the death penalty. On November 30, 1944, three of the prisoners, including the ringleaders Josef Bloderer and Karl Punzer, escaped from the Munich-Stadelheim prison. Punzer was recaptured the same day and killed four days later.[37] Despite the police disruption, some members survived until 1944 when they were finally caught.[38]

Toward the end of 1942 the authorities reported a slackening of Communist activities, which were still mainly concentrated in Vienna, St. Pölten, and the industrial areas of Styria. The resisters found it advisable to exercise restraint, concentrating on collecting contributions for the Red Relief. The remaining Lower Austrian districts, as well as Upper Austria, Salzburg, and Carinthia only infrequently indicated the existence of the KP underground.[39] In particular, the National Socialists pointed out that Upper Austria, with its vast industrial basin around Linz, had remained an island of tranquillity.[40] They credited the lack of agitation to the satisfactory food supply and the severe punishment inflicted on KP militants.[41]

In contrast, in 1942 the armed actions of Yugoslav Partisan units affected events in the old Carinthian-Yugoslav borderland. The mass eviction of the Slovene population in the occupied former Yugoslav territories of Upper Carniola and Lower Styria and the start of the deportation of Slovenes from Carinthia in April 1942 contributed to the Slovene opposition.[42] The early resistance mostly involved the provision of hideouts and food for small parties of young deserters who lived in the mountains and for units of the Communist-run Slovene Partisans who came across the Austrian border from Carniola.[43] While some deserters did not engage in any action, native soldiers on leave or those who refused to report to the Wehrmacht or to be drafted for the compulsory labor services often joined the Partisans. They built underground shelters or log cabins high in the wild mountains where they cooperated with the Yugoslav Partisans, providing them with local support. The Gestapo penetrated one of the groups near Ferlach in the Carinthian borderland, and on November 11, 1942, an SS unit surrounded a farmer's house where it rounded up a party of local insurgents. In all, about 100 persons were arrested. At a special VGH session in Klagenfurt in April 1943, fourteen members received the death penalty, and twenty-two associates were sentenced to lengthy imprisonment.[44]

One of the native guerrilla commanders was the Carinthian Ivan Županc, who had fled with his friends to Ljubljana after the Nazi takeover and had joined the Tito Partisans in June 1941. In the spring of 1942 he returned to his homeland to organize support for a partisan combat unit of sixty men who had crossed the border to Austria in the summer of 1942. The partisans were intent on exterminating particularly rabid Nazis. On August 12, a party of eight executed game-keeper Urban from Ebriach, who was known for his anti-Slovene attitude, and was working as a police informer.[45] However, these few violent actions did not mar the peaceful life in the province. A casual observer at that time would not have seen any discernible signs of a disturbed domestic peace or of a breach of public security.

THE DOWNFALL

The KPÖ's growing difficulties inspired its finest achievements. On October 22, 1942, Radio Free Austria in Moscow broadcast an appeal by forty Austrian exiles to the Austrian people to form a resistance movement uniting all Austrians in the Austrian Freedom Front (ÖFF.)[46] The Party center attempted to prepare the common ground for a unified resistance front that would eventually become a core organization for Communist efforts at infiltration at the regional and local levels of administration.[47] However, such efforts were greatly hampered because of the downfall of the KP networks in 1941-42. External developments, however, quickly brought the Party prestige in Resistance circles. The demise of the Comintern in May 1943 and the Soviet policy of cooperation with the Western democracies helped to improve the Party's image as a respectable political movement. The first issue of the new Communist-run paper, "Das Signal," which was published in August in the name of the "Union of Austrian Freedom Fighters," thus appealed, as the Gestapo reported, "to all Austrians who love freedom and their fatherland."[48] National democratic slogans, acceptable to the non-Communist majority of the people, also tried to gain support for the KPÖ.

Numerous KP militants and their contacts in the Viennese factories had become involved, directly or indirectly, in underground work. The KPÖ apparatus in France, actively supported by the French Communists, had conceived the operation. In France the KPÖ assembled its clandestine cadres through its special wing called *Travail anti-Allemand* (TA), largely made up of Austrians who had fought on the Republican side in Spain and exiles who had resided in France and Belgium.[49] It organized the transportation of the activists to Austria, where the latest disasters had left the Party without a centrally organized network. From October 1942 some forty Communist officials reached Vienna by joining the transports of French workers to the Reich.[50] French Communists provided them with French identity papers. In Vienna, some operators managed to slip underground and to live in safe houses; others acted as French workers and were put to work in the armaments plants, where they made useful contacts and set up cells. In the spring of 1943 the newcomers succeeded in starting a Lit-ap, which circulated some 3,600 copies of thirteen pamphlets and Party appeals between mid-May and August 1943.[51]

The returned activists put together a small network based in Vienna and continued to keep in touch with the officials back in France. In March 1943 they created "the Vienna Directorate of the KPÖ." It was led by the blue-collar workers Ludwig Beer, a former combatant in the Spanish Civil War, and Gottfried Kubasta, former head of the Floridsdorf KP, who had fled the country in November 1937, by Frieda Günzburg, a nurse from the Spanish Civil War, and by Dipl.-Ing. Walter Greif, a former member of the International Brigade in Spain.[52] As usual, the clandestine press proved the Communists' undoing and led to the Gestapo's dismantling of the network on August 24, when they captured Beer and his five accomplices. Without effective escape routes, the other organizers and their followers were trapped within Austria and were gradually rounded up.[53] By February 1944 the last centrally directed, but still rather embryonic, network with French connections lay shattered.[54] At the start of 1944 only some scattered nuclei remained of what had once been a powerful force. The Party never again succeeded in regrouping its wrecked central cadres.

Up to the final collapse of the last home center, the Communist underground was primarily a mass political propaganda operation, not an intelligence-gathering one, run by a few selected leaders.[55] Separate, tightly knit, well-organized sections under Soviet control usually managed intelligence. It was only in the last war years, in the mountains of Upper Styria, Salzkammergut, and Carinthia, that the Communists built up small armed parties of local inhabitants. However, their overall political effect was minimal. Throughout 1943-44 marked insistence on relief activities kept some nuclei at work despite the harsh repression and brutal punishment meted out to their followers. As late as February 1944, the VGH voiced its surprise at the workers' continual involvement in relief work in some Viennese enterprises.[56]

To be sure, the population scarcely noticed KP activities. The Führer still commanded considerable prestige and respect, whereas public opinion opposed the KPÖ. After July 1941, the severest repression was imposed on members of the Communist networks. They suffered more than any other movement, in terms both of the number of resisters arrested and of the severity of the sentences. The situation reports of the VGH Oberreichsanwalt presented the number of the cases (largely KP groups) brought before the Court. The number of the new KP cases rose to 412 and 300 on February 4 and June 1, 1943 before dropping in February 1944.[57] A similar trend emerged from the Vienna Gestapo list of 6,272 arrested Communists in Vienna and Lower Austria:

Year	Arrested Communists	Year	Arrested Communists
1938	742	1941	1,507
1939	1,132	1942	881
1940	837	1943	1,173

In all, 364 resisters received the death penalty, and 293 went to their death, in the two provinces alone.[58]

The Party's strident rhetoric, its engagement in demonstrative gestures of little practical value, and its occasional spasms of violence did not in themselves threaten the regime, but they had a corrosive effect. It is true that the KPÖ could at one time or another be charged with a lack of political tact, or with intending to impose its values on the rest of society, or with a narrow view of its ideological mission. The Party did, for instance, find itself under attack when, at Moscow's instigation, it opposed the war as "imperialist." But in its struggle with National Socialism, it was forced at the same time to fight for democratic institutions and Austrian independence.

The Party's work was crucial to the growth of the underground. In a Resistance initially divided into politically self-contained islands, the Communists recruited beyond their traditional constituency, transcending old differences within the left. Insofar as there was a community between the KPÖ and the non-Communists, it was above all based on a negative consensus: a denunciation of the regime and of Nazi victory. As time passed, the trauma of the occupation undermined the well-established pre-1938 alignments and beliefs. Whatever political community had existed in the Republic vanished. On the other side of the political divide, the KPÖ, or what was left of it, continued to reveal its distinctive ideology and to preserve its organizational identity. Notwithstanding the liquidation of their urban strongholds, the Party's fragmented remnants proceeded with their risky enterprise, extending their links outside their own circles in Vienna and the other provincial capitals into the mountainous areas of southern Austria.

NOTES

1. DÖW, ed., *Widerstand Wien,* 2:15-16, 100; "Bericht über die Herausgabe der illegalen Zeitschrift der KPÖ 'Die Rote Front' 1941/1942," Otto Tropper, 1971, DÖW 7213; Genner, *Mein Vater,* pp. 162-70, 191.

2. The driving force behind the domestic leadership was Adolf Neustadtl, a worker, who had escaped from jail on July 13, 1941. Until May 1942, he was responsible for the work in the provinces as the Provincial Organizer and helped to run the remnants of the central Lit-ap in Vienna. His fellow CC members were Gajda, whose responsibility embraced both the KJV and intellectuals; Franz Jirak, a dentist, who had been active in the Vienna apparatus since 1939 and had had no party affiliation until then; Franz Däninger, a policeman, head of a Schutzpolizei-cell and an old-time SPÖ member; and CC candidate Emil Voreiter, a worker, who had joined the KPÖ in 1941. "Tagesbericht, Gestapo Wien," DÖW 5733d, f; GSAW O Js 622/43, December 12, 1943, DÖW 159.

3. Some of the heads of the sectors and the members of the new City Directorage enrolled in the KPÖ as late as 1941-42 and were new to clandestine life. The collapse of successive KP centers catapulted them into key network positions. DÖW 3382, 4286, 4290, 5734a.

4. U, 7J 247/43-5H 79/43, DÖW 10962; DÖW 5732d.

5. In April and May the CC collected RM 860, mostly from membership fees. About RM 360 was spent supporting full-time militants living underground, and procuring supplies for the press. AS, 7J 513/43, November 30, 1943, DÖW 4178.

6. Some leaflets commemorated the anniversary of the October Revolution and recalled the date of the German attack on the Soviet Union. Five thousand copies of a proclamation issued on May 1, 1942, European Labor Day, called for a slowdown and for sabotage in the factories. Ibid.; DÖW 1448c.

7. The police arrested Springer and his three followers in February 1943. He was executed in 1943. "Tagesrapport, Gestapo Wien," DÖW 467, 573a; U, RKG, StPL (HLS) II, 54/43, DÖW 3402, 4178.

8. The Schutzpolizei was the regular uniformed police. The cell was broken up in July 1942. Däninger was discharged from the police in 1940 but still had a wide circle of friends among the policemen on active duty, including Schneider and the other three Hauptwachtmeisters. All five were executed; another five received prison sentences. After the death sentence was passed, Däninger told Anton Mayer, his co-defendant: "Tell our friends, when you come out, why we die and that I am dying as a Marxist. Fight as long as it is necessary to construct socialism in Austria." DÖW 1131. Five other Viennese policemen went to their death before the end of the war. "Bericht über die Tätigkeit der Gruppe Däninger," DÖW 1131; DÖW 5733e, 4178, 4273.

9. DÖW 5080, 8479; DÖW, ed., *Widerstand Wien,* 2, 313 ff. In all, forty-eight firefighters came before the Supreme SS and Police Court special session in Vienna in March 1944. The thirteen-day trial, which the local press covered, drew much sympathy for the defendants from the public. Five received death sentences and were transported to the execution place at Kagran. Watched by the assembled Vienna firefighters, the SS detachment shot only two of the five men, Plackholm and his deputy Johann Zak. Mitteräcker, *Kampf,* pp. 62-63.

10. Plackholm and Zak helped to distribute Communist literature brought from France in the winter of 1942. Their carelessness apparently drew the Gestapo's attention. *Volksstimme,* August 15, 1948.

11. DÖW 1448 c, 4935.

12. DÖW 5733 d. Voreiter and Neustadtl committed suicide or were tortured to death in 1943; the other two leaders were killed.

13. Jirak suspected that the Gestapo had very early infiltrated the network and shadowed his movements. DÖW 4178.

14. Thus, in August and September 1942 the police seized 244 suspects. DÖW 4934.

15. For the numerous cells in the industrial and municipal enterprises in Vienna, see DÖW, ed., *Widerstand Wien,* 2; passim; for other parts of Austria, see Szecsi-Stadler, *Die NS-Justiz,* pp. 71-73. Most rank-and-file activists were old-time Socialists or former adherents of Socialist-run unions.

16. The OLG and VGH sentences often indicated that the regime regarded the contributions as politically motivated defiance. DÖW, ed., *Widerstand Wien,* 2:309, 357.

17. Ibid., 2:381-82; DÖW 897, 4934.

18. AS, VGH, 7J 359/43, September 10, 1943, DÖW 4400, 6903; Flanner, *Widerstand,* pp. 105-7, 114-18. For other groups, see DÖW 7408, 7788, 11543.

19. Flanner, *Widerstand,* pp. 107 ff; U OLG Wien, 7 0 Js 702/43, DÖW 8981.

20. For the reports on the activities at the Gustloff Works and at the Wiener Neustädter Aircraft Works, and on the harboring of parachuted Allied agents, see DÖW 4350.

21. The majority were former Socialists and two were old-time Nazis. DÖW 5733 f, 8981; DÖW, ed., *Widerstand Burgenland,* pp. 169-70, 201-4.

22. Josef Stalin, *The Foundations of Leninism. On the Problems of Leninism* (Moscow, 1950), pp. 130-31.

23. Henri Michel, *Histoire de la Résistance en France (1940-1944)* (Paris, 1975), pp. 61 ff; Gross, *Polish Society,* p. 252.

24. DÖW 5733 d; Gestapo Innsbruck, "Schlussbericht" and "Vermerk," November 27, 1942, DÖW 9225.

25. Interviews by T. Marek-Spiegel, September 1965, DÖW 2795.

26. DÖW, ed., *Widerstand Wien,* 2:454.

27. DÖW 9225. For the Uhrig group, see below, pp. 148 ff.

28. DÖW 9225.

29. The group embraced about sixty followers, mostly former Socialists. Vogl, *Eisenbahner,* pp. 199 ff; "Bericht, Gestapo," DÖW 1448 d.

30. Vogl, *Eisenbahner,* pp. 199-200.

31. DÖW 897; Vogl, *Eisenbahner,* pp. 145-46, 151-52.

32. Hiebler had been a member of the SPÖ since 1927. During World War I he was decorated several times for bravery. U 7J 599/42 - 6H 44/43, DÖW 361; "Tagesberichte, Gestapo," DÖW 1448 d; 448 a,d.

33. DÖW 1448 a, 4307.

34. DÖW 418, 4348; Vogl, *Eisenbahner,* pp. 159-62. Those cells that remained active included some Communist trade union nuclei and a section of the Graz firefighters. AS, VGH, 7J 415/42; DÖW 1448 d, 10970.

35. DÖW 897.

36. U, VGH, 7J 35/44 - 5H 28/44, DÖW 488; AS, OLG, O Js 220/43, April 20, 1943, DÖW 171; DÖW 6908, 13459.

37. U, VGH, 7J 109/43, DÖW 2997; Mitteräcker, *Kampf,* p. 56.

38. In another development, a cell at the oil refinery in Moosbierbaum near Tulln was liquidated in 1944. Mitteräcker, *Kampf,* p. 56.

39. The Gestapo July 1942 monthly figures of the number of arrested Communist and Marxist-Socialist suspects give some indication of the strength of the provincial Resistance:

Gestapo Office	KPÖ	RS	Protective Custody
Linz	10	2	8
Wien	51	8	26
Graz	46	38	10
Klagenfurt	25	5	20

DÖW 2507. The Vienna Gestapo reported the circulation of thirty-six pamphlets and 268 leaflets.

40. Marek, "Im Kampf," *Weg und Ziel,* 881; KPÖ, ed., *Opfer,* p. 15.

41. "Lagebericht, GSAW Wien," to the RMdJ, January 30, 1943, BA R 22/3388, and GSAW Linz, June 9, 1943, BA R 22/3371. The GSAW in Vienna noted that after every public announcement of "the execution of the Communist political criminals," the judges and public attorneys received anonymous letters threatening their "extirpation" and that of their families ("Ausrottung mit Kind und Kegel"). As a result, the GSAW suggested restricting such announcements to a strict minimum.

42. Luža, *Austro-German Relations,* p. 177-79. On April 14, 1942, 1,075 Carinthian Slovenes were suddenly deported to Germany. Stefan Karner, *Kärntens Wirtschaft 1938-1945* (Klagenfurt, 1976), p. 120. The Nazis, who needed domestic peace in time of war, eventually shelved further evictions. Helga H. Harriman, *Slovenia under Nazi Occupation, 1941-1945* (New York-Washington, D.C., 1977). An estimated 55,000 Slovenes resided in Austria before 1938. Thomas M. Barker, *The Slovenes of Carinthia. A National Minority Problem* (New York, 1960), p. 229; Hanns Haas-Karl Stuhlpfarrer, *Österreich und seine Slowenen* (Vienna, 1977), pp. 84-86.

43. For the story of the Tito-led guerrilla warfare in Carinthia, see Karel Prušnik-Gašper, *Gemsen auf der Lawine. Der Kärntner Partisanenkampf* (Vienna, 1980). In the wake of the occupation of Yugoslavia in April 1941, some young Slovene recruits went into hiding as deserters. Some served as liaison men to the Tito Partisan movement. DÖW 3315.

44. *Kärntner Zeitung,* April 6-9, 1943; DÖW 891; Mitteräcker, *Kampf,* pp. 109 ff; Szecsi-Stadler, *Die NS-Justiz,* pp. 74-75.

45. AS, VGH, 7J 142/245/43, H 283-286, DÖW 3315; Fein, *Die Steine,* pp. 127-45; Karl Prušnik-Gašper, "Die Kärntner Slowenen im bewaffneten Kampf gegen den Faschismus," 8. Koroški kulturni dne . . . 17.-19. Februar 1977, Klagenfurt, 1977, pp. 3-4.

46. KPÖ ed., *Die Kommunisten,* pp. 141-42; Göhring, "Der Jugendverband," pp. 358-59; Aichinger, "Sowjetische Österreichpolitik," p. 47; Elizabeth Barker, *Austria 1918-1972* (London, 1973), p. 124.

47. Bollmus, "Österreichs Unabhängigkeit," *Zeitgeschichte,* 57, 68 ff.

48. "Tagesbericht, Gestapo Wien," DÖW 8475. The non-Communist underground also issued various publications and circulated them by mail or scattered them on the streets of Vienna.

49. A member of the CC KPÖ, Othmar Strobl, was responsible for arranging the transport of militants to Austria. He had radio contact with the Soviet Union. AS, VGH, 7J 137/44, August 26, 1944, IfZ; "Tagesbericht, Gestapo Wien," DÖW 8475-76; Ernst Schwager, "Die österreichische Emigration in Frankreich in der Zeit vom 'Anschluss' Österreichs an das Deutsche Reich im März 1938 bis zum Kriegsende 1945" (Ph.D. dissertation, University of Vienna, 1979), pp. 155-59; Willibald Ingo Holzer, "Die österreichische Bataillone im Verbande der NOV i POJ. Die Kampfgruppe Avant-garde Steiermark. Die Partisanengruppe Leoben-Donawitz. Die Kommunistische Partei Österreichs im militanten politischen Widerstand" (Ph.D. dissertation, University of Vienna, 1971), p. 146; DÖW 5080; Mitteräcker, *Kampf,* pp. 99 ff; KPÖ, ed., *Die Kommunisten,* p. 140.

50. "The Appeal to Austrian Men and Women," AS, VGH, 7J 137/44, IfZ; KPÖ, ed., *Die Kommunisten,* p. 140; Schwager, "Die Emigration," pp. 171-72.

51. 7J 137/44; DÖW 310, 425.

52. DÖW 1132; DÖW, ed., *Widerstand Wien,* 2:126-27.

53. There were eighteen workers in a sample comprising twenty-six persons. DÖW 8475-76.

54. "Tagesberichte, Gestapo," Wien, DÖW 8475-78; *Volksstimme,* August 15, 1948; Tilly Spiegel, *Österreicher in der belgischen und französischen Resistance* (Vienna, 1969), pp. 36, 57-62; Tilly Spiegel, *Frauen und Mädchen im österreichischen Widerstand* (Vienna, 1967), pp. 38-39.

55. This was also true of the clandestine Communist movements in other occupied countries of West and Central Europe. For similar KSČ operations, see Hájková, *Strana,* passim, and Oldřich Janeček, ed., *Z počátků odboje* (Prague, 1969), passim.

56. Wagner, *Der Volksgerichtshof,* pp. 456 ff; DÖW 3906, 9123, 9574, 9720-9729, 9741-42,

9744. The GSAW Wien situation report of June 12, 1943, indicated that the declining production of illegal propaganda material was accompanied by a rise in the number of activists participating in the Red Relief actions. BA R 22/3388.

57. Wagner, *Der VGH,* pp. 453, 459.

58. DÖW 5080. For the Vienna Gestapo's monthly reports, see DÖW 8476, 8479.

14

The End

THE CALL FOR A NATIONAL FRONT: THE "ANTI-HITLER MOVEMENT"

Side by side with the Party chain of command ran parallel Communist apparatuses. In 1941, a Slovene locksmith, Karel Hudomalj, had built up an independent network in Vienna parallel to the KP organization. Hudomalj was not an ordinary Communist. After years of study in Moscow, he had returned to Yugoslavia to become a member of the Yugoslav KP's Central Committee. After 1936, he had worked in France among Yugoslav workers. In 1941 he proceeded with his conspiratorial work in Vienna.[1] A practical man of strong character and steady nerves, Hudomalj set up the "Anti-Hitler Committee" in November 1942 that, two months later, published the first issue of its newspaper "Die Wahrheit" ("The Truth"). The paper's motto read: "Peace, Freedom, Austria"; it attempted to appeal to all political persuasions and regarded the attainment of independence "as the actual, vital question [confronting] Austria."[2] Its circulation soon increased from the initial 100 copies to more than 250, distributed among former prominent Austrian public figures, including those in the conservative and Catholic camps.

Leaning on the existing, experienced Communist-inspired cadres, Hudomalj formed a cluster of local anti-Hitler committees among various non-Party individuals and groups. At the beginning of 1943, a leading organizer of a Socialist group, Dr. Alfred Migsch, a City civil servant, agreed to coedit the paper with Hudomalj.[3] A former Socialist Youth functionary, Migsch, in the fall of 1942, began to collect information on the mood among former SAJ and SPÖ adherents and to identify the cadres of the future unified Socialist movement. He had secured the confidence of

Ludwig Kostroun, Karl Mark, Franz Pfeffer, and other former SAJ and trade union officials and had the support of the central figure in the illegal SPÖ, Dr. Adolf Schärf.[4]

Migsch also established links with the Christian Social circles in Vienna. In the early summer of 1943 he and Dr. Felix Hurdes, an influential figure in the progessive Catholic wing of the CSP, agreed that the Socialists and Christian Socials should cooperate in the postwar Republic. To publicize the idea of cooperation, "Die Wahrheit" began to report news of interest to the Catholic intelligentsia and issued a proclamation to the academic community written by a senior member of the Catholic student association, Dr. Eduard Chaloupka. The political impact of Migsch's drive, directed at the politically conscious segments of the Austrian elite, is difficult to exaggerate. For the first time, the Socialists, Communists, and Christian Socials came together to consider a united opposition to National Socialism.

Communications with Moscow became difficult after the invasion of Russia, so Hudomalj searched for a means through which he could receive further instructions. Acting on Hudomalj's directive, Franz Burda, a young Communist, deserted to the Red Army in June 1943, and transmitted a situation report on Hudomalj's work to the Moscow CC.[5] It appears that as the result of the report, Moscow launched a special operation. It sent an organizational team to Poland in the fall of 1943. Led by Gregor Kersche, an old-time KP official, it included two Viennese Communists, Hildegard Mraz and Aloisia Soucek. The team made its way to Austria where it traveled along Hudomalj's line. It was caught in Vienna on January 2, 1944. Under severe duress, Mraz transmitted news to Moscow for the Gestapo using Kerche's name. The Gestapo exploited the line by establishing direct wireless contact with Georgi Dimitrov and Koplenig, whom the Nazi ploy allegedly duped.[6]

Undoubtedly, Hudomalj's most remarkable achievement was the organization of collective resistance among the conscripted Soviet labor force shipped to work in Vienna. Soviet workers were treated worse than were other foreign workers, and their work conditions were harsh. The concentration of Soviet labor in the Viennese industrial belt made the Soviet workers, who resented their inferior status, a potentially disruptive element of the Nazis. Early in 1943 Hudomalj and his blue-collar aide Gustav Schwella formulated a plan for an "Anti-Hitler Movement of the Workers from East Europe" among the Soviet labor force.[7] Under Hudomalj's political direction, Michael Zenenko and First Lieutenant Michail Iwanow, an escapee from a German prisoner-of-war camp, ran the organization.[8] A net of combat committees was located in most of the war production plants and spread through every Vienna district. As soon as favorable situation presented itself, the Soviet workers planned to engage in direct actions; in the meantime, they awaited the order to act.

The accidental seizure of some notes referring to the publication of "Die Wahrheit" during one of the random police searches of foreign workers put the Gestapo on the track of the Soviet network. On November 27 and 29, they rounded up the families of Schwella and of other Hudomalj associates.[9] At this time the Gestapo was still ignorant of the real scope and nature of the conspiracy. But on learning of the arrests, Karl Suchanek, a member of the Anti-Hitler Committee, and his parents committed suicide. Eventually, contact with the Soviet workers caused Hudomalj's downfall. The absence of any adequate cut-out system had made it almost inevitable that the Nazis would break into the Wahrheit network. The Gestapo placed the suspects under surveillance, and on January 4, 1944, after a short exchange of fire, it captured Hudomalj at his flat. The Wahrheit group collapsed in the following days. Migsch was picked up on January 7 because the Gestapo had found in Hudomalj's apartment the drafts of manuscripts hand corrected by Migsch. Under torture, Hudomalj had cracked and revealed Migsch's identity.[10] Migsch himself gave nothing away and was deported to Mauthausen KZ.[11]

The tragic fall of the imaginative and intelligent Slovene operator was compounded by extensive Nazi actions that dealt his network a deadly blow.[12] Hudomalj had been determined to keep in touch with Austrian political reality. He had cast a wider net politically than had the handpicked senior operators regularly dispatched by the Moscow center. His banding together of individuals and cells drawn from various political affiliations made his work a political success. Insofar as the Resistance forged unity out of diversity, the Hudomalj network forcefully displayed that Austria's interests required the establishment of a tripartite coalition to ensure the country's independence. The disaster of the winter of 1943 did not destroy the beginnings of the coalition. It only postponed its implementation until the end of the war.

THE GERMAN COMMUNISTS IN TYROL

A segment of the revived German Resistance had spread to the western part of Austria, where it worked the east Tyrolian area, assembling the German and Austrian cells in one organization. Toward the beginning of 1940, a German metalworker and political head of the Berlin KPD, Robert Uhrig, regrouped the Communist resistance in Berlin. For Uhrig the network represented the culmination of his early efforts. In 1934 he had been sentenced to eighteen months' imprisonment for his political activity. By 1938 he had started recruiting among the Communist and Socialist militants as far away as Tyrol. Ing. Leopold Tomschik, from an old SPÖ family in Kitzbühel, Tyrol, where he had been active in the Socialist youth, enlisted in Uhrig's network in Berlin in 1938 and joined its inner core in the summer of 1940.[13] During his winter holidays in Kitzbühel, Tomschik approached his

Socialist friends, who subsequently joined the group. Among those friends were a former SPÖ deputy mayor of Kitzbühel, Josef Pair, and the head of the local consumer cooperative, Anton Rausch. Tomschik also gained the support of Werndl in Innsbruck.[14]

Uhrig too vacationed in Kitzbühel, where he formed a local branch, as well as others in Kufstein, Kirchberg, and even in Vienna. His followers were largely former Socialists. Uhrig's poor grasp of political reality is evident from his statement to his followers in Kufstein on June 20, 1941, that "no war will ever be declared [by Germany] against the Soviet Union."[15] He again toured among his Tyrolian followers from October 16 to 19, but he was constantly shadowed by the Gestapo, who succeeded in penetrating most of his Tyrolian cells.[16] On February 4, 1942, the Gestapo arrested Uhrig and his Austrian associates. Rounding up the thirty-two local activists who appeared before the VGH, and their thirty associates whom the OLG Wien tried, continued up to midsummer 1942.[17] Pair and Graus died during the brutal interrogations, and Rausch, Viktor Da-Pont, Georg Gruber, Vogl, Obernauer, and Adele Stürzel were executed.[18] The Tyrolian cells were destroyed.[19]

A more loosely associated nucleus in Schwaz and its surrounding areas, run by a former Communist worker, Max Bär, functioned on a limited scale for a longer time. To build and sustain his followers' political morale, Bär circulated special schooling letters. He continued to operate even after the decapitation of the Uhrig organization. Bär was apprehended in January 1943, after his relatives with whom he was hiding became so apprehensive that they reported him to the authorities.[20]

In Tyrol, more than anywhere else in the country, the Socialist and Communist underground had common features. Their assertive Tyrolian regionalism provided a healthy corrective to the Greater-German idea. With their spirit of activism and the ethic of rebellion, the groups paid little attention to past differences between the Socialists and Communists. Close to Munich and far from Vienna, militant German connections, such as the Haas-Knoeringen and Uhrig networks, strongly influenced the local cells. In both cases, the dedicated Germans provided direct channels of communication and wielded considerable political influence. Reflecting the more conservative character of the province, the KP-oriented cells, however, remained isolated, unable to recruit a significant following. They prospered only so long as they associated themselves with the former power of the SPÖ. When they no longer had Socialist supporters, they returned to their usual isolated state.

THE TROTSKYITES

In striking contrast to the behavior of the Communists, about one hundred followers of Leon Trotsky, who were almost exclusively concentrated in

Vienna, remained politically intact, shunning any contact with other organizations. The movement was given to chronic factionalism, and even the Nazi occupation did not lead to any closing of their ranks. Their sectarian tendency to attune activities to their beliefs and to solicit support among only a few selected radical militants reinforced their political isolation. Because of differences over the war and the Soviet Union, several activists broke away in 1938 from the majority group, the Fighting League for the Liberation of the Working Class, and formed their own nuclei. Fierce dissensions led to constant feuding throughout 1943 and 1944, so the work of the circles was restricted to internal ideological discussion, with each splinter group jealously guarding its clandestine identity through the promotion of its own revolutionary message.[21] What emerged was a curiously vague mixture of radical talk and revolutionary platitudes. From their complete isolation, the Trotskyite groups were unable to challenge the regime. Indeed, their primary objective seemed mere survival and not anti-Nazi action.[22] The heaviest blow came in April 1943 when the police seized seven organizers of the "Gegen den Strom" faction. Because of their isolation and clannish character, the other circles escaped persecution.

THE ROLE OF THE KPÖ IN THE RESISTANCE

During 1938 the KPÖ had become the biggest clandestine force in Austria. No other movement maintained as much discipline, showed as much willingness to take risks, and sacrificed as much during nearly five years of Nazi rule.[23] Its CC, which was safely ensconced abroad, had, in 1937, dropped its references to a dictatorship of the proletariat and endorsed the concept of Austrian national identity. Claiming to represent Austria's national interests, the Party opposed the tutelage of the German Communists. During the KPD, KSČ, and KPÖ discussions on the draft of the November 1939 joint declaration, the German Communists proposed the fusion of the three parties, implying their full recognition of the Anschluss and the dismemberment of Czechoslovakia.[24] Only gradually did the KPÖ reaffirm its independent political stance.

The main purpose of Moscow's continuous assignment of Stalinist-trained operatives to Austria was to ensure the political reliability of the fragile underground structure. The practical arguments for this policy were impressive. When the RS abandoned its underground work in 1938, the KPÖ moved quickly to fill the organizational and political vacuum. The KPÖ, even when reinforced by the influx of Socialist militants after 1934, was still largely restricted to a few industrial areas.[25] Initially, the KPÖ could not challenge the Socialist influence in the urban-industrial strongholds without winning over numerous Socialist militants. The history of the Communist Resistance was, then, the gradual superimposition of the well-structured Communist cadre organization on the broader Socialist following. When the RS resistance vanished or collapsed, the Socialist activists had had no choice but to participate in the Communist underground, which gradually absorbed the bulk of the Socialist militant base. After 1938, a centralized hierarchical organization, strictly disciplined, appeared particularly fitting to clandestine work. The very existence of the underground appealed to the activists, who viewed Communism as the answer to the twin evils of Nazism and Austro-Fascism. In turn, as the Communists made inroads into the Socialist base, a danger arose for the KPÖ that the influx of Socialist veterans would upset the Party's apparatus and thus begin a shift away from the trusted core of Party cadres who controlled the Party. Moscow consequently kept a close watch on events.

There was something pathetic and tragic in a movement steadily sending its best people to their death. The Party's emphasis on organization and indoctrination seemed inevitable, since Communist doctrine was aimed both at demonstrating the necessity for the Party's existence and at justifying its policies, but the almost suicidal tendency to engage in easily traceable propaganda work subordinated the principles of security to political expediency. This belief was the most important factor in the gradual destruction of the Communist-Socialist fighting elite up to the collapse of the centralized organization in 1943. The mass arrests of the first six years shifted the foci of Party activity to the Moscow center and to the guerrilla warfare in Styria and Carinthia.

The decimation of the Communist-oriented native Resistance, which had been one of the prime movers in the struggle for national independence, was an important element in clearing the way for the postwar prominence of the old guard. The absence of independent-minded cadres partly explains the KPÖ's failure to emerge after 1945 as a mass party. In the final analysis, the downfall of the KP underground helped to assure the primacy of the dominant SPÖ-RS cadres, who eventually abandoned their Austro-Marxist past and firmly committed themselves to the pluralistic democratic party system. As the ultimate paradox, it was not the KPÖ nor the RS officials and resisters but the Socialist leader Karl Renner, who had warmly welcomed the Anschluss and endorsed the Munich Agreement in 1938, who reappeared in 1945 as the symbol of Austrian unity, securing general acceptance for a coalition government.

The majority of the population never saw in the KPÖ a possible alternative nor did the Communist Resistance ever reach mass proportions. The Communist mix of political slogan and clandestine action never awoke any popular response because of its contents and its limited circulation. Moreoever, the Socialist tradition and influence were sufficiently strong to withstand Communist penetration, no matter how moderately the KPÖ talked. In the war, depth of moral commitment and emotions mattered more than coherence of ideas, but after 1945, most significantly, a host of those Socialists—although by no means all—who had made common cause with the Communists within the Resistance hastened to rejoin the SPÖ. The other problems hindered the KP: the centralization of the Communist resistance made it insufficiently resilient against the inroads of the security organs; and its propaganda was too public an activity. Although propaganda mobilized dispersed sympathizers, disseminated ideas, broke the isolation of the underground, and temporarily strengthened emerging cells, the clandestine press also drew police attention. Consequently, the Party spent much valuable time recruiting, organizing, and regrouping.

Decision-making and power largely remained in the hands of long-time Party veterans, a small nucleus of embattled officials with common backgrounds, common experiences, and common attitudes and beliefs. However, out of sheer necessity many former SPÖ-RS militants had to be appointed to positions of responsibility within the clandestine structure. In essence, the KPÖ welcomed Socialists on an individual basis, viewing their incorporation as the natural complement of the Party's drive toward a unified workers' party, in which ultimate control would fall to the Communists. In particular, the illegal KP was organizationally as well as politically closely tied to the Socialist cadres in the industrial enterprises. Although the cells in the factories were largely Communist-directed, they served primarily to organize anti-regime activities and only occasionally reflected Communist views. The enrolled activists were usually associated with the SPÖ before 1934, and their participation in the underground was their individual choice. They had entered into a temporary alliance with the KPÖ after the RS had ceased to function. A large number of them, however, retained their democratic Socialist values. Their goals were above all to destroy the regime and create a new social order that would promote greater social justice and fraternity than had the selfish, class-ridden prewar society. Their principal loyalty belonged to the Resistance and to Socialist traditions, not to the KPÖ.

Overall, the members of the Communist-run groups were working-class people, sharing similar social and educational backgrounds. They were close in age, many having shared experiences in the post-1934 era. Because they lived in an era of dramatic change, a forceful leadership was crucial, and the close-knit Communist nucleus provided that leadership in an extraordinary crisis. But the concentration of decision-making in the closed Moscow-oriented center made it difficult for the Party to respond to new, alert, and imaginative militants who aspired to meet broad popular expectations in the post-Hitler regime. During the early war years, however, the woeful effects of the Moscow center's politically sterile Stalinist stance were partly cloaked by the dedication of activists and Socialist sympathizers, who had joined the Resistance with a vision of a democratic future. They plunged headlong into struggle, bearing the brunt of the regime's attack with devotion, zeal, and perseverance.

In the winter of 1943-44 the KPÖ in Austria ceased to exist as a centralized movement. In the meantime, as the Eastern front drew closer to Central Europe, the Soviet Union's primary concern became the securing of the broadest possible support for the increased war effort. Under strong Soviet pressure to intensify active struggle, the KPÖ sought to adapt to the new international situation. However, the expected mobilization of a popular resistance under the Austrian Freedom Front banner never materialized, and the ÖFF remained largely a paper organization. The Moscow Declaration of November 1, 1943, reminded the Austrian people to contribute to their liberation. The Allied powers called for the promotion of clandestine activists in Austria at the very time the KPÖ home apparatus was destroyed.[26]

In response to the Soviet and Allied demands, the Moscow KPÖ center issued a statement on "The Rebirth of Austria," purporting to be prepared by the home underground in June 1944, and calling for a popular uprising.[27] The center saw the guerrilla warfare in Carinthia as a stepping stone to such an insurrection. It also viewed itself as the future core of the Austrian left with a mass following attracted by the prestige gained during the underground struggle. The Party's fresh national image was to form the basis for its rebirth as a mass movement that would pledge to maintain national unity and to work with other popular forces toward a democratic people's republic.[28] The Party well realized the impossibility of openly using the Resistance movement as a springboard for a possible takeover. Despite the prominent role of the KPÖ underground, the Resistance remained a broadly national movement. Moreover, Socialist preferences and the democratic tradition of most old-time SPÖ followers limited the Communist drive to dominate the working class.

Despite the radicalization of the militant forces of Austrian society, both on the NSDAP and Resistance sides, most people showed no inclination to listen to the Communist slogans or to follow the Resistance. For the population at large the Resistance offered only risky experience. In unguarded moments, most people realized that they had no choice but to come to terms with the problem of their German and Austrian identity. But what they desired most of all was political stability and independence. In the early summer of 1944, a Nazi situation report indicated that, "the great bulk of the population have begun to anticipate the unfavorable outcome of the war, and . . . large segments would even favor the German defeat had they not become apprehensive of the Bolsheviks."[29] Given the cautious current of public opinion, neither the calls for a Communist-inspired insurgency nor the Communist claim to a leading role in the future Austrian state could have had any popular support.

The Communist-oriented underground was, above all else, adept at surviving. Since 1938, it had shown an astonishing capacity for regeneration after each Gestapo attack. But by the end of 1943 the Communist-dominated segment of the Resistance lay severely crippled; it was not, however, dead—in particular not in Vienna and the Styrian industrial complex.

NOTES

1. *Volksstimme*, August 18, 1963, DÖW 15479.
2. DÖW 916, 5934; "Berichte, Gestapo Wien," DÖW 8477-78.
3. "Wie entstand unsere illegale Zeitschrift 'Die Wahrheit'?" Friedl Burda, DÖW 329; "Bericht," Dr. A. Migsch, November 10, 1969, DÖW 5934; interview with Dr. Migsch; "Tätigkeit der Widerstandsgruppe Dr. Migsch," June 16, 1946, OM, 21/XIX; Molden, *Der Ruf*, pp. 136-38. I followed the 1969 report, which seems to be more accurate.
4. The Migsch-Mark group was also called the "Socialist Union Movement." Friedrich Weber, "Die linken Sozialisten 1945-1948" (Ph.D. dissertation, University of Salzburg, 1977), p. 66. After 1945 Migsch joined the Austrian government; Schärf became Vice-Chancellor and President of the Republic, and Kostroun and Mark were prominent members of Parliament. Pfeffer died in 1945.
5. *Volksstimme*, August 18, 1963. Hudomalj sent some information to France in a Rumanian diplomatic pouch. DÖW 916.
6. DÖW 5080, 5934, 8912 b, 10016; Genner, *Mein Vater*, pp. 161-62.
7. "Tagesberichte, Géstapo," Wien, DÖW 5080, 8477.
8. DÖW 8477-78.
9. In all, of fifty-eight foreign workers picked up by the Gestapo, fifty-three were of Soviet origin. DÖW 8478.
10. Some thirty-five adherents were arrested in Vienna up to February 1944. At least seven persons, including Hudomalj and Schwella, were executed. Hudomalj's wide range of contacts embraced a newly organized KJV cell in Vienna and reached to Upper Austria, Styria, and Carinthia. DÖW 1040, 1448 d, 5934, 8477-78. A sample of twenty-six arrested members presents a strong working-class character. Eleven women played a prominent part.
11. DÖW 5080.
12. DÖW 5934; DÖW, ed., *Widerstand Wien*, 2:211-13.
13. For the Uhrig network, one of the most important KPD organizations, see Luise Kraushaar, *Berliner Kommunisten im Kampf gegen den Faschismus 1936 bis 1942. Robert Uhrig und Genossen* (East Berlin, 1981), passim; Institut des Marxismus-Leninismus beim Zentralkomitee der SED, *Geschichte der deutschen Arbeiterbewegung*, 5:*Von Januar 1933 bis Mai 1945* (East Berlin, 1966), 227, 278-82, 307-8; Horst Duhnke, *Die KPD von 1933 bis 1945* (Cologne, 1972), pp. 460-61; Peter Altmann, et al., *Der deutsche anti-faschistische Widerstand 1933-1945. In Bildern und Dokumenten* (Frankfurt a.M., 1975), pp. 212-19; Günther Weisenborn, *Der lautlose Aufstand. Bericht über die Widerstandsbewegung des deutschen Volkes 1933-1945* (Hamburg, 1962 ed.), pp. 158-60; Hoffmann, *Widerstand-Staatsstreich-Attentat*, p. 36.
14. Kraushaar, *Berliner Kommunisten*, pp. 181 ff, 241-44; AS, VGH, 9J 777/43g - 1H 59/44, February 15, 1944, DÖW 3365; "Schlussbericht, Gestapo," Innsbruck, November 10, 1942, DÖW 1786; DÖW 1874; Szecsi-Stadler, *Die NS-Justiz*, pp. 65-67; Stadler, *Österreich*, pp. 368-72. Also see above, p. 137.
15. DÖW 2705. The remnants of the Knoeringen network in Tyrol headed by the Socialist high school principal, Johann Vogl, also joined Uhrig. Stadler, *Österreich*, pp. 368-72; DÖW 2673, 12298.
16. In the winter of 1941-42 Uhrig became one of the leaders of the KPD and established links with the Comintern agents Alfred Kowalke, Willi Glatzer, and Wilhelm Knöchel, a top KPD organizer who had arrived in Germany in January 1942. DÖW 3365. Of about 200 arrested militants, sixteen died during interrogations, and thirty-six were sentenced to death in 1944. SED, *Geschichte der Arbeiterbewegung*, pp. 280-81, 307-8.
17. DÖW 2705.

18. DÖW 12298. Tomschik committed suicide in prison. Uhrig and his main aides were executed in 1944. The Gestapo fed its two informers into the network both in Berlin and Tyrol. The Berlin informer ("Ernst"), a KPD member, and another agent were executed in the German Democratic Republic after the war. Kraushaar, *Berliner Kommunisten*, pp. 264, 295.

19. DÖW 2705. Many members were former Socialists, some were Communists, and a few were tainted with a Home Front past.

20. Bär was executed. AS, VGH, 7J 379/43, DÖW 9242; DÖW 2705.

21. DÖW 9414; Fritz Keller, *Gegen den Strom* (Vienna, 1978), pp. 171 ff; DÖW, ed., *Widerstand Wien*, 2:410. The small number of copies published by the underground press were the most visible sign of work.

22. DÖW, ed., *Widerstand Wien*, 2:418-21; DÖW 8477.

23. Over 80 percent of the more than 2,000 records of the OLG Wien (O Js Acts) proceedings dealt with the organized Communist resistance. Similarly, a majority of the VGH's available records on proceedings based on Gestapo and SD-reports involved Communist-inspired activists. See also Dr. Neugebauer in DÖW, ed., *Widerstand Wien*, 2:79.

24. Ústav dějin KSČ, "Materiály z vědecké konference věnované 50. výročí Československé republiky" (Prague, 1968), p. 143; Duhnke, *Die KPD*, pp. 312, 537; O. Janeček et al., eds. *Odboj a revoluce* (Prague, 1965), pp. 97-98; Josef Novotný in the mimeographed bulletin "Odboj a revoluce" (1966), No. 4, p. 50.

25. Before 1934 the KPÖ membership in Vienna amounted to about 400 persons, mostly unemployed and intellectuals. The collapse of the SPÖ February 1934 uprising made a party out of what had been a small workshop. Ruth von Mayenburg, *Blaues Blut und rote Fahnen. Ein Leben unter vielen Namen* (Vienna, 1969), p. 144.

26. After the Moscow Conference, the Soviet journal *Voina i Rabochii Klass* praised the Austrian Resistance but criticized both the RS and the Legitimists. Vojtech Mastny, "Soviet War Aims at the Moscow and Teheran Conferences of 1943," *Journal of Modern History* 47 (September 1975): 499.

27. *Die KPÖ im Kampf für Unabhängigkeit, Demokratie und Sozialistische Perspektive. Sammelband* (Vienna, 1978), pp. 136 ff.; DÖW 573; Maimann, *Politik im Wartesaal*, pp. 212-14; Holzer, "Die Bataillone," pp. 139-40; Vogelmann, "Die Propaganda," p. 56.

28. The statement criticized the Greater-German orientation and the national indifference of the Austrian Social Democracy. DÖW 573.

29. OLG President in Linz to the RMdJ, August 7, 1944, BA R 22/3377.

PART FOUR
The Revival, 1943-1944

15

Preparations

After 1938, political opposition in Austria ceased. A host of political leaders were imprisoned in the concentration camps or were in forced retirement. In the camps, the former politicians formed a loosely knit community, cutting across party line, age, and social position. In Dachau, Socialists and Christian Socials, formerly bitter enemies, exchanged views, fully understanding that there could be no return to the wrecked post-1933 regime. They discerned among themselves a need for frank discussion and scrupulous self-examination, a readiness to accept the responsibilities for fatal past errors, and a fervor to cooperate in the future. In setting forth their common perspective, they spoke openly and succinctly. They wanted to isolate and contain the Nazi penetration and to undermine the German will to fight. They aspired to create an embryonic all-Austrian Resistance coalition and to cooperate within a society traditionally divided into politically hostile camps.

Opinion did indeed change among the conservative elements, disillusioned with the post-1933 regime. They struggled to rediscover the values of democratic life and to provide new leadership. To prevent the divisive effects of ideology from again prevailing, they planned to found a reformed political movement. In effect, reactions to the concentration camp ordeal produced the idea of a future People's Party, situated outside both the old Catholic-oriented CSP and the discredited corporate regime.[1] Thus, following the liquidation of the traditionalist centers in 1940, the concentration camps at Dachau, Buchenwald, and Mauthausen became the largest recruiting grounds for the Resistance, which former inmates joined on their release.

Undoubtedly, the principal figure among the conspirators was Dr. Hans Sidonius von Becker, former Fatherland Front (VF) propaganda chief who had been decorated many times in World War I. By 1937, he had already prepared for the post-1938 clandestine work by creating, within the information Bureau of the VF Secretariat, an operations office to coordinate the struggle against National Socialism.[2] After his release from concentration camp, Becker provided the drive and initiative that resulted in the clandestine reestablishment of the office in May 1941, and in the creation of its liaison branches in Linz, Salzburg, Wels, Innsbruck, Graz, Klagenfurt, and Vorarlberg. Within this skeleton structure of cadres, Becker decentralized his network into a cluster of small circles that kept him informed of events in the provinces. He used as his couriers former civil servants who had been imprisoned; they usually worked as salesmen or insurance agents who could move freely throughout their assigned territories. Gradually, in the fall of 1942, Becker expanded his office into an "Austrian Central Committee."[3]

By the end of 1944 Becker's movement had become a clearing place for a vast array of heterogeneous groups.[4] The result was a tribute to Becker's tireless diplomatic skill and endless work. Imaginative but practical, the shrewd and hard-bitten Becker single-handedly fulfilled the important tasks of integrating and consolidating the fragmented groups. He operated within existing pro-Austrian traditionalist attitudes, but was at ease with the motivations of a variety of resisters. Although his sympathy and affection lay with the Austrian imperial past, he knew only too well its historical fragility. Becker's industry and energy, his political connections with former public officials, and his apparent skill in handling the wheeling and dealing that accompanied recruiting and organizing made him useful to the top leadership.

The influx of new recruits, most of whom were politically to the right of the Socialists, came at a moment particularly suited to the Resistance. The Nazi Reich was visibly weakening, and the Moscow Declaration of November 1943 strengthened the resolve of the anti-Nazi forces ardently working for Austria's liberation. Austrian independence found its greatest advocates in the concentration camps, prisons, and in the Resistance. Initially Greater-German sentiments banished the concept of a separate Austrian identity to the political periphery, but after 1943 the course of military events led to its reemergence. Paradoxically, German military reverses and Allied diplomacy made the post-1938 political underdogs credible Austrian representatives and helped build the basic consensus on which the Austrian state would be recreated. The Resistance moved much faster than general public opinion, which still refused to espouse the Resistance's aspirations. However, the specter of a Nazi collapse fundamentally changed the nature of politics. With the German reverses on the Eastern front and in North Africa, the non-Communist underground seemed to be rediscovering its distinct identity without losing its diversity.

By 1943-44 the balance of power had shifted dramatically from younger, politically inexperienced men, who had perished in the line of duty, to more professional cadres, who understood that the undergound could not be rebuilt on the first springtide of excitement. Despite having been badly mauled in its initial phase, the infrastructure of the Resistance was not entirely dismantled. Regrettably, the failure to develop a central leadership hampered the building of contacts with the Allied powers abroad. Unlike in Norway, Holland, Belgium, Denmark, France, or Italy, "no official aid to the incipient underground groups was given from the outside." Clearly, up to the closing months of the war, the Austrians had still not succeeded in "developing an effective underground," because they lacked "that publicity of local underground activities, propaganda and continuous active encouragement from the outside" which "were decisive factors in the creation in those other countries of conditions conducive to the growth and organization of strong underground organizations."[5] The turn of military events did, however, help to overcome the initial political polarization. By 1943-44 the diverse elements of the widely dispersed democratic Resistance had unreservedly committed themselves to national unity and independence. The long, common struggle created an embryonic national community and finally brought about a reconciliation between Socialists and Conservatives. And, in a display of allegiance to Austria, remaining Communist resisters joined the national Resistance. Whatever their private thoughts they had to acknowledge the predominantly patriotic character of the Resistance. For their part, the Socialists and Communists never developed a common working-class front against Hitler, and, even at this late date, were doing nothing to overcome their rivalry.

THE 05 AND THE COMMITTEE OF SEVEN

After 1942, clandestine groups varying in size from half a dozen to several hundred persons joined the activists' ranks. New cells and groups arose out of the initiative of a few personalities who consolidated their authority by recruiting and organizing their adherents. Their parallel efforts played a decisive part in inspiring the second stage of the Resistance. By 1944, Becker had organized the numerous groups into a single bloc that became known as the 05.[6] The appearance of the mysterious 05 sign overnight in Vienna acted as a psychological impulse, binding a variety of groups in one movement.[7] Throughout 1944, its numerous small cells carried out acts of sabotage. They also committed acts of arson against military supplies and undertook diversionary actions in the local telephone and electricity systems. In Vienna a sabotaged transformer held up the streetcar traffic in some districts for a few hours in June 1944. At times, the members disrupted railway traffic to and from the oil fields of Zistersdorf, and engaged in other industrial sabotage, such as inflicting damage on two automobile repair workshops in Vienna.[8]

Other groups also hindered the Nazis. The circle "West" began its actions in the fall of 1942. The conservative "Prinz Eugen" group, represented by Prince Thurn-Taxis, and the "Neulengbach" group, joined Becker's network in 1944.[9] The traditionalist-inspired "Österreichischer Kampfbund" was linked to Becker through Dr. Zimmer-Lehmann and Herbert Braunsteiner, a medical student. Former adherents of the "Helmuth Wenger" Free Corps, who had suspended their work in 1938-39, formed the nucleus of the "Kampfbund." One of their leaders, Johannes Eidlitz, resumed the work in 1941 when the group became a secure network concentrating on sabotage and propaganda. It expanded its contacts into the military sector, where it acquired some small arms. At the end of 1944, two military cells were set up in Vienna in the Radetzky Military Barracks and in the Army Medical Service Section 17. About the same time, the local leaders were providing shelter to deserters and escapees near Waidhofen a.d. Ybbs and Göstling and building up an escape route across the Alps to Yugoslavia. The route eventually carried between seventy to eighty men to the area that the Slovene Partisans controlled in Carinthia.[10]

The Nazi successes had affected some original adherents of the traditionalist formations. Tempered by past experiences, Baron Maasburg had settled down. But encouraged by Becker, he deserted the Wehrmacht in the summer of 1944. His special concern was to handle liaison between the center and the Tito Partisan movement. Accompanied by Dr. Zimmer-Lehmann and Count Rudolf Thun-Hohenstein, a Viennese lawyer, he established from his castle Wisell in Lower Styria (a former Yugoslav part of Styria) a courier line with the Fourth Zone of the Tito military administration. With the Partisan contact man, Ing. Kankel, head of the Viennese Agency for the Supply of Manpower from the Balkans, he envisioned the formation of an Austrian legion in the Bacher Mountains in Northern Yugoslavia, grouping the Austrian military deserters and activists. In 1944 the Viennese militant Hubert Ziegler, charged with the command of such a unit, succeeded in creating in Lower Styria a nucleus composed mainly of Austrian deserters. He set up radio liaison with the Allied Headquarters in Caserta and communicated with U.S. Scout Liaison officer Captain Rudolph Charles von Ripper who parachuted into Carinthia in 1945 to establish communication with the local 05.[11] In March 1945 the SS killed Ziegler and Kankel.[12] It was only in 1945 that the Gestapo liquidated the Yugoslav support center in Vienna.

Not wanting to remain isolated, other organizations worked under the 05 umbrella. They displayed a heartening political moderation and a willingness to talk with each other. The "Vindobona" group arranged contacts with Yugoslavia from Styria and Carinthia. In 1943 naval Captain Josef Posser established a cell called "Lainz" in the Reserve Military Hospital XXVI. It produced false papers and medical reports to help soldiers avoid duty at the front. In June 1944, Posser was appointed to the Wehrmeldeamt in Vienna, where he obtained false official identity cards for Austrian soldiers. At the end of 1944, his group, numbering thirty people, began to cooperate with the groups run by Leopold Kunschak, a nephew of the Christian Social labor politician,[13] police Oberleutnant Franz Fassl, Major Alfons Stillfried, and Georg Fraser.[14]

Another circle, "Free Austria," largely composed of workers, concentrated on industrial sabotage. Its section in the large Styrian enterprise Alpine-Montan gained contacts with foreign workers and the Yugoslav Partisans. Another cell in Gmünd kept in touch with French prisoners of war. It damaged the railroad bridge on the Prague-Vienna line during March 27-28, 1945. The "Union of the Democratic Freedom Fighters" near Vienna, headed by the chaplain of the Maltese Order Leopold Hauck, also sabotaged war production. In 1944, a left-wing youth cell in Trattenbach, Lower Austria, sabotaged small airplanes and their parts in the aircraft park in Gloggnitz. The boys were seized in December 1944.[15]

In the military medical service, the Resistance assembled a highly competent and enthusiastic staff of activists whose purpose was to aid the Austrian draftees. In Vienna, Ing. Curt Reinisch and his aides at the Army Medical Service Center enabled many Austrian soldiers to remain in the hospitals to avoid active service and to obtain medical reports based on incorrect diagnoses. Many physicians and medical personnel in the barracks, military hospitals, military medical commissions, and Army medical service administration in Vienna, Linz, Salzburg, and Innsbruck worked in dangerous conditions outside their normal medical practice. The physicians thus enabled many Austrian soldiers to evade their military duties.[16]

Two organizations reflected the unexciting, prudent approach of the major formations who were steadily expanding in size and scope. The "Austrian Freedom Front" (ÖFF) had emerged in the post-1934 era, banding together Schutzbund-members. After 1938 the network linked up with a Czech circle in Vienna and with the Czech group "Viktoria" in Brno. During 1943 and 1944, several cells emerged in Vienna, Styria, and Carinthia. Initially, the ÖFF mainly engaged in propaganda. It accumulated its forces gradually, acquiring small arms from the military hospitals in Vienna, where they were deposited by wounded soldiers but not yet registered by the hospital administrations. Military physicians assisted ÖFF members to escape duty at the front. But the arrests of militants in 1944 created great difficulties for the movement. However, their losses did not stop the remaining activists from participating in the final battle for Vienna in 1945.[17]

Another network associated with 05 was the "Austrian Freedom Movement" (ÖF), which had emerged from an agreement concluded in April 1944 by four smaller groups. It issued its first "Information Bulletin" ("Mitteilungsblatt") on May 1, 1944. Its leaflets strewn in the streets of the working-class districts in Vienna appealed to the population to fight for peace, freedom, and Austria. In one instance, The Movement damaged over ninety public telephone booths in five Viennese districts in one night. The ÖF assisted military deserters and Jews and arranged their transport to Tito-controlled Yugoslavia. The ÖF's influence was, however, rather limited, although its members joined the combat teams during the last weeks of the war in Vienna.[18]

Becker and his second in command, Dr. Raoul Bumballa-Burenau, relentlessly recruited and organized throughout 1944.[19] They established a communication line with the circles around L. Kunschak and Ing. Gerhard Schwarz, who supplied arms to the activists and controlled the military automobile park in Prater. Later in the year, the two leaders contacted their former Dachau fellow inmates, Georg Fraser, a Viennese writer, the Socialist Eduard Seitz, and the Conservative Viktor Müllner, who had built up their organizations after Fraser's second release from Dachau in January 1944. A former deputy of St. Pölten, Müllner worked among the peasantry in the Lower Austrian countryside and penetrated the Volkssturm (People's Militia) in Vienna. Fraser befriended some Viennese intellectuals and reached out into the local Communist ranks where he first met Mathilde (Clotilde) Hrdlicka, through whom in July 1944 he approached Mitja Gutov, a Soviet agent in charge of clandestine action among the deported Soviet laborers.[20]

The difficult tasks of creating organizations and recruiting volunteers generated no visible changes in the underground structure. The activist groups kept their ranks tight and their tasks separated. They acted alone, refusing to give up their identities. However, the groups did seek to assure the presence of a central leadership that would coordinate the struggle in the final stages of the war. The recognition of the advantages of close cooperation prompted acceptance of the 05 as an alliance of different activist movements and individuals. In contrast to the development in other countries, the process of centralized coordination did not involve any incorporation of groups into one superior movement nor did it reach national proportion. The stress placed on cooperation and coordination of separate movements rather than on their unification can be explained by the relatively rudimentary, amateurish, and diffuse nature of the underground movement, which lacked strong personalities and a sympathetic public outside its own circles.

The 05 serviced a large range of individuals and groups. However loosely structured the 05 might have been, it provided the local chiefs a means of strengthening their authority and an opportunity for spreading their influence and mobilizing dispersed sympathies. With the end of the war in sight in the fall of 1944, the 05 had to decide whether the chiefs ought to prepare for broad political-military action against the regime. To achieve unity of planning and to rally the dispersed activists, Becker, Bumballa, Fraser, Müllner, Seitz, and Oswald created a steering Committee of Seven in November 1944.[21] Hrdlicka joined the Committee to represent the

Communist tendency; Becker became its head. After Becker's arrest on February 28, 1945, Bumballa replaced him; Dr. Franz Sobek, a civil servant from an Austro-Bohemian family took the vacant place on the Committee.[22]

Riding the crest of a favorable international situation, the Committee operated as a coalition of the main political currents and coordinated the resistance activities of scores of scattered groups. On both political and practical grounds, the Committee reflected the need for a central organization to represent Austria's claim to independence. In fact, however, the Committee, which was mainly confined to Vienna and Lower Austria, had little real political strength compared with the still firmly entrenched individual, mostly liberal-conservative, networks and with the skeleton organizations of the political parties. The Committee's main concern was to tackle the immediate postwar problems: mobilization of public opinion to prevent economic disintegration after the German defeat, and preservation and rapid restoration of the public services. Its priority was to prevent physical destruction by the retreating German armies and their removal of the large war supplies stored on Austrian territory.[23]

Despite their slender resources, the 05 chiefs made good progress in attracting important groups. Dr. Sobek successfully planted 05 seeds among the more conservative movements. He secured the collaboration of the St. Pölten group, directed by head of the Schutzpolizei in St. Pölten, Dr. Otto Kirchl.[24] Another of Becker's friends contacted other networks. Hofrat Bernhard Scheichelbauer provided liaison with the influential Christian Social cell around Dr. Felix Hurdes; with a circle around former Landbund (Peasant's League) minister Vinzenz Schumy; with the Austrian National Committee; with Dr. Schaginger who was associated with the former Austrian telegraph employees; with the Viennese group around the young student Walter De Comtes which was linked to Dr. Karl Gruber in Berlin; and with various other cells and individuals.[25]

The decision to assemble a cluster of combative groups around Becker and the Committee of Seven in Vienna and Lower Austria required continual exchanges among the networks. These exchanges also prevented any artificial centralization around any one group, which would have fanned the flames of personal rivalry. Despite the increased pressure from the Gestapo, cutting back contact at that time would inevitably have damaged the Resistance. In encouraging cooperation among the main ideolgial currents, the Committee considered itself to be in step with the course of war events. The Moscow Declaration was a clear sign of renewed and firm Allied support. With broad segments of the population in agreement with the principle of Austrian statehood, the Resistance had begun to enjoy a limited but comfortable sense of self-worth that came with the approaching Allied victory. After 1944, its stable core developed a crash program to overcome the Resistance's isolation and to become the country's voice and conscience.

NOTES

1. Hans Becker, *Österreichs Freiheitskampf* (Vienna, 1946), pp. 10-14; Ludwig Reichhold, *Geschichte der ÖVP* (Graz, 1975), pp. 44-47; Molden, *Der Ruf,* pp. 97, 207; Ernst Trost, *Figl von Österreich* (Vienna, 1972), pp. 111-27; Rudolf Kalmar, *Zeit ohne Gnade* (Vienna, 1946), passim.

2. "Dr. H. Becker Nachlass," DÖW 12032 a-b.

3. Becker, *Freiheitskampf,* pp. 10-11, 13-14, 28.

4. Becker and his friends in Prague fostered contacts with the important Czech clandestine network around Jaroslav Kvapil and Dr. Emil Lány. Becker's Prague cell provided valuable intelligence to the Czech Resistance. DÖW 12032/8. Allegedly, Becker and his friend Dr. Raoul Bumballa supplied the British Intelligence Service with data. DÖW 12032/4.

5. "Anti-Nazi Resistance in Vienna from 1938-1945," October 18, 1945, Headquarters United States Forces in Austria. Office of the Political Adviser. The perceptive report, published as an appendix to USFA Intelligence Summary No. 20, stated that "no evidence has come to light of any material aid to the underground in Vienna, either by the Russians or by the western Allies, although some intelligence was accepted from Austrian sources." DÖW 8502.

6. The name comes from the letters O and E in "Oesterreich" (Austria). E is the fifth letter in the alphabet. Becker, *Freiheitskampf,* p. 20; DÖW 12032/3.

7. Molden, *Der Ruf,* pp. 170. See also Becker, *Freiheitskampf,* p. 20; Kudrnofsky, *Vom Dritten Reich,* pp. 55-56.

8. Becker, *Freiheitskampf,* p. 17; DÖW 8503; Romanik, *Der Anteil,* pp. 27-28. "Auszug aus dem Tätigkeitsbericht des Gustav Jelinek-Donner," DÖW 8394. No less important was the systematic attempt from October 1940 until 1942 to mail appeals to Austrian soldiers at the front. OM, No. 62.

9. Thurn-Taxis's task was to keep in contact with other still widely scattered groups. Moreover, he successfully established links to the Czech Resistance and to Carl Goerdeler in Germany. Interview of Prince Willy von Thurn-Taxis; "Notizen über Bericht Thurn-Taxis," March 17, 1949, OM, No. 9.

10. "Bericht von Hanns Eidlitz," OM, No. 49; interview with H. Eidlitz. In 1945 the "Kampfbund" numbered a little over 100 members. At the end of December 1944 two men introduced themselves to the network as "Nowotny" and "Areof," American agents dropped by the Allied Mediterranean Command. The men demonstrated their *bona fide* status by arranging for the BBC to broadcast "Kampfbund" messages from London. Unfortunately, the men were SD agents who replayed to England the transmitters captured from British operators in December 1944. OM, No. 49.

11. Ripper was an Austrian artist who after 1936 had fought as a pilot in the Republican Army in Spain. After the Republican defeat he left for the USA. In 1941 he enrolled into the OSS. Molden, *Fepolinski,* pp. 316-18.

12. Molden, *Der Ruf,* pp. 210-211; F. Molden, *Fepolinski,* pp. 318-319; Kudrnofsky, *Vom Dritten Reich,* p. 56; "Bericht Dr. Zimmer-Lehmann," March 17, 1949, OM, No 4. In February 1945, Croatian Ustascha men assassinated Thun-Hohenstein near Maasburg's castle.

13. Following his desertion from the Wehrmacht, Kunschak went underground in Vienna where he set up a nucleus of policemen and other officials including members of the telegraph service. Georg Fraser, "Memorandum," May 3, 1945, DÖW 7936.

14. DÖW 8393; Becker, *Freiheitskampf,* p. 19; Romanik, *Der Anteil,* pp. 23, 27-29; "Berichte," OM, XIX.

15. Romanik, *Der Anteil,* p. 22; Becker, *Freiheitskampf,* pp. 14, 28; OM, DO 21.

16. "Berichte," DÖW 8393; OM, XIX, No 21; Romanik, *Der Anteil,* pp. 25-26, 36; Becker, *Freiheitskampf,* p. 17; *Neues Österreich,* May 18, 1954; OM, DO 21.

17. "Die Österreichische Freiheitsfront (ÖFF) und die Österreichische Freiheitsbewegung (ÖF) in den Jahren 1938 bis 1945. Ein Tätigkeitsbericht," Vienna, DÖW; "Bericht für das Rotbuch der österreichischen Regierung," DÖW 8389.

18. Ibid.

19. Dr. Bumballa participated in World War I as an Austrian Air Force pilot. In 1938 he was imprisoned in Dachau until the fall of 1942. Molden, *Der Ruf,* pp. 206-7.

20. Ibid.; DÖW 7936, 8393.

21. Molden, *Der Ruf,* pp. 206-8.

22. Ibid. Sobek returned from Dachau in the summer of 1943 and acted as an 05 liaison man.

23. Ibid., pp. 209-10. As elsewhere in the occupied countries, some resistance leaders nourished the hope that democratic forces, whose leaders would be selected from among the resisters, would rule the liberated Republic.

24. The group mainly engaged in sabotage and in assistance to the families of political prisoners. On April 13, 1945, the SS executed Kirchl and twelve of his associates in St. Pölten. Romanik, *Der Anteil,* p. 23; Molden, *Der Ruf,* pp. 206-9. Allegedly, a Gestapo informer, Swoboda (alias "Walter Vogl"), betrayed the group. He had also informed on the large cell in the Moosbierbaum oil refinery in January 1945. DÖW 8337; Fein, *Die Steine,* p. 186.

25. For Dr. Hurdes and Dr. Gruber, see below; DÖW 9393.

16

The Consolidation
of the Resistance

Although the circle around Becker had successfully established the 05 and the Committee of Seven, it never exercised effective control over the individual networks. Many groups, including not a few that cooperated with the 05, worked independently. But coordination was gradual. In this clandestine world, Major Stillfried played a key part in building a flexible line, composed of civilians and military, reaching out from a core in his Office of Censorship of Foreign Letters in Vienna in 1939 to the German military in Berlin and eventually in Italy.[1] In Vienna he cooperated with Colonel Count Rudolf von Marogna-Redwitz, head of the *Abwehrstelle Wien* and a Bavarian conservative Catholic, who became his link with the German military Resistance. Stillfried also worked with Hauptmann (later Major) Karl Biedermann, the commander of the important *"Heeresstreife Gross Wien"* (Military Police of Greater Vienna), with Hans Jörg Unterrainer, a former Tyrolian Free Corps official, and with various military and civilian circles. In the fall of 1944 he managed to become one of the patrons of the 05.[2]

A pragmatic man, Stillfried intensified the contacts with active groups so as to coordinate their activities. With Becker and other civilian and military leaders, he regarded the resistance movements as auxiliaries of the Allied armed forces. The former were to control the country after the withdrawal of the German troops. To help weaken the regime, Stillfried had, since September 1944, regularly communicated to the Americans in Switzerland the location of German troops and war production centers in eastern Austria. In the winter of 1944-45, he speeded up preparations for the formation of a coordinating organ of the Resistance that would, he hoped, be acceptable to the Allied authorities as a representative of Austrian public opinion.[3] The favorable course of the war bolstered the confidence of the

Resistance chiefs, who lost no opportunity in quickening the pace of their work, so that the entire underground might adhere to a unified political and military line.

This is not an exhaustive account of the Austrian Resistance. It concentrates on its main elements and what seems most relevant about them. What follows is a description of several groups, but reflects the history of nearly all.

Often the groups grew out of small cells founded earlier in the war. At the beginning of 1942 the dormant Catholic-conservative network "Astra" was reactivated with the support of Colonel Marogna-Redwitz, who provided the leading members Dr. Raphael Spann and Dr. Karl von Winkler with Abwehr covers. The group conducted some industrial sabotage and established connections with the Tito Headquarters and with the United States officials in Switzerland through Dr. Theodor Veiter in Vorarlberg. Spurred by hostility to Hitler, "Astra" had originally started in 1936. Through a member of the German Embassy in Vienna, Emanuel von Ketteler, it was linked with Nikolaus von Halem, who worked the German end of the network. Eventually, the Nazis murdered Ketteler in Vienna in March 1938 and Halem in 1944.[4] In contrast, another group weathered the occupation successfully. The Viennese student Gustav R. Weihs von Mainprugg organized about thirty people in Alt Aussee and Vienna in 1940-41. He stockpiled small arms and ammunition high in the mountains. After 1943 he supplied the British Consulate in Switzerland with secret documents taken from the Vienna *Wehrkreiskommandantur* and with situation reports. The activists participated in the military uprising headed by Major Carl Szokoll in Vienna in April 1945.[5]

Although a Jew required an extraordinary degree of courage to engage in resistance, some Jews found it difficult to remain inactive. Otto Andreasch assembled a special Jewish underground unit (Sonderabteilung "NN"), which was dispersed in 1942 when the Jews were deported. The remaining cadres, mainly composed of half-Jews, formed the "Racially Mixed League of Vienna" in March 1943, which they renamed the "Anti-Fascist Party of Austria (APÖ)" in the fall.[6] The APÖ had its own combat squad and saw itself as the nucleus of an organization combining conservative, Socialist, and Communist elements. In the summer of 1943 it secured contact with the Tito Partisans by way of Maribor. The Jewish fighters supplied Tito's troops with medicine and radio material. The activists organized as a paramilitary detachment were readying themselves to join the Partisans in the spring of 1944 when in February the APÖ was betrayed and rounded up.[7]

The small Czech community concentrated in Vienna played a limited but nevertheless important part in the creation of the resistance movement during the initial period. A number of Czech Socialists participated in the Communist Resistance. On the Catholic side, the initiative for clandestine work came from a young priest, Josef Pojar, a religion teacher at the Czech Komensky School in Vienna. A handful of his compatriots helped him search in vain for connections to the Austrian underground. Instead, they made contacts with the Czechoslovakian exile authorities in London in 1942. When these were broken in 1943, Pojar set off in 1944 with his Czech friend Joachim Hajl for Bari in South Italy, where he reported to the Czechoslovak Military Mission on May 13. After volunteering for service in the Reich and undergoing special intelligence training, he returned to Vienna where his cell soon grew to over thirty companions. Operating in Austria and the Protectorate of Bohemia and Moravia, Pojar reported valuable intelligence to London by way of Yugoslavia and by direct wireless link. Ultimately, the operation ran into difficulties. The liaison man with Yugoslavia, Viktor Dolinček, was apprehended and murdered. Shortly afterward on December 12, 1944, Pojar and sixteen others were captured, three of whom never returned home.[8]

"THE DEMOCRATIC AUSTRIAN RESISTANCE MOVEMENT"

After 1938, Catholic student activists scattered all over the country. Most had belonged to student fraternities that held vague anti-Nazi attitudes. A sense of continuing the tradition of Austrian civic patriotism drew some of them together. In particular, the problems of Austrian loyalty agitated some youthful physicians and medical students. In January 1942 at the Wehrmacht City Command in Vienna, these youths founded a clandestine cell to aid the Austrian soldiers. They won over the local military medical personnel in the barracks. In October 1942, they approached a former fraternity colleague Dr.-Ing. Karl Gruber (1909), who after 1938 had been appointed to the Telefunken Company in Berlin, where he had joined the network known as "Blumengarten," ("Flower Garden") comprising Austrians residing in the Reich.[9] Passivity was not a Gruber trait. Assertive, blunt, and persevering, Gruber was a good negotiator and conciliator who retained complete liberty of judgment on party politics. Energetic and possessed of a strong ego, he was a dashing leader to his admirers.[10] Gruber ran a line to the American diplomats and to the Gördeler resistance movement.[11] In the fall of 1944 he contacted the U.S. Office of Strategic Services in Switzerland through Schedler, the son of the high government official of the principality of Liechtenstein.[12] In the meantime, he established a group in Vienna that, as "The Democratic Austrian Resistance Movement," eventually participated with 05 in the military actions directed by Major Szokoll in April 1945.[13]

In the winter of 1944-45, Gruber was transferred from Berlin to Bavaria and then to Innsbruck. In the Tyrolian capital, he transformed the stumbling local movements into one central network. On March 12, 1945, he arrived in Vienna to communicate last instructions to his friends and to gather intelligence data to be transmitted to the Americans in Bern. He then rushed to Innsbruck to organize the Tyrolian groups before returning to Vienna. In Tyrol, he helped reverse the atmosphere of polarization and division hampering organizational consensus. Appointed head of a Tyrolian command by the leaders of the main networks, he successfully coordinated the resistance.[14] As a newcomer, Gruber was the only Tyrolian figure with sufficient authority whom the indigenous groups would allow to stage an armed revolt and negotiate with the Allies.[15]

THE MAIER-MESSNER GROUP

The energetic young chaplain at the Vienna-Gersthof parish, DDr. Heinrich Maier, was concerned more with issues of morality and politics than with theology and, despite his leftist leanings, he was not above supporting the Schuschnigg regime. However, he perceived that the brutal realities of Nazi rule overshadowed the initially positive social aspects. By 1940, he and his friends had been drawn into clandestine work.[16] Maier, a dynamic man with an engaging personality, worked in the shadow of legality.[17] After 1942, his intelligence circle consisting of a dozen persons used its access to important military and industrial information to supply the OSS in Bern with a steady flow of valuable material. One of the main sources was the Director General of the Semperit Rubber Works, Dr. Franz Messner. In the main, Maier and Messner moved in military and business circles in Vienna and collected much priceless economic intelligence, including data on the development of tanks and the new V-2 rocket. In response to American requests. the group provided the location of industrial targets for Allied air attacks.

From 1943 Maier's group collaborated with the Catholic Monarchist network run by Dipl-Ing. Walter Caldonazzi. The group's downfall came with Caldonazzi's arrest on February 25, 1944, and with the Gestapo seizure of the Hungarian intelligence files when the Germans occupied Hungary in March 1944. The files contained information from the Hungarian agents in Istanbul, which allowed the Germans to identify Messner as an OSS contact.[18] Apparently a sum of RM 100,000 was also confiscated. Messner had transferred the funds that the OSS allegedly supplied from Budapest to Vienna to help cover the cost of his intelligence-gathering.[19] Maier was arrested on March 28, 1944, and Messner in Budapest the next day.[20] But the wreck of this most effective Austrian network did not completely end its work.[21]

In September the 05 man Fritz Molden returned from Switzerland to Vienna on OSS instructions to seek out the remnants of the Maier-Messner group who had been cut off from the American contacts. A school colleague, an American student named Harald Frederiksen, helped contact the Maier group and build an intelligence network of forty people. Up to his arrest in January 1945 Frederiksen supplied the OSS via Innsbruck with vital weekly intelligence.[22] In closely cooperating with the Americans, the Maier-Messner network successfully carried out a highly hazardous intelligence operation. Its leaders hoped that their achievements would not only contribute to Austria's liberation but would also convince the Allies that the Austrian Resistance could be a valuable ally.

ATA

Clandestine work often started with the self-assertion of individuals whom Hitler's destruction of their country had aroused to indignation.[23] These people then generated dispersed nuclei, which grew in strength and expanded into groups.[24] Often when the leaders were imprisoned, no one could fill the void and the disparate nuclei split, vanished, or joined another movement. In this way the distinctions between the sustained individual efforts and the work of a network are often blurred.

One example will illustrate the general course of events. In 1939 a university lecturer (Dozent) Johannes Krebs-Waldau started a network called "ATA," from his office at the *Reichsstatthalterei* (Provincial Government) Lower Danube in Vienna. Drafted in 1940 into the Air Force as Oberleutnant, he served as a *Bataillon-Wehrbetreuungsoffizier* of an Air Force unit that included over 4,000 wounded and sick men on the road to recovery. From his position, he protected and rescued many soldiers from the front line duties. Later, as an air courier officer for the Balkans, attached to the Southeast Liaison Office (Verbindungsstelle Südost-Kurierstelle) of the Luftgaukommando XVII in Vienna, he arranged outside contacts in France, Athens, Saloniki, Belgrade, Nisch, Bucarest, and Sofia. Released from the Air Force in 1942, he returned to Vienna, where he set out to organize clandestine activists. Toward the end of the war, he moved his office to Giesshübl near Amstetten. He played a part in the activities of the Artillery Reserve-and Training Unit 109 under Hauptmann Dr. Manfred Schneider-Wehrthal, with whom he participated in an operation that two American agents and the approaching United States 80th Division coordinated. The operation resulted in the early American seizure of the huge cellulose plant in Lenzing on May 4.[25]

THE RISING TIDE IN THE PROVINCES

Upper Austria

At the time of Becker's release from Dachau, another Austrian prisoner, Dr. Josef Hofer, left Buchenwald KZ. Almost immediately, this former senior police official at the police Headquarters in Linz started to build a following in Upper Austria at the strategic gateway to the important industrial basin in and round Linz. As in insurance agent, Hofer could easily travel throughout the province and start small nuclei. Loosely structured, with bases in both rural and urban areas, Hofer's network had widespread connections to the foreign labor force, to prisoners of war, and to the Nazi security apparatus. In Wels, Hofer contacted a Socialist trade unionist, Franz Grüttner, whose apartment soon served as the center of the intelligence-gathering of his union friends. Grüttner's arrest on October 1, 1944, did not substantially interrupt the work. Released in January, he again operated until the arrival of American troops.[26] Another of Hofer's companions was a former Heimwehr official, monarchist, farmer, horse-dealer, and innkeeper, Ferdinand Roitinger. Arrested in 1938 but soon released, Roitinger proved himself a successful resistance oganizer among the peasants. As a horse-dealer, he could travel freely in the countryside.[27]

A wide range of people animated this rather heterogeneous network, people such as the prominent Socialist Richard Bernaschek, the leader of the Socialist uprising in February 1934. A man of moral courage, integrity, and perseverance, but one who was politically naïve, Bernaschek stunned his Socialist comrades by voluntarily returning from Paris to Linz in January 1939. Previously he had earned a reputation as a radical, romantic individual, driven by his impulses and fiery temper to pursue his revolutionary ideals. But back at home, the revolutionary mellowed. Closely watched by the Nazis, Bernaschek placed himself squarely in the midst of clandestine activity and collaborated with his former political opponent Hofer, who helped him to get a job as an insurance agent. When the Socialist Dr. Hans Frenzel and his eight associates founded the "Gegenbewegung" (G.B.) in Linz on August 9, 1942, Bernaschek saw an opportunity to help recruit the G.B. following. He was imprisoned after the assassination attempt on Hitler on July 21, 1944. On September 7 the Gestapo rounded up some 150 persons in Linz, Wels, Lambach, Gmunden, Ebensee, and Steyermühl. An informer planted by the Linz Gestapo into the Wels network allegedly reported on Bernaschek's clandestine work. Bernaschek suffered brutal treatment at Nazi hands in Mauthausen. Tortured, but refusing to give away his companions, he was murdered on April 18, 1945.[28]

Responding to the mood of the population, who wanted above all to survive, the G.B. did not engage the Nazis in armed combat. Its activists acted mainly as propagandists, recruiters, and organizers. They disseminated news about the progress of the war, sent information on the domestic situation to the soldiers at the front, rendered assistance to foreign workers, prisoners, and Wehrmacht deserters, and conducted some diversionary action against the German war machine.[29] Throughout 1944, members took preparatory steps to prevent Nazi demolition of public installations during the Nazi retreat. More important, the Linz movement closely cooperated with the one-thousand-strong organization of Italian military internees

(F.G.-M.I.), headed by Marco Cortelazzo, with a group of four hundred Dutch workers, and with a group of fifty Soviet prisoners of war.[30] Curiously enough, the G.B.'s followers wore a yellow flower as identification. Such semipublic demonstration betrayed a singular lack of common sense.

After the war it was calculated that the Upper Austrian Resistance numbered at least 1,208; some 1,947 persons were put into Upper Austrian jails and were eventually sent as political prisoners to the concentration camps or other prisons.[31] The losses did not stop underground activities. A number of local groups were at work in the closing weeks of the conflict.[32] One such organization suffered a grievous blow when the Gestapo arrested scores of persons in Freistadt. The prewar Social Democrat Ludwig Hermentin, a managing director of the *Landkrankenkasse* (Provincial Health Insurance) and a white-collar worker, Willibald Thallinger, created in 1943-44 a group called "New Free Austria." Except for recruiting and collecting funds, its actions were insignificant. Nevertheless, the Nazi judicial authorities sentenced twelve members to death in two VGH sessions on February 26 and 29, 1945. The sentences were carried out on May 1—four days before the first American armed columns arrived in Linz.[33]

Salzburg and Styria

As the war swept toward the Reich, railroad and industrial sabotage activities intensified in the Province of Salzburg.[34] Production in local plants such as the Iron Works at Sulzau-Werfen and the Grill Works at Hallein slowed down, and factory machinery was temporarily put out of action. Small bands of Austrian military deserters found refuge in the sparsely populated mountains. They were, however, mainly composed of people whose chief aim was to survive the war. In the summer of 1944, special security commandos combed the Alpine ranges between Goldegg and Radstadt for deserters. When in the fall of 1944 the Volkssturm—the general levy of all able-bodied men between sixteen and sixty—was organized, resisters infiltrated its ranks. They stole arms and ammunition from a number of Volkssturm battalions and slowed down conscription. In the closing stage of the war, teams of militants successfully protected from demolition bridges, water- and electrical power plants, radio transmitters, and other vitally important installations. In Styria, the year 1944 saw the creation of clandestine cells in the districts of Graz, Hartberg, Bruck a.d. Mur, Mürzzuschlag, Fürstenfeld, Liezen, Deutschlandsberg, and Weiz. There were losses, too. In Fischbach the Nazis broke into a local section of a Styrian group, shot four resisters, and arrested twenty persons.[35]

Despite rumblings of dissent in the provinces, a truly mass resistance movement had not yet developed. The pervasive political paralysis, an underdeveloped sense of moral obligation, and the hierarchical nature of traditional Austrian society offered no great prospects for the Resistance, which grew in intensity only among those few who realized the extent of the willful destruction of the Austrian morale and traditions. The same basic contradiction as in other nations in Nazi-occupied Europe—the heroism and enormous losses of a handful of like-minded men and women and the political passivity of the rest—was also prevalent in Austria. The resistance movements had to face not only the overpowering brutality of the regime but also an inert population, which failed to render meaningful aid to the beleaguered patriots and, in the early stage of the war, seemed not even to realize that a battle for the rediscovery of Austrian identity was taking place. As the degradations of the system increasingly affected the country, the underground opted for an activist course. As the war front drew nearer, the resisting patriots became more impulsive and assertive and less instrumental and calculating.

Obviously, apart from the resisters and the prudent majority, there always existed people who opposed the regime, even if they did not engage in organized dissent. Independent of the underground were many spontaneous individual actions, blind impulses of rejection,[36] such as uttering and writing anti-Nazi profanities, listening to foreign broadcasts, and aiding the politically, ethnically, and racially persecuted.[37] Such actions, of course, achieved little in practical terms.[38]

NOTES

1. "Bericht Major Stillfried," OM, II, No 16; F. Molden, *Fepolinski;* O. Molden, *Der Ruf,* p. 94; OM, XIX, No 21; Alfons Stillfried, *Die österreichische Widerstandsbewegung und ihr Rückhalt im Volk. Vortrag im grossen Musikvereinssaal gehalten am 17.6. 1946* (Vienna, 1946). Stillfried was in contact with the senior Abwehr aide and former chief of the Austrian Abwehr Colonel Erwin von Lahousen in Berlin.

2. After 1942 the remnants of Professor Meithner's group under Gererstorfer and Professor Felix Romanik, and the circle of Dr. Hans Dorrek (after 1945 secretary of Federal Chancellor Leopold Figl) organized a network that worked with Stillfried. Romanik, *Der Anteil,* pp. 52-56; "Auszug aus dem Tätigkeitsbericht des Prof. Felix Romanik," May 27, 1946, DÖW 8393.

3. OM, XIX, No 21.

4. Von Halem, who was a member of the German Legation in Prague before 1938, was arrested in 1942. Molden, *Der Ruf,* pp. 140, 144; OM, XI, 78.

5. Molden, *Der Ruf,* pp. 115-16; DÖW 8393.

6. Under the 1935 Nuremberg laws, persons with three or four Jewish grandparents were full Jews, those with one or two Jewish grandparents were of "mixed blood."

7. AS, VGH, 7J 72/44 - 5H 64/44, June 5, 1944, DÖW 989; DÖW 988, 7162; DÖW, ed., *Widerstand Wien,* 3:350.

8. DÖW 9348.

9. Dr. Gruber was associated with the Anti-Fascist Front circle of the former Austrian Telegraph -and Telephone Office employees transferred to the *Störbefehlstelle* in Berlin. Run by Karl Hirnschrott, the group secured valuable intelligence in 1943-44. In 1943 it contacted the Innsbruck cell of the postal telegraph and telephone employees. DÖW 8390.

10. In May 1945, the American occupation forces appointed Dr. Gruber the first postwar Provincial Governor of Tyrol. Later in 1945 he became Austrian foreign minister. Born the son of a locomotive engineer in Innsbruck, he joined the Socialist youth. In 1934 he switched with

his trade union to the Christian Socials. Karl Gruber, *Ein politisches Leben. Österreichs Weg zwischen den Diktaturen* (Vienna, n.d. [1977]), pp. 7 ff; *Das Fenster,* No. 19 (Winter 1976-1977), p. 1972; Karl Gruber, *Zwischen Befreiung und Freiheit* (Vienna, 1953), passim. See below, pp. 245 ff.

11. He communicated with the circle around Carlo Mierendorff, a former SPD member of the German Parliament. Weisenborn, *Der Lautlose Aufstand,* p. 167.

12. Schedler reached Vienna on March 15, 1945, and was given data on the location of industrial plants, storage areas for war material, and zones for possible arms and ammunition drops. He was also given plans for wireless communication. Schedler was urged to meet with the Soviet Mission in Switzerland and to discuss the Austrian plans to coordinate the advance of the Red Army with the activities of the underground. The Soviets were given the names of the Wehrmacht officers in Vienna who were to serve as liaisons to the Red Army. Eventually, a wireless transmitter was installed at the Viennese apartment of Professor Dr. August Maria Knoll at the beginning of April 1945. OM, XIX, No. 21.

13. De Comtes, OM, XIX, No. 21; Molden, *Der Ruf,* pp. 298-99.

14. Molden, *Der Ruf,* pp. 298-99; Gruber, *Ein Leben,* p. 34.

15. For the Tyrolian Resistance, see below.

16. See Franz Loidl, "Kaplan Heinrich Maier-ein Opfer des nationalsozialistischen Gewaltsystems," in Herbert Schambeck, ed., *Kirche und Staat. Fritz Eckert zum 65. Geburtstag* (Berlin, 1976), pp. 271-92. Maier contacted various representatives of the German resistance groups, in particular the former Catholic trade unionists around Jakob Kaiser. O. Molden, *Der Ruf,* p. 111.

17. "Bericht Dipl-Ing. Karl Schaden," OM, X, No 66. Maier was a frequent guest of Lieutenant General Heinrich Stümpfl, the commanding officer of the City of Vienna. Maier got valuable data on these visits. The well-known Viennese pianist Barbara Issikides, who toured extensively, and the technical director of the Wanda Company, Dr. Theodore Legradi, acted as couriers. Issikides used to meet an Austrian lawyer resident since May 1938 in Zurich, Dr. Kurt Grimm, who then transmitted the information to Allen Dulles, the OSS chief in Switzerland.

18. Molden, pp. 71-74; Anthony Cave Brown, ed., *The Secret War Report of the OSS* (New York, 1976), pp. 298-301, 325. Messner traveled regularly to Turkey, where he transmitted information to the OSS. The group supplied to the OSS the extemely valuable reports on the construction of the V-2 and its assembly plant and testing ground at Peenemünde. Ibid., pp. 298, 325, 330.

19. OM, X, No 66; "Berichte Gestapo," Wien, DÖW 8478; Hans Holzner et al., eds., *Zeugen des Widerstandes,* pp. 18-20, 63-64.

20. U, VGH, 5H 96/44 - 6J 158/44g, OM, X, No 66; Molden, *Der Ruf,* pp. 110-13; *Der neue Mahnruf,* February 1952; DÖW 1553. Eight men, including Maier and Messner, were sentenced to death. Issikides was arrested but survived. As Messner was a Brazilian citizen, OSS Bern tried to secure Messner's release in exchange for a German agent in Brazil. Brown, *The Secret War,* p. 325. Nothing came of it and Messner was gassed at Mauthausen on April 23, 1945. Persico, *Piercing,* pp. 393-94; Holzner et al., *Zeugen,* p. 64. Of the ten men on trial, nine had university degrees and the tenth was a noncommissioned police officer. Four were NSDAP members or Party candidates. For the execution on March 22, 1945, see Hans Rieger, *Verurteilt zum Tod. Ein Dokumentarbericht* (Wuppertal, 1967), pp. 36 ff.

21. DÖW 1553.

22. Harald Frederiksen, OM, No 37; F. Molden, *Fepolinski,* p. 287. The communication line worked smoothly. Railwaymen transported the reports to Innsbruck where a clandestine transmitter began working in November 1944. A special courier carried the most important news to Switzerland. The very valuable source was Dr. Frederik Berkovits from the Luftgaukommando Vienna. Frederiksen met Stillfried and other 05 members as well as the Yugoslav, Greek, and Dutch underground composed of forced labor draftees. Alfons Stummer, a student, established another intelligence circuit. The communication line to and from

Switzerland ran through the 05 Vienna liaison Center, directed by Molden's cousin Neda Rukavina from her reception desk at the Grand Hotel and by Dr. Staretz, who had deserted to the Americans in Milan in the summer of 1944 to join the OSS office in Switzerland. He returned with F. Molden to Vienna.

23. Notburga Tilt's reconstruction of her post-1941 clandestine work in Austria, Yugoslavia, France, and Germany for what was probably a British-run circuit located in Leoben, brings to life the personal experiences of a young woman engaged in risky underground operations. *The Strongest Weapon* (Elms Court, Devon, 1972).

24. Dr. Hans von Müllern's "O.M." group tried to support and shelter Jews, deserters, and foreign workers and to supply them with false medical reports. It also helped the Tito Partisans to obtain badly needed medical supplies. DÖW 8393.

25. Krebs-Waldau was in contact with Becker and the group "Orel" in Upper Austria. Becker, *Freiheitskampf,* pp. 24-25; DÖW 4308; 14603; Molden, *Der Ruf,* pp. 217-18; DÖW 4308; *Rot-weiss-rot-Buch,* pp. 142, 158-59. For the action in Lenzing see DÖW 5179.

26. Josef Hofer, *Die Weggefährten. Vom österreichischen Freiheitskampf 1933 bis 1945* (Vienna, 1946), pp. 15-16, 19-20, 30, 41-44; Molden, *Der Ruf,* pp. 99-106. Hofer vividly describes some extraordinary exploits of the sabotage teams of Austrian soldiers and officers, who apparently worked for Allied intelligence in Yugoslav Slovenia and Austria. Hofer, *Die Weggefährten,* pp. 31-40.

27. Hofer, *Die Weggefährten,* p. 45; Molden, *Der Ruf,* pp. 105-6.

28. Inez Kykal-Karl R. Stadler, *Richard Bernaschek. Odyssee eines Rebellen* (Vienna, 1976), pp. 207-26; Molden, *Der Ruf,* pp. 106-8; Hofer, *Die Weggefährten,* pp. 71-72; DÖW, *Widerstand in Oberösterreich,* 1:199-200. On April 29 between thirty-eight and forty-three selected Austrian resisters were murdered in Mauthausen. Ibid., p. 226. The total G.B. membership allegedly amounted to 472 persons. "Bericht," Dr. Hans Frenzel, DÖW 2129/2. Gabriele Hindinger indicates that Bernaschek, his brother Ludwig and the railwayman Alois Wimberger rallied to the "Free Austria" network, *Das Kriegsende und der Wiederaufbau demokratischer Verhältnisse in Oberösterreich im Jahre 1945* (Vienna, 1968), p. 19. See also Kykal-Stadler, *Bernaschek,* p. 215. In 1945 Wimberger became a Socialist member of Parliament and Ludwig Bernaschek was elected a Deputy Provincial Governor of Upper Austria.

29. "Die Linzer Widerstandsgruppe G.B.," December 1946, DÖW 2129. Physicians and medical personnel were involved. Military intelligence was transmitted to the "Viennese center," apparently to Becker's 05. After the war Frenzel became the Austrian Minister of Food.

30. DÖW 2129.

31. "Bericht," April 25, 1946, Ludwig Bernaschek, DÖW 2127. For the RS group of railway employees in Attnang-Puchheim, see DÖW, *Widerstand in Oberösterreich,* 1:185, 201-3. There were other groups connected with Frenzel and Bernaschek. Hindinger, *Das Kriegsende,* p. 19. For the "Kampfbrigade Münichreiter," see DÖW 14521. For the guerrilla warfare around Aussee, see below. This Styrian territory was attached to Upper Austria during the Nazi period.

32. Hindinger, *Das Kriegsende,* pp. 19, 23-25.

33. U, VGH, 5H 39-41/45-7J 205-207/44, OM, XIV, No 20; 5H 42-44/45-7J 208-210/44, DÖW 314; 14654; Edmund Merl, *Besatzungszeit im Mühlviertel. Anhand der Entwicklung im politischen Bezirk Freistadt* (Linz, 1980), pp. 14-17; DÖW, *Widerstand in Oberösterreich,* 2:356-65. Politically, the members belonged to the Christian Socials and Socialists.

34. See Becker, *Freiheitskampf,* pp. 30-33. Becker tends to inflate the 05 achievements, the scale of sabotage, and the number of organized activists.

35. For Carinthia and Tyrol, see below. I follow the documentation for the *Rot-weiss-rot-Buch,* which the Styrian Provincial Government prepared on May 10, 1946, DÖW 834. See also *Rot-weiss-rot-Buch,* p. 210. The Styrian report indicated that at one time or other about 36,000 political prisoners passed through the Graz police prison. In the period from January to April 1945, 143 persons were reported executed in Graz alone. Ibid., p. 209; Leopold

Hohenecker, "Das Kriegsende 1945 im Raum Fischbach," *Österreich in Geschichte und Literatur* 19 (1975): 196-97.

36. See Dr. Neugebauer in DÖW, ed., *Widerstand Wien,* 3:432-35.

37. About one-half of the almost 45,500 cases tried before the Special Courts of the OLG Vienna from 1938 to 1945 were politically motivated, and most dealt with antiregime utterances. The culprits were usually tried under the 1934 Reich Law against malicious gossip. Only in exceptional cases was the much stricter 1938 Reich Law against the undermining of military morale used. Listening to foreign broadcasts was prohibited by a decree of September 1, 1939. By a decree of November 25, 1939, the authorities prohibited social intercourse with foreign prisoners of war. Ibid. See also Frei, *Der kleine Widerstand,* pp. i-ii, 4-9.

38. For acts of individual resistance in Vienna, see DÖW, ed., *Widerstand Wien,* 3:437-527.

17

Christian Democracy

THE EMERGENCE OF THE AUSTRIAN PEOPLE'S PARTY

Between 1939 and 1945, the democratic elements of the former Christian Social party (CSP), who had been pushed into the background after 1933 by the authoritarian regime, gained momentum in and through the Resistance. Within the elements, three main tendencies emerged that were as much the product of historical precedent as the reflection of new needs and opportunities. These tendencies were those of the democratic Catholic activists, the Christian trade unionists, and the Austrian Peasants' Union.[1]

The first rather loosely structured tendency, that of the democratic Catholic activists, saw Allied victory as the only way to obtain Austrian independence. Some of these activists had been influenced through personal contact with those who had opposed CSP policy in the recent past.[2] Repudiating the clerical and anti-parliamentarian Christian Social past, the Catholic democratic circles aligned themselves with those forces who claimed to be building a new order rather than restoring the old Republic.[3] Opposition to Austrian assimilation and to the Nazi dictatorship played an important part in bringing the Christian-oriented conservatives into sympathy with the democratic militants. Chilled by the failure of the Dollfuss-Schuschnigg regime and by the Nazi violence, they eschewed the old extremist anti-Socialism that had so soured the political mood of the Republic and helped devastate the country. The resisters saw a parliamentary democracy as a starting point, and in their talks forged the beginnings of a grand coalition with their Socialist counterpart that would shape the nation's political future. In restructuring the political movements, the underground chose cooperation as the basis for national politics in the future.

Historically, the Austrian Christian trade unionist (CTU) tendency had played a subordinate political role within the CSP. Its distance from the Party mainstream, which was burdened with responsibility for the anti-parliamentary excesses of 1933 to 1938, enabled the Christian's movement to become the moving force behind the Christian Democrats. Supporting an accelerated pace of social reform and a progressive economic policy, the Christian unionists attempted to build with the Socialists a united trade union movement that would cut across ideology and party loyalty. Their perspective enabled the CTU to create a broad-based pressure for a leftward shift of the future party that would allow it to join the Socialists in a na-tional coalition. The CTU's association with the main body of the German Resistance, already firmly committed to a Conservative-Socialist alliance, helped convince the Socialists that their former enemies had outgrown their anti-Socialist bias and had begun to act with a new awareness of their democratic responsibilities.

The third tendency, more conservative but traditionally democratically oriented, was that of the Austrian Peasants' Union (Bauernbund, ÖBB). The peasants' contingents, at once stable, homogeneous, socially conser-vative, and democratic, had been the strongest interest group within the CSP. After 1938 the peasant movement withdrew into silence for the dura-tion of the occupation. Initially, no resistance organization was planted in the peasants' ranks; only late in the war in Lower Austria did the ÖBB assume importance.

THE CHRISTIAN WORKERS' MOVEMENT
AND CHRISTIAN DEMOCRACY

After 1918 the Christian Workers' movement, including its trade unions and workers' associations, sided with the moderate proparliamentarian fac-tion within the CSP. From the ranks of this politically not very important organization, headed by Leopold Kunschak, voices arose supporting a com-mon front with the SPÖ in the struggle against the National Socialists.[4] In 1934 the CTU was dissolved, and its cadres joined the newly founded single trade union movement under state authority (Gewerkschaftsbund — GB). The new organization came under the influence of the young disciples of Kunschak and his associates.[5] In 1938, a handful of Christian Workers' cells in Vienna, joined by followers in Linz, Vorarlberg, Tyrol, Styria, and Salzburg, secretly collected funds to aid the families of imprisoned col-leagues.[6] Members met in the shoemaker's workshop of Ferdinand Rechberg (former chairman of a section of the GB).[7]

The members were dedicated to building a new labor movement. In meetings in 1939-40 the younger members around Erwin Altenburger, Lois Weinberger, and Dr. Franz Latzka committed themselves to building a united trade union organization while other ranking trade unionists were more reluctant to abandon those old unions to which they had devoted much of their lives.[8] In 1940 to reconcile their differences, the opposing factions of Heinrich Woboril (a former head of the Christian Textile- and Leather Workers Trade Union) and of Rechberg chose as their spokesman Weinberger, who as a former chairman of the Union of Bank- and Insurance Employees of the GB stood outside political controversies. Kunschak, the respected former leader, confirmed Weinberger's selection. Into the organization with Weinberger came his school friend and former member of the Carinthian Provincial Government in 1936-38, Dr. Felix Hurdes.[9] The two men were determined to unify the shattered unions, and both played a decisive part in the evolution of the CTU cells into a spearhead of the rejuvenated Christian Democratic Resistance.[10] Backed by Kunschak's authority, they restructured the labor movement, giving it a renewed sense of identity.[11]

Generally recognized as an eloquent orator, an able and articulate negotiator and conciliator, Weinberger was in line to succeed Kunschak. In conjunction with Weinberger, Hurdes became the main architect, as well as one of the main representatives, of the Christian Democratic underground. As the principal inspirer of political regeneration, he maintained ties to the Catholic Church, the farmers, the middle classes and the world of culture. Hurdes made the movement's factions blend their voices in something approaching harmony. He played a strong role in committing the CSP cadres to democratic pluralism. On the vital issue of formulating "in an embryonic form" a new political model that could reunite the country, Hurdes, Weinberger, and Kunschak championed the historical compromise between the two previous opponents, the SPÖ and the reorganized Christian Socials. They had a realistic respect for the power of the Socialists.[12]

The National Socialist occupation not only had originated the rapprochement between the two movements but also had transformed the old CSP into a socially progressive umbrella movement, embracing all the social strata. Both the former CSP and VF officials in Dachau and the clandestine cadres independently agreed to surmount the outdated ideologies of the CSP and of the defunct authoritarian system that had prevented the attainment of political democracy and economic prosperity.[13] When on November 11, 1941, Weinberger, Kunschak, Hurdes, and Latzka met to celebrate Kunschak's seventieth birthday at the Rechberg's apartment, they reaffirmed their intention to integrate the Christian workers as an autonomous group within a new Christian-oriented political party after the fall of Hitler.[14] Only the trade unionists initiated general political debate on the need for a truly modern Christian political party. In contrast, the clandestine peasant, trade, craft, and industry circles, who assembled much later, were more intent on building separate organizations to pursue their own interests than on pursuing national renovation.[15]

To widen the political spectrum, Weinberger and Hurdes relied primarily on personal contacts. Hurdes arranged liaison with the Socialists and met one of their ranking members, Dr. Migsch, whom, unfortunately, the Gestapo apprehended shortly before their second meeting in January 1944. In the early summer of 1943, Hurdes communicated directly with Dr. Schärf.[16] The confidence of the German Socialist unionists in both Weinberger and Hurdes helped overcome the initial Socialist hesitation and distrust that accompanied the discussion of Hurdes' proposals for cooperation. In his turn, Schärf allegedly met Kunschak and former CSP Finance Minister Josef Kollmann in Baden in 1943 or 1944.[17]

Deeply concerned about the country's plight, the Christian Democrats were seeking out potential sympathizers in public life and assessing their future role in the reconstituted Republic. They related their plans to the former Christian Social peasant leader Josef Reither, and to Dr. Eugen Margaretha, who represented industrial interests. In the end, they were running a varied set of effective political lines.[18] One network included scores of former postal employees and unionists dismissed by the Nazis and subsequently employed as sales agents by the Ostmark Insurance Company for whom Weinberger also worked. He used the apartments of some of his friends as safe houses. His associates continued to move in postal circles in Vienna and Lower Austria, maintaining touch with Dr. Gruber's network and the Christian Social cell in the Telegraph Service Headquarters in Vienna.[19]

The clearest evidence of the effectiveness of the call for national reconciliation was the electorate's unreserved acceptance of it after 1945. The abandonment of some of its past convictions later secured power for the new Christian Democratic movement. In the meantime, the underground offered the different groups a common commitment to the Austrian cause, and the clandestine action succeeded in achieving a degree of coordination. More important, it provided them with a banner to which they could all rally.

THE GREAT CONSPIRACY

The Christian unionists worked effectively with the mainstream of the German Resistance, which had drawn together a welter of conspiratorial groups, ultimately centering on Carl Goerdeler, a former mayor of Leipzig. Since 1934, the leader of the German Christian unions, Jakob Kaiser, had maintained close contact with Johann Staud, who presided over the unified Austrian Trade unions (GB). Kaiser also collaborated with Wilhelm Leuschner, a former Socialist Minister of the Interior for Hessen and a former Deputy Chairman of the German Trade Union Association. Leuschner provided a link to other German unionists and Socialist militants. They formed a part of the central civil-military network. After the Anschluss, Staud and his colleague Otto Troidl, chairman of the GB Union of Free Professions, were interned at Dachau, where Staud died in 1939.[20] Troidl was released and in July 1941 he introduced Kaiser and Max Habermann, former head of the German National Association of Commercial Employees, to Weinberger.[21]

As preparations advanced in Germany for a national resistance coalition to overthrow Hitler, Kaiser and Leuschner hastened to establish a direct link to Goerdeler in 1941. When Hitler failed to achieve a military breakthrough in the summer of 1942, Goerdeler's major effort began. Convinced that the interest of the German Resistance demanded Austria's incorporation in the Reich, the conspirators sought political allies in Austria. In October 1942, Kaiser accompanied Goerdeler on a trip to Vienna where the latter met Weinberger, Hurdes, and Troidl. Goerdeler explained his clandestine plans to former CSP Federal Chancellor Otto Ender and the prominent Greater-German historian Professor Dr. Heinrich Srbik. To win the Socialists over to the conspiracy, Hurdes and Weinberger urged Goerdeler and Kaiser to approach former Socialist mayor of Vienna Seitz. Kunschak wrote a letter introducing Kaiser to Seitz. The Germans pleaded for a unified Germany that would recognize Austria's special position. However, Seitz's reaction was noncommittal.[22]

Because of the rapid pace of the war, Kaiser requested that Leuschner visit Vienna in the early summer of 1943 to secure Socialist cooperation. Leuschner came to Vienna to win the support of the SPÖ and CSP for the conspiracy and for the preservation of the union of Austria and the Reich. But when Leuschner saw Schärf and Seitz, it was difficult to find common ground.[23] Leuschner, confident that the conspiracy could destroy the regime, suggested that Goerdeler would head the post-Hitler cabinet and that he would be Vice-Chancellor. Dr. Kurt Schuschnigg was expected to join the cabinet as Minister of Education. At this time, to Schärf and to many of his friends, the "thought that the Anschluss . . . could be revoked was . . . new and unusual." Schärf reportedly said that "The Anschluss is dead. Austrians have been thoroughly cured of their love for the German Reich. . . . I foresee a day when the Reich Germans will be expelled from Austria as the Jews were expelled before." Leuschner left in deep distress. Schärf immediately informed his Socialist friends, above all Seitz and Renner, about his conversation. "Thereupon all of us slowly came to the conclusion that had for the first time so abruptly come to my lips at my discussion with Leuschner. In November 1943, the Moscow Declaration on the reconstruction of a free Austria was published. It only strengthened our conviction."[24] The German conspirators strenuously attempted to win over the Austrians, who generally, however, supported the reestablishment of the Republic.[25]

THE MILITARY ACTION IN VIENNA

As the moment for action against Hitler approached, the German resisters had to undertake a great deal of concrete work, all of which they successfully carried through in Austria. In June 1943, Kaiser pressed Weinberger, Hurdes, and Troidl for the names of prominent politicians whose prestige would enhance the conspiracy's public image. After much hesitation, Kaiser put forward the names of Seitz and Reither. These two men of integrity had won excellent reputations during their public service.[26] When the coup successfully started in Vienna on July 20, 1944, the cables from the Berlin military headquarters to the Vienna Military Command charged Seitz and Reither with the conduct of political affairs in the area. Onetime Provincial Governor Dr. Franz Rehrl and Dr. Anton von Mörl, a former Security Director of Tyrol from 1933 to 1938, were appointed political plenipotentiaries in the Salzburg Military Command area, but no military action took place there. One of the organizers of the coup in Vienna, Colonel Marogna-Redwitz, was put in charge of the liaison to the Supreme Army Command in Berlin.[27] The coup collapsed in a few hours.[28]

Obviously, the close association of the Christian Democratic circle with the men of July 20 was very important. Exclusively concerned with political organization, it was the only Austrian political group that the plotters in the German Army High Command and in the civil sector took into their confidence and directly involved in the political preparations for the 1944 coup. It provided the German organizers with useful information on the Austrian political arena. Its role was less that of a combatant than of a political group discussing future public affairs. Its members were firmly committed to a free Austria, but they never doubted that they should cooperate with their German friends and colleagues. The common platform of the German July 20 Resistance and the equal share in the assignment of political responsibilities among labor, military, and conservatives presented a broad democratic consensus that certainly impressed the Austrian leaders of the two main pre-1934 political blocs.

THE PEASANTS' UNION

The farming population with its many independent small landowners constituted a traditionalist pool within Austria. Before 1938 the peasants overwhelmingly followed the ÖBB, a Christian-Social bastion opposed to the Heimwehr's proto-Fascist forces and to National Socialism. The Union preserved its own democratic institutions, which served to keep the peasants together in the confusion of the authoritarian regime after 1933. In 1938, its officials, among them Reither, its head and Provincial Governor of Lower

Austria, and Ing. Leopold Figl, its administrative director, were sent to concentration camps.[29]

Peasant attitudes largely reflected dissatisfaction with the war, but the peasants were cautious about active involvement in the Resistance. The leaderless rank-and-file was still under the influence of the officials of the Peasants' Union, who reflected a Catholic and conservative orientation. As the news of Mussolini's downfall in July 1943 reached the rural areas, a mood of uncertainty set in. However, widespread disgruntlement with local or national matters did not translate itself into political opposition, because the majority of the peasants did not as yet seriously question the regime's legitimacy. Besides, affiliated as they were with the Nazi's compulsory peasant association, they had no organizational forum to which to turn.

After his release from Dachau in May 1943, Figl decided to engage in clandestine work. A few days after his return from Dachau, Figl went to see Reither, who had been freed in 1941. He wanted to begin his clandestine activity in full agreement with his quiet, unassuming old mentor, to whom their common experience in Dachau had closely attached him.[30] Figl's good friend Julius Raab, a former Christian Social leader, helped him get an assignment with the Kohlmayer Road and Bridge Construction Firm in the Zistersdorf oil fields.[31] As a construction supervisor, Figl moved freely throughout the province inspecting projects.

Figl, not a reflective man, was temperamentally disinclined to speculate on what lay decades ahead; but his conduct was distinguished by a keen political interest. His audience consisted largely of former functionaries of the Peasants' Union and of the Chamber of Agriculture who had been familiar with his past work. Concerned with mobilizing former peasant officials, he did not want at any point to act without their support. A professional politician of the old school, he cautiously probed the feelings of the peasantry, who appeared ready again to entrust their affairs to their former representatives. He also strove to restore the peasants' faith in themselves.[32] Instead of building up a conspiratorial organization, be became a "crystallization center" drawing peasants' support and rebuilding morale among the former Peasants' Union officials.[33]

In the early morning of May 4, 1944, three men took their places in three different cars in a train at the Francis Joseph Railroad Station in Vienna. The men were Figl, Josef Kraus, an expert on agricultural cooperatives and later Federal Minister of Agriculture, and Edmund Weber, Figl's future press secretary. They went to visit Reither's wine cellar in Judenau.[34] From his Dachau days, Reither attached great importance to the formation of a farm association embracing all the peasantry. He reflected that "the Peasants' Union cannot be too strong in the new state . . . so that the events of 1938 could never happen again. Only the peasantry and the workers can guarantee Austria's freedom and independence. When these cannot stand together, then democracy cannot exist any longer in Austria.[35]

Reither envisioned a rejuvenated peasant leadership. "I have grown old, but I still want to help rebuild our Peasants' Union. It is the young people who should take over. Figl is a man who has the ability to build a new Peasants' Union. He is of peasant origin; he is a democrat." Reither put forward the names of other personalities who should lead the Union hierarchy. At the end of the meeting, the ÖBB was reborn.[36] The participants however, were not prepared to develop prematurely an all-Austrian network. The organization remained restricted to senior cadres in Vienna and Lower Austria, and no corresponding buildup took place in other Länder.[37]

THE AUSTRIAN PEOPLE'S PARTY (ÖVP)

In his effort to reach agreement on common objectives with other Christian Democratic groups, Figl and his friends elaborated a concept of a new political party that not only would permit the political center and right to avoid isolation but would project the party into the middle of Austrian political life. Figl discussed structural reform in the Christian Democratic movement with Raab and the Weinberger-Hurdes circle. Raab was a spokesman of the small entrepreneur, whose rights he asserted. He proposed that trade, industry, and handicraft assemble in a single organization, thereby establishing an effective businessmen's constituency (Austrian Economic Union, Österreichischer Wirtschaftsbund, ÖWB). Economic problems might vary in intensity from branch to branch, but the aspirations for the protection of business interests remained the same. Anxious to avoid precise commitments, especially to uncontrolled clandestine situations, Raab never pressed his friends for a formal involvement. Nevertheless, he met Figl at Figl's Viennese apartment on Saturdays. Often Hurdes, Pernter, Weber, Weinberger and Fritz Eckert joined them.[38] The informal nature of the talks proved instrumental in drawing the various factions closer together.

In the spring of 1944, a pattern of commitment was evident among the leading members of the three principal groups around Figl, Weinberger, and Raab. At Easter 1944, Figl, Weinberger, Hurdes, and Pernter finally agreed on the organizational form of the future movement that would bind the three interest groups into a single political and ideological community called the Austrian People's Party (ÖVP).[39] The renovated party was to look to rural and urban workers as its constituency. Clerical influence vanished. The overall moderate tendency was part of a broader shift of the center of gravity within Austrian society from the rural areas to the cities. The new model of a progressive political center had genuine possibilities in the country, strengthened as it was by prevailing anti-capitalist social and economic objectives in which social reforms were predominant.[40] The loose collection of three groups in a federal-type party structure reflected the special conditions of clandestine work and corresponded to the great diversity of the future constituency. Eventually, the reformist aspirations were scaled down, out of respect to the more conservative views of some of the interest groups. But in the immediate postwar period, the ÖVP thrived in a political climate hospitable to the organized pursuit of democratic reform.

It was the uncertain image of the future party and the willingness to search for new solutions that intensified this variety among the Christian Democratic tendencies. The growing Christian Democratic community was not entirely new; its resurfaced leaders generally owed their positions to their affiliation to the CSP or to its associated organizations. Represented by a close-knit circle of veteran politicians, it was a middle-class, intensely patriotic, skilled, lay-dominated group, numerically small enough to know one another. They could no longer tolerate the flabby inertia of the Schuschnigg era and the paranoia and repression of Hitlerism. Their gallant behavior reduced the stigma attached to those politicians of the pre-1938 regime who survived the war remarkably well, because they had learned to respond adequately to the accelerating pace of change. As the liberation became imminent, the professional politicians showed more signs of life. The resisters did not oppose the restoration of the political parties, although they wished that it would take place within the unity fostered by the Resistance. Figl persisted in supporting cooperation with the SPÖ. Through his prison-mate Sobek, who returned from Dachau in July 1943, Figl found links to the 05, and contacted the former Socialist Deputy Provincial Governor of Lower Austria, Oskar Helmer.[41] For Figl, a man of simple ideals, his activity was not merely a question of a political stand: it was above all a question of morality to behave according to one's beliefs.

The conspiracy of July 20 drew the Gestapo's attention to the former political parties' personnel. In September and October, the Gestapo arrested Weinberger, Hurdes, Troidl, Figl, Pernter, and scores of other suspects, including the prominent actor Paul Hörbiger and the future president of the Association of the Industrialists, Dr. Frank Mayer-Guthof, and threw them into Mauthausen. On January 21, 1945, Figl, Hurdes, Weinberger, Pernter, and their accomplices were moved to Vienna to be tried before the VGH. They survived mainly because the rapid advance of the Red Army brought their release from the prison on April 6. A few days later they were able to appear at the Auersperg palace, headquarters of the 05. On April 17 the ÖVP was constituted. Not surprisingly, it counted numerous resisters in its top echelon: Bumballa, Hurdes, Figl, Pernter, Weinberger, Kunschak, Eidlitz, Braunsteiner, Oswald, and others.[42]

Although the Resistance's decision to rebuild the ÖVP largely conditioned the Party's fortunes throughout the initial era of the Republic, the reconstituted ÖVP soon found itself in conflict with some members who refused to endorse what they considered the Party's minimization of their role in the Resistance. They persisted in the suspicion that the Party wanted to deny the resisters their proper place in its ranks.

NOTES

1. For a discussion, see Reichhold, *Geschichte der ÖVP,* pp. 53-54.

2. In 1934, the CSP dissolved itself and its cadres joined the newly formed Fatherland Front.

3. Ibid., pp. 55-56.

4. See Anton Pelinka, *Stand oder Klasse? Die Christliche Arbeiterbewegung Österreichs 1933 bis 1938* (Vienna, 1972), passim. Kunschak was a member of the Vienna City Council from 1907 to 1938 and a CSP member of the Parliament from 1907. After 1945 he became the first chairman of the ÖVP and President of the Austrian Parliament.

5. CTU membership increased from 64,478 in 1920 to 130,000 in 1932. Pelinka, *Stand,* pp. 25, 31.

6. Stiftung für die Pflege der Tradition der christlichen Arbeiterbewegung, *Die christlichen Gewerkschaften in Österreich* (Vienna, 1975), pp. 252 ff.

7. Reichhold, *Geschichte,* pp. 30, 446; *Die christlichen Gewerkschaften,* pp. 253-54.

8. Reichhold, *Geschichte,* p. 31. In 1945 Altenburger became deputy chairman of the unified Austrian Trade Union Association.

9. After 1945 Weinberger became a member of the Austrian cabinet and Deputy Mayor of the City of Vienna. Hurdes became the first Secretary General of the ÖVP and later Federal Minister of Education. Lois Weinberger, *Tatsachen, Begegnungen und Gespräche. Ein Buch um Österreich,* (Vienna, 1948), pp. 87-88; interviews with Erwin Altenburger, Anton Hyross, and Dr. Franz Latzka.

10. Reichhold, *Geschichte,* pp. 30 ff; *Die christlichen Gewerkschaften,* pp. 258 ff; Weinberger, *Tatsachen,* pp. 92 ff. In March 1938, Hurdes and Altenburger were arrested and Hurdes sent to Dachau. Kunschak was detained for a short time in 1938.

11. This model of a unified trade union movement, to replace the former party-oriented and politically heterogeneous trade unions, reflected the prevailing mood favoring cooperation with the Socialists. The German Resistance, which endorsed the plan of the Christian Democrats and Social Democrats for a unified movement, strongly supported the concept. Reichhold, *Geschichte,* p. 57. The German Christian unionist Jakob Kaiser used the idea of a unified labor movement to good effect in his Vienna talks with Weinberger and Hurdes. Ludwig Reichhold, *Arbeiterbewegung jenseits des totalen Staates. Die Gewerkschaften und der 20. Juli 1944* (Vienna, 1965), p. 15.

12. Reichhold, *Geschichte,* p. 42. Hurdes saw in the constitution of the new party the Christian Resistance's most important contribution. *Österreichische Monatshefte,* no. 4 (1965).

13. Reichhold, *Geschichte,* pp. 44-47. Professor Lugmayer's apartment in Vienna became the meeting-place for Weinberger, Hurdes, former Minister of Education Hans Pernter and Karl Kummer, the first postwar Secretary General of the ÖAAB. Ibid., p. 56; Weinberger, *Tatsachen,* p. 232; Gustav Blenk, *Leopold Kunschak und seine Zeit* (Vienna, 1966), p. 213.

14. *Die christlichen Gewerkschaften,* p. 259.

15. Reichhold, *Geschichte,* p. 56.

16. Ibid., pp. 41-42; Weinberger, *Tatsachen,* pp. 102-4.

17. Blenk, *Kunschak,* p. 209; Adolf Schärf, *Österreichs Erneuerung 1945-1955. Das erste Jahrzehnt der Zweiten Republik* (Vienna, 1955), p. 25; Reichhold, *Geschichte,* pp. 41-42; *Die christlichen Gewerkschaften,* p. 259; Weinberger, *Tatsachen,* p. 102.

18. Ibid., pp. 95-100.

19. DÖW 8381; interview with Anton Hyross.

20. Elfriede Nebgen, *Jakob Kaiser. Der Widerstandskämpfer* (Stuttgart, 1967), pp. 35, 83 ff; Weinberger, *Tatsachen,* pp. 120-27. Kaiser's confidante Dr. Elfriede Nebgen went to Vienna several times to help secure Troidl's release in the spring of 1939.

21. Reichhold, *Arbeiterbewegung*, *pp. 9-11;* Reichhold in Ludwig Jedlicka, *Der 20. Juli 1944 in Österreich* (Vienna-Munich, 1965), pp. 158-68; Nebgen, *Kaiser*, pp. 86-88, 91-93.

22. Manfried Rauchensteiner, *Der Sonderfall. Die Besatzungszeit in Österreich 1945 bis 1955* (Graz, 1979), p. 59; Nebgen, *Kaiser*, pp. 128, 140-47; Weinberger, *Tatsachen*, p. 128; Gerhard Ritter, *Carl Goerdeler und die Deutsche Widerstandsbewegung* (Stuttgart, 1955), pp. 294-95; Archiv Peter für historische und zeitgeschichtliche Dokumentation, ed., *Spiegelbild einer Verschwörung. Die Kaltenbrunner Berichte . . . über das Attentat vom 20. Juli 1944 . . .* (Stuttgart, 1961), p. 358; Tesarek, *Unser Seitz*, p. 141. Seitz was arrested and dismissed by Dollfuss from his post as Mayor of Vienna in February 1934.

23. Schärf, *Erneuerung*, pp. 23-25; Weinberger, *Tatsachen*, pp. 137, 142. Weinberger recalls that Leuschner had complained of the evasive and hesitant attitude of the Austrian Socialist leaders toward the German conspirators.

24. Schärt, *Erneuerung*, p. 24. For Nebgen's observations, see *Jakob Kaiser*, pp. 148-50. Other Austrian candidates in the cabinet were Seitz and Dr. Heinrich Gleissner, a former senior official of the Peasants' Union, who moved to Berlin after 1938. Kaiser talked to Gleissner, who turned down the proposal. In Berlin, Gleissner kept in touch with the major figures of the Resistance, including former SPD deputy Mierendorff, former editor of a Hamburg Socialist paper, Adolf Reichwein, Dr. Theo Haubach, Count Helmuth James von Moltke, and Count Peter Yorck von Wartenburg. Gleissner introduced the members of the Kreisau Circle to Dr. Gruber and to other Austrians. Nebgen, *Kaiser*, pp. 148, 171; Ger van Roon, *German Resistance to Hitler. Count von Moltke and the Kreisau Circle* (New York, 1971), p. 214; Joachim G. Leithäuser, *Wilhelm Leuschner. Ein Leben für die Republik* (Cologne, 1962), p. 226.

25. The German resisters associated with the so-called Kreisau Circle assiduously worked for a union of Austria with Germany. Count Moltke's acquaintances included the new Archbishop of Salzburg, Andreas Rohracher, and the former Christian Social Provincial Governor of Salzburg, Dr. Franz Rehrl, whom Moltke probably recommended to Goerdeler for political plenipotentiary for the Military Command XVIII in Salzburg. In the summer of 1943, Moltke met professor of economics and former Minister of Trade, Dr. Wilhelm Taucher, in Graz. Rehrl had access to the principal activists in the Kreisau Circle, Yorck von Wartenburg, Dr. Hans Lukaschek, and the Bavarian Catholic lawyer Dr. Josef Müller. Similarly, the German Jesuit Father Alfred Delp exerted his influence through Prelate Karl Rudolf in Vienna. Jedlicka, *Der 20. Juli*, pp. 32-33, 78-79; Ger Van Roon, *German Resistance*, pp. 215, 238; Freya von Moltke-Michael Balfour-Julian Frisby, *Helmuth James von Moltke, 1907-1945. Anwalt der Zukunft* (Stuttgart, 1975), pp. 210, 257-58, 284, 298; Kunrat Freiherr von Hammerstein, *Spähtrupp* (Stuttgart, 1963), p. 218.

26. Nebgen, *Kaiser*, pp. 157-58, 178-79; Weinberger, *Tatsachen*, p. 144 ff. Nebgen places Kaiser's last visit to Vienna in 1943, whereas Weinberger places it in 1944. Nebgen believes that Kaiser had informed both Reither and Rehrl of their nominations in 1943, while Leuschner or Goerdeler apparently discussed in general terms with the reluctant Seitz the problem of his participation. Nebgen, *Kaiser*, p. 179; Archiv Peter, *Spiegelbild*, p. 359; Tesarek, *Seitz*, p. 141. After the war Seitz stated that he had not consented to the July conspirators' use of his name. He referred to his answer as "evasive."

27. Jedlicka, *Der 20. Juli*, pp. 61, 69, 76-77, 169-70. See below, p. 228.

28. Marogna-Redwitz was executed; Reither returned from prison in the summer of 1945 and died in 1950; Rehrl passed away in January 1947. Seitz, too, returned with broken health, and died in 1950. Schärf was apprehended but released in September. Weinberger, Hurdes, Pernter and others were later arrested and their case went before the VGH. Goerdeler, Leuschner, the German trade unionists, and the members of the Kreisau Circle were put to death. Kaiser went into hiding and survived to become a member of the West German Federal cabinet. Mörl knew nothing about the coup, although the conspirators had chosen him as their political adviser for Tyrol. Jedlicka, *Der 20. Juli*, pp. 76-78; Schärf, *Erneuerung*, pp. 26-27; Tesarek, *Unser Seitz*, pp. 141-4; Wolfgang Huber, ed., *Franz Rehrl. Landeshauptmann von*

Salzburg 1922-1938 (Salzburg, 1975), pp. 31-33; Anton Mörl, *Erinnerungen aus bewegter Zeit Tirols 1932-1945* (Innsbruck, 1955), pp. 129 ff, 148 ff; Molden, *Der Ruf,* pp. 145-60; Hoffmann, *Widerstand,* pp. 543-45, 553-60.

29. Born near Tulln in Lower Austria, Figl was director of the Peasants' Union in Lower Austria. Ernst Trost, *Figl von Österreich* (Vienna, 1972), pp. 102-3. From December 1945 to 1953 he was head of the Austrian government, and from 1953 to 1959 its Foreign Minister.

30. Edmund Weber in *Der "Österreichische Bauernbündler,"* August, 1, 1945; Trost, *Figl,* pp. 133-34. After his return from Dachau, the police shadowed Reither at his farm in Langenrohr, but he succeeded in maintaining contacts with former peasant officials.

31. Trost, *Figl,* pp. 104-9, 129 ff; Karl Heinz Ritschel, *Julius Raab. Der Staatsvertrags Kanzler,* (Salzburg, 1975). Raab, a builder from St. Pölten, entered Parliament for the CSP in 1927. In February 1938 Schuschnigg appointed him Minister of Trade. He was Federal Chancellor from 1953 to 1961.

32. It is difficult to find specific reasons for the rather passive mood of the Lower Austrian peasantry. The answer might be that Austrian society was in transition from the small-town stage to the large-scale industrialization stage.

33. This is also the view of L. Reichhold, *Geschichte,* p. 37.

34. Figl in Trost, *Figl,* p. 134.

35. Weber published the account of the five-hour discussion in *Der "Österreichische Bauernbündler,"* August 1, 1945.

36. The first postwar Peasants' Union (ÖBB) presidents were Reither (1945 to 1947) and Kraus (1947 to 1960). After meeting his friends, Figl confided his plans to his political associates. Reichhold, *Geschichte,* p. 38.

37. Interview with Professor Reichhold.

38. Trost, *Figl,* pp. 135-36; Reichhold, *Geschichte,* pp. 38 ff; O. Molden, *Der Ruf,* p. 208. Eckert was another of the Dachau CSP inmates rearrested in 1944. He became Secretary General of the ÖBB from 1945 to 1972. Schambeck, ed., *Kirche und Staat,* pp. 603-6.

39. Reichhold, *Geschichte,* pp. 59 ff. On May 11, 1944, both Reither and Raab endorsed the agreement.

40. The pluralist form of the future ÖVP aimed to realign the membership into three main sections: The ÖAAB, represented by Kunschak, Hurdes, and Weinberger; the ÖBB led by Reither and Figl; and the ÖWB headed by Raab. The autonomous structure of the interest groups made their displacement of the old bonds of loyalty to the CSP easier.

41. Molden, *Der Ruf,* p. 208.

42. Reichhold, *Geschichte,* pp. 72 ff, 108-11.

PART FIVE
From Conspiracy to Armed Action

18

Guerrilla Warfare

THE CARINTHIAN AND STYRIAN BORDERLAND

The Communist-led insurgency continued in the rugged mountain terrain of the Carinthian-Yugoslav border country, where the nature of the territory allowed combat parties to survive, and where their small size did not initially provoke the Nazis into large punitive expeditions. Guerrilla activity increased in 1943. The Slovenes fiercely resented their persecution and the Nazi resettlement plans.[1] The Austrian Slovenes had been made to feel second-class, which stung even more bitterly when the end of the regime seemed in sight.

As traditional Slovene grievances against the Greater-German nationalists intensified after 1938, some young Carinthian Slovenes in the Rosen and Gail Valleys fled to the mountains, seeking closer ties with the Slovenian Tito Partisans in Yugoslavia and their political arm, the Slovenian Liberation Front (LF). Partisan reconnaissance patrols moved from Slovenia across the frontier into Carinthia in the fall of 1941. The Slovenes Johan Županc and Stane Mrhar became the first armed fighters to go into hiding near Eisenkappel. Throughout the Slovenian rural communities they gathered supporters and set up committees of the emerging LF. Unfortunately, a Gestapo informer broke up a supporting group in Zell in November 1942. The arrest and execution of thirteen followers severely limited activities among the Slovene segment of the population that was unprepared and unwilling to wage guerrilla warfare. Sick and shaken, the two militants retired to Ebriach for the winter. In the winter of 1942-43 twelve armed Carinthian Slovene insurgents installed themselves in the almost inaccessible mountains at Petzen. In March 1943, the squad became the First Carinthian Battalion. Its operations, which Franc Pasterk conducted on

193

both sides of the border area from Bleiburg to the Loibl Pass, spurred the underground new activity.[2]

After the withdrawal of the First Carinthian Battalion to Yugoslavia in the summer of 1943, the Yugoslav Partisans in Carinthia only gradually strengthened their first combat unit ("odred"). It numbered some 400 combatants organized in three detachments, which managed to launch hit-and-run raids into the eastern areas stretching from Rosen Valley to Dravograd. In the spring of 1944 a second, smaller unit was based in the Gail Valley in the western part of the province. The detachments included mostly Slovenes from Carniola, some Carinthian Slovenes, some escaped Soviet war prisoners, and a few Austrians. Initially independent, the units in the eastern and western sections of Carinthia eventually came under the command of the LF regional committee for Slovenian Carinthia, constituted in March 1944. Gradually, the operations took an increasingly political turn when the activity of LF's Slovene Communist elements increased. The Communist regulars pressed their propaganda drive to create sympathizers for their quest for political control of the nationally oriented Slovenian local underground, which was preparing to confront the German-Austrian majority.[3]

One of the largest early actions was the armed engagement of a Partisan combat group under Pasterk with the German forces in the Meža Valley in the early spring of 1943.[4] On May 9 or 10, 1943, seventy rebels seized Feistritz in Rosental, ten miles south of the provincial capital, Klagenfurt. They freed forty Soviet prisoners of war, set the local sawmill on fire, and destroyed a factory producing war material.[5]

Fanned by the Tito Partisan forces, guerrilla warfare spread from the Yugoslav part of Slovenia across the border into Austria during the second half of 1943 and continued throughout 1944.[6] In October and November 1943, insurgents were active in Bad Vellach, Ebriach, and Meža and Rosen valleys, and near lake Klopeiner, where their activity hurt industrial production especially in the armaments industry. At the end of December 1943, patrols of the German 438th Division were positioned as guards around vulnerable industrial plants in Feistritz, Ferlach, Kühnsdorf, Rechberg, and Mežica (first raided on April 4, 1943).

The presence of German forces did not impede the insurgents in escalating their operations against military and industrial targets. Despite the German ripostes, the aggressive Tito Partisan parties continued their widely scattered but devastating armed raids. About 100 uniformed rebels raided the railroad station Maria Ellend on the main line to Yugoslavia on February 25.[7] The sporadic guerrilla hit-and-run actions led Heinrich Himmler on August 8, 1944, to place the southern area of Carinthia and the Slovenian territory in Yugoslavia (the so-called *Bandenkampfgebiet*) under a special command in Ljubljana.[8] A confidential German situation report from Graz on August 1 discussed Partisan ambushes, which were "causing great alarm'' among local populations in Upper Styria, Carinthia, and Carniola.

The German forces operating against the bands are still quite insufficient. Raids on public buildings, installations, villages, and farm houses and acts of robbery against individuals have been going on day and night. The bands are not afraid to stage raids against targets close to the provincial capital Klagenfurt. A band even attacked the old, former teacher of the Führer, Professor Loisl in his home.[9]

The report of September 28, 1944, stated that "the bands' activities are particularly bad in Carinthia—they spread as far as Wolfsberg. The town itself became the scene of some fighting."[10] While the Partisan offensives were under way, special Allied reconnaissance field missions had reached the Yugoslav battle zone in the spring of 1944, bringing arms, equipment, and clothing.[11]

From the start of 1943 the Slovenian LF underground press summoned the local population to fight against the regime. The LF's Central Committee for Carinthia set up near Feistritz an illegal printing work to publish its Slovenian and German newspapers, *Slovenski porocevalec* and *Die Einheit*. Clandestine bulletins and leaflets circulated among the civilians and the soldiers stationed there. Accomplices working at the NSDAP offices of Radmannsdorf and Klagenfurt supplied paper, ink, and stencils. But the intensive German-language propaganda addressed to German soldiers and Austrian workers met with little success.[12] A Gestapo agent located the literature apparatus at the end of 1944, and some urgently needed supplies fell into police hands on the discovery of an underground bunker. The informer, a forester, was executed by the insurgents.

The national differences in Carinthia failed to undermine the common political interest that the Austrian anti-Nazi elements and the Slovene insurgents shared. In places, Wehrmacht soldiers established clandestine contacts with the Partisans. A cell of the Wehrmacht Communication Company installing telephone and radio lines in Carinthia and Carniola cooperated with the rebels, and the Company was never ambushed. The Partisan detachment supplied the Company's kitchen with fresh meat in exchange for paper, salt, newspapers, sulphur ointments, and bandages. A Slovene butcher in Krainburg served as the secret go-between.[13]

Without local support, no guerrilla insurgency could develop in a province largely populated by Austro-German elements. Most of the guerrillas gathered in underground bunkers they had constructed in remote forests. The Slovene highlanders of the impoverished border region challenged the Nazi regime by collecting weapons and food, providing shelters, and arranging contacts, safe houses, and couriers. They helped the insurgents to survive in the mountains and to slip through police dragnets by providing information on Nazi collaborators and on the movements of the security patrols. But because the Gestapo used a wide net of informers, many fighters were caught. Johann Klantschnik, a courier, was arrested with twelve others from the Wolfsberg and Völkermarkt area in May 1944. In 1944 the Gestapo closed in on a cell of twelve that had organized like-minded foreign workers.[14] At times, the native German nationalists, serving in the auxiliary police troops and in the Landwacht (the loose rural militia largely manned by peasants), took revenge on the captured Partisans. On November 18, 1944, the local security force near Velden ran into twenty-two Partisans, who suffered heavy losses. The badly wounded fell into enemy hands and were brutally mistreated by the escorting force of the Velden *Voksturm*.[15] By the end of the war about 500 Slovene resisters lay buried in Carinthia.[16]

MUTUAL CONTACTS

The Tito insurgency movement attracted keen attention from the Austrian resisters, who hoped to establish contact with the Western Allies and assumed that the LF could provide communication lines to the British and Americans. In its turn, the Partisan command was alert to the importance of the Austrian territory as the base for the German troops fighting in the Balkans. Some mutual contacts were established after 1941. In 1944 Lieutenant Willibald Zechner, a member of the military circle around the City of Vienna Commander General-Lieutenant Stümpf, came to the village of Eisenkappel to visit his brother Johann, a mountain troops soldier who had deserted and subsequently enlisted in the Partisans at the outset of 1944. There the head of the Partisan detachment Janko Pototschnig joined the two brothers. They discussed a British suggestion to set up wireless communications between Vienna and the Allied powers. Soon afterward, on October 10, Johann Zechner was caught. Willibald was arrested in November.[17]

In another instance of cooperation with the Tito insurgents, Widmayer, a former Socialist and trade union official, managed to operate a highly effective intelligence network transmitting information to the Allies in Switzerland and Istanbul. Widmayer cooperated with the Yugoslav Partisans and repeatedly met their emissaries in the Semmering Pass at the Styrian-Lower Austrian border. He succeeded in delivering military intelligence to Great Britain, enlisting Partisan help to do so through the former Styrian Socialist official Fritz Matzner who traveled to the Partisan-occupied territory with the data to be forwarded to the British.[18]

For their part the Austrian Communists felt closely identified with Marshal Tito's Partisan forces. The caravan of Communist visitors who had converged on the Carinthian border area for talks with the Partisans signaled the importance of the Partisan role in shaping Communist action.

When the resisters returned to their Austrian bases, they carried the promise of cooperation. In October 1942 the Communist militants around Leoben in Upper Styria collected RM 2,500, which they forwarded with medical supplies to the Partisan bases in Carniola through Hermine Sagmeister in Klagenfurt. In their turn, Partisan emissaries journeyed to Styria. In 1943 Josef Filz and Anton Wagner, members of the Leoben group, traveled to Carinthia to contact the Slovenian LF. On their return to Styria in the summer, they played a prominent role in creating the nucleus of a combat group. Another Styrian emissary, Willi Muchitsch, went to Villach to see Konrad Bucher, a senior Communist functionary who had contacts with the Partisans and the Slovenian KP. Bucher's nucleus worked with Hubert Kness, the KP regional chief, who was on the run. Kness animated Communist underground activity in the province until his arrest on May 15, 1944.[19]

THE AUSTRIAN BATTALIONS

With victory in sight, the KPÖ Moscow center elaborated a well-devised plan in cooperation with Josip Tito's military mission, which arrived in Moscow in April 1944. Because the Carinthian borderland was remote from those Partisan bases in Yugoslavia where the rebels carried on guerrilla warfare, the Austrian Communists stationed some men in the Partisan-occupied territory. From here the newly created detachments of Austrian nationals would penetrate into southern Carinthia. Moscow saw these groups as the nuclei of the future Communist-led guerrilla movement in Austria comprising the Communists, Socialists, and Catholics. A special KPÖ mission headed by Honner was dropped near Črnomelj in Tito-occupied Slovenia in August 1944.[20] Honner was followed by another senior Party official, Siegfried Fürnberg, who parachuted in with twenty Communists in October. The Partisan stronghold became the headquarters of the KPÖ political and military mission.

In a manifesto reportedly originating on June 10-11, 1944, the top KP officials reiterated the call to armed insurgency of the Moscow Declaration of 1943. They believed that guerrilla warfare on Slovenian soil would arouse the desire of the Austrian population for a people's war against the German invaders. The Communists hoped to build up the Austrian Freedom Front (ÖFF) as their political organ so as to unify all patriots. As the new version of the Popular Front, the ÖFF would become a multi-party façade for the KPÖ unity-of-action policy, the intent of which was to control the future government. As its most urgent task, the ÖFF formed combat units within the Yugoslav People's Army in Partisan-held Slovenia. Eventually, in the Communist view, these Austrian battalions controlled by reliable cadres flown in from the USSR would form the fighting core of the future Austrian army and security forces.

Specially trained Party personnel recruited and organized the planned five battalions. For the most part, the veterans of the International Brigades in Spain controlled the military command. The First Battalion, which had 94 to 100 men, took part in combat on Slovenian soil and fought on the front in January 1945. Most of the combatants were recruited from among Austrian prisoners of war. Some volunteered and were put into a training camp in Ljubno near the Carinthian border where they underwent their first screening. At first, the volunteers set out in separate parties from Ljubno on guerrilla actions in the Austrian border country. They hoped that local recruits would join their units.[21] Unfortunately, the bulk of the Styrian and Carinthian German-speaking populace viewed the insurgents as irresponsible hotheads who could bring disaster upon local communities. In many places the villagers responded with fear, contempt, or hatred to the insurgents, denouncing them to the authorities. Engaged in a difficult struggle with the security forces, the twenty-nine volunteers from Ljubno who did enter Austrian territory retreated to their base camp in December, their expectations unfulfilled.[22]

For successful actions, the insurgency depended on the assistance of the population. Support from the anti-Communist and deeply religious natives could not be gained without a representative political leadership reflecting the mood of the country. The KP leaders Honner and Fürnberg were fully aware that cooperation with the Socialists and Catholics was essential to the success of the Communist plans for the ÖFF. Honner contacted Erwin Scharf, an SPÖ member, and Dr. Tschubar, a Catholic from Völkermarkt. After his release from prison in 1940, Scharf had returned home to Velden in Carinthia, where in 1941 he contacted the remnants of the Revolutionary Socialist group around Ferdinand Wedenig. Wedenig, who worked in a consumer cooperative, had been arranging supplies of food, clothing, and comforts for the Slovenian Partisans near Velden. Scharf then gained access to the clandestine LF representatives in Klagenfurt. To avoid arrest, Scharf went into hiding on August 22, 1944 and traveled along the escape line across the Alps to Slovenia. Under the cover name of Wallner, Scharf emerged as the Socialist representative on the ÖFF Provincial Committee for Styria and Carinthia and worked as a recruiting agent and political instructor for the Austrian battalions. With Honner and other ÖFF members, he was flown to Vienna on April 21 to become one of the SPÖ's Central secretaries.[23]

"THE STYRIAN COMBAT GROUP"

The former Spanish Civil War combatants and Schutzbündlers flown from Moscow and dropped near Črnomelj in the summer of 1944 were excellent soldiers. On August 7, a combat team of twenty-five men marched north to Austria, crossing the Carinthian border on the evening of September 17, to seek refuge in the Saualpe mountain range. From the beginning, the Nazi authorities launched massive dragnet operations against the insurgents, whose fate depended on peasant support. However, the unfriendly villagers all too often denounced the insurgents to the police. Lacking food and suffering from the cold, the squad moved fast, so that neither the gendarmes nor the local Nazi auxiliary forces ever quite caught up with them. Finally, the men decided to break out of the Carinthian mountains and journey through the forests to the Koralpe ranges along the Styrian-Yugoslav-Carinthian border.

The vast Alpine forests now became a new base for the detachment, which broke up into several independent parties. Alarmed by the existence of an armed squad cooperating with other Slovene Partisan units, the Nazis fought several short engagements with the guerrillas, who were finally reduced to thirteen men, "The Styrian Combat Group," wearing the red-white-red insignia of the ÖFF.[24] During the last winter of the war, the news about German reverses affected the population; the reputation of the partisans grew in proportion to Red Army advances. The rebels also began to build up local links to gain the confidence of the mountain inhabitants. To counteract the anti-guerrilla propaganda, they appealed to the natives' patriotic sentiments.[25] Slowly, some of the Austrian-minded villagers began to provide aid.

During the late winter and early spring, German deserters, escaped Soviet prisoners of war, and Soviet laborers created new combat units that were attached to the Styrian Combat Group.[26] The guerrillas established wireless communication with the LF and the KPÖ command in Slovenia. On March 2 and again around mid-April, Soviet planes dropped weapons, ammunition, and medical supplies. In an attempt to control the insurgents, the Germans assembled several thousand men—local gendarmerie, police, and Volkssturm—who pursued the guerrilla squads through the borderland area from Lavamünd and Deutschlandsberg to Maribor.[27] When the security forces ventured into the mountains, guerrilla bands tormented them with sniper fire. In several skirmishes Nazi units suffered heavier losses than the insurgents, who broke up into smaller detachments and slipped away into the mountains.

At the end of the war in May, the Group fielded three battalions, one composed of Austrians, one of Soviet prisoners, and one of mixed nationalities. Only eight men of the original combat team stayed with the Group. In all, seventeen combatants survived.[28] Evidently, the assistance from the Slovene Partisan detachments whom the Group had the good luck to meet in the winter months of 1945 helped them remain an organized force. Although the Styrian Combat Group did wage guerrilla war in Germany's rear, it did so not as an instrument of the Austrian national struggle for independence, but as one of the Slovene movement, acting in concert with the Slovenian High Command and following KPÖ directives.

THE LEOBEN-DONAWITZ GROUP

The industrial basin of Leoben, Bruck, and Kapfenberg in Upper Styria had been one of the labor movement's traditional strongholds. In 1942-43 the surviving members of the Communist conspiracy, who had escaped Nazi imprisonment, united in the area of Leoben, Donawitz, St. Michael, Vordernberg, Eisenerz, and Hieflau. Responding to Radio Moscow's call for direct action, the surviving militants decided to form guerrilla squads. The Communist ringleaders Filz and Wagner went into hiding on April 3, 1943, to lay the foundations for guerrilla warfare. They understood that an effective combat organization required that a wide range of adherents actively participate and that they create an organizational base in Leoben and the surrounding mountains. They also used women extensively, over 100 of whom supplied ration cards, medical supplies, food, clothing, and information that they had gathered in their jobs at telegraphy, municipal, railroad, and military offices. The resisters penetrated the district military command and the district administration of Leoben. They collected arms and, thanks to two Austrian soldiers, they stole weapons from a military depot.[29] Small farmers provided them with hideouts and safe houses in the mountain valleys. The members constructed bunkers and equipped them with supplies.

In the fall of 1943, the group named itself "Austrian Freedom Front" (ÖFF).[30] Its principal concern was to persuade dispersed sympathizers to support guerrilla insurgency and to prepare for armed actions the following spring. To overcome its isolation and to encourage the underground, the ÖFF sought to improve contacts with the Tito Partisans in the Bacher Mountains in Yugoslav Lower Styria and in Carinthia. The Communists were numerically few, but from their leadership positions they exerted the dominant influence in the group. The group's expanded activities attracted the attention of the Gestapo, who countered the threat by offering awards of RM 10,000 for the capture of ÖFF leaders. The Gestapo actions had little effect on the fiery advocates of direct action who, at a meeting in Donawitz in April 1944, prevailed over those activists who viewed guerrilla activity as premature and who instead wanted to form small sabotage teams.

The first action occurred during Whitsuntide 1944 when an ÖFF combat team failed to disrupt the main railway line at St. Michael. In June a combat squad blew up the railway tracks near Kapfenberg, drawing the local military, SA, and *Landwacht* force to the mountains that served as its hideout. On June 22 during an armed encounter, the first insurgent died when he was wounded, captured, then murdered by the SS. On July 11, a freight train was damaged in Leoben. In the following months the guerrilla detachment of about twenty men broke up into smaller parties and retreated to escape massive Nazi sweep operations.[31] At the beginning of August the combat parties dispersed, to reassemble in the late fall. Forced to remain in the harsh mountainous terrain during the severe winter, the insurgents split into several parties for security reasons. The different parties constructed bunkers in inaccessible places. However, a hunter who accidentally uncovered one of the winter bunkers informed the police. Surrounding the dugout on December 1, the Nazis clashed with the partisans, who managed to escape, losing two wounded men, one of whom the security forces then killed. Filz, the second partisan, took months to recover from his wounds in his hideout.

The Nazi authorities made every effort to stamp out the insurgency. As early as the summer of 1944 they were already trailing the partisans. When arrested, a combat team member agreed to act as an informer and caused the arrest of a number of resisters.[32] Furthermore, the Gestapo had already broken into the noncombatant ÖFF support organization. Rainer, one of the major Communist organizers, was captured during a visit to his family at the beginning of May. Agreeing to inform, he was fed back into the organization.[33] The Nazis fully exploited the new information and in the second half of 1944 destroyed almost the entire network.[34] Still, its remnants held out, and when in the winter of 1944 the Allied victories indicated an early end to the regime, they rebuilt the ÖFF. However, the cells were reactivated too late to engage in action.[35] No open guerrilla fighting broke out, but at the local level, the ÖFF managed to prevent wanton destruction of bridges, roads, and factories.[36]

It is difficult to overlook the contrast between the catastrophe that befell the ÖFF and its initial high expectations. For a brief period, the fighting in Styria weakened Nazi confidence, but by mid-1944, after only a few months of sporadic harassment, the untrained guerrilla parties were in disarray, fleeing before the ruthless security force composed of fellow Styrians. Apparently in 1944, most of the Styrian population was still favorably disposed toward the Nazi regime.

SALZKAMMERGUT

In Salzkammergut the Communist Party's initial instinctive response to the occupation was often unselective recruitment and the hasty buildup of Party cells.[37] Many Party activists dispersed or enlisted in the Wehrmacht in 1941-42. A Spanish Civil War veteran, Sepp Plieseis, reactivated the dormant cadres after his escape from the Hallein branch of Dachau KZ on August 20, 1943. Five days later, accompanied by his companion Fritz Gitzoller, who had helped rescue him, Plieseis met a handful of trusted Party and Communist Youth activists in Bad Ischl to weld the Catholic, Communist, and Socialist underground into an All-Austrian group named "Willy."[38] With the cooperation of Socialist and Catholic-oriented cells in Goisern, Bad Aussee, and Mitterndorf, the group made new contacts in Ebensee, Obertraun, Gmunden, and Liezen.

By September 1943 about fifty resisters were at work mainly in Ischl and Goisern. Many were local draft dodgers or soldiers evading further military service. During the winter of 1943 they found refuge in the Dead Mountains (Totes Gebirge), an almost inaccessible range. Local gamekeepers, foresters, and highlanders assisted the parties and told them of the whereabouts of the security forces. But most of the population was initially indifferent or even hostile. That attitude changed, however, in the winter of 1943-44 when the populace expressed some sympathy and even provided support in some localities, villagers supplying the partisans with food, shelter, and financial aid. The organizational base among the inhabitants of the neighboring villages grew to more than 500 followers at the end of 1944. More Austrian Wehrmacht soldiers also joined the hiding deserters.

Another element played an important role in the development of the underground. In Alt Aussee, miners and employees working in the salt mines had to help safeguard the priceless art treasures from Germany and German occupied territories that Hitler stored there to protect them from air raids. In April 1945, Hitler issued an order prohibiting the authorities to destroy these invaluable works of arts. Disregarding the Führer's directive, Upper Austrian Gauleiter August Eigruber ordered the mines to be blown up before the arrival of the United States troops. Even the head of the Reich Security Main Office Ernst Kaltenbrunner, who managed to reach Aussee, personally interceded with the Gau authorities against this senseless destruction. Fortunately, the art treasures survived through the intervention of the local resistance, who safeguarded over 7,000 irreplaceable works of art, including paintings (*Mona Lisa*, the *Ghent Altar*), and rare collections of weapons, books, sculpture, coins, jewels, and porcelain from Austria, Germany, Belgium, France, Italy, and elsewhere.[39]

Throughout 1944, the sense of urgency among the militants increased. Some were ready to show force, planning such acts of terror as the killing of local Nazi bosses. Plieseis and his aides persuasively argued that such actions would only cause brutal reprisals, alienate the local inhabitants among whom they lived, and isolate the underground. Although victory appeared close, survival remained the most urgent task.

When in the early fall of 1944 the authorities learned that a party of deserters was roaming the Dead Mountains, a small task force set out to destroy the resisters. Warned by the local gendarmes, the men fled to other areas and no one was caught. Opting against guerrilla warfare, they confined themselves to local activities and refused to stage an armed resistance. Their organizational activity picked up again in the winter of 1944 when the underground turned the mountain region from Bad Ischl to Alt Aussee, Mitterndorf, Hallstatt, and Obertraun into a self-controlled base. In the end, the group, which was constantly on the move to avoid the Gestapo, found some opportunities for political propaganda. However, it engaged in direct action only in the closing weeks of the war, when the second important clandestine organization under the command of Albrecht Gaiswinkler, a former health insurance official and a Social Democrat, seized the initiative.

Gaiswinkler had formed his network on February 23, 1940, in cooperation with Valentin Tarra, a gendarmerie inspector, and Hans Moser, a clerk in the Salt Mines. The three worked hard in the Aussee area and made contacts with Plieseis, Matzner in Graz, and Frenzel from the G.B. in Linz. In 1943 Gaiswinkler was drafted by the Wehrmacht. When sent to France, he joined the French Resistance in the summer of 1944. In the fall of 1944, a Ukrainian Gestapo informer betrayed Moser, who was killed in an air raid in 1945. Other arrests followed in Bad Aussee and Alt Aussee in February 1945, and even included some members of the local gendarmerie. Tarra alone escaped the Gestapo's attention and remained free.

Gaiswinkler's sudden appearance marked a radical improvement. On the night of April 8, 1945, Gaiswinkler and three other Austrian operators, equipped with wireless transmitters, were dropped in the Höllen Mountains near Ebensee as part of a British circuit.[40] Returning to Aussee, Gaiswinkler had, within a few days, appointed Tarra his deputy and established a base there. The organization grew to about 360 volunteers, overlapping territorially with the "Willy" group.[41] By mid-April the gendarmes in Bad Aussee had joined. They were placed under Tarra's authority together with the auxiliary police members of the resistance. Arrangements were made for the gendarmerie to provide small arms for the resisters.

The area around Aussee became a vast refuge for fleeing prominent Nazis, officials of the satellite governments of Bulgaria, Rumania, Hungary, and the retreating German Sixth Army. Local patriots collected intelligence. In the process, they forced Gauleiter Eigruber's secretary and three Gestapo agents to hand over police files and to provide Gestapo forms, stamps, and passes. These made it possible for two resistance emissaries using faked papers to reach the advancing United States Army near Vöcklabruck and to reveal the position of the German forces at the Pötschen Pass in the Alps between Aussee and Goisern, where the troops offered an ideal target for Allied air strikes. Later during the confusion of the Nazi retreat, the resisters disarmed a few isolated units of the Sixth Army and equipped themselves with captured arms and two German tanks.

Gaiswinkler's men controlled the administration even before the area was cleared of German troops. In one incident, a combat unit succeeded in holding General Fabianku as prisoner at his headquarters to force the release of an underground courier. At the beginning of May, fifteen guerrillas seized the radio transmitter Vienna II stored in Bad Aussee and began broadcasting as Radio Freedom Ausseeland. In the end, the insurgents could claim outstanding success in pinning down Nazi forces, in preventing the willful destruction of the art treasures, and in confiscating stores of gold and other valuables from the fleeing German forces in this last refuge of the collapsing Reich.[42]

THE WECHSEL MOUNTAIN GROUP

Irregular warfare in other provinces was progressing at a fast pace. In the Wechsel mountain range near Hartberg in eastern Styria, insurgency expanded on such a scale that the Nazis sent in an SS column that quickly acquired a reputation for mistreating civilians.[43] SS troops murdered five men when searching Pongratzen on April 27, 1945, and carried away a woman and her two sons, whom they shot on May 8. In April 1945, the region saw almost daily actions against the retreating German and Hungarian troops.[44] Behind the battleline the guerrillas disarmed small scattered SS and Wehrmacht units before they could regroup. On April 2 the partisans set three light airplanes on fire at a field near Penzendorf. By April 20, the guerrillas under Gustav Pfeiler had more than 200 men concentrated around their base in Pongratzen.

The guerrillas fought several battles with the SS and a police task force was brought in to restore order. In one skirmish with the local SA at the beginning of April, partisans entered a farmhouse sheltering the family of the local NSDAP chief in Hartberg, Erich Heumann (Ortsgruppenleiter), and shot to death his wife, two children, and six other family members and friends. In retribution, the Nazies rounded up scores of suspects. On May 4 the Special Court sentenced thirteen locals, mostly peasants, to death. They were executed in Hartberg town park.[45]

The local guerrillas did not seem to act in concert with the advancing Red Army or the Western Allies. Supplied with food by their contacts in the villages, the partisans operated in small squads, without any centralized system of command. No underground sprang up in the countryside to strengthen the insurgents.

GUERRILLA INSURGENCY

The defining feature of the Resistance was its wish to reunite the Austrian provinces into an independent state. Armed guerrilla groups emerged in various parts of the country at the very moment when the Resistance was seeking Allied acknowledgment of their struggle and of their commitment to Austrian independence.[46] But armed encounter between the insurgents and the Nazi forces never grew intense and widespread until the closing weeks of the war. Railway and industrial disruption was never more than an irritant, provoking harsh retribution. The few armed parties who took to the mountains could not persist as fighting units unless they drew support from the local populace and received Allied assistance through drops of equipment—as was the case in France and other subjugated West European countries. In Austria, the Resistance was left to itself, which, of course, affected the nature and results of armed resistance. Hiding in the mountains, inspired by patriotism or a mixture of nationalism and social radicalism, the insurgents were mainly preoccupied with survival.

The Communists played a crucial role in organizing armed resistance in southern Austria, linking the local underground with the KP center in Moscow. But their militants were often too busy trying to stay alive to engage in violent actions. Nevertheless, they did harass, sabotage, and fight the security forces, tying up army, security, and auxiliary contingents. The Communists sought to impose themselves as the dominant element, and to lay the foundations for their future penetration into Austrian political life. But their activism backfired because by their pro-Soviet and pro-Yugoslav line, they were at odds with public opinion. Despite their assertive and insistent propaganda, they had remained outside the political mainstream.

Because the partisans requisitioned food and clothing, they made it easier for the Nazi authorities to brand them as outlaws. In view of the public passive hostility and unfriendliness to the few isolated combat parties and the overwhelming forces massed against them, it was remarkable that the few resisters had exercised any psychological and political effect on the public at all. With no massive propaganda support nor material help from the Western Allies, armed resistance never developed as a form of popular opposition. The situation radically changed in the winter of 1944 when Allied support was forthcoming in Vienna and Tyrol.

If individual combatants did not seem to ask whether under the circumstances armed struggle was counterproductive, certainly other people did—up to the early spring of 1945. When initiated too early, without links to outside resources, armed resistance was doomed to destruction. The usefulness of combat operations naturally varied with the extent to which they imperiled future actions by attracting too much attention from the authorities. The usefulness also depended on the strength of the partisans' links with the Allied powers and on the flow of Allied support. The hundred-odd partisans who bore the brunt of the fighting until 1945 lived in daily expectation of death.[47] With no uniforms, no war rules, no possibility of surrender, they expected no mercy; capture meant brutal torture and certain death. Survival in the forests was possible only for the fit and healthy, those with arms and skill who could elude the pursuing security forces, and those who could depend on at least a handful of supporters among the local inhabitants.

The combat detachment was an alternative institution improvised by the Resistance, a community of dedication imparting a sense of purpose to its members. Members shared a sense of comradeship, of solidarity, of combat experience, of tenacity, and of sacrifice that others did not have. Unlike the situation in Yugoslavia, Poland, or France, lack of training, small size, and isolation made it generally impossible to form and operate parallel, complex military and administrative structures. Also in contrast to the organizational structure in France, Yugoslavia, Poland, or Czechoslovakia, the combat groups were not affiliated with any representative Austrian political organ at home or in exile; and the military benefits of the guerrilla exploits seemed to many not worth the heavy suffering and lost lives. As happened to the Resistance movements elsewhere in Europe, the Austrian Resistance very likely "received more blows than it dealt . . . [and] more deaths to grieve than it inflicted upon the adversary."[48]

In terms of economic disruption, political disorder, and military redeployment, insurgency caused the regime only marginal embarrassment. Yet its struggle was indeed of political and moral significance and unsettled the popular mood, irritating National Socialist sympathizers. Political and moral, not military, repercussions and considerations were of importance.[49] In the Austrian circumstances, the armed action and the Resistance itself were instruments for the recognition of the legitimacy of the country's national and political aspirations. They contributed towards the restoration of the soul of Austria. The Austrian experience was not unique, but its elements—the absence of both a central political organ in exile and of Allied help, the attitude of large segments of the population favorable to the Nazi regime—did not occur elsewhere.

NOTES

1. Hanns Haas-Karl Stuhlpfarrer, *Österreich und seine Slowenen* (Vienna, 1977), pp. 84-87. Josef Rausch offers a detailed description of guerrilla warfare in *Der Partisanenkampf in Kärnten im Zweiten Weltkrieg* (Vienna, 1979) and in an article of the same name in *Österreichische Osthefte*, 23, no. 1 (1981), 53-76; for the Slovenian view, see Prušnik-Gašper, *Gemsen*, passim.

2. Karl Prušnik-Gašper, "Die Kärntner Slowenen im bewaffneten Kampf gegen den Faschismus," 8. Koroški kulturni dne . . . 17.-19. 2. 1977 (Klagenfurt, 1977), pp. 2-12. The first armed encounter between the insurgents and the German security forces occurred in Carinthia in August 1942. Ibid., p. 2. For the most part, the young Slovenes regarded their fight as a struggle for national survival. The peasants among the Austrian Slovenes appeared to support the attachment to Yugoslavia of the Carinthian territory predominantly populated by the Slovenes. Rausch, "Der Partisanenkampf," *Österreichische Osthefte*, p. 75.

A native of Lobnik, a village set in the heart of the Alpine ranges near the Yugoslav-Carinthian border, Pasterk enlisted in the Tito-led Partisans in October 1942. Gravely wounded in combat, he died in April 1943. His brother was executed in 1943. Fein, *Die Steine*, p. 145.

3. Malte Olschewski, "Die psychologische Kriegsführung und Propaganda der Tito Partisanen in Kärnten und Slowenien" (Ph.D. dissertation, University of Vienna, 1966), pp. 44-45. Prušnik-Gašper, "Die Slowenen," pp. 3-8. The Communist Party of Slovenia had complete political control of the LF. The Carinthian Partisans included a small number of German Austrians, among whom the Catholics played an important part.

4. Olschewski, "Die Kriegsführung," pp. 44-46.

5. "Berichte über die allgemeine Lage an RMdJ Dr. Georg Thierack," Der Oberlandesgerichtspräsident, Graz, November 26, 1942; GSAW Graz, January 27, May 28, 1943, BA, R 22/3365.

6. Rausch, *Der Partisanenkampf*, pp. 34, 40, 49 ff, 68. By July 1943 soldiers on leave were

prohibited from returning to the territory south of the Drau river. Haas-Stuhlpfarrer, *Österreich*, p. 87. The reports of the Rüstungskommando, Klagenfurt, recorded the deteriorating situation in the borderland areas. NA, T 77, roll 748, 981318—349, 981379.

7. Ibid., 981536-722.

8. Ibid., 981977; Rausch, *Der Partisanenkrieg*, pp. 53, 102-4. The number of police and gendarmerie stations went up from forty-three in 1938 to 152 in 1945. On October 19, 1944, the Partisans severely damaged an important industrial plant producing fluorescent bulbs, which had just been dismantled and removed from Carniola in occupied Yugoslavia to St. Andrä. Reichministerium für Rüstung, November 10, 1944, T 77, r. 751, 986197.

9. "Bericht. Der Oberlandesgerichtspräsident," BA R 22/3365.

10. "Bericht, GSAW," Graz, ibid. For a discussion on the extent of guerrilla insurgency in Carinthia, see Rausch, *Der Partisanenkrieg*, passim; Barker, *The Slovenes*, pp. 236-39; Prušnik-Gašper, *Gemsen*, passim.

11. Prušnik-Gašper, "Die Slowenen," p. 11; David Stafford, *Britain and European Resistance 1940-1945. A Survey of the Special Operations Executive with Documents* (Toronto, 1980), p. 189. Reports on the guerrillas had eventually reached the Western capitals. On June 22, 1944, George Hall, British Parliamentary Foreign Under-secretary, stated in the House of Commons: "There is some anti-German activity in Carinthia." H. C. Debates, 5th Series, vol. 401, col. 353 in John Mair, *Austria in Four-Power Control in Germany and Austria 1945-1946. Survey of International Affairs 1939-1946* (London 1956), pp. 290 ff.

12. Olschewski, "Die Kriegsführung," pp. 62-63, 70-72, 149; František Hejl in *Slovanský přehled* (Prague, 65, 1979),: 434-35.

13. Olschewski, "Die Kriegsführung," pp. 70-71.

14. AS, VGH, December 18, 1944, DÖW 3364; U VGH, 1H 380/44 11 J 418/44, December 18, 1944, DÖW 1138; Prušnik-Gašper, *Gemsen*, passim.

15. *Die Einheit*, November 17, 1950. The Carinthian population was deeply divided along national lines, but a common heritage formed a bond between the Slovenes and the Austrians.

16. Prušnik-Gašper, "Die Slowenen," p. 12; Rausch, *Der Partisanenkrieg*, pp. 82-83, 101.

17. The two brothers were sentenced to death in March 1945 but Willibald escaped execution because the war ended. DÖW 6198.

18. For Matzner, see DÖW 13415; for seven groups in Carinthia, see DÖW 15197. Widmayer was arrested three times, DÖW 8912/a-b; Stadler, *Österreich*, pp. 71-72, 375-76. He became a Socialist member of the Parliament after 1945. Some Allied field operatives made their way to Austria across Yugoslavia. The British SOE sent a party to the country in 1943 but it soon returned. Foot, *Resistance*, p. 212. For the British mission in Slovenia in 1944, see Prušnik-Gašper, *Gemsen*, pp. 171, 307-308. The OSS dispatched Lieutenant-Colonel Franklin Lindsay to southern Austria in the winter of 1944-45. R. Harris Smith, *OSS. The Secret History of America's First Central Intelligence Agency* (Berkeley, 1972), p. 161.

19. AS, VGH, 11 J 49/45-5H 64/65, March 17, 1945, DÖW 14885; Prušnik-Gašper, *Gemsen*, p. 175. Forty-nine persons from the Villach and Klagenfurt area were apprehended in December 1944. They had provided food and hiding places to Kness and assisted the Partisans. DÖW 887; 993; 5509. "Bericht über die Parteiarbeit des Bezirkes Leoben ab 1937," DÖW 900-901; Max Muchitsch, *Die Partisanengruppe Leoben-Donawitz* (Vienna, 1966), pp. 18, 21, 23, 25; DÖW 895-96.

20. I follow Willibald Ingo Holzer, "Die österreichischen Bataillone im Verbande der NOV i POJ. Die Kampfgruppe Avantgarde-Steiermark. Die Partisanengruppe Leoben-Donawitz. Die Kommunistische Partei Österreichs im militanten politischen Widerstand," Ph.D. dissertation, University of Vienna, 1971, pp. 137-40, 244 ff; Willibald I. Holzer, "Die österreichischen Bataillone in Jugoslawien 1944-1945. Zur Widerstandsstrategie der österreichischen kommunistischen Emigration," *Zeitgeschichte*, 4 (November 1974), 46 ff. See also Friedl Fürnberg, *Österreichische Freiheitsbataillone. Österreichische Nation* (Vienna, 1975), passim. An experienced top-ranking operator, Honner participated in the Spanish Civil War. After October 1939 he worked in Yugoslavia. In May 1940 he went to Moscow where he

reported on the Yugoslav situation as Josip Tito had instructed him to do. Herbert Steiner, "Die jugoslavische Kommunistische Partei im Mai 1940," *Zeitgeschichte* 7 (October 1979): 1-8. He became State Secretary of the Interior in the first postwar Austrian government.

21. Holzer, "Die Bataillone," *Zeitgeschichte,* pp. 50-52.

22. Ibid., p. 47; Holzer, "Die österreichischen Bataillone," pp. 422-23; Fürnberg, *Freiheitsbataillone,* pp. 16-18. Holzer stresses the lack of cooperation from the rural population: "At the end of 1944 the majority of the Austrians had seen their Fatherland threatened. However, they did not consider Hitler the principal culprit" (p. 494).

Central to another action, the top KP officials Willi Frank and Laurenz Hiebl flew with eight other Communists from the USSR to Belgrade in December 1944. With fifteen combatants they traveled to Carinthia on February 17, to encourage native resistance. Two days later, the band ran into the Germans, who killed Frank. The party had to withdraw from Austria. Holzer, "Die Bataillone," pp. 50-53.

23. A firm promoter of unity with the Communists, Scharf eventually broke with the SPÖ and became Secretary of the KPÖ. Interview with Erwin Scharf; Erwin Scharf in Danimann, ed., *Finis Austriae,* pp. 224 ff. Fürnberg, *Freiheitsbataillone,* pp. 15-16; DÖW 1967.

24. I follow the narrative of the Group's political commissar, Walter Wachs, *Kampfgruppe Steiermark* (Vienna, 1968), passim; W. Wachs, "Die Partisanen auf der Koralpe," DÖW 1a. For an analysis, see Willibald I. Holzer, "Am Beispiel der Kampfgruppe Avantgarde-Steiermark (1944-1945)," in Gerhard Botz et al., eds., *Bewegung und Klasse. Studien zur österreichischen Arbeitergeschichte* (Vienna, 1978), pp. 377-424. For the activities of the Slovene Partisans in the Saualpe range in the fall and winter of 1944, see Prušnik-Gašper, *Gemsen,* pp. 194 ff.

25. DÖW 1a; Wachs, *Kampfgruppe,* pp. 49-51.

26. By January 1945 the group's fighting force numbered 200 to 250; by the end of April it increased to about 500. Most Austrians who enlisted in the unit were Catholic, Austrian-oriented, non-party men. In early April, nineteen well-armed Wehrmacht soldiers, mostly Austrians, joined the Group. Ibid., pp. 29, 36, 40.

27. Ibid., pp. 30-37; Holzer in Botz, *Bewegung,* p. 413. On April 1 a patrol of the Reich Labor Service captured five members of the Combat group near St. Oswald ob Freiland. The local NSDAP Kreisleiter, Dr. Hugo Suette, ordered their immediate execution. Wachs, *Kampfgruppe,* pp. 34-35, 40.

28. Ibid., pp. 43-44.

29. I follow Muchitsch, *Die Partisanengruppe;* Sepp Filz, "Der Widerstand in Obersteiermark," DÖW 896; DÖW 900. As late as the summer of 1943, twenty former Socialists, predominantly miners, were picked up in Tragöss. DÖW 13351.

30. Muchitsch, *Die Partisanengruppe,* pp. 25-26; DÖW 17146.

31. On August 15 the security forces killed the guerrilla military commander Hanns Kren.

32. Muchitsch, *Die Partisanengruppe,* p. 48.

33. DÖW 896, 900.

34. Eleven members died in action, forty-four were murdered or died in concentration camps, and twenty were executed (eighteen workers and two women). In October and November, ninety-four women—mostly members of the resisters' families—were dispatched to the concentration camps; some never returned. Muchitsch, *Die Partisanengruppe,* pp. 59-64. For the informers, see ibid., pp. 33-34.

35. The military reverses in 1944 did not affect the morale of the regime, whose war-making machine ran smoothly. Many former Communist officials still obeyed their draft orders and ignored the Party directive to enroll in the underground.

36. In a rare outburst of violence, the Partisans summarily executed the chairman of the military court martial in Hieflau and the chief of the Volkssturm Company in Eisenerz. The retreating SS troops behaved with customary brutality. DÖW 8828; Muchitsch, *Die Partisanengruppe,* pp. 51 ff.

37. AS, VGH, September 8, 1942, OM, XIV.

38. I follow Peter Kammerstätter, Materialsammlung über die Widerstands- und Partisanenbewegung Willy-Fred. Freiheitsbewegung im oberen Salzkammergut-Ausseerland 1943-1945, 2 vols. Manuscript, 1978; Sepp Plieseis, *Vom Ebro zum Dachstein, Lebenskampf eines österreichischen Arbeiters* (Linz, 1946; Albrecht Gaiswinkler, *Sprung in die Freiheit* (Vienna-Salzburg, 1947); interview with Plieseis in DÖW 1966; DÖW 631, 3759, 8377; Gaiswinkler-Tarra, "Bericht," OM, No 39; Göhring, "Der Jugendverband" pp. 311-26.

39. The United States armed forces assumed control of the stored artworks on May 8, 1945. As early as 1943, one of Becker's network responsible for the storage of the art treasures had contacted the underground in Alt Aussee and at the Salt Works. In 1945 the security guards of the collections were drawn from reliable adherents of the Resistance. For the rescue action, see DÖW 631, 8377, 8342; E. Pöchmüller, *Weltkunstschatz in Gefahr* (Salzburg, 1948).

40. Joining the Allied forces in France in September 1944, Gaiswinkler received special training in Great Britain.

41. The members were mostly blue- and white-collar workers with past Socialist, Communist, and Christian Social loyalties. DÖW 8342.

42. The American military government appointed Gaiswinkler head of the district administration. After 1945 he was elected to the Parliament. The representatives of the intelligence (CIC) branch of the United States 80th Infantry Division recorded on June 10, 1945, their deep appreciation of Gaiswinkler and his men for their aid in preserving the art works, and in capturing Kaltenbrunner and scores of other SD and Gestapo agents.

43. For the Anselm Grand group, see Anselm Grand, OM, 28/III; DÖW 8377. For the Johann Schöller group, see DÖW 15644.

44. See the reports by G. Pfeiler, January 25, 1946 and by the Hartberg gendarmerie station, DÖW 2124; interview with A. Grand.

45. On April 23 a noncommissioned officer and forty-two of his soldiers from a transport regiment joined the guerrillas, bringing military equipment and trucks with them. SS-report, April 29, 1945, DÖW 5373.

46. In the summer of 1944 a detachment of escaped prisoners of war, deserters, and East European forced labor draftees assembled in the southern part of Lower Austria near Scheibbs and Gaming. A column of German soldiers, gendarmerie, and policemen, with the usual complement of *Landwacht* guards, pursued the men, who eventually escaped. Three policemen were killed. "Lagebericht. Der GSAW an RMdJ," October 1, 1944, BA R 22/3388.

47. Scores of Austrian deserters were left alone in their forest hideouts since they did not want to join the underground or had only a tenuous connection with it. However, some did join to avoid capture or to fight the Nazis.

48. Henri Michel, "L'aide apportée aux Alliés par la Résistance clandestine française," *Revue des Travaux de l'Académie des Sciences Morales & Politiques,* 115e année, 4e série, 1962, 66.

49. It is of interest to cite the Office of Strategic Services' estimate of the Austrian armed resistance's efforts. "Maquis groups in Austria consist chiefly of deserters from the Wehrmacht, foreign workers, and escaped prisoners of the Germans. The majority of the maquis fighters are believed to be non-Austrian. The largest and most active maquis units are apparently located in southern parts of Styria and Carinthia, where the Slovene population has been waging warfare on the Germans for several years. POEN relations with these Slovene maquis are admittedly poor, since the Slovenes oppose the incorporation of this region into any future Austrian state. Maquis units also are reported to be operating in the Judenburger Gebirge area, the lower Tauern region, the southeastern part of the Burgenland, the Leithagebirge area, the Vorarlberg, the Tirol, and the vicinity of Berchtesgaden. . . . The effectiveness of their operations remains almost as obscure as their numerical strength." OSS, Research and Analysis Branch, Current Intelligence Study No. 9, R & A 3038S, 13 April 1945, DÖW 12667.

19

The Constitution
of a Resistance Center and
Its International Recognition

By the fall of 1944 the establishment of links to the Western powers seemed as important as gathering support in the country. Having reduced the underground's initial fragmentation, the 05 and the Committee of Seven looked for international recognition.[1] But the difficulties in breaking out of political isolation were almost insurmountable. Without any contact with Austrian exiles and without any effective link with the Allies, they could not relay political intelligence to the West. In turn, the Allies could not commit supplies to the Austrian movements, whose existence they had ignored, nor could they execute subversive actions without a logistical base provided by the Resistance. All this changed when the Fritz Molden mission set the clandestine work in a new context.

The son of former deputy editor of the *Neue Freie Presse*, Dr. Ernst Molden, and of Paula von Preradovic, a noted writer and poet from an old Croatian military family, Fritz Molden joined the Resistance in March 1938 as a Free Corps student.[2] A young, impish man of nerve and determination, a dedicated idealist with independence and self-possession, Molden impressed his friends with his energetic approach. He volunteered for the Army to escape the Gestapo and had the good fortune, thanks to Major Stillfried and former Austrian intelligence chief Colonel von Lahousen, to be finally posted to Italy in 1943.[3] There he made contact with the Italian and German underground. At the end of April 1944, during his leave in Vienna, Molden received a directive from Stillfried and Major Biedermann to help form an Austrian guerrilla detachment in Lombardy, to establish liaison with the North Italian partisans, and to meet with the British Intelligence officer at the British Consulate in Lugano, Switzerland.[4] Unfortunately, the police broke into his circuit at the German 356th Infantry Division near Pescia. Warned by a fellow German noncommissioned officer,

Molden left his unit and managed to travel along various Italian underground lines to Switzerland. During a short stay in Milan, Stillfried's courier, an officer of Austrian origin, urgently repeated the April directive to him.

In Switzerland Molden agreed to help both the Swiss authorities and the staff of the Bern OSS post. He brought a mass of vital intelligence about the situation in Austria and North Italy, and within the Wehrmacht. At this point, in July 1944, the Austrian Resistance had entered the final phase of its existence, which would, for the first time, bring about a tangible result on the international scene. As the first underground courier to come out from the country, Molden made an excellent impression on his Swiss and United States contacts. Sensing the urgent need of the Swiss for continuous fresh information on the deployment of German forces near the Swiss borders, Molden concluded a written agreement with the Swiss intelligence authorities. This agreement provided substantial help for the development of an Austrian intelligence network in Italy, Austria, and the Reich, and for the establishment of a communication system with the Austrian underground. For this purpose, a special Austrian liaison office was set up in Zurich.[5]

Molden's plan to launch Austrian operations reached a high point when he won the confidence of Allen Welsh Dulles, the OSS representative in Switzerland.[6] Within weeks of his arrival, Molden worked out with his new Austrian friends, Dr. Kurt Grimm and Hans Thalberg, a plan of action that both the liaison group and the 05 central command in Vienna subsequently endorsed.

> The intensifying of the activities of the various Austrian resistance groups made it necessary to weld the more important groups into one disciplined body and to set up a steady, smoothly working line of communication with the Allies. Austrian clandestine operations could be carried out successfully provided these Allied contacts were put to good use. . . . This task cannot be achieved without material aid (supply of arms, transmitters, etc.) and increased psychological support (improvement and intensification of Allied propaganda in a form comprehensible to the Austrian population). Therefore it is indispensable to increase the . . . confidence of the Allies in the seriousness and capability of the Austrian Resistance.

"In order to achieve the above mentioned objectives," Molden proposed to take two steps:

> 1) The organization of a smoothly working intelligence service and communication line between Austria and both the German-occupied area of North Italy and our liaison group in Switzerland which has already established links with the Allied powers and has been recognized by the Swiss authorities.

2) The fastest possible unification of all known resistance groups under one central command, and the formation of a central political committee in Vienna, embracing all parties and groups actively participating in the Resistance, which would direct clandestine work. The already existing 05 would become its military branch. It has already become evident that only such a committee could convince the Allied powers to support the Austrian Resistance and eventually officially recognize it.[7]

In planning Austrian operations, Molden believed that the underground had to play an active role, and that its centralization and strengthening should precede any American-run supply operation. He agreed to return to Italy and Austria to organize his contacts as intermediaries between the OSS and the Resistance. The aim of Molden's first trip was to build a network of escape routes, courier lines, safe houses, and reception parties for Allied agents and to form a political center in Vienna to coordinate clandestine work.[8]

In August Molden set up a safe house in Milan and arranged an effective military intelligence network there. On September 6, 1944, supplied with forged military documents, and disguised in the uniform of a Wehrmacht non-commissioned officer assigned from the RSHA, Kommando Meldegebiet Munich to Meldekopf Zeno in Milan, Molden departed for Innsbruck and Vienna.[9] In Vienna he concluded arrangements with the underground securing its centralization. He also held a series of talks with his father Ernst, Major Stillfried, Major Biedermann, Becker, Heinrich Otto Spitz, and Oberleutnant Wolfgang Igler, who provided liaison to the head of the military network in Vienna, Major Carl Szokoll. The Austrian officers organized cells in various Wehrmacht units stationed in Vienna and Lower Austria.[10]

On December 12, during Molden's third journey, organizational unity was achieved under the banner of POEN, the Provisional Austrian National Committee.[11] Its members generally assumed that POEN was the nucleus of a future provisional Austrian government.[12] Working in POEN initially were the representatives of liberal, conservative, Christian Social, and Monarchist tendencies, Becker, Ernst Molden, Spitz, Stillfried, Professor Dr. Alfred Verdross, Dr. Josef Count Ezdorf, a Monarchist attorney, and Friedrich Maurig, director of the Schoeller Bank. The Socialists Dr. Schärf and Bertha Lemberger joined POEN on February 26, 1945.[13] Dr. Viktor Matejka represented the Communists. For the first time since the early years of the Republic, a united political front including the former feuding political movements was constructed.

During his journeys in September and November, Molden prepared safe houses and reception parties in Innsbruck, Salzburg, and Vienna for the Allied liaison officers to be stationed in Austria. In the winter of 1945 special OSS missions in the guerrilla zones in Carinthia near Bleiburg and in the Kematen Alm near Innsbruck began training resisters for combat duty.[14] Two special circuits in Vienna were exclusively concerned with gathering intelligence. Run by Molden's former fellow students, Frederiksen and Stummer, they provided the Allies with valuable intelligence via Innsbruck. Of special importance was the intelligence that Ms. Nam Brauer de Beaufort provided. She was an Abwehr aide in Milan and a former associate of Marogna-Redwitz and Lahousen. Brauer, who had belonged to the resistance community in Berlin from the very outset, volunteered to supply Molden with valuable Abwehr records. As a start, she gave him the Abwehr codebook when he was returning to Bern in September.[15]

Back in Bern, Dulles and his aides Gero von Gaevernitz and Gerhard van Arckel were delighted with the results of Molden's trips, which won full OSS support for the Austrian Resistance. The Allies still anticipated that Austria would form one of the last armed bastions of the Nazi defense and viewed the area as strategically important. When POEN was constituted as the political symbol of Austrian independence, Dulles officially informed Molden in January that the United States had agreed to give de facto recognition to POEN and 05 as its Austrian partners.[16] Molden was appointed the Liaison Officer of the Austrian Underground Forces at the Allied Forces Headquarters in Caserta.[17]

During his Vienna visit, Molden was requested to act carefully in his sensitive talks with the Allies. The POEN leaders asked him not to take sides in any inter-Allied squabbles. Arriving in Paris in January, Molden outlined, in his talks with the United States, French, British, and Soviet representatives, his mission's main objectives as POEN saw them:

1) To inform the French, English, American, and Russian authorities in Paris of the existence, organization, and aims of POEN in particular, and of the military situation in Austria . . . in general.
2) To propose an eventual dispatch of French, English, American, and Russian observers to POEN. Similarly, POEN would send a representative to Paris to inform the Allied powers of developments in Austria and of POEN's activities.
3) To discuss eventual material and moral aid for a fighting Austria.
4) To propose cooperation between the POEN intelligence service and the other Allied intelligence services.
5) To submit proposals on the possible creation of an Austrian Legion in France composed of Austrian exiles and possibly of Austrian prisoners of war as well.
6) To engage in propaganda activities for a free Austria (radio, pamphlets, etc.)[18]

In Paris, Molden strove to build conditions for cooperation with the four Allied powers. During his visit to the Paris Supreme Headquarters of the Allied Expeditionary Forces, a plan for launching special OSS teams into Austria was adopted.[19] Jean de Chauvel, Secretary General of the French Foreign Ministry, gave a pledge of support that encouraged Molden. On many occasions thereafter, the French fully backed the Austrian demands for increased Allied assistance.[20] Both in Paris and Caserta the Americans, in particular the OSS, were convinced that Austrian armed Resistance in Tyrol, Carinthia, and Salzkammergut where the partisans were strong would prove useful when the retreating German forces reached the Alps. The Commanding General of the United States Fifth Army responsible for military operations in Italy and Austria, Mark Clark, received the youthful Austrian resister, whose reports Dulles and his staff had so highly evaluated, at his Caserta headquarters in January.[21]

What mattered at this juncture more than individual achievements and their inspirational effect abroad was the political credibility of the 05 and POEN — they still lacked Socialist political support. The Allied Commission for Austria decided to send the exiled Austrian Socialist Dr. Eugen Lemberger, Major in the French Army, on a fact-finding mission to Vienna. Lemberger was authorized by the SPÖ groups in London, Paris, and New York to urge the Socialists and RS at home to join POEN.[22]

Disguised as German soldiers, Molden and Lemberger reached Vienna on February 23. Lemberger's intensive efforts were crowned with success. Through his mother, Bertha, a Socialist veteran, he acquired the necessary Socialist and trade union contacts and won Schärf's approval of SPÖ participation in POEN. The two emissaries briefed POEN members and discussed future military actions with Becker, Unterrainer, Biedermann, and Spitz in Stillfried's house in Vienna-Döbling on February 25. At the meeting, Igler turned over the 05 organization table with the list of the 05 groups and cells within the Wehrmacht units to the emissaries. The military command also provided the Allied Air Command with a list of military targets in Austria together with a request to stop Allied air raids of the war-weary Austrian cities, and, above all, to save the center of Vienna.[23] As for future military operations, the Americans and British favored the development of 05 assault parties to harass the rear of the retreating German Army and its communication system. Plans were elaborated for the selection of dropping zones and reception parties in the Vienna Forest for air drops of weapons, food, and other stores to equip the assault teams.[24]

Later in the night, a regular Schutzpolizei patrol ran into a special commando unit of the Viennese military police guarding the clandestine meeting. After a short exchange of fire, the Schutzpolizei withdrew. The resisters quickly dispersed, and the security forces that soon arrived to search the houses found nothing. Lemberger and Molden left the city in a military train the next morning.[25] But the Gestapo was hard on POEN's trail. On March 2 it started to round up the suspects. It picked up Becker, Stillfried, Spitz, Ernst Molden and his wife, Ezdorf, and others. POEN was wiped out.[26] The performance of the Nazi security apparatus until the collapse of the regime was superb. Through a network of busy informers and agents, it effectively monitored clandestine activities, mainly because many activists talked too much and did not cover their trails.

Back in the West, Lemberger and Molden requested on March 20 that the three Allied governments recognize POEN as the representative organ of the former political parties and of the Resistance. Lemberger rushed off to London to meet with State secretary Geoffrey Harrison and Sir William Henry Mack, the designated British High Commissioner in Austria. This time, the British Foreign Office seemed more anxious to accommodate the Austrians and assured Lemberger that it supported POEN.

The trend of military events increasingly disturbed the Resistance. It realized that the Soviets would emerge as a power strong enough to counterbalance the Western Allies. Whatever their political opinions of Communism, POEN and 05 opted for close military cooperation with the Red Army when they learned that the Soviet Union had been assigned the eastern part of the country as its occupation zone. Lemberger and Molden agreed to a POEN proposal that they seek permanent contact with the Soviet authorities. In Paris, they held several talks with General Ivan Susloparov, head of the Soviet Military Mission at the Allied Supreme Headquarters. They gave Susloparov the necessary data on the 05 plans for a military uprising in Vienna and even provided him with the code and wavelengths of Igler's radio transmitter, which linked Vienna to OSS Secret Operations Branch in Caserta. It was agreed that the Red Army would dispatch its own liaison officer to Vienna. Moscow was informed that the military underground's plan to fight the Nazis in Vienna depended on the cooperation of the Red Army. On March 30, the head of the military network, Major Szokoll, wired an urgent message via Caserta to the Soviets asking them to receive an Austrian emissary who would put forward the plans for a military uprising in Vienna, and to define for him the terms of Soviet military support so as to ensure close collaboration. Apparently, the Soviets were inclined to accept some cooperation.[27]

While the talks with the Soviets went on in Paris, Molden flew to Caserta on March 12 to convince the Commanding General of the Fifteenth United States Air Group, Charles P. Cabell, and his aides to stop the air raids on Austrian civilian quarters, hospitals, churches, and monuments and to concentrate on bombing military targets. After a somewhat heated debate, General Cabell issued an order on March 14 instructing his men to avoid civilian targets in Austria.[28]

The problems of increased assistance to the home front were more easily resolved when the OSS began to concentrate its resources on its ventures in Austria and Germany. Special OSS teams were dispatched to Austria. Scout Liaison agent Fred Mayer with his aide and a wireless operator parachuted into Tyrol in February. The Austrian-born Lieutenant Josef C. von

Franckenstein-Horneck and Karl Novacek, his wireless operator, were sent to Innsbruck as a liaison team, accompanied by Otto Molden, Fritz's elder brother.[29] These were primarily support operations to enable the underground to collect the promised drops of weapons and explosives and to establish wireless contact with the OSS. Couriers from 05 transported five transmitter sets from Switzerland to the 05 branches in Bozen, Innsbruck, Salzburg, and Vienna. As another way of passing messages, secret Allied broadcasts to Austria began, and the BBC's Austrian program and the Voice of America transmitted coded messages to the 05, announcing drops or arrivals of agents. Eventually, the message "Monika ruft Dampfschiff" was passed announcing to the underground the start of clandestine operations on the home front.[30]

The collapse of POEN made the Tyrolian 05 sections in and around Innsbruck, welded by Molden and his friend Helmut Heuberger into a network in the fall of 1944, into a new western POEN headquarters. To keep strengthening the 05, in April Otto Molden and Franckenstein pressed on from Innsbruck, with the coordination of combat groups in Ötz Valley, Kematen Alm, Paznaun Valley, and Vorarlberg,[31] and the Moldens picked up the 05 threads they had left behind in Salzburg and Linz.[32]

THE 05

The exact nature of the 05 network was complicated and even today much about the organization remains unknown.[33] According to its own reports, the umbrella alliance, headed by General Staff (GS) and politically responsible to POEN, was divided into three main sections: (1) direct action; (2) intelligence, communications, supplies; and (3) propaganda. It was run from Vienna. The regional command posts in Vienna, Linz, Salzburg, Graz, Innsbruck, and Carinthia supervised the work in the provinces. The important cells inside the Viennese police,[34] Wehrmacht,[35] Vokssturm,[36] and Reich Railways acted as independent bodies under the GS. The cells in the radio station, electrical and gas works, the Danube harbor, and other enterprises in Vienna were attached to the 05 through separate lines. The GS ran a special armed Action Group to conduct sabotage, direct actions, and some security tasks.[37] The GS controlled courier and intelligence services, radio contacts, and propaganda. The GS had received from the United States a strong wireless transmitter and expected two others. The communication lines from Vienna to Klagenfurt, Graz, Innsbruck, and Bludenz were run by railwaymen. The groups in the provinces were running smoothly and built up contacts with the deserters and escapees in the mountains in Lower Austria, Styria, Salzburg, and Tyrol. In Vienna, the painting of the 05 signs on walls carried the Resistance's message to the public.[38]

The civil and military sectors developed closer working arrangements in

November with the creation of a liaison team.[39] After the decimation of POEN, the Committee of Seven assumed command of the political organ, and Bumballa replaced Becker.[40] POEN's abrupt downfall disrupted the overlapping circles of the dangerously widespread 05, whose security two Gestapo informers, "Walter" and "Franke," compromised. During January and February ranking members were rounded up. The number of arrests ran into hundreds when some captured resisters cracked under severe pressure.[41]

On March 25 talks between the military underground and the major 05 organizers were held at Auersperg Palace in the center of Vienna, where Maasburg had settled in January.[42] Because the arrests had temporarily cut off the links to the Committee of Seven, an ad hoc military-civilian Steering Committee was set up as a substitute. It included Prelate Jakob Fried, Felix Slavik, Bernhard Scheichelbauer, General Luschinsky, and Szokoll's close aides, Hauptmann Alfred Huth and Oberleutnant Rudolf Raschke. However, in the closing weeks of the war, the deep complexities and ambiguities of the roles of the Committee, of the various other networks, and of the political parties deprived the Vienna Resistance of a strong leadership.

In many ways, the 05 movement was as much a heterogeneous coalition of sectional, party, class, and provincial interests as a focus for the still mute hopes of the Austrian patriots.[43] The release from jail of Slavik and Fried, who were soon anxious to start clandestine work, helped. The Committee had lost its contact to Schärf, who had built up the network of personal relationships on which the Socialist underground depended; Slavik and Fried relieved the political strain on the 05. As the exponent of the Revolutionary Socialists, Slavik linked the 05 with the Social Democrats,[44] and Fried pushed the concept of a unified Resistance among even the most ardent anti-Marxist Catholics.[45]

At the beginning of 1945, under the pressure of the young militants, a special Central Council of the 05 was set up as an organ of the squads of armed civilians. It consisted of the individual chiefs of the various combat units, including Eidlitz and Braunsteiner from the "Österreichischer Kampfbund," Thurn-Taxis from the "Prinz Eugen," a student, Erich Rubak, from the "Adlon," and Ralph Svetlik and Herbert Baumann from the "Kampfgruppenkommando I-Free Austria."[46] Because of the Red Army's rapid advance, the Council decided to concentrate all the available paramilitary teams in the Vienna area.

The process of coordinating underground work speeded up an agreement at the end of March between the military conspiracy in Vienna, represented by Oberleutnant Otto Scholik, and the Central Council. Unable to organize the armed insurgency, because it had too few men and scarce resources, the Council proposed to join the military section in preparing for an uprising. The military entrusted the civilian assault teams with the major task of occupying the less heavily guarded public buildings, such as the City Hall, the Parliament, the Police Presidium, and the seat of the Provincial Government, while the Army troops would occupy military and police installations.[47] At this stage in 1945, the chiefs of the combat units decided to adhere to the Committee of Seven.[48] Changing circumstances expanded the role of the paramilitary forces. After the arrests of Becker and of POEN members, the military and the combat teams regarded the 05 movement as one that they could commandeer when open warfare would break out.[49] When the plan for armed insurrection in Vienna had been adopted and the military resistance strengthened into a solid organization, the weakened civilian counterpart moved into a temporary shadow, although it had helped to assemble a wide array of clandestine forces for the final battle.[50]

THE SOCIALISTS

Thanks to Schärf, Slavik, Oskar Helmer, Paul Speiser and other prominent prewar figures representing the Revolutionary Socialist and Social Democratic connections, Socialist competition with the Christian Democrats presented no serious problem. The two main political currents espoused similar political objectives for the immediate future. Above all, the domestic Socialist leaders succeeded in casting off the revolutionary myth that had equated the struggle against National Socialism with the struggle for an All-German Socialist revolution. They were aware of political realities and realized that although the Austrian people wanted necessary reforms, they had no desire for revolutionary change.

To some extent, events themselves determined the Socialist response. Socialist policy was basically defensive, reacting to events rather than initiating them. Such a posture had a solid foundation in public opinion, which differed from that in other liberated countries. There was a sober realization of Austria's exposed international position and of the need to protect the country. However, the temptation to seize on the series of Nazi defeats as a gratifying foretaste of the victory to come developed a momentum of its own among the Socialists and drew together the RS and the SPÖ veterans.[51]

During the war the Socialist exiles in London hoped to establish links with the home front. In 1943 they availed of a British offer to parachute a team of Socialists into the country to communicate with the Socialist underground. In the fall of 1943 Stefan Wirlandner, an RS veteran, left England for Istanbul to build up a line to Austria. In the summer of 1944 his contacts fell. In September he moved with seven companions to Bari in South Italy. Three of them parachuted in to Styria and Lower Austria in December or January.[52]

The Socialist party had no countrywide clandestine organization but rather a welter of informal groupings, confined to personal friends and former Party colleagues. Underground activity had mostly been the work of a few individuals such as Schärf. Despite a certain aloofness in his bearing and a somewhat pedestrian style, Schärf emerged as one of the most respected Socialist leaders. His active involvement in the underground and the experience in parliamentary tactics that he had gained in the Republic served him well in negotiating political understandings. More than any other Socialist, he symbolized caution, decency, and tenacity. In no way a typical party boss, Schärf was thorough, methodical, and orderly to a fault. Through the sympathy and quiet inspiration that he had offered the Resistance, he emerged in 1945 as the recognized leader of the reorganized SPÖ. He was committed to a pragmatic view of politics and was closer than some of his colleagues to the dynamics of Austrian society and to the social and economic realignments that resulted from the war.

Because they did not engage in much clandestine work, there were no disasters among the Socialists. Caution tempered the revolutionary impetus, and doctrinal impulsiveness gave way to more immediate security concerns. At the end, there was general agreement to offer a Socialist support to POEN and 05. The international development completed the Party's changed orientation from a Greater-German to an Austrian framework. Their major effort had been to design a postwar organizational Party structure and to maintain a nucleus of Party veterans in Vienna and provincial capitals ready to emerge at the appropriate moment to take over the administrative machinery of the new Republic. Ultimately, old-line regulars, whom the ideological excitement of the liberation struggle left largely untouched, formed the hard core of the postwar SPÖ cadres.[53] The lack of sympathy between the Resistance leadership and the old Party traditionalists created the postwar Socialist strategy, personified by Schärf, based on the belief that the basic stability of national politics depended on the coalition of two large disciplined parties committed to parliamentary democracy.

THE ALLIES AND THEIR MISSIONS

The Soviet advances on the Eastern battle fronts in the winter of 1942-43 forced the Kremlin to reexamine its strategy. The Soviet chieftains worked out their policy in terms of national roads to Socialism. They visualized a concerted effort of the native Communist parties to liberate the Nazi-occupied countries. As the most active elements, the parties would then win popular confidence and become the dominant political force in their countries. To back up its objectives, Moscow began to establish regular communication lines with the domestic Communist networks by parachuting Party officials and Soviet agents behind the front lines. In February and

March 1943 the Moscow center dropped a few small parties, led by reliable Austrian and Czech Party officials supplied with radio transmitters, in Poland and Burgenland.[54] They carried Moscow directives for the organization of armed struggle to the native cadres in Vienna and in the Reich Protectorate of Bohemia and Moravia.

The Reich security organs methodically followed the intensified Soviet activity in Austria.[55] Since 1942 the Vienna Gestapo had captured agents play back their radios to Moscow and London.[56] The Gestapo agent Franke was responsible for the downfall of the Hans Strohmer group, an organization of some seventy Socialists. Radio contact with London was the group's undoing. Franke impersonated a British agent resident in Vienna and had his identity checked by a password broadcast on the BBC Austrian program. On March 16, 1945, the organizers were captured and twelve were murdered.[57]

The Gestapo's radio ploy exposed many brave men and women and sent them to their deaths. In 1943 the Gestapo ran some of the important Soviet and Communist lines. It had discovered the dropping zone and the time of the drop of Hermann Köhler, a senior KP official, and his radio operator Emilie Boretsky even before Köhler jumped in Burgenland at the beginning of February 1943.[58] The two operators were trailed from their jump up to their capture at the end of March. Köhler and some of his associated endured dreadful torture before being slain in Mauthausen KZ in 1945.[59] In another development Josef Angermann and Georg Kennerknecht were picked up soon after their arrival. They had been dropped in German uniforms in Poland on May 10. On June 11, through an informer, the Gestapo discovered their presence in Vienna and seized Angermann five days later.[60] Gregor Kersche had a special assignment to coordinate the mostly self-contained cells in Vienna. With his capture, the last Moscow-directed undertaking collapsed. As a viable future alternative, the Moscow CC shifted its attention to the preparations for guerrilla insurgency in Carinthia and Styria.

The November 1943 Declaration of the Allied governments to reconstruct a free and independent Austria reflected the increased strategic importance of the Austrian area in the course of the war. After the Declaration a new stage in the underground struggle commenced.[61] American, British, and French intelligence operators were parachuted blind into the open country to work in Vienna and southern Austria.[62] They were provided with addresses of safe houses and contacts and kept in wireless contact with London. The main purposes of their dangerous assignments were to locate the sites for air raids and to guide the Allied aircraft with special radar sets, called Eureka, to their targets in the industrial areas around Vienna, Wiener Neustadt, and Linz.

Among the first volunteers for this hazardous duty were Josef Sasso and Karl Brezina, who jumped near Lake Neusiedler in February 1944. Sasso was born near Wiener Neustadt. As a Communist Youth follower, he was sentenced to three years' imprisonment in 1939 and after release in 1942 was drafted in the special Wehrmacht 999 unit for politically unreliable elements. In May 1943, he was captured by the Americans in North Africa. Sasso volunteered for special services behind enemy lines, selecting military objects and guiding incoming aircraft on raids against targets in Wiener Neustadt. He was apprehended on April 4 after shooting a Gestapo agent to death.[63] The capture of Sasso and Brezina led the Gestapo to a larger group headed by N. Dworschak (a cover name), who was dropped in June 1944 and had, with his circuit, directed the air raids against Vienna in the second half of 1944. He was caught on December 22. His circuit alone transmitted over 150 messages to England, located targets, and guided the aircraft to the areas around Vienna, Linz, Prague, and Banská Bystrica in Slovakia.[64]

A wide-ranging intelligence circuit was run by Widmayer, an old-time Socialist labor official and journalist who had established lines to Turkey, Switzerland, and Tito-occupied Yugoslavia. He ran into difficulties because of a double agent. The Gestapo arrested him on September 23, 1944.[65] As the Red Army advanced, Soviet military reconnaissance parties of five to six soldiers, dropped behind the swiftly moving battle lines and maintaining radio contact with field bases, dominated the last phase of the special parachute operations in eastern Austria.[66]

NOTES

1. "Gedächtnissprotokoll Nr.6," Dr. Franz Sobek, OM.

2. See above pp. 45.

3. I follow Fritz Molden, *Fepolinski;* "Bericht," Fritz Molden, OM.

4. Molden, *Fepolinski,* pp. 218-19, 236. Molden also kept in touch with the Maier-Messner group. Also see Brown, *The Secret War,* p. 325-26.

5. Molden, *Fepolinski,* pp. 248-52; O. Molden, *Der Ruf,* pp. 173 ff. Relations with the Swiss remained close until the end of the war. Among the members of the office were the Austrian exiles Hans Thalberg, Dr. Kurt Grimm, Dr. Emanuel Treu, Prince Johannes Schwarzenberg, former Socialist member of Parliament Anton Linder, and Ludwig Klein. Grimm took part in meetings with the OSS in Bern. Molden, *Fepolinski,* p. 271. The Austrian railwaymen were Klein's and Linder's contacts with Austria. O. Molden, *Der Ruf,* pp. 179-80. Toward the end of 1944, Gary van Arckel from OSS Bern discovered an RS cell in Zurich. Its contact in Austria, a track inspector for railway lines in western Austria, provided military intelligence on the movements of German troops and armaments along Austria main lines. The track inspector passed his reports to the RS confidant at Buchs, the Swiss border station. The information was rushed to the U.S. Fifteenth Air Group in Italy, whose bombers then attacked the targets. Persico, *Piercing,* pp. 340-41.

6. Dulles's aide Gero von Schulze-Gaevernitz served as the OSS liaison man to Molden. After the war, Molden became Dulles's son-in-law.

7. Molden, *Fepolinski,* pp. 261-62; "Bericht," Fritz Molden, OM.

8. In the summer of 1944 clandestine passage into Austria was only feasible via North Italy and South Tyrol. Stringent control of the Swiss-Austrian frontier shut Austria off from Switzerland. Molden established an escape and courier line that ran from Lugano in the Swiss Canton of Ticino across the frontier to Lake Como and on to Milan. The journey from Zurich

to Milan usually took one day. From Milan he took the German military train to Innsbruck and then continued on to Vienna, Munich, or Berlin. The line remained the only functioning escape route to Switzerland from the German-occupied areas of Central and Eastern Europe up to the end of the hostilities. Not only Austrian agents but also Vatican, French, and OSS couriers used it. Still another, although very risky and difficult, route for resourceful couriers ran across the mountains from Liechtenstein into Vorarlberg in Austria. This auxiliary line became important in the final months of the war when the Brenner Pass was closed. F. Molden, *Fepolinski,* pp. 262-64, 291, 351.

9. After September 1944 Molden went to Innsbruck twelve times and to Vienna seven times. Ibid., p. 290.

10. For more information on military resistance, see below. The owner of a moving company, and a well-known activist during the Schuschnigg regime, Spitz formed a wide intelligence network.

11. Ibid., pp. 285 ff; 298 ff. Fritz and Otto Molden saw no real difference between the POEN serving as the political center for the Allies and the Committee of Seven, coordinating the various groups at home. Interviews with Fritz and Otto Molden.

Molden contacted many groups, among them the 05 organizations of Becker and Stillfried, the Maier-Messner circuit, a fairly effective network of former Schuschnigg adherents headed by Spitz, and Dr. Karl Rudolf's cells. The groups overlapped socially. In turn, Ernst Molden started a small loose circle of his friends, called "Bereitschaft" ("Readiness"). Ernst Molden received encouragement from the noted businessmen Franz Mayer-Gunthof and Manfred Mautner-Markhof, and from Cornides, the director of the Oldenbourg Publishing Company in Munich. "Bericht Dr. Ernst Molden," OM, No 29, III.

12. The U.S. Department of State viewed with sympathy the efforts of the Austrian Resistance:

> Resistance movements in Austria have apparently been increasing in size and importance during recent weeks, and there is accumulating evidence that this resistance is becoming organized under a Provisional Austrian National Committee, generally referred to as POEN. . . . Its supporters appear to include practically all shades of Austrian political groupings. . . . A statement of the objectives of POEN, given to the American Embassy in Paris by its emissary, states emphatically that it is not seeking to establish itself as a government of Austria, but merely to organize resistance to the Germans.

The Department of State to the British Embassy. Memorandum. April 20, 1945. [USA]. *Foreign Relations of the United States. Diplomatic Papers.* Vol. 3, Washington, D.C., 1968, 563-64. In the report of its Research and Analysis Branch, *The Current Intelligence Study No. 9,* 13 April 1945, the OSS commended the activities of POEN, considering it likely that POEN "will serve as an important nucleus for the revival of political life in the Austrian state." DÖW 12667. See also NA, Record Group 226, Records of the OSS.

13. F. Molden, *Fepolinski,* pp. 298-99; 342-43; Hans Thalberg, "Ernst Lemberger," *Die Zukunft,* nos. 1-2 (January 1975): 6-7. See below pp. 214-15.

14. F. Molden, *Fepolinski,* pp. 292 ff, 316 ff.

15. Ibid., pp. 289-90.

16. In March 1945, "with the resistance movement more and more in evidence," the OSS received reports from Vienna that the Austrian population "has been turning more and more anti-Nazi." The radiotelephone report from the OSS Bern representative, which the OSS Director William J. Donovan gave to President Franklin D. Roosevelt on March 7, 1945, Collection PSF OSS, Container No. 171, folder 1, Franklin D. Roosevelt Library, Hyde Park. As of early April 1945, the OSS viewed POEN as

> a broad leadership coalition . . . charged with the central direction and coordination of underground activities, both political and activist. . . . POEN is said to be

regarded by its affiliated groups as a temporary body with no official program and with no pretensions to post-war power in Austria. It gives itself no publicity in Austria and is apparently unknown to the rank and file of the underground. POEN's activist affiliated 05, however, is widely publicized in order to promote resistance among passive elements of the population. . . . Though POEN apparently has no formal platform, the political groups which it unites appear to have four basic and common aims: (1) the reestablishment of Austria on the basis of the 1920 democratic constitution, (2) the nationalization of key industries, transportation, banking, and insurance, (3) the punishment of war criminals by the Austrian resistance, and (4) the expulsion of all Germans from Austria.

OSS, Research and Analysis, *Current Intelligence Study No. 9,* 13 April 1945, DÖW 12667.

17. Molden, *Fepolinski,* pp. 305 ff. Molden was granted the rank of Lieutenant-Colonel in the United States Army. Dulles briefed him on the Allied postwar plans for the formation of occupation zones in Austria. POEN was thus well informed of the Allied planning for the country.

18. Fritz Molden, "Bericht I, Mappe I," OM.

19. According to F. Molden, the domestic underground was amply provided with funds supplied by former wealthy Nazi sympathizers. In contrast, the Swiss group lived on a very tight budget, having turned down the United States offer of subsidies. Molden, *Fepolinski,* pp. 328-31. This situation differed sharply with the conditions in France, where the Resistance was generously funded by General Charles de Gaulle from London.

20. Ibid., pp. 314-16; O. Molden, *Der Ruf,* pp. 183 ff. The British were skeptical of the work of the Austrian underground. Soviet officials were reserved.

21. Molden, *Fepolinski,* pp. 321 ff.

22. Ibid., pp. 333 ff; O. Molden, *Der Ruf,* pp. 187-88; "Bericht Dr. Ernst Molden," OM, Nr. 29, III; "Bericht Major Stillfried," OM, Nr. 16, II; "Bericht des Generalstabs 05. Organisation und Aufbau von 05," March 3, 1945, OM, X/D6; interviews with Dr. Ernst Lemberger, Karl Czernetz, and Karl Hartl.

23. Molden, *Fepolinski,* pp. 344 ff. The 05 military command, represented by Igler, communicated with Caserta through an OSS-supplied transmitter. The OSS was thus kept informed of the military resistance plans to liberate Vienna, and transmitted to the Soviets the 05 request to set up direct contact with the approaching Third Ukrainian Front. Ibid., pp. 354-55.

24. In February Stillfried made contact with British Intelligence. "Bericht, Major Stillfried," OM.

25. Lemberger arranged for a transmitter to be left in Salzburg. In both Salzburg and Innsbruck he sought Socialist support for the 05 network. Interview with Dr. Lemberger.

26. The SS murdered Spitz on April 10; the others survived. O. Molden, *Der Ruf,* pp. 249-50.

27. Molden, *Fepolinski,* pp. 352-55; O. Molden, *Der Ruf,* pp. 193-97.

28. Molden, *Fepolinski,* p. 356; O. Molden, *Der Ruf,* pp. 199-200; William J. Donovan, OSS Director to President F. D. Roosevelt, March 7, 1945, OSS Report, PSF OSS, Cont. 171, Franklin D. Roosevelt Library, Hyde Park, N.Y.

29. Molden, *Fepolinski,* pp. 292 ff., 316 ff., 364 ff; Persico, *Piercing,* passim; O. Molden, *Der Ruf,* pp. 264 ff.

30. O. Molden, *Der Ruf,* pp. 198-99; F. Molden, *Fepolinski,* p. 300.

31. Molden, *Fepolinski,* pp. 288, 364, 365; O. Molden, *Der Ruf,* pp. 269 ff.

32. In April, Otto Molden worked the Salzburg area, where he formed a nucleus of a provincial National Committee. O. Molden, *Der Ruf,* pp. 276-80.

33. I follow Lemberger and Molden's joint report prepared in Zurich on March 3 on the basis of reports that POEN members submitted to them at their February 26 meeting in Vienna. The OSS adopted the main points of the report in its secret statement of 13 April 1945, DÖW 12667. The somewhat inflated data have to be adjusted by the use of other reports and

recollections. "Organisation und Aufbau von 05," OM, X/D6; "Bericht Dr. Zimmer-Lehmann," March 17, 1949, OM, No. 4; "Report of the activity of the Austrian Resistance Movement later united in the '05'," OM, No. 62; and its German version Nr. 51, "Die österreichische Widerstandsbewegung," OM, "Bericht 38/IV"; "Bericht über die politische Lage in Oesterreich Ende Feber 1945," OM, X/D14.

34. The Viennese police with a force of 7,000 men was strengthened by 5,000 Ukrainian auxiliaries as reserve police troops. 05 won over those senior police officers who were neither Germans nor SS.

35. On the military side, in Vienna, underground cells worked in the staffs of the Wehrkreiskommando (WK) XVII, the Wehrmachtstadtkommandantur, the Prisoners of War Command WK XVII, the WK XVII Administration, the Streifendienst WK XVII, and the Armament Inspection. Circles existed in a number of units stationed in and near the City. Report of March 3, 1945, OM.

36. Activists from 05 worked at the Viennese command center of the Volkssturm (People's Militia) and infiltrated many of its units. Ibid.

37. The report rather optimistically estimated the 05 strength at 18,000 to 20,000 members and put the number of followers in the factories at some 40,000 to 50,000 men. The Action Group allegedly consisted of some 1,500 men. In comparison with the estimates in other countries, these figures do not seem to be overly inflated since the availability of arms and the opportunity to enlist might have enabled a group of 100 or 1,000 people to suddenly grow to a strength of over 1,000 or 10,000 respectively. Such estimates have been made for the French and Czechoslovak Resistance.

38. A sign may still be seen at the main gate of St. Stephen's Cathedral. See also Becker, *Freiheitskampf*, p. 20. Cells from 05 worked in Krems, St. Pölten, Wiener Neustadt, and Salzburg, and action teams in Graz, Zell am See, and Innsbruck. Outside Vienna, military cells developed in the Dolmetscherkompanie, Studentenkompanie, and Panzerjäger Ersatz-und Ausbildungsabteilung 137 in Innsbruck, and in the Landesschützenbataillon and Funkstelle at Schlossberg in Graz. Report, March 3, 1945, OM.

39. The team consisted of Maasburg, Zimmer-Lehmann, Thurn-Taxis, and Dr. Willfried Gredler. "Bericht Dr. Zimmer-Lehmann," OM; letter from Dr. Gredler, former Austrian Envoy to Bonn, to Professor H. Steiner, February 18, 1976, DÖW 11409.

40. O. Molden, *Der Ruf*, pp. 206 ff, 247-49. Maasburg, who went into hiding in Vienna, became the liaison man between the military and the 05. On April 9 he was appointed Secretary General of the Committee of Seven.

41. Group Strohmer, the organization "P" in the City Military Command, among others, was destroyed. Becker, *Freiheitskampf*, pp. 19-20. At the end of January 1945 a Croatian Lieutenant from the Stockerau Training Brigade was picked up by the Gestapo and in the course of his brutal interrogation he gave away the name of Fritz Molden as one of his contacts. This brought his captors to Molden's parents. Molden, *Fepolinski*, pp. 339-41.

42. With scores of couriers and organizers visiting the Palace, a few unexpected visitors traveling along the 05 line could always be expected. One day a "blind" man with dark glasses, a stick, and a yellow armband knocked at the gate. After some introductory talk, he removed his glasses and introduced himself to Maasburg as a Red Army officer dropped behind the front lines. Mitja Gutov was in charge of the Soviet prisoners of war and forced labor draftees in and round Vienna and had been fed into the line by Mathilde Hrdlicka, a Communist 05 member. Kudrnofsky, *Vom Dritten Reich*, p. 57; O. Molden, *Der Ruf*, p. 247; DÖW 7936; OM, IX; "Bericht," J. Eidlitz, OM.

43. "Bericht Prinz Thurn-Taxis," OM, No. 9, I; Molden, *Der Ruf*, pp. 223, 247-49; Georg Fraser, "Memorandum," DÖW 7936; "Die österreichische Widerstandsbewegung," OM, 38/IV.

44. Adolf Schärf, *April 1945 in Wien* (Vienna, 1948), pp. 71-72; Stadler, *Österreich*, p. 376; DÖW 12504. Some former RS officials operated clandestinely.

45. Schärf, *April 1945*, passim.

46. "Adlon" and the "Kampfgruppenkommando I-Free Austria," each of which had about thirty men, had been activated out of the remnants of older groups at the beginning of 1945. In particular, the "Kampfgruppenkommando I" was assigned to guard the Central Council meetings. Its members had established a link to 05 in 1944. Securely organized, it became one of the busiest groupings within the 05 network. Many members used the Volkssturm identity cards and wore special Volkssturm arm bands so as to move more freely throughout Vienna. OM, Nos. 46, 69; O. Molden, *Der Ruf*, p. 245.

47. Molden, *Der Ruf*, pp. 223-24.

48. OM, 38/IV; O. Molden, *Der Ruf*, pp. 244-45; "Bericht Hans Eidlitz," OM, No. 49, V; OM, Nos. 46, 69, I.

49. The name "05" came to be generally applied to a variety of clandestine groups and services in 1944-45, and has remained to this day, loosely used, the name for the active non-Communist Resistance network in the closing years of the war. The BBC broadcasts in March 1945 spread its reputation throughout the country.

50. Maasburg estimated the number of widely scattered organizations in Vienna at over 200, but a great many were small cells with few followers. Such extreme fragmentation and proliferation naturally generated the formation of a large umbrella organization. Kudrnofsky, *Vom Dritten Reich*, p. 58.

51. The Socialist Party of Austria, combining Revolutionary Socialists and Social Democrats, was reconstituted on April 14, 1945. Adolf Schärf, *Österreichs Erneuerung*, pp. 25-26.

52. Oskar Pollak in London was made responsible for the few Party communications with the home country. Pollak and Karl Czernetz dispatched a courier on a Swiss passport to Austria as early as 1941-42. Interviews with Dr. Stefan Wirlandner, Walter Hacker, Karl Czernetz.

53. Interviews with Dr. Bruno Pittermann and Dr. Johann Dostal; Bruno Pittermann, "Österreichs Befreiung und Wiederaufbau," *Zeitgeschichte* 2 (April 1975): 175; Stadler, *Österreich*, p. 376; Schärf, *April 1945*, p. 10; O. Molden, *Der Ruf*, pp. 138, 209.

F. Molden complained in his report written after the war, that, "it proved to be almost impossible to win any Socialists over into the Austrian resistance movement because frequently one could not find any of them in western Austria prior to the liberation of Vienna." OM, "Bericht 1/I."

54. Ústav marxismu-leninismu, *Komunistická Internacionála*, pp. 500 ff; Rudolf Vetiška, *Skok do tmy* (Prague, 1966); Radomir Luza, "The Communist Party of Czechoslovakia and the Czech Resistance, 1939-1945," *Slavic Review* 28 (December 1969); 571; "Lage-und Wahrnehnumgsbericht," GSAW Wien, June 1, 1943, BA R 22/3388.

55. GSAW, June 1, 1943, BA R 22/3388. By a strange coincidence, the Gestapo penetration of the KSČ was as deep as that of the KPÖ. It so devastated both parties in 1941-43 that they had ceased to exist as organized movements by the late summer of 1943.

56. The head of the Vienna Gestapo Section for Enemy Parachutists and Sabotage, Johann Sanitzer, was responsible for the "Funkspiele" (radio games). Sanitzer reported in 1949 that the Vienna Gestapo had worked twenty-four such operations and had captured over 100 Soviet and Western agents and over 500 of their accomplices. Allegedly 102 agents worked for the Gestapo. The wireless games began in 1942 when the first Allied agents were dropped to transmit weather forcasts. "Strafverfahren des Volksgerichtes Wien," 1949, DÖW 8912/1-b; Leopold Banny, "Ihre Namen sind verweht . . . Österreicher bei Geheimunternehmen in ihrer Heimat während des 2. Weltkrieges, 1938-1944." Manuscript, 1981. DÖW. See also Persico, *Piercing the Reich*, pp. 174 ff.

57. OM, XIX, No. 21. From 1943 the Strohmer network supplied industrial intelligence via Switzerland to the USA and provided forged Wehrmacht identity papers to deserters and other opponents of the regime. *Rot-weiss-rot-Buch*, p. 157; Romanik, *Der Anteil*, p. 23.

58. Interview with Berta Lauscher; Genner, *Mein Vater*, pp. 177-78. Köhler had been in charge of the KPÖ up to 1935. According to Sanitzer, Köhler's main assignment was to

activate the Soviet intelligence ring, which had been lying low in Austria since the 1920s. DÖW 8912 a, b; 15468.

59. Interview with B. Lauscher; DÖW, ed., *Widerstand Wien,* 2: 456 ff; Banny, "Ihre Namen," pp. 211 ff.

60. "Tagesberichte, Gestapo Wien," DÖW 5743c. Caught in 1942, Börner was the first Soviet agent forced to undertake the radio-game with Moscow. For the list of sixty-eight Soviet agents and the description of their radio-games with Moscow, see Banny, "Ihre Namen," passim. Some of the Soviet agents were dropped by the British. For Angermann, see above and DÖW 15468.

61. For the American infiltration of Austria by some 200 OSS operators in 1944-45, see Persico, *Piercing,* passim. For other supply, infiltration, and leaflet missions in Austria, see also Military Affairs/Aerospace Historian Instant Publishing Series. "Special Operations: AAF Aid European Resistance Movements 1943-1945." Manhattan, Kansas, [n.d.] pp. 106, 189, 204, 230. The first operation sorties to Austria was flown in June 1944. The main effort came in March 1945 with nineteen special sorties from South Italy. Ibid., p. 106.

62. DÖW 8912 a-b; Smith, *OSS, The Secret History,* pp. 104, 161; DÖW 2756, 16623.

63. DÖW 8912 a-b. After ten months of severe interrogation, Sasso was transported to a concentration camp. The Gestapo changed his name on the transport list to Josef Mayer for security reasons, and next to the name inserted the notorious red letters RU (return not desired). During the journey, American airplanes damaged the train. When the list was check-ed in Linz, Sasso reported his true name, stating that he had been arrested for a minor offense. The Gestapo found the error after some time but, in the meantime, a Czech typist in the concentration camp exchanged Sasso's card with its fatal initials for another one. Sasso returned alive. Flanner, *Widerstand,* pp. 225-30.

64. DÖW 8912 a-b.

65. Ibid.; Stadler, *Österreich,* pp. 72, 375-76. For Widmayer, see also p. 196; DÖW 16511.

66. DÖW 8912 a-b.

20

The Military Resistance
and the Liberation of Vienna

For the few soldiers whose primary loyalty was to Austria, clandestine action remained the natural option. To defy Hitler, however, they had to overcome moral issues that civilians did not have to face. Contrary to the tradition of disciplined military service, they had to ignore their military oath to the Führer and disregard the time-honored principle of keeping out of politics. The National Socialist refusal to allow purely Austrian units further restricted the possibilities for clandestine work in the military sector. By the end of 1943, the military realized the great disadvantages of the traditional conspiratorial methods. They decided that they would have to mount a major military challenge to the regime from within and not from outside the existing military power structure—a lesson the planners of the July 20, 1944 coup applied.

Deeply concerned that the country might soon be engulfed in battle, the military underground grew in strength in Vienna. By 1944 military-backed clandestine work began to be fueled from the lower military echelons. Bruno Schmitz, a noncommissioned officer, assembled a cell within the Military Police Detachment of Greater Vienna. In 1944 this fairly effective group concentrated on minor sabotage on military trains passing Vienna. "Such operations included misassembling trains, shunting priority traffic on dead-end or damaged tracks, and losing shipments." Schmitz did attain some of his objectives:

> Arson at a large grain elevator in Vienna Second District; blowing up of an ammunition dump in Enzersdorf near Vienna; . . . damage to an airplane factory at Wiener Neudorf, damage to Borgward and Tarbuk automobile workshops; sabotage of Vienna power system four times in June 1944 alone; blowing up of Ebenfurth ammunition factory.[1]

Although Schmitz was apprehended in the fall of 1944, clandestine work within various army units continued unabated. The deliberately lax attitude of the Viennese military police aided the desertion of Austrian soldiers. Administrative sabotage, such as issuing wrong instructions to soldiers returning to the front, was rampant. Similarly, many physicians helped Austrian recruits evade military duties.[2]

Among the active officers whose conscience could not accept the Nazi onslaught on the Austrian identity, military tradition, rule of law, and values of decency Carl Szokoll, Major in the General Staff, stood out conspicuously. A professional soldier, determined, ambitious, and highly intelligent, Szokoll was drawn to clandestine work in Vienna in 1942 in his key function as head of the Organization Section (Ib/Org.) in the Military District XVII (Wehrkreis) Headquarters.[3] He was responsible for the formation of new reserve units, destined for frontline service.[4] Along with Colonel Marogna-Redwitz, Szokoll was apparently the only officer in Vienna whom the military conspirators in Berlin under Colonel Claus Schenk Count von Stauffenberg trusted enough to contact directly. Long before July 20, Szokoll was readying troops for the mobilization order code-named "Valkyrie" for an outbreak of internal disorders. When the order finally arrived in Vienna after the attempt on Hitler's life on July 20, 1944, the troops occupied military installations and railroad stations and arrested senior NSDAP, SS, and police officials.[5] When the revolt was crushed in Berlin, hundreds of former public figures from Austria were rounded up as hostages on the basis of special lists that the Gestapo had prepared well in advance.[6]

Both the Austrian Resistance and the civilian population were excluded from involvement in the July events. The Gestapo never learned of Szokoll's involvement. After the Putsch, he joined the front ranks of the Resistance. His clandestine activity was motivated by the lesson he learned from the July 20 disaster that only an armed uprising could assure an orderly transition to an Austrian administration toward the end of the war. He considered the military forces as the backbone of the uprising. He planned on assuming power in Vienna, when the proper moment arrived, "through the ostensibly legal use of the military forces" which would conceal the true objective of the clandestine action.[7] Subsequently, the unified Resistance, who would provide political leadership and most of the paramilitary combat units, would continue the insurrection and seize political power. But Szokoll also realized that the collapse of the July 20 coup and the Allied invasion of France made insurrection in Austria contingent on outside help: the call for uprising and the subsequent insurgent actions had to be carefully planned and coordinated with the Allied troops.[8]

Szokoll's operations expanded in the fall of 1944 when, as head of a Special Branch in Vienna, directly subordinated to the Reserve Army Command in Berlin, he extended his authority to the Protectorate of Bohemia and Moravia, Slovakia, and sections of Hungary and Yugoslavia.[9] Szokoll concentrated on organizing battalion-size units consisting largely of Austrians, on assigning Austrian military personnel to influential positions, and on collecting arms, ammunition, and gasoline.[10] He formed a small staff of dedicated anti-Nazi Austrian officers and fully threw himself into organizing a clandestine structure within the military forces. Through his liaison officer Oberleutnant Igler, Szokoll was linked to Major Stillfried and Becker. In September 1944 Igler met Fritz Molden in Stillfried's apartment to discuss expanding the military clandestine organization to other Wehrmacht units. Encouraged both by Molden's important new line to the United States, and by the deteriorating military situation in the rapidly shrinking Greater-German Reich, the military and civilian sectors of the Viennese Resistance moved toward more effective cooperation of their activities. One concrete product of the greater cooperation was the formation of the Committee of Seven in November.[11] Igler and Szokoll aides — Oberleutnant Scholik, Raschke, and Hauptmann Huth, set up a small liaison team to 05.[12]

At lower echelons, the Wehrmacht still largely managed its own affairs, despite the recent presence of the so-called National Socialist political officers in its ranks. Generally it was strongly rooted in a German reality, and its ideas reflected the changes then occurring in the public mood. Its recruits could remain politically aloof without incurring their superiors' wrath. The Wehrmacht's political insulation and its spirit of soldierly camaraderie amounted, practically, to toleration of a variety of opinions within the military services and thus facilitated clandestine work. The main focus of the Szokoll-run underground was the penetration of the Reserve Army units. In the fall of 1944, Igler, Scholik, and Szokoll's other aides were building a secret military task force in and around Vienna. Soon, a genuine military organization emerged, with contacts to individuals or cells in 80 percent of the military units stationed in the Vienna area.[13] Not infrequently, some cells had already had past experience of underground activity.

Much of the military's early effort involved establishing nuclei around individual officers. At the Vienna Military District Headquarters, Feldwebel Franz Studeny had created a nucleus in 1939. In 1943, Szokoll discovered the cell that consisted of Austrian soldiers and noncommissioned officers whom Studeny had saved from front-line duties by assigning them to posts in the military administration.[14] Another important nucleus operated, even before the July coup, under Major Otto Schick in the Landesschützen Bataillon 866. Schick helped some of his men seek closer ties with the underground.[15] In early 1945, as commanding officer of the eastern sector of Vienna's defense line, Schick devised a scheme for cooperating with the approaching Soviet troops; he would withdraw his men, leaving the flank of the German front open. In mid-March he was apprehended. His battalion abandoned its sector near Schwechat and disbanded on April 6, allowing the Russians to advance without resistance.[16]

An exceptionally important organization had been working close to Szokoll in the 1,600-man Vienna military police. Its head was Major Biedermann who for years stood at the center of the conspiracy. The clandestine task force involved mostly Reserve Army units. One main combat unit was that in the Second Reserve and Training Battalion of the Viennese Regiment 134, "Hoch-und Deutschmeister," under Lieutenant-Colonel Franz Hofer; another was that in the Croatian Reserve and Training Brigade based in Stockerau where Hauptmann Josef Rothmayer and Oberleutnant Walter Kraus organizd two squads of carefully selected soldiers.[17] Hofer started to work with Hauptmann Huth from Szokoll's staff in 1943. Kraus met Igler in the fall of 1944 when Kraus began organizing an Austro-Croatian artillery unit in the Stockerau Brigade. In July 1944 Hofer was transferred to command the Reserve- and Training Regiment in Stockerau. Studeny brought Rothmayer to the Regiment in September to accelerate the formation of a clandestine striking force.[18]

In February 1945 Szokoll conveyed his plans for the long-awaited uprising to Hofer, whom he instructed to activate the military combat teams, which were to play the decisive role.[19] Numerous other officers accepted the authority of Szokoll's command. Their cells were active in the Motorcycle Unit (Feldwebel Gruza), the Bicycle Platoon (Holper), the City Military Command (Major Bosina), the Communication Troops Command (Lieutenants Herbert Nossek and Weninger), the Press Section (Hauptmann Lachmaier), Reserve Unit "Reiter 11" in the Rennweg Barracks (Oberleutnant Fritz Grohs), and the 177th Reserve Infantry Division (Hauptmann Sedelmeier and noncommissioned officer Moser).[20] The group called the "Austrian National Committee" operated in the Air Force District Command XVII, providing fake personal and travel documents to Austrian deserters and, within its own jurisdiction, replaced the Reich German staff with Austrian personnel. A former Socialist, a noncommissioned officer B., worked in Section IIb dealing with personnel affairs. Using only a small nucleus, he succeeded in keeping many Austrian soldiers on the home front.[21]

In time, the military expanded their contacts as far as Upper Austria. Oberleutnant Janauschek, whose transfer from Brno to Amstetten in December 1944 Szokoll arranged, organized the liaison to the Artillery-Reserve- and Training Unit 109.[22] Commanded by an Austrian, Hauptmann Viktor Estermann, a cell of fourteen helped prevent 150 men from going to the front and, by falsifying reports, helped store weapons, gasoline, ammunition, trucks, and horses. The resisters were eager to establish links to other Wehrmacht units in the Upper Austrian towns of Enns, Steyr, and Wels and to the civilian underground in and around Amstetten, Enns, Steyr, Hollenstein, and Lunz. In January a section of the Unit moved to the village of Hollenstein in the rugged Ybbs Valley to create a secure defense base which the Unit would eventually hold. On May 4, having learned of the arrest of some civilian supporters, the Unit retreated to the prepared defense positions in the Lower Austrian Alpine area of Hollenstein-Weyer-St. Georgen, closing the road from Göstling to Weyer and stopping the westward retreat of the Wehrmacht columns. The Unit, named the Second Austrian Liberation Brigade, fought a reinforced SS-regiment for several days. Pursued by overwhelming German forces, the men successfully extricated themselves and dispersed in the mountains.

The military underground struggled against heavy odds, finding it difficult to replenish its ranks and to reestablish contacts each time sudden transfer of its members to the front or their removal to other units interrupted. Its structure, which Szokoll devised, reflected its nature and objectives. Whereas the civilian resistance was organized into small, scattered groups that could be easily re-formed, Szokoll infiltrated the Wehrmacht units with a few carefully chosen officers in positions of command, thus deploying his clandestine network throughout the German war machine.[23] As Otto Molden put it,

> While Stauffenberg had nominated field marshalls, generals, and senior staff officers as liaison men to the Army Groups and Army Corps, and the entire German-occupied Europe had become his operational Base, Szokoll's associates were Colonels, Majors, and Captains in the brigades, regiments and battalions in Army District XVII and in Hungary and Czechoslovakia.[24]

THE UPRISING IN VIENNA

The retreat of the German armies roused many Austrians from their passivity and encouraged those who had been calling for resistance. The impending Nazi defeat awoke a spirit of open commitment to Austrian independence among some Austrians, making the dream of national insurrection possible. The civilian sector of the underground began to coordinate its efforts, and it endorsed the idea of an armed uprising. There was a growing realization that the Red Army was much more likely to liberate the city than were the Western Allies. The provinces would be liberated at different moments, usually determined by the arrival of Allied troops.[25] The knowledge that the Allies intended to divide the country into three or four occupation zones rendered unrealistic the concept of an All-Austrian Resistance center. The Resistance was thus geographically, militarily, and politically divided into several segments. Austria's future seemed gloomy indeed, as the final days of the occupation approached without central political leadership abroad or at home.

Szokoll and his aides seemed confident that they could successfully carry out the uprising in Vienna. The rapid advance of the Soviet southern front and the costly failure in March of the German counteroffensive in Hungary convinced Szokoll that Austria was about to become a major battlefield. With the German southern front disintegrating, the German High Command deployed at sensitive points some of the formations and combat units that Szokoll had originally reserved for the uprising, and thus removed them from the conspiracy.[26] Despite this setback, the renewed Soviet offensive of March 16 was viewed as a clear indication that the proper moment had finally arrived for the military to appeal directly to the Soviets for assistance.

Szokoll expected to coordinate the uprising since the success of the military insurgency lay in the Red Army's active support of insurgent Wehrmacht troops, strengthened by paramilitary combat teams. He expected the Soviet attack to trigger mass anti-German activity in Vienna. At the end of March he conveyed his plan to the top 05 officials and the chiefs of the paramilitary units and decided to implement it as soon as he had established working contact with the Soviet Command. The military and civilian sectors agreed to set up a joint body to assume responsibilities.[27] The military-civilian agreement laid down a coordinated plan, creating a center of disruption behind the front lines that would act in coordination with the Red Army operations. It directed the insurgent military units to occupy military installations and the Vienna radio transmitter and radio station and to interrupt road transport during the initial assault, while the civilian combat teams waiting in their assembly centers were ordered to seize the seats of government and of the Nazi Party.

On April 2, Szokoll's emissary, Oberfeldwebel Ferdinand Käs, and Szokoll's personal driver, Gefreiter Johann Reif, headed toward the front lines with false military orders to contact the retreating Hungarian Army High Command in the Semmering area.[28] After being fired at by both sides, the couriers finally crossed the front to the Soviet Army Ninth Guard Headquarters in Hochwolkersdorf near Gloggnitz, where they briefed the Soviet military chiefs headed by Colonel-General Alexei S. Scheltov.[29] At a long meeting, Käs revealed the deployment of the German troops and outlined Szokoll's insurgency plan. He also requested that the Anglo-Americans stop their aid raids on Vienna, that the city water supply not be interrupted, and that Austrian prisoners of war receive special treatment, and, when possible, be released.

On April 4 the Soviets approved Szokoll's plan and agreed on special arrangements for its application. Red flares dropped from Soviet planes above Vienna would signal the beginning of the Soviet offensive. The insurgents would wear white cloth on their right arms and the password would be "Moscow." Six communication points would be clearly marked to facilitate mutual contacts. The Red Army, marching through the Vienna Forest, would attack the City from the unprotected west, thus outflanking the German's main southern defense line. Austrian irregulars who would forge an entrance from the west into the inner city would meet them at the Hütteldorf-Weidlingau Road. In this way they hoped to prevent the crack SS units, fighting on the eastern outskirts, from falling back. In the meantime, insurgent troops would seize the public buildings, railroad stations, and bridges, and selected police parties would take over the police headquarters.

When Käs returned to Vienna on April 5, he immediately reported to Szokoll. In the late evening, the main military conspirators' meeting at the Wehrkreis Headquarters agreed on the final details of their operations. They resolved to strike on Friday, April 6.[30] Raschke would occupy the Wehrkreis Command building, and Biedermann's men would take key positions throughout the city and prevent the demolition of the bridges. A motorcycle platoon was to seize the radio transmitter on the Bisamberg.[31] Kraus's four howitzers would fire on the SS headquarters. A special assault team would be held in reserve. At 8:00 P.M. the Socialists and Communists were to assemble to provoke public unrest and disturbances in the outer districts of Simmering, Meidling, and Floridsdorf. This agitation would spread to reach the inner city by 9:00 P.M.[32] Barricades erected in the southern part of the city would cut off the retreat of the SS troops deployed south of the city. Arms would be distributed from depots in the Rennweg Barracks to the assault teams who, at 10:00 P.M., would storm public buildings, occupy bridges, and round up the prominent Nazis.[33] Major Stillfried's policemen would occupy police headquarters. Szokoll and a group of officers would force General of Infantry Rudolf von Bünau, the newly appointed commander of the Vienna Defense Zone, to sign the prepared capitulation order. At 11:30 P.M., a proclamation would be broadcast over the captured radio station, calling on the population to welcome the Soviet soldiers as liberators.[34] By midnight on April 5, the insurgents had left to issue the last orders. Later Szokoll summoned Bumballa and other 05 chiefs to inform them of the negotiations with the Soviets and to outline the final timetable. The day of revolt began well. As agreed on, the Russians fired their red flares shortly after 1:00 A.M. Civilian combat groups who had received their instructions went on alert.

Nevertheless, the conspiracy collapsed before it really started. At 4:00 A.M. on April 6, an agitated Raschke rushed into the Wehrkreis building to report to Käs that Biedermann had just been apprehended. The shattering news reached Szokoll ninety minutes later. He resolved to go on with the original plan despite the danger that the plot might have been betrayed.[35] Before breaking the frightful news to his 05 companions, Szokoll issued new directives.[36] He ordered Raschke to hold the Wehrkreis building against any approaching troops unless they identified themselves by the password "Radetzky." He rushed the Croatian storm unit to reinforce the insurgents at the Wehrkreis Headquarters. He instructed Huth and his motorcycle platoon to capture the Bisamberg radio transmitter immediately, and ordered

Kraus's battery supported by combat units to rescue Biedermann from von Bünau's command post.[37]

Everything seemed to depend on the rapidity with which Szokoll's new instructions were implemented. But now events began to unroll in a manner that the insurgents could no longer control. In the early hours of April 6, the Gestapo made Biedermann reveal the password and disclose names. Nazi countermeasures immediately began. SS-Jagdkommandos were deployed around General von Bünau's command post, and at 7:30 A.M. an SS detachment broke into the Wehrkreis building and apprehended Huth and Raschke.[38] The occupation of the conspiracy's headquarters, the confiscation of the motor park, the arrest of the leaders (Hofer and Rothmayer were seized later in the day), and the temporary interruption of the contact between the scattered units left the movement in disarray. Only some remnants escaped the downfall. Moreover, amid the initial chaos it was not clear how many groups had avoided the Nazis and how many addresses and names had been divulged. Szokoll immediately shifted his hideout to elude the Nazis, who were searching for him, but desperately attempted to renew his contacts despite the great personal risk.[39] To restore order, the chiefs of the assault teams gathered in the evening on April 6. Their morale high, they were still ready to fight although SS troops had raided some of their assembly points and they suffered from a shortage of machine guns and ammunition, which the SS had seized at the Wehrkreis headquarters. They regrouped their forces and swore to hold out for the Russians to arrive.

In his new command post, Szokoll reestablished contact with Biedermann's unit and secured Volkssturm arm bands and passes for his teams, which allowed them to move freely between Schmerling Square in Favoriten, which Resistance combat teams occupied, and Auersperg Palace, where the 05 military and civil command moved in on April 7.[40] Lest the Soviets be caught unaware, Szokoll's driver Reif crossed the battle lines to inform the Soviet Command of the disaster that had befallen the Resistance.[41] The sense of urgency among the insurgents increased when they learned that at around 7:30 A.M. the Red Army had launched the final assault against Vienna from the south and the west. In the evening some Soviet columns fighting their way through the outer districts stood not far from the city center. A handful of 05 members with some volunteers guided the Soviets through the western outskirts of the city, bypassing German gun positions, tanks, and barricades.[42] Although the authorities still did not realize the full extent of the military conspiracy, great unease and serious doubts about the reliability of some Austro-German formations spread among the officers of the SS-Sixth Armored Army and of the Vienna City Command and helped weaken their resolve to defend the city.[43]

Within the inner city, any organized action by the poorly armed civilians was impossible, because of the heavy concentration of German armored columns around the parliament. Some combat teams not notified in time of the roundup engaged the German troops, and some resistance fighting erupted spontaneously where antagonism against the regime ran high.[44] Civilians offered shelter to deserting Volkssturm members and persuaded Austrian soldiers to throw away their uniforms and weapons, and to put on civilian clothing.[45]

From April 7, the insurgency was directed from the Auersperg Palace. As the weight of the fighting shifted from the military to the civilian ringleaders, so did its control. The Committee of Seven filled the seat of leadership that POEN and the military had vacated.[46] From April 9 the Committee convened at the Palace every morning. However, with the possible exception of Bumballa, those in authority at headquarters were members of the permanent staff headed by Maasburg, the secretary general of the Committee. Maasburg, Zimmer-Lehmann, Gredler, Thurn-Taxis, and Braunsteiner maintained contact with the combat squads and the underground groups through intrepid couriers. The Central Council of the 05 was also on alert, and produced leaflets spreading 05 appeals to the population.[47]

On April 8, Lieutenant Scheichelbauer got hold of the closely guarded new plan for the defense of the inner city at the Vienna Fortress Command. Because of the plan's importance, Szokoll and his bodyguards crossed the front line at about 4:00 A.M. on April 9 to hand the plan to the Third Ukrainian Front Command.[48] Similarly, braving SS controls and artillery fire, Mainprugg and Suppan reconnoitered the forward SS defense positions and forwarded the information on their locations and strength to Szokoll.[49] On the morning of April 10, while the first Soviet patrols advanced toward the Hofburg, which the Germans had abandoned the night before, an 05 commando team stormed the Vienna police headquarters.[50] Throughout the city, local resistance members assisted the Russians in clearing their neighborhoods of Germans. On wiping out the last pockets of German resistance, however, the Soviets saw a potential threat in the irregular forces and hastened to disband them. On April 11 Soviet Marshal F. I. Tolbuchin summoned Bumballa to his command post. After congratulating Bumballa "for his achievements," Tolbuchin "summarily ordered Bumballa to have his men surrender all their arms."[51]

With military leadership wrecked by the last-minute police raids, control of the Resistance was finally lodged in its civilian sector. The scattered military who had evaded the SS commanded no particular influence. They suspended their activities or joined the civilian commando forces. To the career and reserve officers, who had no attachment to any particular political tendency, the Resistance had been above all an opportunity to struggle for the liberation of their homeland. After the liberation, they retreated into the shadows of the infant Second Republic. Having performed what had been a bold and difficult task, Szokoll has since become a controversial figure, for not a few former officers and citizens have shunned this most prominent of the resistance military men. Many believed that Szokoll had failed to live up to his military oath and had collaborated with the Soviets in an undertaking of no military value, whose success might have resulted in the destruction of the Inner City of Vienna.

THE DISSOLUTION OF 05

The battle for Vienna raged until April 13. After April 10, the Committee of Seven and the 05 command in Auersperg Palace acted as the highest Austrian authority in Vienna. They entered into some arrangements with the Communist elements, who emerged during the battle under the cover of the Austrian Freedom Front. The Communists were intent on avoiding anything that might impair their close ties to 05, but they were busy spreading propaganda and occupying positions in the new city and police administrations.

The real advantage that the Communists gained lay in their temporary appointments to the district offices in Vienna by the local Soviet commanders. As early as April 11, backed by the Red Army City Command, 05 decided to nominate former SPÖ City Councillor Anton Weber and Communist Rudolf Prikryl, respectively, as provisional Mayor and Deputy Mayor of Vienna.[52] The next day, to gain acceptance for his nomination to this critically important post, Weber informed Schärf of the offer, leaving the final decision to the SPÖ. But the SPÖ leadership resented Weber's candidature, which the Soviets and the Communists had suggested, because Weber's public endorsement of the Anschluss in March 1938 had come under strong Socialist fire. Weber would thus be almost certainly subject to strong Communist pressure. Instead, the Socialists nominated their official General Theodor Körner, who won wide approval. Eventually, a provisional city government was installed with Körner as the Mayor.[53]

The political vacuum after April 11 and the presence of the Red Army administration gave the Communists opportunities to assume positions of influence far beyond their actual strength. The remnants of the illegal KP cadres regrouped around Prikryl, welcoming all patriots into their ranks, and giving political support to the swollen ranks of the resisters.[54] As word about the distributing of resistance membership cards and the issuing of recommendations at Auersperg Palace spread rapidly, hundreds of quasi-resisters swarmed the City Hall, where Prikryl and his Communist aides nominated, in a most haphazard way, resistance card holders to various branches of the city administration. Through such procedures, the Communists undoubtedly aspired to play a dominant role in the capital.

These first Communist representatives, however, vanished when Koplenig and Ernst Fischer arrived from Moscow in the first half of April.[55] After meeting Hrdlicka, Thurn-Taxis, and other 05 officials in Auersperg Palace the two KP leaders made no attempt to hide their contempt of this "band of rogues, crooks, and naïve people." Infuriated by the "foolish babblers from 05" who had attempted to build a semi-political organ "behind their backs," the Communists preferred to deal with the more experienced party politicians.[56] The early formation of the SPÖ and ÖVP as the nuclei of political power discouraged any efforts to band the resistance group into a single movement.[57] Because the Austrians were still attached to their traditional political loyalties, the parties did not want to see 05 exercise any political authority. Having ceased to function as a political organ, the Committee of Seven vegetated for a few days after April 13 before it disappeared.[58]

Both the public and former party activists, when they envisioned the reconstruction of political life, again looked to the political parties as symbols of continuity. The Communists acted politically independent of the Resistance centers. Party concerns prevailed on the Socialist side as well. A few SPÖ leaders, usually men of experience in prewar politics, such as Dr. Schärf, rose to positions of political importance because of their Party connections. But they usually operated on the Resistance fringe and rarely administered the Socialist underground circles. With no profound desire for political and social renovation, the public and the Resistance were reconciled to the reemergence of the old political parties. In the postwar conditions, the experienced party veterans easily outshone the resisters, whose abilities and skills usually were not conducive to political activity.

In Vienna, the politically inexperienced resistance groups did not seek to arrogate political power for themselves. Their immediate concerns were to fill the executive-power vacuum after the collapse of the Nazi regime and not to allow sectional interests to destroy national unity. The most urgent tasks involved the establishment of public transportation, the feeding of the population, and the reconstruction of water, gas, and electricity supplies.[59] One of the Committee of Seven's first measures was the rapid reconstruction of the central administrative body.

The Resistance was not a cohesive and coordinated movement with a definite chain of command. It played down the need for any specific ideological orientation, and its propaganda was primarily focused on Austrian patriotism and hostility to the Germans. Although the military objective of the non-Communist Resistance was clear—to defeat the Nazis—its political ideas were generally vague. In a nation where hierarchy and tradition were all-important, the Resistance was more concerned with restoring the First Republic than with transforming society. Unlike its image in many other countries, the Resistance in Austria was seen more as a rallying point for gaining an independent Austria than as an instrument for forming a new democratic state, infused with principles of social justice that would sweep away antiquated socioeconomic and political structures. In fact, one of the most important effects of the absence of an organized

Socialist resistance and of the collapse of the Communist underground was the predominance of the traditionalist elements, who had recaptured their political legitimacy in various underground organizations in the closing years of the war. Consequently, a truly progressive character and revolutionary spirit was absent in the Austrian underground.

The Resistance, reflecting the general mood of uneasiness, tension, and uncertainty, could not commit itself to progressive social and economic reforms. Without a general popular desire to build a new Austria, the perspective of profound social structural changes could not develop a momentum of its own. The moderate tendency of the Resistance was one of the specifically Austrian elements that prevented it from playing an effective role on the postwar political scene.

The politically diverse and ideologically amorphous 05 groups were united around the vision of a "free, independent, democratic Austria."[60] But when the reconstitution and coalition of the SPÖ and ÖVP seemed to promise the early formation of a national government that would give the new state viability, 05 dissolved itself on April 23.[61] Despite the moral boost that clandestine work had given its rather colorless leaders, 05 had never become a real alternative to the political parties. Lacking political expertise, the resisters found it easier to help dismantle the creaking fixtures of the old regime than to construct a new one. Moreover, they found themselves with no political base from which to grapple with the momentous political and economic issues.

The clear danger facing most parties was that in the immediate postwar vacuum, the Communists, under the cover of the unified resistance, would bore into Socialist ranks, make inroads in the central and local administration, and spread their influence.[62] But it was Austria's fortune that both the ÖVP and the SPÖ emerged from clandestine life with a coalition government in mind. Thanks to their cooperation, new Austria entered the democratic mainstream on April 27 when the top officials of the three political parties issued a declaration of Austrian independence, which was, in ways, the product of experiences shared in the concentration camps and in the Resistance. Indeed, the great strength of the Resistance experiment had been the willingness of its Socialist and Christian Democratic activists to talk to one another. Conscious that a combination of fear and ideological orthodoxy had led the hostility that had wrecked the First Republic, Austria's democratic political leadership displayed a heartening moderation, courage, and opennes to dialogue—one of the silent legacies of the war sacrifices and of the Resistance.

NOTES

1. "Anti-Nazi Resistance in Vienna, 1938-45," October 18, 1945, Headquarters U.S. Forces in Austria, Office of the Political Adviser, DÖW 8503; "Tätigkeitsbericht der Gruppen der Österreichischen Widerstandsbewegung, . . ." April 15, 1945, OM. No 51/VI.

2. Ibid.; Kudrnofsky, *Vom Dritten Reich,* pp. 49-50.

3. The District comprised the territory of Vienna, Lower- and Upper Austria and northern Burgenland. Vienna's geographic position made the city a garrison center. In July 1942 about 25,000 men, including 11,000 Wehrmacht- and SS troops, 123 Wehrmacht agencies, and 10,000 Air Force men were stationed there. Manfried Rauchensteiner in DÖW, ed., *Widerstand Wien,* 3:395-96.

4. Manfried Rauchensteiner, *Krieg in Österreich 1945* (Vienna, 1970), pp. 107, 113. When the Wehrkreis XVII Headquarters moved out of Vienna on April 2, 1945, Szokoll joined the staff of General Rudolf von Bünau, who commanded the military forces in Vienna, as General Staff officer (1b).

5. Weinberger, *Tatsachen,* pp. 144 ff.

6. Szokoll gave his personal account of the action in *Die Presse,* January 31, and February 7, 1948.

7. "Nur durch eine dem Schein nach legale Übernahme der Befehlsgewalt konnte der Putsch glücken." O. Molden, *Der Ruf,* p. 238. Szokoll's plan adopted Stauffenberg's brilliant idea that had been central to the preparations for the July 20 Action. See his printed report of May 1946, *Tätigkeitsbericht über die militärischen Planungen und den Einsatz von Österreichern zur Beschleunigung der Befreiung vom Nazismus,* pp. 6, 9, DÖW 590.

8. Szokoll reportedly contacted the British Intelligence Service through his own office in Budapest in the fall of 1944. Ibid.

9. Szokoll never managed to contact the units of the Salzburg Military District. Only in the last weeks of the war did he establish links with Tyrol through the 05. Ibid., p. 4.

10. About 100 machine guns and 3,000 rifles were hidden. "Unternehmen Szokoll," OM, 26/III.

11. F. Molden, *Fepolinski,* pp. 285-86; O. Molden, *Der Ruf,* pp. 160, 205-6, 211; "Unternehmen Szokoll," OM, 26/III.

12. Maasburg and Zimmer-Lehmann also belonged to the team. OM. No. 4.

13. O. Molden, *Der Ruf,* p. 212.

14. "Bericht Franz Studeny," OM, 11/II; O. Molden, *Der Ruf,* pp. 202 ff.

15. The nucleus developed contact to the Hofburg Group in the Reserve Military Hospital XV in Hofburg, Vienna, where about twenty members, led by the orthopedist Professor Dr. Philipp Erlacher, had assisted Austrian recruits to evade military service since the summer of 1943. In April 1945 the Hofburg Group damaged the electrical and telephone installations in Reichsstatthalter von Schirach's command bunker. O. Molden, *Der Ruf,* pp. 212-13, 233-34.

From 1940 to 1945, a group of noncommissioned officers in Communication-Reserve Unit 17 specialized in forging medical documents for Austrian soldiers to help them evade front-line duties and occupy positions in the military administration. The widespread network so controlled the military hospitals and barracks in Vienna that hardly any Wehrmacht unit stationed in the City was outside its influence. OM, 21/XIX.

16. Schick escaped from jail on April 7. Since the summer of 1944, Schick had been working with the OSS operator Jack Taylor, who was arrested in January. Taylor's mission was to investigate the possibilities for a combined operation by the Allied airborne force flown into Lower Austria from Italy and supported by an Austrian uprising. "Auszug aus dem Tätigkeitsbericht des Major a. D. Otto Schick," DÖW 8393; Friedrich Vogl, "Österreicher im grauen Waffenrock im Widerstand und vor den Kriegsgerichten," Manuscript (Vienna, 1974), pp. 160-62; O. Molden, *Der Ruf,* pp. 215-17, 256; Banny, "Ihre Namen," pp. 482, 488.

17. Vogl, "Österreicher," pp. 172-74; "Bericht," OM, No. 42.

18. A first World War veteran officer, Rothmayer had first been active in the "Hoch-und Deutschmeister" Regiment where after 1942 he created a special training cell within the Fifth Company. Eventually, he organized over 120 like-minded patriots. "Bericht von Hauptmann a. D. Josef Rothmayer," July 6, 1945, DÖW 4623; "Bericht," OM, 21/XIX.

19. According to Szokoll's plan, the combat groups were to occupy the Wehrkreis Headquarters and the Danubian bridges. Szokoll ordered the battery commanded by Kraus to move to Vienna on April 3. "Bericht," W. Kraus, OM, No 42; Vogl, "Österreicher," pp. 173-74;

"Auszug aus dem Tätigkeitsbericht des Oberleutnant a. D. Walter Kraus," DÖW 8393.

20. "Unternehmen Szokoll," OM, 28/III; O. Molden, *Der Ruf,* pp. 217-18. In the spring of 1942, Feldwebel Rudolf Fiedler, a former Socialist, set up a circle inside the City Military Command, where he built links to other Wehrmacht units. In 1944, he communicated with the Austrian Freedom Front (ÖFF) which was preparing, in connection with its British SOE contacts, to assist the Allied airborne troops. Unfortunately, one of his ÖFF contact men was a Gestapo informer. Fiedler was picked up in November 1944, but his group continued to store arms, ammunition, and gasoline for the uprising. *Arbeiter Zeitung,* October 13, 1946; "Gruppe Fiedler, Bericht," July 17, 1946, DÖW 5988/a.

21. Becker, *Freiheitskampf,* pp. 17, 19-20; Romanik, *Der Anteil,* p. 28; *Arbeiter Zeitung,* October 13, 1946.

22. Becker, *Freiheitskampf,* pp. 24-26; O. Molden, *Der Ruf,* p. 217.

23. Szokoll, *Tätigkeitsbericht,* pp. 3, 9.

24. O. Molden, *Der Ruf,* p. 219.

25. See Szokoll's outline of May 29, 1946, for the planned *Red-White-Red Book,* DÖW 8333. He correctly asserted that "there had never been either unified leadership or centralized direction" in both the civilian and the military sectors of the Resistence.

26. Szokoll, *Tätigkeitsbericht,* p. 10.

27. O. Molden, *Der Ruf,* 222 ff.

28. For Käs's journey, see his account, DÖW 2495; Ferdinand Käs, *Wien im Schicksalsjahr 1945* (Vienna, 1965); Szokoll, *Tätigkeitsbericht,* pp. 10-12; Rauchensteiner, *Krieg,* pp. 101 ff; John Toland, *The Last 100 Days* (New York, 1967). pp. 375-78; O. Molden, *Der Ruf,* pp. 229 ff; B. V. N. Želanov, "Vzaimodejstvie sil Avstrijskogo dviženija soprotivlenija s vojskami Krasnoj Armii v bojach osvoboždenie Avstrii aprel 1945," *Vtoraja mirova vojna* (Moscow, 1966), 3:118. A professional noncommissioned officer, Käs had known Szokoll since 1934 when they had served together in the Austrian Army. They met again in the fall of 1944. "Bericht," Hanns Eidlitz, OM, 49/V.

29. F. Molden, *Fepolinski,* pp. 354-55.

30. "Bericht," F. Käs, DÖW 2495.

31. Ibid.

32. The civilian sector included a number of activists who did not favor working with the Communists. The inclusion of the Communist Hrdlicka on the Committee of Seven, and the cooperation with Communist groups during the uprising seemed to indicate that the conservative majority was ready to take account of the present international situation. For Hrdlicka, see Wilfried Aichinger, "Sowjetische Österreichpolitik 1943-45" (Ph.D. dissertation, University of Vienna, 1977), pp. 161-64. The KPÖ rebuked Hrdlicka in April 1945 and shortly thereafter the Soviet security organs apprehended her.

33. Rauchensteiner, *Krieg,* p. 133.

34. Szokoll, *Tätigkeitsbericht,* pp. 12-14, 22-23; OM, No 62; OM, 38/IV. The conscripted Soviet laborers under the Soviet emissary Gutov were instructed to operate on the western outskirts of Vienna.

35. A telephone conversation between Szokoll and Biedermann was intercepted on April 5 by "NS-Führungsoffizier" Lieutenant Walter Hanslik, who denounced Biedermann to the authorities. Kudrnofsky, *Vom Dritten Reich,* p. 60. After the way, Maasburg accidentally encountered Hanslik in St. Gilgen near Salzburg and had him arrested. In 1947, Hanslik was sentenced to life imprisonment. Ibid., p. 124.

36. In 1970 Szokoll wrote that in 1945 he had assembled ten battalions of regular troops and fifteen civil combat teams. "Der österreichische Widerstand und seine Zusammenarbeit mit der russischen Befreiungs Armee," *Die österreichische Nation* 22 (June 1970): 84. The civilian underground claimed to have mobilized 6,000 men and 14,000 civilians. Rauchensteiner, *Krieg,* pp. 121, 123; O. Molden, *Der Ruf,* p. 236.

In his study, Rauchensteiner offers new figures on the numbers of German troops deployed in and around Vienna (*Krieg,* pp. 102 ff, 115-16). Molden used Szokoll's and Käs's figures, but they are subject to revision (*Tätigkeitsbericht,* passim; *Wien im Schicksalsjahr,* pp. 9, 12). General von Bünau had only fifteen weak battalions, one light battery, and two Flak regiments. On April 4 he was put under the command of the SS-Sixth Armored Army. However, the SS Army existed only on paper as it had suffered great losses in its March counteroffensive in Hungary; its three armored divisions numbered twenty-eight tanks. The only intact unit was the regular Army Division, which Hitler rushed from Germany in April. *Krieg,* pp. 112-16.

37. "Bericht," F. Käs, DÖW 2495; O. Molden, *Der Ruf,* pp. 235 ff; Szokoll, *Tätigkeitsbericht,* pp. 14-17.

38. A court-martial sentenced Biedermann, Huth, and Raschke to death. They were publicly hanged in Wien-Floridsdorf on April 8. DÖW 4623, 6384b; Ludwig Jedlicka, "Dokumente zur Geschichte der Ereignisse in Wien im April 1945," *Österreich in Geschichte und Literatur,* No 3 (1961): 127-32.

39. To pass through the numerous military controls, Szokoll wore a lieutenant's tattered uniform. He tore the breast pocket to explain the loss of his military papers. OM, 69/I.

40. O. Molden, *Der Ruf,* pp. 242 ff; "Bericht," OM. No 62.

41. Želanov, p. 119, in Rauchensteiner, *Krieg,* p. 122.

42. Szokoll, *Tätigkeitsbericht,* p. 17; "Bericht," OM, No 67; Toland, *The Last 100 Days,* pp. 386-87; O. Molden, *Der Ruf,* pp. 247-53; Kudrnofsky, *Vom Dritten Reich,* p. 113.

43. Szokoll, *Tätigkeitsbericht,* pp. 16-17; O. Molden, *Der Ruf,* pp. 243-44; Rauchensteiner, *Krieg,* p. 129.

44. On April 7 General von Bünau painted a dark picture of the situation in Vienna in his report to Hitler's Headquarters: "The civilian population directs heavier fire against German troops than does the enemy." *Salzburger Nachrichten,* December 29, 1945, in O. Molden, *Der Ruf,* p. 247. For the unrest in the working-class quarters, see the SD situation report, March 10, 1945, BA NS 6/377, and Kreisleiter Hans Arnhold's report to the NSDAP Chancellery, April 2, 1945, ibid.

45. See excerpts from the war diary of the Wehrmacht High Command in Rauchensteiner, *Krieg,* p. 126; "Anti-Nazi Resistance in Vienna, 1938-45," DÖW 8503. Schärf reported that Socialists provided some 3,000 Wehrmacht and Volkssturm deserters with civilian clothes. *April 1945,* pp. 15-16.

46. Schärf, *April 1945,* p. 54.

47. O. Molden, *Der Ruf,* p. 248; Kudrnofsky, *Vom Dritten Reich,* pp. 113 ff; OM, No 49/V; No. 62.

48. Toland, *The Last 100 Days,* p. 389. Szokoll sets the date on April 10 and was far less specific in his account, *Tätigkeitsbericht,* p. 17. Also see O. Molden, *Der Ruf,* pp. 253-55. Szokoll visited the Soviet headquarters again on April 12 or 13. This time, he submitted a note requesting that the Red Army adopt measures that would restrict the wild confiscations, allow the Viennese authorities to organize an auxiliary police, and reestablish public transportation. *Tätigkeitsbericht,* p. 17 and *Anlage 5.* The Soviet police apprehended Szokoll as an alleged Western spy at the City Hall in the late afternoon of April 14. "Unternehmen Szokoll," OM, No 26/III; Toland, *The Last 100 Days,* p. 392. He was released, rearrested, and with twelve other resisters jailed for more than five months. DÖW 15658. Szokoll was not reactivated when the Republic began to build up its armed forces. Interview with Carl Szokoll. The Austrian authorities' treatment of Szokoll has been a particularly outrageous case of insensitivity.

The Soviets also arrested Maasburg soon after the liberation and interrogated him about his Abwehr activities. He escaped and retired to the United States occupation zone. Kudrnofsky, *Vom Dritten Reich,* pp. 115 ff; Rauchensteiner, *Der Sonderfall,* pp. 68-69.

49. Molden, *Der Ruf,* p. 254.

50. OM, 49/V; DÖW 8503; Rauchensteiner, *Krieg,* p. 136.

51. DÖW 8503.

52. Rauchensteiner, *Der Sonderfall,* p. 76. The KPÖ took charge of the local administration

in thirteen districts, the SPÖ in seven, and the ÖVP in one. The respective ratio of the district police chiefs was sixteen, three, and two. Schärf in Weber, "Die linken Sozialisten," pp. 73-74; Ulrike Wetz, "Geschichte der Wiener Polizeidirektion vom Jahre 1945 bis zum Jahre 1955 mit Berücksichtigung der Zeit vor 1945" (Ph.D. dissertation, University of Vienna, 1971), pp. 180-81.

53. Schärf, *April 1945,* pp. 53 ff; Schärf, *Österreichs Erneuerung,* pp. 33-34.

54. OM, No 41.

55. Schärf, *April 1945,* pp. 60-62. Ernst Fischer disagreed with Schärf's account of the initial talks, *Das Ende einer Illusion. Erinnerungen 1945-1955* (Vienna, 1973), pp. 45-50. OM, No 41; Kudrnofsky, *Vom Dritten Reich,* p. 119.

56. Diary of E. Fischer in Aichinger, "Sowjetische Österreichpolitik," p. 163; Ernst Fischer, "Der Weg der Provisorischen Regierung," *Weg und Ziel* 4 (January 1946): 3-5. Fischer depicted 05 as "a political air balloon . . . a soap bubble . . . a group of monarchists and fortune hunters . . . ghosts of the past." Ibid.

57. The representatives of the three political parties in the provinces (SPÖ, ÖVP, KPÖ) frequently played down the authority of the Resistance groups. In fact, even ÖVP and SPÖ resisters such as Hurdes, Weinberger, Schärf, and Lemberger disliked associating with 05. Weinberger, *Tatsachen,* pp. 245-48; Aichinger, "Sowjetische Österreichpolitik," p. 164; Weber, "Die linken Sozialisten," pp. 72-75, 77. In contrast, many youthful fighters expressed their disgust for some veteran politicians seeking power despite their inactivity during the occupation. Interview with J. Eidlitz.

58. None of the members of the Committee of Seven had enjoyed his own party's support. All in all, the Committee, a colorless group without distinction or political experience, comprised personalities of insufficient stature to cope with the problems at hand.

59. OM, XI.

60. Ibid. Unlike in Austria, the resistance programs in France, Czechoslovakia, Italy, and elsewhere eagerly sought to build a new power structure to replace the old party system. The leaflets distributed in Austria in 1944-45 predicted an early Nazi defeat and called for public disobedience and retaliation. But nowhere do we see a text detailing the Resistance's political program.

61. OM, IX. The silencing of 05 was engineered by Soviet and Communist pressures. To the Communists 05 lacked proper political credentials and was pro-Western and anti-Soviet. OM, No 41; Aichinger, "Sowjetische Österreichpolitik," pp. 169 ff. The Soviet distrust was not diminished when the Soviets apprehended at Auersperg Palace the operator who had maintained wireless communication with Caserta. On April 21, the Soviet authorities requested 05 to register with them, and the Communist chief of the Vienna police ordered the 05 files seized. Ibid.

The Soviets charged the last president of the freely elected parliament, the Social Democrat Karl Renner, with the organizing of the first postwar Austrian cabinet. Apparently Marshal Josef Stalin saw in the old Socialist leader a comfortable figurehead. Renner lived in retirement in Gloggnitz near Wiener Neustadt and had been in loose contact with Schärf during the war. Renner formed the provisional government, initially recognized only by the Soviet Union, in Vienna on April 29. Renner became its head and Schärf, Figl, and Koplenig formed the political cabinet. Representing the ÖVP, the prominent resisters Gruber, Bumballa, and Weinberger functioned as under-secretaries. Schärf, *Erneuerung,* pp. 33 ff; Jacques Hannak, *Karl Renner und seine Zeit* (Vienna, 1965), pp. 669-75; Aichinger, "Sowjetische Österreichpolitik," p. 122.

62. The rising Communist influence alarmed SPÖ officials, who saw in the Resistance concept of national unity an instrument for Communist infiltration of the parliamentary system. They were afraid that such a national Resistance front would force them to cooperate closely with the double-dealing KPÖ and would put pressure on the SPÖ to drop its independent stance. The SPÖ reasserted itself in the industrial and urban areas, and its leaders opposed any leftist bloc with the Communists. Interview with Dr. Lemberger.

21

The Insurgency in Tyrol

Outside of Vienna, Tyrol became the locus of clandestine work. Its compact geographical position, enclosed by extensive Alpine ranges, helped shape a strong political subculture that firmly entrenched itself in the mountain valleys. That the inhabitants were active Catholics further bound them together in a province where the National Socialists continually encountered difficulties. The social and economic structure of the region, based mostly on the small independent farmer, the traditional guarantor of Tyrolian patriotism, also strengthened the vital regional sentiment. The strong geographical local boundaries between various subareas discouraged wide-ranging social relations and helped to insulate the traditional Catholic hegemony.

That this world of rural communities remained circumscribed accounted for the containment, insulation, and fragmentation of the Tyrolian Resistance. Generally, the segregated local groupings refused to expand beyond their boundaries, thus reinforcing their isolation. Although the Resistance activists tolerated a variety of basically conservative groups, they were unable to transcend the specifically local engagement of the groups. This special situation called for a patient wait for the mobilization of the local peasantry, whose leaders had to adapt clandestine work to local circumstances.

Because of its deep regionalism, the loosely structured Tyrolian Resistance possessed specific features of importance. First, the Resistance had to extend its influence among an extremely diverse array of local groups. Second, this wide-ranging diversity in no way lessened the overpowering sentiment of regional identity. Third, the isolated groups were more easily activated by outsiders, who could cut across cleavages of geography and personal and local differences and who could maximize the all-Tyrolian and Austrian ties. The participation of Knoeringen, Uhrig, Molden, or Gruber was central to the prospects for upgrading and consolidating clandestine activities. The adoption of central leadership weakened the regional impulses, lessened the impact of the physical barriers, and lowered the dependence on local concerns. Tyrol's historically distinct individuality provided the channel through which strong Austrian self-awareness asserted itself. In the country at large, the Resistance implanted itself as a counter-culture of Austrian zealots. In Tyrol, the underground had more chance to sustain this distinctiveness, and it found a more intense pattern of pro-Austrian commitment among the populace.

The origins of the traditionalist resistance go back to 1940 when, after the defeat of France, a handful of former high-ranking civil servants, whom the Nazi regime demoted in 1938, formed a small circle that met weekly in Innsbruck. Although the participants did not engage in any direct activity, through their contacts they exerted increasing political influence on the shaping of the underground. They were pragmatists rather than ideological militants. With the help of Ing. Anton Hradetzky and his close friends, Dr. Anton Melzer and Ing. Wilfried Egger, the circle started a larger network in the countryside, embracing the traditionally oriented Catholic elite in the Stubai Valley, Landeck, Hall, Seefeld, Zams, Matrei, Gurgl, and reaching into the City Works in Innsbruck.[1] Hradetzky and Dr. Leo Praxmarer maintained contacts with former Christian Social minister Pernter and with conservative circles in Vienna. Still other organizations were formed, overlapping both territorially and socially with the Innsbruck network. Melzer and Dr. Robert Skorpil were in close touch with the Catholic circle around the prominent Innsbruck physician Dr. Flora.[2]

The impetus for coordination among the emerging group came from Dr. Friedrich Würthle, a Liberal Catholic journalist and writer.[3] As a noncommissioned officer, he was transferred in 1940 to the Wehrmeldeamt, the Military Registration Office, in Innsbruck where a small circle around Praxmarer and Dr. Oskar Peterlunger worked. Würthle provided the resisters with forged documents and identity cards. He moved energetically in underground circles that included both the Christian Socials around Dr. Hans Gamper and the Social Democrats under Dr. Karl Höflinger. Through Gamper he encountered the Communist cell under Joseph Ronczay, who supplied propaganda material from Paris and ensured the link to other circles.[4] In the summer of 1942 the impetuous Jörg Sackenheim, one of the most dedicated, hard-working militants, met Würthle and Flora.[5] Würthle provided him with false identity papers so Sackenheim could travel more easily across southern Germany and Austria, renewing contacts and organizing the activist segment of the Innsbruck underground.

In 1943 the network became affiliated with the shoemaker Anton Haller's well-organized group in Hall and with the cells of former Tyrol Attorney General Dr. Ernst Grünewald and his son Eduard. In 1940, Dr.

Franz Mair, a professor of English in an Innsbruck gymnasium, had formed the nucleus of the Grünewald group, largely from his own students.
Thanks to Eduard Grünewald, liaison was established with a circle around
the writer Michael Brink in Munich, but the Gestapo liquidated the Brink
group as early as 1943. The Mair-Grünewald youth organization produced
an illegal newspaper and engaged in some violence against NSDAP property. Eduard, a student, provided false forms and rubber stamps to his friends
to help them avoid the draft for labor or military service.[6]

Würthle and his companions prepared to build up a united underground
in the province. They first convened a meeting in 1943 of the representatives
of the scattered groups in and around Innsbruck to discuss common action.
The widely respected Würthle found much understanding for his call for a
joint organization. Würthle, Sackenheim, Praxmarer, and Ing. Ortner,
among others, agreed to establish a combat squad under Sackenheim and to
procure arms. But it was not yet any part of their purpose to provide intelligence or to engage in sabotage. They confined their activities to propaganda and exchange of information and opinion.[7] At the end of 1943, the
Gestapo rounded up Flora, Steinmayer, and Ronczay. In December, Melzer
and Skorpil fell into Nazi hands.[8]

The process of growing together proved a success for the Tyrolean
underground groups. Late in 1943 Dr. Gruber arrived in Innsbruck for a
short visit from Berlin.[9] Würthle received Gruber with open arms. During
his visit Gruber established a strong reputation within the divided
Resistance. At about this time, Würthle's circle contacted the nascent
groups of deserters and young men who instead of reporting for compulsory labor in Germany took to the mountains in Ötztal, Gnadenwald,
and Schwaz.[10] Outside of the Innsbruck-Hall urban agglomeration,
numerous cells steadily expanded in the small towns and communities.
Among the first to establish contact with Hradetzky on April 1, 1943, was
Josef Stockhammer, who in November 1941 had assembled a circle in the
town of Landeck and in the adjoining valleys. A local businessman and a
former Schuschnigg adherent, Stockhammer was approached on November
21 by Stefan Zechner from Innsbruck, who had ties to the military. The circle grew in strength throughout 1944, and Stockhammer reached out to the
prisoner of war camps and to the officers of the Mountain Troops Reserve
Battalion 136 (Gebirgsjäger) stationed in Landeck.[11]

Further east things had been going well since 1941-42 for a nucleus of
partisans hiding in the forty-km long Ötz Valley, which Italy bordered in
the south. The partisans included poorly equipped and inexperienced young
soldiers evading their front line duties in high mountain hideouts. Approached in 1941 by his friend, Max Manl, by the postbus driver Peter
Falkner, and by the student Wolfgang Pfaundler, the Socialist locomotive
engineer Hubert Sauerwein of Innsbruck decided to travel to the Valley to

form an organizational base to help the irregulars. There Sauerwein and Pfaundler enlisted the help of two local gendarmes Hans Köll and Franz Alexander. By the end of 1942 some fifty men had joined them and their strength had risen to sixty by the end of 1944. The inhospitable mountains provided favorable terrain to which they could withdraw whenever the Gestapo launched search parties. Local peasants offered food, shelter, clothing, and other stores to the youthful cadres. The deserters put some of their arms— five machine guns, fifteen automatic rifles, hand grenades — into underground caches. The reports of their existence soon spread throughout Tyrol, and their deepening entrenchment created insecurity for the regime.

The irregulars remained compact and secure up to the end of the war, mainly because they were a self-contained local force, which held a well-protected natural base between the Italian frontier and the Inn Valley.[12] The men, augmented by local supporters, never ventured beyond their isolated area. Contrary to the usual practice, they never challenged the local security forces nor did they engage in significant violence. They did not operate as a guerrilla unit, and up to the closing weeks of the war they engaged in clandestine action on an individual rather than on a group basis.[13] In early May 1945, the men descended from the surrounding forests to overpower and disarm the retreating German troops. On May 4 the American forces, greeted by flowers thrown by the population, entered the valley without a single loss of human life.[14]

TOWARD THE UPRISING

In 1944 the dispersed clandestine organizations were plotting tactics to topple the regime. These activities prompted the establishment of contacts with the military. Among the Austrian officers and soldiers in the Wehrmacht units stationed in Tyrol, there was much concern about the outcome of the war. Some officers believed that the German defeat would promote Austria's independence. They accepted the need for outright resistance. Much of the initiative came from the Commander of the Mountain Troops Reserve Battalion 136, Major Werner Heine, a highly decorated officer (Ritterkreuzträger), and from his adjutant Lieutenant Ludwig Steiner. The professional soldier's sense of duty, indomitable combativeness, and daring impelled Heine to rally to the Austrian Resistance. Yet another resister was already locked in combat with the regime. Obergefreiter Oskar Görz had develped a nucleus of soldiers and noncommissioned officers at his Panzerjäger Reserve Company 137. A friend of Gruber and Würthle, Görz delivered arms to resisters and stored some in the celler of his apartment. Eventually, he was much involved in the running of numerous cells throughout Tyrol.[15]

In February 1945 the arrival of the OSS scout liaison mission galvanized the underground. The head of the team, Frederick Mayer, was dropped near Innsbruck with his Tyrolian aide Franz Weber and Dutch radio operator Hans Wynberg to train the resisters and to provide intelligence. The team soon established an intelligence chain penetrating the local Gestapo. The Allies were also concerned about a possible last ditch fight by the Nazis in the Alps. In mid-April Otto Molden slipped across from Italy with an Austro-American OSS liaison officer, Lieutenant Franckenstein, and his wireless operator, Novacek-Totzenberger. They journeyed to Innsbruck to secure the underground's cooperation in the expected battle for Tyrol.[16] As the liberation approached, the motivators behind the efforts to create a united resistance front were persons outside the fiercely independent Tyrolian underground, unconnected with its personal jealousies. Apparently only outsiders could secure the cooperation of all to make action work. Gruber, designated to coordinate the activities, many believed to be the only person capable of succeeding in this delicate job.

Earlier, Gruber had cooperated from Berlin with the United States authorities in Switzerland. He had a following in Vienna and had remained in touch with the major resistance figures in Innsbruck. Coming from Vienna, he arrived in Tyrol on March 14, 1945 to resume his talks with the underground. In past discussions, he had impressed his friends with his perseverance, quiet resolve, and stamina. He sensed that the vast majority of the underground desired a united organization. On April 9 at a meeting with Würthle, Haller, and their two associates, Gruber set forth four main tasks for the immediate future. First, all groups should cooperate, and he stressed that until the liberation, "let us not talk about politics. Before everything else, the Nazis have to disappear." Second, they should set up a military staff to direct military actions. Third, they should provide intelligence. Fourth, they should procure arms.[17]

The objective toward which Gruber and other resisters moved was a popular uprising launched at a proper moment, in conjunction with the advancing Allied forces. The Resistance seizure of power, which would place Tyrol under Austrian sovereignty, would go a long way toward demonstrating the credibility of the Austrian struggle for independence.[18] On April 13 at a conference at Sackenheim's residence, those groups who saw most urgently the advantages of unity selected Gruber as their chief and Würthle as his deputy.[19] Sackenheim was put in charge of the combat teams and Görz the liaison with the military.[20]

In the following weeks, the central command under Gruber's unflappable leadership worked out a common policy. Gruber made Resistance unity and national cohesion his central themes. He immediately involved the military and others in his preparations for armed uprising,[21] and with the assistance of Hirnschrott, an experienced radio technician, Gruber was in a radio communication with the American authorities. His own associates did useful work in the Post, Telegraph, and Telephone Office.

Leaning heavily upon Heine and Görz, Gruber devoted himself to bringing the cells in the Wehrmacht units in and around Innsbruck into the orbit of the unified Resistance. He also concluded working arrangements with the underground in Ötztal, Landeck, and Seefeld.[22] In almost daily meetings, Gruber and his entourage urged the separate clandestine movements to unite for final action. The leadership felt that, at this crucial time, the Resistance should express the unity of the nation. Eventually, the cluster of assembled networks included the groups of Haller, Hradetzky, Ronczay, Flora, E. Grünewald, Mair, Gamper, a gendarmerie cell of Rittmeister Winkler, and a police circle of Dr. Rudolf Junger, who had just returned from Germany.

From the outset, the Molden brothers had conducted a separate effort. In September and November 1944, while combing the Innsbruck area for activists, Fritz Molden created an 05 group. In the past the Greater-German-oriented members of the family of Professor of Geography at Innsbruck University, Dr. Richard Heuberger, Molden's uncle, had supported National Socialism. But they had become disillusioned by the regime's inhumanity. When Molden visited Innsbruck, he enlisted them in his network. The family's apartment served as a contact point for the 05 couriers coming from Switzerland, and the Professor's university office was used by two French liaison officers whom F. Molden had brought to Innsbruck.[23] On Richard Heuberger's son Helmut rested the responsibility for making contacts with the provincial and Innsbruck organizations. These organizations were internally rent, marked by great differences of views. They had no unified chain of command and no contacts with the world abroad, the absence of which in the end ensured their survival. Their fragmentation made it almost inevitable that Heuberger could make only indirect approaches to Grünewald, Mair, and Heine. Otherwise his achievements were small as he continuously met a rigid wall of distrust and prudence.[24]

Within weeks of his arrival in Innsbruck in April 1945, O. Molden, assisted by Heuberger, created a respectable 05 network. He also enlisted the help of E. Grünewald and Hartl Pezzei, a student with links to various groups of deserters and young peasants.[25] Of particular help were some remarkable, mostly young, women couriers who provided shelter and safe houses, arranged contacts, and carried out innumerable missions with aplomb and energy.[26] Students carried out most of the organizational work. The task of molding the various groups into a fighting organization received an important boost with the arrival of OSS operatives, because their presence implied Allied moral and political support for the Resistance cause.[27]

Constantly advocating a unified center, the 05 organizers tried to enlist the support of other groups.[28] The energetic Lieutenant Steiner joined 05 through Dr. Willibald Stricker, a prominent throat-nose-ear specialist who headed a clandestine line in the military hospitals in Tyrol, and through Count Hans Trapp, both of whom were looking for new recruits in the Wehrmacht. Steiner further widened the basis of 05. As Heine's adjutant up to February 1945, Steiner thwarted the Nazis by helping to purge the Mountain Reserve Battalion 136 of Nazi elements and by bringing his own reliable men to Innsbruck, where he assembled helpers in the military barracks. The Battalion's former physician, Dr. Emil Eckl, who had been busy recruiting police officials, aided him. Outside the provincial capital, Steiner gained the cooperation of Hauptmann Schlick, a battery commander in the town of Kufstein, and of the partisans in the Ziller (Sorg) and Navis Valleys (Richard Baumgartner).[29]

Apparently at this juncture word reached 05 that the Resistance in Tyrol had begun to figure seriously in American military planning. Undoubtedly this information accelerated the range of 05 activities and encouraged the 05 leaders to press for a joint political effort and to institute a coordinating political committee. On April 18, the first 05 leadership meeting, attended by O. Molden, H. Heuberger, Pezzei, and Dr. Grünewald, discussed the formation of the executive political organ in Tyrol, which became known as POEN.[30] On April 22 the 05 operational staff members gathered for a strategy session in Stricker's apartment, prompted by a request from the United States military authorities to work out a plan for the possible landing of Allied airborne troops and parachutists in Tyrol.[31] The members committed 05 to launching an armed uprising to accompany the Allied landing. O. Molden took the plan to Caserta on April 24.[32]

UNIFICATION AND LIBERATION

Early in the spring of 1945 the Resistance leaders feverishly made final plans for the impending uprising. They argued over how to prevent the Nazis from destroying power plants, bridges, and public installations, and made their revolt contingent on the rapid advance of the Allied troops. They concluded that, to be ready to act, the underground forces had to be unified.[33] The parallel existence of both the Gruber network and 05 duplicated and hampered preparations and worried the leading activists because it gravely affected the chances of success. To deal effectively with their tasks, the two organizations resolved mutual problems and fused into the united resistance movement, gradually absorbing all underground elements in Tyrol. Introduced by Görz, Heuberger met Gruber on April 26. Impressed by Gruber's leadership, he placed himself and 05 under Gruber's command.[34]

The fusion of both networks made the Resistance into an operative force. Having lost their contacts with Vienna, both organizations devoted all their energies to Tyrol. Activities were intensified. The acquisition of arms proceeded smoothly, and quantities of small arms and ammunition were smuggled from the military barracks into the cellar of the Hotel

Munich in Innsbruck.[35] Gruber rapidly gathered his military and civilian staffs and put together a small operational command. Heine's military aides were Major Schneeberger, who commanded the vital front sector in Seefeld, north of Innsbruck, Steiner, and Oberleutnant Anton Huber.[36] The civilian staff was put in charge of political, organizational, and technical matters.[37]

The greater activity demonstrated on Hitler's birthday, April 20, in Innsbruck, where 05 posters covered the walls and a red-white-red Austrian flag was hoisted at the police presidium building, attracted the Gestapo's attention. They closed in on a number of cells in a series of raids on April 12. On April 27, the police struck again, but on a much larger scale. Dr. Grünewald and his son, the entire Kematen Alm group, and many other militants fell into Nazi hands. Heine, Moser, Steiner, and Stricker were forced to keep moving, hide, or leave the city. The arrests interrupted some of the contacts, which had to be reestablished, destroyed a few groups, frightened some followers, imperiled the entire network, and disrupted several military and combat lines.[38]

However, the reverses did not deter Gruber and his companions from acting on a large scale. They rightly assumed that the advance of the United States Seventh Army in Germany would hamper cooperation with the Fifth Army in Italy, who cooperated in running the clandestine operations in Tyrol. The resisters had no direct link to the Seventh Army, which would probably be the first American force to occupy Tyrol. Furthermore, the speedy Allied operations made any air landing highly improbable, since the anticipated date of the first airborne action was May 10. Facing this development and overruling the objections of less courageous minds, Gruber decided that the only sensible thing to do with his weakened forces was to abandon a widespread insurrection and limit his actions to the seizure of the more important public installations in Innsbruck alone — the barracks, radio station, main post office, and bridges.[39] The military chiefs made the final decision on April 28, when they resolved to occupy the four military barracks as soon as the United States Seventh Army launched an attack through the Seefeld area where Schneeberger's unit held a sector.[40] On April 30, Gruber moved to a safer command post. There followed in the ensuing days a host of actions in Innsbruck, and the insurgency gradually extended to a number of areas throughout the province. Assisted by a few Gestapo agents, Sackenheim stormed the Gestapo archives at Schillerhof and seized invaluable police documents. In Sollbad Hall, a town near Innsbruck, the National Socialist Mayor offered to transfer the power to the chief of the local underground, Haller.[41]

At a less exalted political level, the representatives of the three main overlapping movements around Hradetzky, Gamper, and the 05 began their delicate talks about a unified political organ. Naturally, the competition for political power among the organizations was strewn with personal and political pitfalls, each of the networks claiming for itself the post of chairman. Personality and ambition probably caused more strain than did ideology. Finally, in early May, Gruber emerged as a compromise candidate who could win the allegiance of the temporary underground coalition, which was named the Executive Committee of the Austrian Resistance in Tyrol.[42] This heterogeneous body assumed the role of the supreme organ of the unified Resistance.

On May 1 Gruber issued final instructions for an imminent uprising in Innsbruck. That very evening Sackenheim gathered his combat group of over 150 armed men. Heuberger tried to get the order through to the enlisted volunteers, but too many of them felt unable to rally for the final assault.[43] Only a fraction of the registered resisters took part in the action. On May 2 the Resistance carried out its first major coup. Between 9:15 A.M. and noon, it captured all four Innsbruck barracks with some 2,000 men and seized large stocks of arms.[44] The combat units entered the barracks with no resistance from the soldiers on guard. At the Inn Barracks, the resisters took over the City Army Command post. As the U.S. troops had not yet arrived, the scattered insurgent forces withdrew in the evening to the Kloster Barracks to prepare for the expected counterattack.

So far no head-on clashes with the SS- or Wehrmacht units had occurred, but as long as the Defense Commander of Tyrol, General-Major Johannes von Böhaimb, could clear the city of insurgents, the uprising could be liquidated within a few hours. It became painfully clear to the insurgents that to preserve their new positions, a combat team would have to raid General von Böhaimb's headquarters, at the summer resort of Hungersburg, situated on mountain slopes above the city. In a spectacular insurgent action, Major Heine hastily recruited a special commando unit of twenty men and raced to Hungersburg. Accompanied by Oberleutnant Huber, he overpowered the sentries, surprised the General and his staff at dinner, disarmed them without a single shot being fired, and returned with the captured General to Innsbruck.[45] This precautionary raid significantly improved the insurgents' security.

During the raid, the combat party stumbled upon two American emissaries, United States Army Major Bland West and Captain Ernest H. Braun, who had arrived in Hungersburg earlier to negotiate a cease-fire and the surrender of the German troops. They were briefed on the situation in Innsbruck and immediately returned to the United States 103rd Infantry Division, urging it to advance to Innsbruck before the SS columns to the east could move up in force.[46] At three A.M., Gruber learned that in the late evening the resistance combat force had withdrawn from the Kloster Barracks and had occupied a fortified camp in the outlying eastern district, facing an area bristling with the SS. After an exchange of fire with a Wehrmacht patrol strengthened by a few SS-men, the resisters scattered without suffering any losses.[47]

Although the Wehrmacht and SS-troops could still drive back the insurgents wherever challenged, the Nazis viewed the spread of the insurgency and its deepening entrenchment in the previous twenty-four hours as alarming. Gruber and his men took heart from this gloomy Nazi perspective and resumed their operations on the morning May 3, when it was still not certain when the American troops would enter the city.[48] At 9:15 Gruber and Hradetzky, assisted by Junger, drove in a police car to Police Headquarters and demanded that Police Director Dr. Dornauer resign. He stepped down peacefully. After 10:00 A.M., an insurgent police team captured the radio transmitter near the city. Once again arriving in a police car, Gruber and Hradetzky occupied the half-empty residence of the Provincial Government. Gruber moved into an office on the second floor to exercise, as head of the Executive Committee, the authority of the Provincial Governor.[49]

In the afternoon mopping-up operations were in progress as resisters cleared the inner city area. They clashed with an SS-detachment near the Provincial Government seat, where a bullet killed Mair.[50] By 5:00 P.M. Innsbruck was safely in the hands of the Resistance;[51] but the situation was tense.

> Heavily-armed Austrians [were] swarming all over the place . . . some were in German uniform, some in civilian clothing, all wearing the white and red armband of the resistance movement. They all seemed excited and keyed up. . . . The halls were stacked with cases of . . . ammunition, and there were long rows of panzerfaust layed out [sic]. The men were loaded with 2 or 3 weapons each and had hand grenades stuck in their belts . . . all seemed excited and apprehensive that SS troops were coming in.[52]

With no sizeable German forces between the American columns and the liberated Tyrolian capital, the road was open for the Americans to follow Gruber's request to enter Innsbruck as early as possible. By the time the city was free, the radio station had performed a very useful service. To counteract any possible Nazi measures, the station broadcast from the early afternoon an appeal from the Executive Committee, calling on the Wehrmacht forces in Tyrol to pass on to their units the cease-fire order issued by the Southwestern Army Group in Italy on May 2. Because Tyrol was still under the command of Field Marshal Albert Kesselring's Army Group in southeastern Germany, which had not yet surrendered, confusion reigned among Wehrmacht units retreating to the Tyrolian Alps.[53]

In a festive atmosphere, thousands of Austrians marched into the streets while the uneasy peace remained in effect. The first United States convoys finally reached Innsbruck in the evening.

> It was like the liberation of Paris. The ovation was tremendous. Men, women, and children screamed greetings and threw flowers before the advancing troops. Bottles of cognac and wine were offered the

doughs, puzzled as to whether or not they should accept. . . . Pretty girls climbed aboard tanks and jeeps to kiss [the soldiers]. Austrian flags fluttered in the town. There were no white flags. The people seemed to consider it a liberation. . . . The Wehrmacht troops still in uniform stood at the curbside. They still carried weapons, but wore 'Free Austria' armbands, and shouted 'Heil Americans!'. The scene was totally different from anything the doughs had ever seen in any German town.[54]

By silencing the German guns, the Austrians themselves had ended the war in Tyrol.

The news of the successful coup in Innsbruck and of the advance of the American troops reverberated through the province where numerous local clandestine groups worked independently of the Gruber command. Spontaneous local uprisings spread across the province. The American advance signaled the open rebellion that began in an outburst of irregular warfare allowing American forces to take over the area without much bloodshed.[55] Before the first United States troops entered the towns, the indigenous resisters had disarmed scattered groups of German soldiers, cleared up their communities, removed weapons from the reach of the Germans, hindered the mobilization of the Tyrolian Volkssturm, protected bridges, power plants, railroad installations, public buildings, and food stores from destruction, and interrupted road and railroad transport.[56] They supplied the American columns with information on the Wehrmacht's disposition and harassed German lines of communication, but, generally, they did not keep ambushing or raiding the retreating German units.[57] Their unwillingness to risk open confrontation with the vastly superior enemy forces accounted, no doubt, for the correct behavior of the Wehrmacht. There were no cases of burnt villages, nor of civilian slayings.[58] However, several SS-units whom the Allied forces had rolled back to the Tyrolian Alps behaved with pitiless cruelty, torturing and killing any armed civilian on whom they could get their hands.

The local Resistance commanders took over the administration of the self-liberated localities. The overall picture was, however, one of constant confusion and flux as German troops passing through reoccupied the liberated areas. One of the ugliest bits of fighting took place near the town of Wörgl around Itter castle, which had sheltered since May 1943 some prominent French hostages, among them Paul Reynaud, Édouard Daladier, General Maxime Weygand, General Maurice Gamelin, and Léon Jouhaux. Concerned that the SS might execute the prisoners, an armed resistance detachment moved to surround the castle, which some of the "Gross-Deutschland" Division held.[59] Failing to penetrate the German roadblocks, the insurgents called on the advancing Americans to save the hostages. On May 5 a United States rescue column of sixteen tanks assisted by a reconnaisance party of thirty resisters finally broke the German ring around the castle and liberated the prisoners.[60] After all this, the surrender of the German Nineteenth Army in Innsbruck on May 5 was something of an anticlimax.[61]

With Tyrol wrested from Nazi hands, the Resistance drew up the balance of its achievements and losses. It estimated its strength at 1,003 active fighters organized into 157 combat teams. (But to this figure should be added all those activists who failed to register after the war.) It claimed to have saved eighty-nine bridges from destruction, to have kept 5,000 German soldiers from the battlefield, and to have preserved from damage thirty-four localities. The toll was twenty-one persons dead.[62] Fearlessness, endurance, ingenuity, and prudence were the hallmarks of the members of the Tyrolian Resistance. Joined in national and human aspirations, they demonstrated that a country physically maimed could become morally free again, not through timidity and caution, but through action and self-sacrifice.

NOTES

1. Interview with Dr. Friedrich Würthle; Molden, *Der Ruf,* pp. 118 ff.; DÖW 8390. After the liberation many activists occupied high positions in public life. Thus Hradetzky became a member of the Provincial Government and Melzer Mayor of Innsbruck.

2. Father Johann Steinmayr, S.J., who belonged to the Flora circle, was executed in November 1944. Flora's son, Paul, later a prominent painter, established contact with the White Rose group in Munich. Holzner, et al., *Zeugen des Widerstandes,* pp. 75-76, 95-97; Molden, *Der Ruf,* pp. 122-23.

3. Interview with Dr. Würthle; "Bericht," Dr. Würthle, March 29, 1949, OM, 25/19. In 1945 he became a member of the Provincial Government in Tyrol. From 1947 he was Dr. Gruber's press secretary in the Foreign Ministry.

4. OM, 25/19.

5. Of Austrian origin, Sackenheim was born in Bavaria and studied architecture in Munich and Vienna. He had participated in the Resistance since the summer of 1936. Jörg Sackenheim, "Tätigkeitsbericht," DÖW 8390; "Bericht," J. Sackenheim, OM, 22/III.

6. Ibid., Dr. Edi Grünewald, "Bericht," OM, 18/II; Molden, *Der Ruf,* pp. 122 ff.

7. OM, 22/III. Würthle quietly stored away some weapons in the Wehrmeldeamt depot. OM, 25/19.

8. "Aus der Tiroler Widerstandsbewegung," OM, 54/VI; "Bericht," Sackenheim, OM, 22. During a roundup of a Communist cell in Linz, the Gestapo found a forged military identity card (Wehrpass) supplied by Ronczay. Thanks to Würthle, Ronczay escaped from the War Court (Kriegsgericht) building in Innsbruck. OM, 25/19.

9. For Dr. Gruber, see above, pp. 169-70; OM, 25/19.

10. Ibid.

11. Josef Stockhammer, "Bericht," OM, 35. Dr. Vinzenz Pezzei became Stockhammer's deputy.

12. Wolfgang Pfaundler, "Widerstand im Ötztal," OM, 20; *Rot-weiss-rot-Buch,* pp. 218 ff; Molden, *Der Ruf,* pp. 127-30; "Kurzbericht," Hubert Sauerwein, 1946, DÖW 13240.

13. F. Molden, *Fepolinski,* pp. 288-89, 316-17; O. Molden, *Der Ruf,* pp. 274 ff; Wolfgang von Pfaundler, "Zum Problem des Freiheitskampfes 1938-1945 an Hand von Beispielen insbesondere des Widerstandes eines Tiroler Tales" (Ph.D. dissertation, University of Innsbruck, 1950), pp. 338, 341-42. In the fall of 1944 F. Molden secured contact with Sauerwein and Pfaundler.

14. *Rot-weiss-rot-Buch,* pp. 222-23. Since armed actions made little sense within this

isolated valley, there was no fighting until the end of April 1945. The resisters consisted mainly of local young peasants. In the last days French prisoners of war assisted them.

15. R. Mackowitz, *Kampf um Tirol* (Innsbruck, 1945), pp. 15-17; Johann Holzer, "Untersuchungen zur Überwindung des Nationalisozialismus in Österreich" (Ph.D. dissertation, University of Innsbruck, 1971), pp. 44-45. A native German, Görz had actively opposed the Nazis since 1933.

16. O. Molden, *Der Ruf,* pp. 269 ff; Molden, *Fepolinski,* pp. 364, 394-95. For the "Greenup" mission led by Mayer, see Persico, *Piercing,* pp. 271 ff, 291 ff.

17. Mackowtiz, *Kampf,* p. 6.

18. Gruber, *Ein politisches Leben,* pp. 33-34.

19. Molden, *Der Ruf,* pp. 298 ff; Mackowitz, *Kampf,* p. 15.

20. Gruber pointed out that of the roughly 1,600 persons who were initially sworn in, ultimately only about 150 actually took part in actions. The rest did not show up. *Leben,* p. 34.

21. Although a number of military-organized cells in many towns came into contact with the civilian resistance, so far neither a battle plan nor a central command emerged to turn the chaotic situation into an organized operation. Ibid.

22. O. Molden, *Der Ruf,* pp. 300 ff; Mackowitz, *Kampf,* pp. 17, 21 ff; OM 22/III; Holzner, "Untersuchungen," pp. 92-98.

23. For the amusing account of how Molden and the two French officers, dressed in German uniforms, moved a large clumsy English wireless transmitter disguised as German war booty from Milan to Innsbruck, see Molden, *Fepolinski,* pp. 292 ff, 312; O. Molden, *Der Ruf,* pp. 260-62. A British MI-6 officer in Bern, Edgeworth Leslie, apparently assisted the 05 efforts. Interview with Dr. L. Steiner; Stafford, *Britain,* p. 189.

24. "Bericht," Helmut Heuberger, OM, 19. For the 05 list of its safe houses and groups in Tyrol, see OM, X/31.

25. "Bericht," Dr. Hartl Pezzei, OM, 21/III. A French liaison agent, Austrian-born Lieutenant Ferdinand Zöllner, met Heuberger in Innsbruck on April 13 and established radio communication with Paris. Tilly Spiegel's interview with F. Zöllner on March 18, 1971, DÖW 7093; "Gesprächsbericht Tirol," April 7-25, 1945, OM, 50/V.

26. Molden, *Der Ruf,* p. 273; OM, 50/V.

27. On April 20, Franckenstein's radio operator Novacek-Totzenberger set up a short-wave radio transmitter at Kemater Alm (at an altitude of 1,600 m) near Innsbruck, linking the 05 group to the U.S. Headquarters in Caserta. The Kemater Alm resistance strongpoint, based on a small Wehrmacht unit stationed on the mountain, was built up around a military cell in the Mountain Reserve Battalion 136 run by Feldwebel R. Mackowitz and his companion Feldwebel Egon Horst. Horst and Mackowitz, who were introduced to Mayer, cooperated closely with Heine and helped contact activists in other Wehrmacht units. The Gestapo destroyed the cell on April 27 when they rounded up the Wehrmacht soldiers stationed at the Alm. During an exchange of fire, Novacek-Totzenberger was killed. Franckenstein, Horst, and Mackowitz were arrested in Innsbruck. "Bericht über den Widerstandskampf . . . auf der Kematen-Alm in den Jahren 1944-1945," DÖW 7447; "Vom Widerstandskampf in Tirol," DÖW 3525; "Bericht," Ludwig Steiner, DÖW 7093; Holzner et al., *Zeugen,* p. 102. The American officers moved around wearing Wehrmacht uniforms.

28. Mayer contacted Alois Kuen, a criminal police officer, who recruited a small cell from the ranks of the Innsbruck criminal police and made friends among railway workers and among groups of German deserters hiding in the mountains. The penetration of the police went so far that Mayer transported 05 couriers in police cars to the Swiss border. Mackowitz, *Kampf,* p. 22; OM, 50/V; Persico, *Piercing,* pp. 293-97. A line run by Ms. Olinowetz from the Cross Sisters' Sanatorium operated within 05 as did the intelligence gathering center of Hauptmann Dr. Artur Andreatta, the owner of the prominent Innsbruck Hotel "Kreid." Andreatta, Mayer, and the organizers of the Kuen group were arrested on April 20. Initially, Mayer was brutally interrogated, but he was soon brought before Gauleiter Franz Hofer of Tyrol, who requested him to serve as a go-between, offering Hofer's terms of capitulation to the United

States Seventh Army Command in Zirl. Mackowitz, *Kampf,* p. 37; DÖW 7093; Persico, *Piercing,* pp. 294-97, 360 ff; Edward Hymoff, *The OSS in World War II* (New York, 1972), pp. 230-34; Brown, *The Secret War,* pp. 557 ff.

29. DÖW 7093; interview with Dr. Steiner.

30. O. Molden, *Der Ruf,* p. 275, 280 ff; "Bericht," Helmut Heuberger, OM, 19/II; Mackowitz, *Kampf,* pp. 22-23; OM, 50/V. Eventually, Prof. Dr. Eduard Reut-Nicolussi, a noted advocate of the freedom of South Tyrol, became the head of POEN, although he had not been active in the Resistance.

31. Apart from Heine and Steiner, the staff included Major Josef Schneeberger, Lieutn.-Colonel (ret'd) Haubold, Oberleutnant Josef Moser, Stricker, Eckl, Pezzei, Heuberger, E. Grünewald, and Winkler. O. Molden, *Der Ruf,* pp. 282-83; DÖW 7093. Moser belonged to a military cell in the popular summer resort of Igls, which the Gestapo soon destroyed. OM, 19/II.

32. O. Molden, *Der Ruf,* pp. 282 ff; OM, 50/V; OM, 19/II. Heine was mainly responsible for the actual planning. Apparently still uninformed about the real capabilities and intentions of the enemy, the Allied planners assumed the Nazis would make a last defense effort in the Alpine region.

33. OM, 19. Some of the differences among the ranking figures concerned tactics. Sackenheim favored direct actions by small armed combat teams without waiting for outside help, whereas Gruber, Würthle, and Heine concentrated on preparing for a large military action. OM, 22/III, 50/V.

34. OM, 19. The cooperation between Gruber and 05 evolved smoothly. The relationship between Gruber and both Moldens became so close that Fritz was appointed Gruber's secretary at the Foreign Ministry at the end of July 1945. F. Molden, *Fepolinski,* passim; Gruber, *Ein Leben,* p. 31.

35. Gruber, *Ein Leben,* p. 36.

36. Heine moved to the military hospital in Sollbad Hall to avoid his impending transfer to Carinthia. From Kemater Alm, he drove almost daily to Innsbruck. The Gestapo just missed him during the roundup on April 20. Gruber, *Ein Leben,* pp. 34-35; OM, 19; Molden, *Der Ruf,* pp. 302-3.

37. OM, 19. Tyrol was divided into two main sectors. Sackenheim and Haller were charged with the Upper Inn and Lower Inn Valley, respectively.

38. Molden, *Der Ruf,* pp. 303-4.

39. DÖW 7093; Gruber, *Leben,* pp. 36-37.

40. OM, No 53; Mackowitz, *Kampf,* p. 38. Unfortunately, Schneeberger had been removed from his command upon Gauleiter Hofer's urging before the clandestine action started. However, he still succeeded in denuding his sector of German troops, and Seefeld fell without resistance. On May 2, Lieutenant Steiner crossed the battle lines to brief the Americans on the situation in Innsbruck. He then accompanied Mayer to Gauleiter Hofer to negotiate Hofer's capitulation. "Bericht," L. Steiner, DÖW 7093.

41. OM, 22/III; Mackowitz, *Kampf,* pp. 35-38; O. Molden, *Der Ruf,* pp. 317-19; OM, 19/II.

42. The Committee's roster, headed by Gruber, comprised Gamper, Dr. Grünewald, Dr. Karl Höflinger, Hradetzky, Melzer, Reut-Nicolussi, Würthle, Franz Hüttenberger, Dr. Franz Kundratitz, Univ. Prof. Dr. Arthur March, Josef Muigg, Thurner, Dr. Alfons Weissgatterer, and Zechner. Mackowitz, *Kampf,* pp. 48-49.

43. Gruber, *Leben,* pp. 36-37; OM 22/III; OM 19/II; Molden, *Der Ruf,* pp. 318 ff.

44. Oberleutnant Huber, Hauptmann Guido Todeschini, Dr. Eckl, and above all Sackenheim bore the brunt of the fighting. Molden, *Der Ruf,* pp. 319 ff; OM 22/III; Gruber, *Leben,* p. 37; Mackowitz, *Kampf,* pp. 39 ff.

45. Gruber, *Leben,* pp. 40-41; Mackowitz, *Kampf,* pp. 41-43; Molden, *Der Ruf,* pp. 320-22; Dr. Gruber in *Wiener Kurier,* May 3, 1946.

46. Mackowitz, *Kampf,* p. 43; "Bericht," J. Sackenheim, OM. On May 2 a representative

of General von Böhaimb was taken blindfolded to the United States 103rd Division command post. The emissary offered the surrender of Tyrol. On May 3, the Division's intelligence officer Major West again drove into German-occupied territory to see Gauleiter Hofer who then "sent a message to the German troops to yield to the Americans." Ralph Mueller and Jerry Turk, *Report after Action; The Story of the 103rd Infantry Division* (Innsbruck, 1945), pp. 141-43.

47. Gruber, *Leben,* pp. 41-42.

48. The insurgents reoccupied the Kloster Barracks and captured the main arms depot at Hofburg. Molden, *Der Ruf,* p. 325.

49. Mackowitz, *Kampf,* pp. 49 ff; Molden, *Der Ruf,* pp. 325-26; Gruber, *Leben,* pp. 42 ff; OM, 54/VI.

50. When an SS-column entered the city, Major Heine commandeered an artillery unit and returned with heavy 7,5cm antiaircraft guns, which he positioned so as to direct their fire against the SS armored vehicles. The soldiers followed Heine, who took command as a higher ranking officer, without ever asking him any questions. They had no idea that insurgents carried out the operation. Gruber, *Leben,* p. 45.

51. Mackowitz, *Kampf,* p. 58. According to the 103rd Division intelligence, about 800 armed men were at the disposal of the Resistance; the number included 300 men from a Wehrmacht unit and 500 armed civilians. DÖW 7812.

Gruber was also worried about the fate of his arrested companions (Mayer, Grünewald, and others) at the local concentration camp in Reichenau and took immediate steps to launch a rescue operation. Fortunately, the inmates were released unharmed. Mayer was brought to Gauleiter Hofer, whom he helped to persuade to abandon Innsbruck. Persico, *Piercing,* pp. 363-69.

52. Report of Operations. *The Seventh United States Army in France and Germany 1944-1945.* Restricted, 3 vols. 3:845.

53. Mackowitz, *Kampf,* pp. 51 ff. Other broadcasts urged soldiers to surrender to the Provisional Austrian Army.

54. Mueller and Turk, *Report after Action,* p. 143; Holzner, "Untersuchungen," p. 119. For their reminiscences, see Molden, *Fepolinski,* pp. 389 ff, and Karl Gruber, *Zwischen Befreiung und Freiheit. Der Sonderfall Österreich* (Vienna, 1953), pp. 7 ff.

55. Some of the cells emerged in late April; the nuclei of many others had been built throughout 1943 and 1944. Well in advance of the insurrection, the underground emissaries had cooperated with French conscripted workers and prisoners of war in the labor camp in the village of Rum near Innsbruck and with the Serbian labor camps in Hall am Kematen. "POEN-05, Aktionsgebiet Tirol," April 21, 1945, OM, X/31.

56. Holzner, "Untersuchungen," p. 132. Preventing the destruction of the Arlberg tunnel and of the Trisanna bridge on the important Arlberg railway line represented the main achievement. DÖW 7803.

57. Revolts erupted in many localities. Holzner, "Untersuchungen," pp. 120-31; various reports by local resistance groups, DÖW 7802-7804.

58. For reminiscences by a noted German anti-Fascist writer who settled in the village of Mayrhofen in the Ziller Valley at the end of March 1945, see Erich Kästner, *Notabene 45. Ein Tagebuch* (Zurich, 1961).

59. "Die Wahrheit über Schloss Itter," OM, 24/III. In another action early in May, the South Tyrolian resistance in North Italy helped free from a hotel in the Pragser Wildsee resort about 200 political prisoners, among them Léon Blum, Hjalmar Schacht, Dr. Kurt Schuschnigg, and British Intelligence officer Payne Best. Allen Dulles, *The Secret Surrender* (New York, 1966), pp. 229-30; *Mitteilungen des Bundes der Tiroler Freiheitskämpfer,* 1, no. 1 (December 1948). Another group of prominent figures including the Polish underground military leaders were freed from a prison camp in the Pongau valley on May 5. Mueller and Turk, *Report,* p. 145.

60. On May 3 Rupert Hagleitner and forty men set out to take control of Wörgl. German Major Josef Gangl and ten of his soldiers joined them. Gangl and Hagleitner feared that the

castle guards would kill its French residents and sought help from Colonel Lynch, commander of the 142nd Regiment of the United States 36th Infantry Division, who had just reached Kufstein. Gangl was killed on May 5 when he took command of the local combat group. "Bericht. Darstellung," Rupert Hagleitner, DÖW 7804.

61. Mueller and Turk, *Report,* p. 144.

62. For the figures given by the Bund der Tiroler Freiheitskämpfer in 1948, see Holzner, "Untersuchungen," pp. 134-35. W. Pfaundler estimated the number of the fighters in Tyrol before 1945 at no more than 1,500 persons. "Zum Problem des Freiheitskampfes," p. 86.

For the OSS mission parachuted near the town of Kufstein on March 24, 1945, see Persico, *Piercing,* pp. 254-58, 378-80. The OSS team specialized in military intelligence and cooperated with the local underground. With its fifty-two radioed messages to its home base in London, the mission ranked as the most productive of the OSS teams sent to the Reich. See also Brown, *The Secret War,* pp. 542, 547-48.

22

The Liberation in the Provinces

TWO MAIN CURRENTS OF RESISTANCE

By late April all of Austria had become a frontline zone as the Allied armies pushed back the outmanned and outgunned Wehrmacht. Behind the battle lines, the Resistance took the lead in anti-German activity. But its actions, which occurred at different times and places, only further divided the underground, already split into different regions and lacking a single center. Some survivors of Gestapo raids on the original networks, who had withdrawn from clandestine work, rejoined in the last years of the war. New adherents joined late in 1944 and in 1945, when victory seemed likely.

At this stage, former party veterans, unable to participate earlier in the conspiracy because of their high visibility, resurfaced. Their role was political. Not anxious to engage in armed combat, they pointed out the risks involved in covert activities. They saw the underground primarily as a means to assure an orderly transfer of power to the Republic and to aid their return to politics. The proximity of the liberation made them more acutely aware of the need for common political agreement. Carrying the authority of the traditional political parties, these political veterans joined in cooperative clandestine efforts to ensure that their joint wartime experiences provide the basis of a future coalition government. The wretched experience of the occupation and the joint struggle crucially changed the two principal parties' views of each other. The Socialists and Christian Democrats exorcised their prejudices against each other as the enemy and thus set a pattern for their future dealings as democratic partners.

If one views participation in the Resistance as a matter of degree, ranging from organizational involvement to participation in armed action, a line may be drawn across that range and all persons above that line categorized as active militants and those below merely organizationally or politically involved resisters. Although no clear line can be drawn between the groups dedicated to action and those more informal groups usually dedicated to their political interests, these two principal impulses, military and political, could often be clearly distinguished. The two strands did not often coincide, but they did overlap. Apart from the activist networks, a welter of political groups mushroomed throughout the country. Because they existed to gain power when the military should collapse, the party-oriented circles were less structured and less effective than the patriotic networks. In their structure and opinion, they reflected the incoming party system more than they did the fighting tradition and activism of the Resistance. In their mood, they represented the ordinary citizens' refusal of Nazi efforts to implicate them in the consequences of the war.[1]

This often ambiguous and blurred bipolar character of the underground in its final stage was linked to the absence of a clear-sighted, strong leadership at home and abroad. Apart from those in Vienna, Tyrol, and parts of Upper Austria and Styria, the cadres of the early networks never quite succeeded in becoming the national nuclei around which the crippled anti-Nazi conspiracy could reassemble. However, the value of clandestine warfare should not be underestimated. Although most underground work did not seriously threaten the regime, activist patriotic movements such as 05 had annoyed the authorities and had gradually created an atmosphere of political insecurity that weakened the regime's confidence and lowered public morale.

The series of German defeats moved the clandestine action into a more political phase, less spontaneous in its nature, more selfish and calculating in its origin. The less vibrant moderates, represented by old party hands, saw the possibility of a peaceful takeover. Their exercise of caution appeared reasonable to many because their stake in the underground was less immediate and less personal than that of the militants who had been at work since 1938.

THE PROVINCES

Various internal changes contributed to popular discontent and unease in the country. The anti-regime motivation was largely patriotic and ideological, and in places the Austrians began to hate all Germans, not just Nazi Germans, as the traditionally more easy-going Austrian life-style fell victim to Berlin's efforts to impose its Prussian self-discipline. War losses, shortages of food, and the terrible hardships of the war combined to create opposition even among apolitical people. Instability and apprehension in the wake of the overwhelming Soviet and Anglo-American victories in 1944 brought Austrians closer together. The increasing sacrifices and the great anxiety, which the ferocious Allied air raids awakened in 1944-45, contributed to the rise of a tense climate for Austro-German relations, a climate that pushed more rapidly the development of Austrian self-consciousness.

After the first omens of disaster, many Austrians strove to disengage themselves from the pernicious consequences of the war of aggression that the Nazis had instigated. They began to look for a shelter. Since responsibility rested with Nazi Germany, Austria was entitled to her national independence. Thus, at the end of the winter of 1944, the Resistance, in striking contrast to its earlier isolation, was gaining in moral influence, if not in prestige and popularity.

For reasons of geography and wartime politics, no nationwide uprising could have been centrally coordinated in a country besieged from four sides. When the Red Army wrested Vienna from the Germans, Germany still controlled the remaining provinces. The Resistance could not act simultaneously all over the country. Its intervention was concurrent with the advance of the four Allied forces. In contrast to this development, which eventually split the country into four occupation zones, the Resistance made national cohesion an objective that overrode regional differences. It never accepted the easy assumption that the Republic should somehow be won by "waiting it out." The spontaneous emergence of the local and regional resistance that had a burning desire to liberate Austria unified the provinces.

UPPER AUSTRIA

The first days of May 1945 were memorable in the history of the war in Upper Austria. No fighting took place in Linz, the provincial capital. Foreign workers and tens of thousands of German refugees, seeking refuge in the United States-occupied territory, flooded the city and the surrounding industrial zone. The underground's role in the liberation of Linz was slight. Native anti-Nazi elements arranged with the local authorities to prevent destruction of the slaughterhouse, food stores, power and water plants, and the Danube bridge. On May 3 and 4 an emissary slipped through the battle lines to the approaching American troops. He brought information on German artillery positions in and around Linz and on the strongpoints on the Traun defense line. Since the Gestapo had departed from the city a few days earlier, the resisters removed anti-tank road blocks during the night of May 4-5, enabling the United States Third Army's armored column to arrive in Linz on May 5.[2]

In the Eferding-Haag am Hausrück area, Josef Hofer called on volunteers to assist the American forces. Activists who had joined the Resistance were organized into small groups in the towns of Ried, Helfenberg, Aigen, Peilstein, Perg, Grein, and Steyr. They roamed behind the front lines eliminating road traps and blocks, taking over control of local government and reporting German dispositions and movements to American reconnaissance parties.[3] Meanwhile, on the morning of May 4, Major Franz Payrl and his men from Motor Car Reserve- and Training Unit 17 established themselves in the barracks in Enns and rounded up the Nazi-oriented officers within the Unit. Payrl carried out a plan devised in conjunction with Hauptmann Estermann's combat teams in Amstetten. The plan expected the teams to set up strongholds within the Enns frontline to harass German columns.[4] But two SS-units crushed the uprising, captured Major Payrl, and surrounded the barracks. A sudden air raid by Allied fighter-bombers enabled the men to escape.[5]

Events in Wels, the second largest city in Upper Austria, went more smoothly. Two Austrian officers who had returned from the front organized a military circle at Artillery Reserve Unit 96 in March 1945. The circle coordinated activity with Amstetten Unit 109 under Estermann and with the trade unionist Franz Grüttner who provided local friends.[6] On May 4 when Nazi officials ordered the machinery in the factories destroyed and the bridges demolished, the two commanders of the Soldatenbund went at once to the commanding officer of the 66th Infantry Regiment of the United States 71st Division to arrange the capitulation of the Wels military command. One hour later, the officers in the Wels artillery barracks joined the conspirators and handed their surrender to American Colonel Regnier whose column had just arrived in the city. In the evening the streets were lined with people celebrating, toasting the Americans, and singing patriotic songs.[7]

Apart from the Hollenstein and Salzkammergut armed revolts, perhaps the Upper Austrian underground's greatest achievement was its preservation of the largest Austrian paper and synthetic fiber plant in Lenzing.[8] On April 21, two Allied agents, J. Staufer and H. Rieder, who had parachuted near Lenzing, asked the group "Bari" to prevent the destruction of the plant. The group had about seventy men, some officers and soldiers of Unit 109 transferred from Amstetten under Hauptmann Dr. Manfred Schneider's command, and some employees of the Lenzing plant. On May 4 a small resistance task force moved into the plant and disarmed sixty-five members of the Factory Guard and of the Wehrmacht Pioneer Company. The next morning the plant was handed over intact to the officers of the United States 80th Division. During the rescue operation, only one resister was killed.

As the advance of the Allied troops accelerated, the resisters took charge of the towns and localities even before the shattered Nazi administrations had been removed. In places, the higher-ranking Nazis fled their posts; elsewhere, as did the Mayor of Linz Franz Langoth and the Carinthian Gauleiter Friedrich Rainer, they negotiated a peaceful transfer of power with the Resistance. Unfortunately, in a few instances the Nazis, like cornered wild animals, committed ugly crimes. On April 6, in the large Stein prison near the Danubian town of Krems, local Nazi officials ordered the massacre of 386 political inmates, just hours before their release, and the hanging of prison director Franz Kodré and his four aides.[9] Eager to assert his authority, Upper Austrian Gauleiter August Eigruber instructed the judicial authorities to carry out all the death sentences passed by the courts.[10] The authorities blindly followed the infamous order.[11] On April 9, forty-six political prisoners taken from Vienna to Stein were shot by their SS guards.[12]

Salzburg, Styria, and Carinthia

In the provinces of Salzburg and Styria, as elsewhere, the principal clandestine activity was not open fighting against the regime, but the marshaling of resistance to prevent wanton destruction. The resisters, flooded by latecomers, busily formed cells and started small actions mainly to protect bridges and other important public installations. In places, clashes developed between German troops and underground parties removing explosive charges.[13] In Salzburg, special units guarded the main post office building, the bridges, and the radio transmitter at Mönchsberg. One armed team even requested of the City Military Commander that he protect the city from destruction. The Resistance missed no chance to hamper and obstruct the organization of the Volkssturm units, often seizing their weapons.[14] Since the beginning of 1945, acts of sabotage had intensified (for instance, at the Sulzau-Werfen Iron Works), and aid was offered to Wehrmacht deserters, whose numbers had swollen since 1944.[15] Ultimately, the city fell without struggle to the American forces on May 4 when Gauleiter Dr. Gustav Scheel recognized the futility of further German armed resistance.[16]

In Graz and Klagenfurt, representatives of the democratic parties took control of provincial governments directly from the Nazi authorities, who quietly stepped aside to avoid a costly battle.[17] The growing restiveness of the underground rarely resulted in open fighting — except for sections of the Koralpe range and of the Austro-Yugoslav border occupied by the Partisans. The underground had done well in the Weiz, Fürstenfeld, Hartberg, and Deutschlandsberg districts of Styria in 1944. In Fohnsdorf and the districts of Feldbach, Liezen, Bruck a.d. Mur, and Mürzzuschlag, numerous cells had even done some work in 1943.[18] Many of the cells had helped individual militants and the families of imprisoned resisters but had not been overly effective. In the last stage of the occupation, the level of resistance activity rose perceptibly, and anti-Nazi teams aided the Red Army by preventing demolitions by the withdrawing Wehrmacht.

In November 1944, the "Styrian Fighting Community" first appeared. Its influence, concentrated in Graz, grew and spread through Socialist and Christian Democratic groups into factories, the Volkssturm, and the Wehrmacht. Eventually, Colonel Leonhard of the Army City Command, a native of Graz, won over by his sister-in-law, supplied the militants with arms and documents. To build up its forces to meet any local contingencies and to emphasize the urgency of underground action, the "Styrian Community" distributed leaflets calling for a "liberation struggle." One of its preoccupations was protection of the city, which German units garrisoned. The Soviets had positioned their ground forces south of the Styrian-Yugoslav border, and the Graz underground realized that it had a limited time to convince the local German military that the Austrians had no interest in the Wehrmacht's combating Soviet troops in and around the city. Pleading for a cease-fire, the commanders of the Graz Resistance approached the Graz commanding officer, General Julius Ringel, at the end of March. They were more successful with Nazi Mayor Dr. Julius Kaspar, who shared their apprehension of the potentially heavy damages to the city. On May 7, parties of resistance fighters tried to safeguard the bridges and power plants. In the afternoon, an armed group seized the police headquarters, and during the night its members contacted the Red Army.[19] The Soviets entered the city the next day without encountering armed opposition. Party politicians had already taken steps to ensure their eventual control. At the beginning of April a few former high ranking Socialists met near Graz to approve a scheme for the peaceful reestablishment of the democratic Provincial Government. On May 8, a temporary Provincial Government took the reins of the provincial administration into its hands.[20]

In Klagenfurt Gauleiter Rainer finally transferred power to the Austrian administrators on May 7. As in Styria, the underground provided the necessary framework for the relatively smooth takeover. The nucleus of the Revolutionary Socialists (RS) became again a focus.[21] It regarded the Communists as unsuitable allies but attempted to deal effectively and amiably with the Yugoslav Partisans. The RS expected to coordinate their efforts with other resistance organizations, the most important of which was a new network, started in the summer of 1944, following the liquidation of the Granig-Krumpl-Kofler movement in 1943. Major (ret.) Friedrich Gressel and the textile merchant Julius Santer led the Klagenfurt group, which found supporters within the police and gendarmerie. Early in 1945 they developed contacts to several Army units, above all to the commander of the 438th Division in Klagenfurt, General-Lieutenant Ferdinand Noeldechen, and to the commander of the 139th Mountain Reserve Regiment, Colonel Meng. The latter arranged a clandestine rendezvous with Tito Partisan emissaries and established contact with the British troops on the Italian border.[22]

Early in May the Klagenfurt group expanded to become a Provincial Action Committee, which embraced former democratic party leaders. The movement included a security team of police and gendarmerie officers headed by Lieutenant-Colonel Josef Stossier, who had secretly been in touch with the Yugoslav Partisans, feeding them false information about the strength of the local German units and thus delaying the Partisan attack upon the provincial capital. Because the British forces were engaged near Tarvis in Northern Italy, and the Germans were withdrawing from Yugoslavia toward the British lines, any German decision to fight in the province would have been militarily senseless; and it would have left the area in a state of anarchy, inviting what the resisters, the military, and the Nazis most dreaded — Yugoslav occupation.

For the Austrians, the main task was to arrange a cease-fire to prevent the outbreak of a destructive British operation, which must be somehow arranged before the Yugoslav Partisan units reached Klagenfurt. The resisters, who felt the same way, sought an agreement with the military and political authorities. On April 15, Santer requested Lieutenant-Colonel Payer to provide General Noeldechen with a liaison to help arrange the takeover of the provincial government from Gauleiter Rainer. On May 4, General Noeldechen, after talking to Santer and Gressel, transmitted to Rainer their demand for an orderly transfer of power to the Action Committee, which would have a free hand to negotiate the surrender of the province with the British Eighth Army. The next day the Gauleiter saw the members of the Committee, who pleaded with him to approve the surrender, but he still refused to resign, making his resignation dependent on the British actually crossing the border. During the next day negotiations continued. The Austrians argued that a cease-fire would allow the British to counter the Partisan threat to occupy Klagenfurt. After more wrangling, delay, and anxious waiting, the obstinate Rainer finally succumbed to reason and declared Klagenfurt and Villach open cities. At 11:10 P.M., on May 7, Radio Klagenfurt announced the constitution of the democratic provincial government.[23] On the morning of May 8, a British column entered Klagenfurt to accept the surrender of the German troops. A few hours later, the Tito forces reached the city.[24] The new administration under Social Democrat Hans Piesch took immediate charge of the province.

Vorarlberg

Vorarlberg, the westernmost province, was administered from Tyrol. Its economic prosperity reflected the westward shift of the Austrian economy after 1938. The ensuing rise in the standard of living helped strengthen Nazi rule in the province and contributed to an enormous increase in NSDAP membership from 1,188 in 1933 to 7,893 in 1938 and to 70,348 in 1942.[25] The great distance from Vienna, the temporary economic boom, and the close ties with neighboring Swabia reduced the chances for widespread clandestine action. Moreover, the Gestapo was vigilant because of the proximity of the Swiss border.

At the outset of the war, the thoroughly independent-minded population, some of it in the more remote mountain areas, had remained relatively untouched by the occupation; there was no serious underground. Isolated circles had cautiously begun to take shape in the western part of the province bordering Switzerland. Various escape lines bringing persons out of Austria ran through Vorarlberg. From Zurich, Klein established safe houses in Vorarlberg with the aid of Socialist railwaymen who smuggled microfilmed reports hidden inside pencils to Austria.[26] Always the Resistance moved cautiously, but it was not until 1945 that the growing tide of military reverses which threatened to submerge the province thoroughly stirred up resistance.[27]

The continued Allied advance found the people deeply disturbed. What they saw in the near future was more of a war that had already lasted too long and that would bring death and destruction to their homes. At this crucial stage, the activists increased their contacts in the larger towns. They concentrated their forces in the provincial capital, Bregenz, which late in April became the prime target for the French troops massed at the Austrian border.[28] To prevent heavy street fighting, the patriots joined forces with the French spearhead at the city outskirts. On May 1 the French fired on Bregenz. Guided by Professor Paul Pirker, two French infantry companies turned the German flank and entered the city from the rear. The beflagged capital prepared a warm welcome for the French soldiers.[29]

Meanwhile, small cells had made progress in the countryside, reflecting a general deterioration in security when the Nazi administration could no longer effectively control the population. A group in Langeneff in the Bregenz Forest was the center of a cluster of supportive cells. At a meeting at the end of April, the patriots prepared to prevent demolitions of bridges, to arrest local Nazi officials and their "fanatical associates," and to disrupt the German lines of communication. On May 1 a combat team occupied the local post office and removed explosives from two bridges. Unfortunately, a column of forty SS-men ran into a six-man party in Langenegg and wiped it out.[30]

In other towns the underground had been built from almost nothing. In Dornbirn a group of over forty persons actively assisted the French troops. Otherwise, its achievements were small. In Feldkirch there existed three parallel organizations. The remnant of the Communist cell that had been wrecked in 1942 collected intelligence for the British in Switzerland and in 1944 drafted plans for the airborne landing of Allied troops in the province. The resisters stored arms and ammunition and enlisted the help of the local gendarmes. Oberleutnant Lorenz Tiefenthaler successfully ran his 05 line for the rest of the war. Firemen and postal and railway employees penetrated the local Volkssturm. Late in April, in the neighboring town of Bludenz, ten firemen and forty-two civilians formed a group whose principal effort was an unsuccessful raid against the NSDAP district headquarters during the night of May 3-4.[31]

As in other places, the underground in Montafon Valley was divided into several nuclei, mostly made up of workers and employees from the factories and power plants.[32] Volunteer units kept their localities intact by disarming German soldiers. The chief task of the Wehrmacht contingent in Partenen was the protection of the Ill Works, the largest Austrian electrical power plant and dam, guarded by an anti-aircraft artillery battery. Between May 1 and 3 local patriots overpowered the battery commander and his officers, disarmed the soldiers, cut off their communications, and blocked access to the Works to prevent the Germans from sabotaging the power plant. They moved the anti-aircraft guns toward St. Gallenkirch to hold in check and to disarm SS and Army groups seeking shelter in the valley.

After May 1, the French presence transformed the nature of the resistance in the province and brought it into sharper focus. The pattern of fighting shifted to larger engagements involving French units. Most of the fighting was concentrated around towns, all close to the main Arlberg railroad line. The irregular forces assisted the French troops but usually avoided armed skirmishes with the Germans. By May 6 the French had achieved their objective—the control of Vorarlberg—in six days. The underground's last achievement was preventing the blow-up of the Arlberg tunnel and the blocking of the Arlberg Pass road.[33] The military underground operated parallel to the civilian groups. In three companies of Mountain-Communication-Reserve and Training Unit 18 in Bludenz, self-contained cells (thirty-one soldiers out of 1,800) encouraged soldiers to avoid fighting, delayed the obeying of orders, and spread alarming rumors. The internal demoralization was so effective that the poorly equipped companies partly disintegrated, unwilling to fight the much superior French forces.[34]

Amid the chaos of the German defeat and the exuberance of victory, the Resistance forces and the emerging political parties represented a stabilizing factor. Not surprisingly, the French authorities chose to have representatives of the two main political parties included in the future provincial government. On May 2 they dispatched several officials to Zurich to bring former Socialist functionaries Klein and Linder back to Vorarlberg, and sounded several former Christian Social leaders on their support of the coalition with the Socialists.[35] The scattered and uncoordinated men of the Resistance did not compete with the leading political figures at the liberation. Almost immediately they departed the political scene. And so, Austrian politics returned to its long-standing practice of operating through political parties.

NOTES

1. Luža, *Austro-German Relations*, p. 343.

2. DÖW, ed., *Widerstand in Oberösterreich*, 1-2, passim; Ludwig Bernaschek, "Zusammenstellung über die Widerstandsbewegung Oberösterreichs," April 25, 1946, DÖW 2127. As in other occupied countries, scores of small cells, previously unknown, surfaced in the last days of the occupation. American soldiers were surprised at the friendly welcome they received in heavily bombed Linz, which had suffered twenty-two air attacks since July 25, 1944. Hindinger, *Das Kriegsende*, pp. 18, 29, 39, 49.

3. DÖW 2127; Hindinger, *Das Kriegsende*, pp. 22 ff, 33 ff; Erich Leimlehner, "Das Kriegsende und der Wiederaufbau demokratischer Verhältnisse im Mühlviertel 1945." Lizentiatsarbeit (University of Zürich, 1972), pp. 18-22. DÖW, ed., *Widerstand in Oberösterreich*, 2:342-44; DÖW 8362, 15061.

4. The Enns military cell had been founded in 1943 and was in contact with L. Bernaschek.

5. The resisters, who numbered 186, wore red-white-red armbands. Hermann Reszentylo, "Freiheitsbatallion Enns," DÖW 2125; L. Bernaschek, "Der Kampf um Enns," DÖW 2127.

6. Oberleutnant Gottfried Teufel and Leutnant Volkmar Vösleitner were chiefs of the Wels six-member military committee. DÖW 2126; O. Molden, *Der Ruf*, p. 104. Grüttner maintained links to the Bernachek group in Linz and to the Hofer network.

7. DÖW 2126.

8. DÖW 5179; *Rot-weiss-rot Buch*, p. 142.

9. *Neues Österreich*, August 4, 21, 1946; Stadler, *Österreich*, pp. 354-55.

10. Stadler, *Österreich*, p. 356.

11. Szecsi-Stadler, *Die NS-Justiz*, pp. 25-26.

12. Ludwig Jedlicka, "Die letzte Kriegsphase," in Erika Weinzierl and Kurt Skalnik, eds., *Österreich. Die Zweite Republik* (Graz, 1972), 1:133. As late as May 3 some Austrian inmates were executed at Mauthausen concentration camp. Leimlehner, "Das Kriegsende," p. 23.

13. Becker, *Freiheitskampf*, pp. 31-33.

14. Ibid.

15. Becker indicates that 650 cases of deserters from Salzburg came before the military tribunals in 1944. Ibid., p. 31. Kaut gives figures on Socialist losses, *Der steinige Weg*, p. 147.

16. Rauchensteiner, *Krieg*, pp. 281-84 and *Der Sonderfall*, pp. 96-97.

17. According to the offical estimate of May 10, 1946, some 36,000 political inmates passed through the police prison in Graz during the NS-era. Between January and April 1945, 143 persons were executed in Graz alone. *Rot-weiss-rot Buch*, p. 209; DÖW 8342.

18. *Rot-weiss-rot Buch*, p. 210. Many acts of resistance remained unrecorded. Participants may sometimes have exaggerated their activities.

19. DÖW 3012, 3095.

20. Schärf, *Erneuerung*, p. 45.

21. In September 1944 the RS were still sympathetic to the Greater-German concept. Early in March 1945 they disowned this view. Weber, "Die linken Sozialisten," pp. 64-65; interview with Erwin Schärf.

22. Amt der Kärnter Landesregierung, "Die historischen Maitage 1945," March 28, 1946; Julius Santer, "Die Aktion Gressel-Santer in Kärnten"; Franz Payer, "Was in den historischen Maitagen 1945 in Kärnten wirklich geschah," December 1945; Julius Santer-Fr. Gressel, "Bericht"; DÖW 8385; *Volkszeitung*, December 16, 1945; Fr. Rainer, "Gedächtnissvermerk," May 5, 1945, Institut für Geschichte der Arbeiterbewegung, SPÖ, Partei Archiv, Mappe 70, Kärnten 1944; Claudia Fräss-Ehrfeld, "Kärnten 1945—Von-Neubeginn und Bewältigung," *Österreich in Geschichte und Literatur* 20 (March-April 1976): 101-2. For a different account, see Rauchensteiner, *Der Sonderfall*, pp. 86-88.

23. The government list was prepared on May 6. The nominees belonged to the SPÖ (three) CSP (two), Landbund (two), and KPÖ (two). The tenth member, Santer, was without party affiliation. DÖW 8385. See also Theo Rossiwall, *Die letzten Tage* (Vienna, 1969), pp. 307 ff.

24. Remembering the post-1918 crisis, Austrians feared Tito's ambition to annex a part of Carinthia. Schärf, *Erneuerung*, pp. 46-47.

25. BA, Sammlung Schumacher, 303I, 376. The figures apply to Tyrol and Vorarlberg, which merged in a Reichsgau in 1938-39. In 1947 the recorded ratio of former Nazi Party membership to the total population was the highest in the three western provinces: Tyrol, 14.5 percent; Salzburg, 10.9 percent; and Vorarlberg, 10.4 percent. Austrian Federal Chancellery in Military Government Austria, Report of the U.S. High Commissioner, November 1947, p. 187.

26. Stadler, *Österreich*, p. 77.

27. In all, 2,684 political prisoners passed through the LG prison in Feldkirch between March 13, 1938, and May 1, 1945. LG, Feldkirch, April 15, 1946, DÖW 8346.

28. For the situation in Vorarlberg, see Dietlinde Löffler-Bolka, *Vorarlberg 1945. Das Kriegsende und der Wiederaufbau demokratischer Verhältnisse in Vorarlberg im Jahre 1945* (Bregenz, 1975), pp. 48-49; DÖW 8346.

29. Paul Pirker, *Citadelle Bregenz* (Bregenz, 1946); Georg Schelling, *Festung Vorarlberg. Ein Bericht über das Kriegsgeschehen 1945 in unserem Lande* (Bregenz, 1947); DÖW 8346.

30. Löffler-Bolka, *Vorarlberg,* pp. 49-51. Gustav Schelling, "Die letzten Kriegstage in Vorarlberg," April 1, 1946, DÖW 8346.

31. On this occasion, a railwayman was captured and shot. Fein, *Die Steine,* p. 279.

32. DÖW 8346; Löffler-Bolka, *Vorarlberg,* pp. 55-57.

33. Schelling, *Festung,* pp. 172 ff; Rauchensteiner, *Krieg,* pp. 274-75. In Kleine Walsertal, an underground cell that started in 1943 assisted deserters and collected arms. On May 1, 1945, local resisters took control of the three communities, rounded up the Nazi officials, and held on for two days until French troops arrived. DÖW 8346.

34. Löffler-Bolka, *Vorarlberg,* pp. 58-59. The OSS helped Hilde Meisel, a member of Internationaler Sozialistische Kampfbund, to slip from Switzerland to Austria early in 1945. She formed an intelligence cell in Vienna. When crossing the Swiss-Vorarlberg border on her way back to Zurich on April 17, she was shot by a border patrol. She committed suicide on the spot by swallowing a cyanide pill. Persico, *Piercing,* pp. 106-7; 114; Fein, *Die Steine,* p. 274.

35. Schärf, *Erneuerung,* p. 48.

CONCLUSION

Conclusion

POSTWAR AUSTRIA

If the average citizens had endorsed the Anschluss in 1938, they had done so to live in peace and prosperity, but by the spring of 1945 they felt that their country had sacrificed its own interests to those of Germany for too long. The prevailing mood reflected national pride, economic fear, and sheer warweariness. But the occupation had had positive effects. In spontaneously reintroducing the party system at the provincial and local level, the citizens certainly demonstrated that they prized democracy the more for having lost it. They understood now that strong political parties were crucial to a democratic system. They also perceived the need for a policy of national reconstruction, for social and political reform and economic modernization.[1]

The elitist Resistance was ill-suited to solve the urgent needs of national reconciliation. It had accomplished its part; it had given to the vision of national community a moral purpose. However, in what appears a unique case in liberated Europe, the resisters received no recognition or thanks from the new authorities or from the public. They were often considered superfluous outcasts, an uncomfortable reminder to the Austrian people of their own timidity. The indifference, distrust, lack of understanding, and glacial manner of many government officials sapped the morale of the resisters, creating much bad feeling and frustration among them.

Almost immediately after the liberation, friction arose between the underground militants and the various party officials. In the heady atmosphere of the provisional government in 1945, the executive organ of all three coalition parties in Salzburg (SPÖ, ÖVP, KPÖ) went so far as to propose to the American occupation authorities that they dissolve the Resistance organizations. The parties did not even inform the movements of the reasons for this highly unusual step.[2] The resisters were not completely to blame for their political insensitivity and naiveté. Many still remembered that their furtive approaches to former public officials in 1938 had achieved nothing because the politicians objected that clandestine work against overwhelming odds was impractical, that only impetuous fools or immature idealists would expose themselves to ghastly reprisals for trifling results. Not infrequently these "realists" assumed power after the liberation, which must have further frustrated the Resistance.

The loss of political influence of the inexperienced Resistance might well have been for the good of the Republic, as it allowed the democratic parties to preserve democracy against Communist subversion.[3] The postwar course, however, started to swing far in the opposite direction. The parties not only actively discouraged all efforts to band the politically disparate underground into a single movement, but they also made possession of the party card, and not merit, the criterion for selection and advancement of public officials. It soon became almost impossible for isolated, powerless resisters to struggle against special bureaucratic interests. The Resistance leadership was in part responsible for its own demise because it allowed thousands of latecomers, who certainly included some dubious characters and swindlers, to claim underground membership during the chaos of the Nazi collapse. Such infractions almost inevitably accompanied the Nazi downfall in all the occupied countries—they were not a specifically Austrian phenomenon.

Unlike the political parties, who sought the support of hundreds of thousands of former Nazi sympathizers, the resisters could not morally take into account the tragic dilemma that for many of their compatriots victory had meant the defeat of their country and the death of thousands of Austrian soldiers. After 1945, hundreds of thousands of people were still waiting in agony for their fathers, sons, brothers, and husbands to return from the prisoner of war camps.[4] Powerful emotional and cultural forces opposing German nationality and Austrian consciousness ran deeply through almost every family.[5] As a reflection of the double role played by the Austrian population, who "either fell victim to the Nazi terror or were forced to offer frightful sacrifices for the National Socialist cause," the balance sheet of final losses bared the terrifying legacy of the Anschluss.[6] The death toll during the National Socialist era amounted to 372,000 persons—5.58 percent of the 1939 population. During their seven years of struggle, the resisters had mourned 2,700 persons who had been executed, 16,493 who had died in concentration camps, 9,687 who had lost their lives in German jails, and 65,459 Jews who had been exterminated. In the jails of occupied Europe, a further 6,420 Austrians, mostly political refugees, died. The military tribunals also passed several hundred death sentences.

Over one million Austrian men were drafted into the armed forces, and approximately 247,000 never returned. Civilian losses amounted to 24,300 persons.[7]

Unlike what occurred at the liberation of Czechoslovakia, Italy, Yugoslavia, France, and other occupied countries, the Austrian liberation did not take place in an outburst of popular indignation and violence. Despite some harassment and looting, the SS troops committed no widespread cruelties on the unarmed population, which would have exacerbated popular feelings. The mood of the country opposed revenge or the rousing of social or national hatred. The ravages of the war, the dire menace of hunger and misery, the uncertainty about the future of the country, divided into four Allied occupation zones, and the urgent problems of reconstruction created this mood of moderation and patience. Furthermore, the general understanding that the fortunate existence of the independent Republic would exempt its inhabitants from the harsh consequences of the Nazi defeat discouraged any activist inclination to engage in divisive political confrontations. Such infighting would have seriously undermined national unity, the indispensable shield against Soviet disruption of the incipient democratic regime.

Under the special postwar threat of Communist domination and the possible dismemberment of the Republic, the Resistance concept of anti-Nazi national unity became counterproductive and played into the hands of the Communists who advocated the formation of a common anti-Fascist alliance. Accordingly, the democratic parties interpreted the concept of unity as a deliberate challenge to the existing delicate political balance. Given the first opportunity to show their opinion after the war in the November 1945 elections, the voters solidly backed the democratic coalition of the ÖVP, which emerged as the largest party with 85 seats in Parliament, and the SPÖ which followed with 76 seats, 49.8 percent and 44.6 percent, respectively, of the total vote. The KPÖ with four seats (5.4 percent) was routed.[8]

When the Republic, which was seemingly paralyzed by its division into four occupation zones, first reemerged in and through its provinces, there were (unlike in 1919) no separatist tendencies anywhere in the country. Throughout the war, the resisters' consciousness of themselves as Austrians had transcended the regionalism of their networks. Soon after the war, many resisters were integrated into political parties, but the loose groups of apolitical militants sank from public sight. Because everything associated with the Resistance reflected unfavorably on all those who had even remotely participated in the discredited National Socialist policies, the public, until the mid-sixties, chose not to recollect the painful Anschluss era. The Resistance had become the outcast of Austrian history.

THE AUSTRIAN STRUGGLE

The German occupation and the Resistance came simultaneously to a country torn between the wish to exalt the glory of the Greater-German national entity and the need to preserve its own identity. The country was split between those who were aware of their centuries-old distinct political and cultural tradition and those whom the Nazi promises of nationalist aggrandizement and modernity attracted. Those groups who were prepared to manipulate that division in Austria's favor constituted the Austrian segment of the "fourth dimension," that wide spectrum of clandestine activities reaching from passive resistance to armed actions. Throughout occupied Europe, the contribution of the Resistance was a cumulative one. But its impact on wartime events still awaits full and final evaluation. Within the countries under Nazi domination, the resisters acted under widely different conditions, and what was possible in one territory might have been impossible in another. Only rarely could the resisters openly claim a victory. In general, however, political concerns played the main role. Although greatly important for morale, and politically significant for European postwar politics, the various achievements of the Resistance played a marginal part in Allied military operations. In short, the underground assisted military operations; it did not supplant them.[9]

As was the case in other countries, the nature, methods, and tactics of the Austrian struggle reflected the specific circumstances of the country. Except for the German Resistance, the Austrian Resistance operated for the longest span of time in Europe. Its four most memorable features were related to its unique circumstances. First, the politically isolated democratic underground maintained almost no contact with the divided and confused exile movement. The absence of a political authority abroad to seek Allied support and to supervise clandestine operations at home gravely hampered work in the country. Without external aid, the non-Communist networks had to stand alone. In contrast, the Communist networks were in touch with Moscow, which dispatched KPÖ operatives to run the networks. The Communists never faltered in their conviction that the unity and close cooperation of the Party organizations at home and abroad had to be preserved under all circumstances.

Second, and peculiar to Austria, as an aggregate of geographically dispersed and politically disparate elements, the Resistance lacked a coordinated centrally organized leadership, except during the final months of the war. Its actions were usually scattered and individual. But the existence of a common enemy and the sharing of common aspirations gave the movement some coherence, especially after 1943 when the monolithic structure of the regime began to crack.

The third memorable feature of the Resistance was the relative absence of an administrative structure. Unlike the organizational structure of the French, Polish, or Dutch underground, the non-Communist organizations were generally not divided into separate branches, each assigned a special task such as providing escape routes or engaging in propaganda or sabotage. On the other hand, the KPÖ had created a special apparatus charged with subversive propaganda. The resisters were mostly amateurs in clandestine work. They were often casual and easy-going but also often obsessed with local prestige and self-importance. Although they were imaginative and amiable, they were also talkative and unsystematic, qualities that often cost them their lives and destroyed their cells.

Fourth, the Resistance was a living tie between the past and the future, a patriotic and ideological struggle by people who shared the same general beliefs. As in Germany or Italy, the political parties were the regime's important adversaries. Associated with the longing for parliamentary democracy and social and economic justice, the political parties reemerged in and through the Resistance. Whereas the Socialist middle and higher echelons were largely content to sit out the occupation, the KPÖ valiantly worked in the underground. It kept its organizational separateness and became the only party engaged in mass political work.[10] The composition of the more conservative CSP, the future ÖVP, was heavily influenced by former Christian Social trade unionists and peasant officials. The main trend of the diversified currents of opinion was essentially patriotic and moral, a call to return to native values.[11] Part of the Resistance's achievement was that by piercing the Nazi fiction of unanimous Austrian support for the regime, it constantly reminded Austrians of their inheritance.

Although the ancient, often bitter, conflict between those who upheld the Austrian cause and those who pursued unification with Germany seemed irreconcilable, those initially rigid boundaries as well as those between the left and the right gradually faded. Common persecution fostered national feeling and helped develop closer personal relationships among former bitter opponents. Indeed, within the concentration camps Socialist and Christian Social inmates evolved common emotional bonds based on shared sufferings. Certainly, the movement from Greater-German feeling to Austrian patriotism was in some cases not instantaneous; nevertheless, national instinct, which the Socialists initially greatly underestimated, revealed itself as a powerful impulse. Some early Greater-German believers such as Major Szokoll converted to Austrian patriotism when confronted with the occupation and belatedly discovered a respect for their new allegiance in the Resistance.

After 1938, the Resistance endured a permanent state of siege. Its growth was partially related to the Nazi setbacks after 1942, but also to its intense activity in the first years of the occupation. The damage which its opponents inflicted on the regime was cumulative; it relentlessly eroded the power of the Reich, and thus it diminished the value of the Anschluss to its Austrian sympathizers. However, if left to themselves, the clandestine forces were individually weak and incapable of more than scattered and merely local actions.

THE MAINSTREAMS OF THE RESISTANCE

As happened in every Nazi-occupied country, the system of occupation shaped the Resistance and its response in Austria. In part, that response was a continuous and spontaneous moral reaction to the regime's brutality and vulgarity. But it was also a personal attempt to maintain a sense of moral decency. Many resisters believed that the only way in which they could maintain their honor was within the underground. But there they sought action, never sure how much their work might resonate at home and how successfully it might expose the evil of the regime.

The phenomenon of widely organized conspiratorial action was new in Austrian history. The occupation produced an array of clandestine movements with a constantly changing cast as arrests continually eroded the front ranks of the activists. The non-Communist protest movement was, at first, little more than an assortment of various inexperienced elements, often merely verbally demonstrating their feelings. They started cells as much by chance as by intent. Resistance statements were more concerned with vague generalities about national independence and the regime's inhumanity than with specific claims. Looking more to the past than to the future, the resisters lacked a vision of a new social order and failed to elaborate proposals for fundamental changes.

The Resistance itself was never a mass phenomenon, despite its becoming widespread in the closing months of the occupation. It was less a national drama than the individual commitment of a personal conscience. An unstable elite, an undefinable fraternity of idealists, the underground "was an unforeseeable phenomenon, born as much from a challenge to 'common sense' as from a scorn for hollow dogma and calculation of the odds. Isolated and vulnerable, it seemed like an undertaking touched with madness."[12] At the outset, the Resistance was made up of parallel, dispersed groups that occasionally cooperated and then separated again. At least nine main groups and tendencies can be identified.

From the beginning, the KPÖ was the major clandestine force. In keeping with its aspirations, it established a compact net of local and regional cells heavily centered on Vienna. The RS, by withdrawing from clandestine work after March 1938, created a political void that offered the KPÖ, as the only remaining Marxist political group with underground experience, an inestimable advantage in recruiting and organizing resistance.

Moscow's unchallenged control over the KPÖ determined its politics. Moscow's about-face in 1941, which reversed its post-August 1939 anti-Western line, encouraged the militants to believe that the Red Army could help install a Communist regime. Consequently, through the Resistance, in which up to 1943 they played an all-important, though not an overwhelming, part, the Communists laid the moral and political foundations for their postwar efforts to penetrate the Austrian central administration. Tightly run by Moscow's KPÖ emissaries, the Communists joined the underground as a party of cadres aiming to become a party of the masses. They failed because they did not appeal to the generally conservative populace and because of the dreadful losses they had suffered. Hundreds and thousands of militants and their sympathizers were killed in Nazi purges, some in accordance with a Nazi internal regulation issued after the invasion of Russia, which stipulated that any convicted Communist militant be sentenced to death.

By 1944, guerrilla insurgency had become an important element in the Moscow center's Austrian strategy. It trained and equipped Austrian battalions on Yugoslav Partisan territory and sent a few selected combat teams to Styria and Carinthia to start guerrilla warfare. But the lack of support the teams received from the local population astounded the Communists and in conjunction with their loss of local links reduced their calls for a broad anti-Fascist Liberation Front, which the KPÖ would obviously dominate. The Party did not see the Resistance as a Revolutionary process but rather as the means to acquire control of the country through the Liberation Front, which would eventually become a nucleus of the legitimate Austrian government. In 1945, the fundamentalist Moscow firmly controlled the KPÖ.

The second major group was the Socialists, who acknowledged no fundamental inconsistency between their aspirations for power after the defeat of Nazism and the relative insignficance of their clandestine work. Largely concerned to sit out the Nazi era, the higher RS and SPÖ echelons argued that the conflict would be resolved militarily and that heroism was useless. The party veterans kept a wary eye on the tortured course of the war and concentrated on surviving. There were exceptions, such as Haas, Widmayer, Schärf, Migsch, Slavik, Wedenig, and others; but the RS's self-imposed isolation and its renunciation of clandestine activity reduced the RS illegal structure to impotence. As the result, many Socialists joined the KP networks and laid the foundations for the Communist-oriented factory cells. The resisters were ready to forget their past political affiliations for the sake of the common struggle against National Socialism. This Socialist willingness to join the common struggle was one reason for the growth and advance of the Communist underground after 1938. It also explains the Communist's subsequent weakness in 1945 when the trend abruptly reversed, as the surviving Socialist activists, clinging to their democratic principles, returned to the SPÖ, which had reasserted its authority in order to play the central role in postwar national politics. The Socialists' tradition of concern for the working man and their historical association with the democratic system proved stronger than the KPÖ's courageous underground effort.[13]

The third group that the blue- and white-collar factory workers constituted operated among disaffected elements in the industrial centers. The regime was fearful that the underground in the crucial war industries would publicize workers' grievances and form ties with the KPÖ factory cells. Even the remote prospects of a coalition between workers and the KPÖ had provoked the most carefully orchestrated police crackdowns on resisters in Vienna, St. Pölten, the Styrian industrial basin, Salzburg, and elsewhere. Obviously the disparate workers' cells had little political impact; the real power lay with the KPÖ cadres.

The Legitimists supporting the Habsburg restoration composed the fourth tendency. Assisted by their connections abroad and by a favorable attitude in the West, the Legitimists were more than a mere assemblage of traditionalists. The Legitimists undertook their essential groundwork in 1938, and remained very much alive in the early Anschluss years, though their importance varied according to region and circumstance. The coherence and effectiveness of the conspiracy was the product of the common efforts of the movement at home and of Otto Habsburg abroad, where he was strong in some Allied circles. The domestic network was a mixed body of officers, youths, and women of both conservative and progressive leanings. The French collapse and the destruction of the cadres at home pushed the members adrift, and the Leigitmist underground folded. Ultimately, its significant feature was simply that it survived more as a tendency than as a unified movement.

The fifth strain of defiance was a medley of former Christian Socials, Catholics, and, to a lesser extent, former liberals who advocated the evolution of a pluralist democracy. Laced with former adherents of the Schuschnigg regime, these traditionalist groups dreamed of turning their country into an independent state sustained by popular approval. The most charismatic and eloquent leader of this first Resistance generation, Roman Scholz, who was more an academic moralist than a prudent organizer, played a leading part in the attempt to establish the widest possible non-Communist platform. The Gestapo quickly focused on these potentially dangerous activists. It struck in 1940 with a blow that decimated the movement. Although the conspiracy gradually replenished its ranks, the losses dulled its activism. Quite independently, the tireless Christian Democratic trade unionists brought to this arm of the movement a political canniness that Scholz, Kastelic, or Lederer had not possessed. Weinberger and Hurdes set up links with the German Resistance and introduced Goerdeler and Kaiser to activists in Vienna. After his return from Dachau, the Christian Social peasant leader Figl contacted former peasant officials. When the liberation appeared close, steps were taken to institutionalize the alliance of trade unionists and peasants in a new political party, the ÖVP, which replaced the CSP.

As the pace of resistance work quickened, the sixth group, a broad array of activists, including civilians and military uninterested in party politics, joined the resistance arena. Central to these independently minded patriotic formations (identified as the All-Austrian tendency—AA) was the umbrella organization 05 and its affiliated combat groups. After the arrests of 1943 shook the underground, the AA-oriented networks sought to organize the widely dispersed patriotic cells. Its groups joined with the military in busily preparing popular uprisings in Vienna and Innsbruck. In the spring of 1945, local insurgencies throughout the country accompanied the advance of the Allied armed forces.

A handful of vigorous and determined military men set up, sustained, and led the seventh formation. Some were old soldiers of the imperial army who bitterly resented the dissolution of the Austrian entity. Others were disaffected younger Austrian Wehrmacht officers who had fallen out of sympathy with the regime. All were sincere in detesting what they viewed as Hitler's and the Nazi Party's appalling political mismanagement of the war and of their homeland. At the outset, little common action or planning occurred. But by 1943-44, individual officers and N.C.O.s provided nuclei around which clandestine military cells could form. In general, these military men were not gifted with any extraordinary insight into political affairs. Indeed, the ideal to which they gave their loyalty was that of a free Austria. Curiously, the Wehrmacht constituted the power base that helped them to plot against the system. They not only cleared out unreliable elements from certain selected Army units but also replaced them with Austrian recruits, thereby ensuring the dependability of selected troops stationed in and near Vienna. As the situation on the fronts rapidly deteriorated, these military men sought contacts with the civilian resisters who demanded arms. In Vienna, Upper Austria, and Innsbruck they concerted their preparations with the civilians and together organized a military-civilian force capable of mounting a local insurgency. The military men's trust in one another and their position of power made them the most effective group in the Resistance in the last years of the war.

The Jehovah's Witnesses made up the eighth tendency. Their religious creed and their refusal to be drafted challenged the regime, and their activities so worried Berlin that it had the Gestapo move ruthlessly against the sect. Their printed materials were confiscated, and members were detained and prosecuted because of their outspoken beliefs.

The ninth, and weakest, current of protest was that of the former Heimatschutz members and sympathizers of the Schuschnigg regime. During the occupation many former Heimwehr followers turned away from their former anti-Socialist stance, which had drawn them to authoritarianism. Some enlisted in the Resistance and some withdrew into silence for the duration of the Nazi era. But after 1945, because of their past association with the authoritarian regime, of which the public was critical, they were considered morally tainted.

THREE PHASES OF THE RESISTANCE

The Resistance evolved gradually in three main phases under the impact of Nazi policies and of the war. In the first period, when German troops entered the country in 1938, the new authorities detained thousands of their former opponents. Many within the silenced opposition hoped for more signs of protest but, much as they hated to admit it, the country widely accepted National Socialist rule. The calls for protest went largely unheeded. With the country at peace and Hitler firmly in control, the opposition of a few disappointed individuals did not seem to matter. The reasons that people backed the National Socialist system were diverse. The principal ones were the pervasive tradition of Greater-German nationalism, the still flourishing belief that Austria formed part of the German nation, and the belief that Austria's huge problems could best be solved within a larger economic and political unit. That the Austrians did not have a separate language that would have kept alive their sense of identity certainly played a role.

In contrast, scattered individuals decided that they could not compromise with the system. They stressed anti-Fascist patriotism, which saw the conflict not only as a national struggle but also as one to uphold basic moral values. In 1938-39 politically diverse groups spread throughout the country recreating an embryonic Austrian national community. These spontaneous cells were principally based on political and moral affinities and on former party affiliations. Only gradually did broader political cooperation develop. This shift to the pre-1933 power structure was facilitated by the detention of former Christian Social politicans and their embattled Socialist colleagues. Veteran members of these camps (Schärf, Kunschak, Reither) formed the nuclei of the future political realignment. The events of 1938 offered a political opening for the Legitimists and similarly for the KPÖ, which was among the first to print clandestine papers and flysheets. While the Nazis tried to exploit the Catholic distrust of Marxism and the Socialist dislike of clericalism, they lured no movement into emotional anti-Communism, although quite naturally some tension arose between the KPÖ and other groups during the 1939-41 period. The main enemy was the pagan swastika. The left-wing contingent of the CSP strengthened as Nazi repression pushed Christian Socials away from their conservative stance. In turn, many Socialists became keenly aware of their past mistaken assumption that Austrian national sentiment rested almost entirely on traditional loyalties and institutional ties. Naturally, there were losses: infiltrated by the Gestapo, the main networks were destroyed by the end of 1940.

The small, still amateurish underground sank to its weakest level after it had suffered shattering blows in 1939-1940. Its momentum was curbed, its political dexterity undermined, and its following disrupted. It experienced a lull, an interim period of somewhat less coordinated work as a new generation of activists took shape in the second stage from 1941 to 1943.[14] Its morale, hurt by the French defeat, was boosted by the entrance of the Soviet Union and the United States into the war. However, a series of arrests sapped the Communists' front ranks, undermined their self-reliance, and led to the virtual eclipse of the KPÖ central networks. After 1943, even the regional Party groups who had formerly flourished in the urban centers of Styria, Tyrol, Salzburg, and Upper Austria were silenced or wrecked, or they engaged in little work of any kind.

The underground started to grow again in the final phase. Now more experienced and less gullible, the political veterans who returned from the concentration camps, the survivors of the early networks, and the recruits developed new nuclei. Their attitude, long unfocused, hardened after the crises in Stalingrad and Italy into a determination to intensify clandestine work. In pursuit of this objective, the skillful minds of Becker and his 05 friends patiently welded the fragments seeking at least a temporary unity of purpose. Until the formation of the short-lived Provisional Austrian National Committee (POEN) in Vienna in the winter of 1944-45 to coordinate the dispersed actions of various groups, no one inspired or gained any effective political allegiance from the various resistance currents.

What was required after the Allied invasion of France was not minor isolated action but collaboration among the active forces so that they could strike an effective blow against the regime. Clearly, any such development—which 05 and the military around Major Szokoll in Vienna foresaw—implied the dispatch of an informed activist abroad to provide the Allies with first-hand information on affairs within Austria, and to establish reliable lines of communication. Recognition of this need coincided with the increased interest of the United States in Austria, which it viewed as possibly the Wehrmacht's last defense barrier. When Fritz Molden finally reached Switzerland in July 1944, he established contacts with Allen Dulles and the Allied military and political authorities in France and Italy. The ensuing American and French support of the Austrian Resistance brought about the necessary close cooperation.[15]

Encouraged by the successes abroad, in the winter of 1944-45 the military organization busily engaged in planning armed rebellion in Vienna in cooperation with the advancing Red Army. Unfortunately, the military operation was betrayed at a critical moment, but the civilian combat teams were able to help the Soviet troops occupy the city in April 1945. In Tyrol, however, Gruber and Heine ably and successfully directed the Resistance uprising. At the beginning of May, in a daring coup, military groups and armed patriots gained control of Innsbruck before the first American columns reached the Tyrolian capital. Insurgency in the mountainous areas of Styria and Salzkammergut developed late in the war, but generally the armed struggle was limited there. The only territory on the soil of the German Reich to experience guerrilla warfare was the Carinthian borderland. Here, helped by Tito's Partisans, the Communist-inspired Liberation Front recruited a contingent of German Austrians, including a number of Catholics.

Apart from the widely dispersed, localized, and sporadic insurgency in the spring of 1945, the gathering of intelligence and active and passive sabotage were the most significant clandestine activities. Yet even these acts caused no discernible material damage to the German war machine. There was industrial action, but no massive strikes straining German forces ever broke out, nor did unrest ever sweep the country. Street demonstrations, rioting, or open clashes between soldiers and civilians never took place, nor was a curfew ever imposed. Under these circumstances, the role of the Resistance in the final stage was small but psychologically, politically, and morally vital. Its international influence became all-important, and its defiance encouraged the sympathy of the passive segment of the population. The political and moral significance of the liberation would have amounted to little without the aspirations of the Resistance, which had provided the basis for the implementation of the stipulations laid down in the Moscow Declaration of 1943.[16]

Equally important was the public attitude in the emotional atmosphere of the immediate post-war years when throughout liberated Europe a wave of repression swelled against the Nazis. The Austrians were almost alone in avoiding the politics of vengeance and quickly surmounted the unsettling divisive effects of the occupation. Most of those who had faithfully served the National Socialist system were left unmolested and indeed were often employed in the service of the Republic. For anyone familiar with the bitter polarizations of French, Yugoslav, Dutch, Belgian, or Norwegian societies during the occupation, such moderation was rather surprising. As for the Resistance, it was largely condemned to silence and even ridiculed by skeptical public opinion in the decades following the war.

The postwar waning of the Austrian Resistance was not an entirely exceptional feature in the history of the Resistance in Europe. For instance, the Czech Home Resistance was relegated to a secondary position by the returning exile politicians who had spent the war in relative comfort of their London and Moscow headquarters. However, such relegation certainly did not apply in Slovakia, Yugoslavia, Holland, Italy, Norway, France, or Denmark. In France some 80 percent of the deputies elected in the National Assembly in 1945 and 1946 came from the Resistance, and 66 percent of the deputies elected in 1951 and 1956 were former resisters.[17] In the Austrian Republic, the resisters had to wait until 1977 when the Bruno Kreisky government granted them long-deserved recognition by awarding them special decorations. In the meantime, innumerable honors, titles, and decorations were bestowed upon some notoriously petty bureaucrats, zealous businessmen, and lofty second- and third-rate public figures who had never lifted a finger to liberate their homeland.

The true significance of the Resistance transcended its practical achievements or failures. During the occupation, the resisters learned to live a life of larger meaning by committing themselves to a national vision and to a social purpose. They formed a temporary community of an elusive character that was intensely personal: it united men and women of divided social background and different political hues, who often could not even reveal their names to their closest friends. For many, their clandestine days were the most exciting of their lives.

Numerically, the Resistance had never been an important force; but the observer of the Austrian scene should perhaps apply some sense of proportion to the study of the Resistance's history. How large, then, was the number of resisters?[18] The question cannot be fully answered because it means bestowing identity on an informal group or on a harmless Stammtisch or imagining names, plans, or aspirations where none probably existed. On the contrary, it may also mean ignoring groups and individuals because nobody survived to report what had happened. Resisters do not usually keep archives. And in Austria after 1945, many resisters found it expedient to play down their underground activities. To this day, a few resisters have refused to disclose their identities—an attitude that reveals the low reputation that the Resistance enjoyed after 1945. The evidence on which historians usually rely in writing about political movements just does not exist in the case of the Resistance.[19] For it, the main sources are the court records, the files of the Nazi security organs, and the reminiscences of participants.[20] One knows quite a lot about the activists who were arrested and tried and also something about their chiefs; but one knows little or next to nothing about many who were never caught, who were slain, or who died.[21]

Yet, burial places, gallows, and prisons forcefully testify to the message and mission of the Resistance. According to inadequate and incomplete estimates, more than 100,000 Austrians were arrested for political acts. One can assume that most were resisters—persons actively involved in the organized anti-Nazi struggle.[22] Likewise, one can assume that a great many political prisoners out of the 16,107 who died in prisons and the 16,493 who died in concentration camps were resisters (a few were political hostages). Similarly, most of those 2,700 persons executed for political crimes had belonged to the underground. Only a fraction of the deported and murdered Jews—largely those emigrants trapped by war in western Europe—were linked with the Resistance. At the liberation, the resisters may have made some exaggerated claims and included a number of latecomers in their ranks. Yet the final figure of about 100,000 resisters gives an approximate picture that is impressive indeed.[23] It should lessen the skepticism of many whose attitude to the achivements of the Resistance has remained at best ambiguous and at worst despicable. Public doubts about the existence of the Resistance have always vexed and tortured those genuine resisters whom the Nazis had vilified for opposing the regime.

At a time of national doom, lacerating divisions, and deadening resignation, at a time when the *furor teutonicus* threatened to destroy the Austrian identity, the mosaic that was the Resistance enabled each different cell and political fragment to cling to its distinctive ways, and made room for the political and social diversity among them. On the international scene, where it insisted that the final peace must involve Austria's right to independence, the Resistance symbolized the Austrian struggle for statehood, augmented proAustrian sentiments, and strengthened Allied efforts. The Moscow Declaration of November 1943 was predicated on the Allied belief that the Austrian people wanted to regain their own state and to maintain their traditions. The Resistance provided the catalytic element that represented that Austrian will at home and abroad.

NOTES

1. In 1946 Ernst Fischer, the Communist leader, stated that in May 1945, "no organized . . . working class existed nor any effective organs of a national revolutionary, anti-Fascist popular movement." What had happened was an "upheaval without revolution." *Weg und Ziel* (1946): 1.

2. Klaus Grasmayr, "Zur Frage der Österreichischen Widerstandsbewegung," OM, X/65.

3. Interview with Dr. Lemberger. See also Fritz M. Rebhann, *Finale in Wien. Eine Gaustadt in Aschenregen* (Vienna, 1969), pp. 222-23; Schärf, *April 1945*, passim.

4. Between 1945 and 1969, 335,334 prisoners of war returned from the West, and 159,605 from the East. Heeresgeschichtliches Museum, *1918-1968, Die Streitkräfte der Republik Österreich* (Vienna, 1968), p. 299.

5. On April 1, 1948, 595,670 National Socialists were listed in the official register, but the figure included some applicants who were free from the duty to register. Civil Affairs Austria, Report U.S. High Commissioner, No. 33, July 1948, p. 41. By July 31, 1948, 9,396 persons in 116,693 cases submitted to the new extraordinary People's Court, specially created to try Nazi war crimes, had been declared guilty. [U.S., Department of State] *Report of the United States High Commissioner. U.S. Element. Allied Commission for Austria. Statistical Annex,* no. 36, October 1948, p. 7. See also Dieter Stiefel, *Entnazifizierung in Österreich* (Vienna, 1981), passim.

6. Luža, *Austro-German Relations,* p. 353.

7. DÖW 1342, 8447; DÖW letter to the author, July 8, 1971; Manfred Rauchensteiner in *Die Presse,* August 13, 1974; "Bevölkerungsverluste Österreichs während des Zweiten Weltkrieges," *Österreichische Militärische Zeitschrift,* Heft 3 (1974), pp. 219-20. Estimates of the number of Austrians drafted for military service vary between 800,000 and 1,200,000 men. Szecsi and Stadler put the number of political prisoners brought before the Nazi courts in Austria at between 16,500 and 17,000. *Die NS-Justiz,* p. 21.

8. Erika Weinzierl and Kurt Skalnik, eds., *Österreich. Die Zweite Republik* (Graz, 1972), 1:156.

9. For the European Resistance, see the surveys by Jorgen Haestrup, *European Resistance Movements, 1939-1945: A Complete History* (Westport, CT, 1981): Foot, *Resistance;* Michel, *La guerre de l'ombre; European Resistance Movements 1939-45. Proceedings of the First and Second International Conferences on the History of the Resistance Movements* . . . vols. 1-2 (Oxford, 1960, 1964). Michel correctly states that the Resistance was built up of heterogeneous geographical, political, and structural elements. Under these circumstances, a single unified French Resistance had never existed. Ibid., 2:577.

10. Within the Czech Resistance as well, the Communist Party was the only political party that worked underground. In contrast, several parties in Poland built up their own clandestine organizations.

11. Social issues were not dealt with extensively, even in the illegal Communist press. The

same applied in the Czechoslovak Communist underground. Janeček, ed., *Z počátků odboje,* p. 502.

12. Vistel, *La nuit,* p. 13.

13. The SPÖ did not find itself on common ground either with the French, Italian, or the Polish Socialists who were deeply absorbed in Resistance ideology and politics.

14. Although in the main the French Resistance in its initial phase from 1940 to 1942 concentrated on building networks and organizing the clandestine press, the Austrians had already lost their first underground cohort by 1940-41.

15. See the U.S. Department of State, Memorandum, March 16, 1945, on the "United States policy toward Austria": "Depending upon the contribution of the Austrians themselves to their own liberation from German domination, extend to the Austrian economy treatment approaching that for the liberated countries, without subjecting Austria to the reparations and other economic treatment to be applied to German." DÖW 12669.

16. "Austria is reminded, however, that she has a responsibility, which she cannot evade, for participation in the war at the side of Hitlerite Germany, and that in the final settlement, account will inevitably be taken of her own contribution to her liberation." So little has been known about the work of the Austrian Resistance, that M. R. D. Foot devoted a mere three pages to it in his *Resistance* (pp. 209-12) and H. Michel left it out in his *La guerre sans ombre.* The Allied intelligence agencies seem not to have mounted any of their circuits in Austria until 1944. Stafford, *Britain,* p. 189; Foot, *Resistance,* p. 212. For the OSS, see Brown, *The Secret War,* pp. 542-43, 547-48, 554 ff; Smith, *OSS,* pp. 161, 224, 233.

17. Mattei Dogan in Dwaine Marwick, ed., *Political Decisionmakers* (Glencoe, 1961), p. 87.

18. I cannot estimate the number of sympathizers or of those additional tens of thousands who felt vaguely well-disposed toward the Resistance.

19. Lack of the usual evidence might be one reason for Henri Michel's assertion: "It is impossible for people who have not taken part in the resistance to relate [its history] without committing grave errors" (the introductory survey to the session on "The History of the Resistance Movements in Europe," at the International Historical Congress in Vienna, August 30, 1965).

20. The source material is incomplete. The Austrian expert Dr. Neugebauer from the DÖW noted that a great many records disappeared or were destroyed at the end of the war. These included those of the VGH, SS- and Police courts, Military-Field-and War courts, Martial-Law courts, and, in particular, the Gestapo files. Of the extensive Special Courts (SG) records, DÖW historians could have seen in their entirety those of the SG Vienna, which contained some 10,000 trials, more than one-half of which were of a political nature, and those of the SG Innsbruck, Linz, and Salzburg. From the Special Senates of the Supreme Provincial Court in Vienna, the files of about 2,800 cases, involving at least 6,000 to 8,000 resisters, mostly Communists, were preserved. All in all, it appears that tens of thousands of persons appeared before the Nazi courts for political offenses and crimes, not counting economic offenses such as black marketeering or illicit slaughtering of domestic animals. However, the boundaries between the resistance and mere opposition remain fluid and subjective. See Dr. Neugebauer's letters to this author, October 1, 1977, No 56/78/N, August 16, 1982, No 1173/82/N.

21. It is not possible, for instance, to check whether the numbers of suspects given at the trials or included in the Gestapo files were correct as the defendants did not generally reveal the names of all their companions. On the other hand, it was sometimes difficult to separate an active resister from an opponent who had been detained because he verbally criticized the regime. Neither do we know the number of guerrilla fighters and their helpers, in particular, those of Slovene origin who had joined the Yugoslav Partisans and were not keen on publicizing their participation after the liberation. Ibid.

22. Ibid.

23. This study has not covered the Austrian Resistance abroad, in France, Belgium, the Soviet Union, Yugoslavia, Italy, England, Sweden, Switzerland, and the United States.

APPENDIX
The Profile of the Resistance as an Elite

Appendix

THE RESISTANCE ELITE

I conceived of this study as an historical account. Originally, I did not expect that the available data would permit a quantitative analysis. However, I now believe that I can provide a social analysis of the resisters as an elite group.[1] Essentially, the combination of moral rectitude, courage, civic responsibility, ideological concern, and expectation of social and material advantage distinguish the elite alignment.[2]

Resistance members usually had little in common. Despite their diversity, activists of all political and professional backgrounds shared the will to join the Resistance. They knew that they represented a tiny minority of the population, out of step with the vast majority. Their early commitment to resistance was a kind of moral instinct, a spontaneous personal act, often taken alone or possibly with the aid of a few trusted friends. As the problems challenging the Resistance during the Nazi occupation became increasingly technical and political, the amateur progressively yielded to the more professional, more specialized, and less ideologically oriented operator who had greater experience in the field.

THE METHODS OF INQUIRY

My analysis of Resistance membership focuses on the personal, social, and political characteristics of 3,058 individuals. The sample is purposive: it was not possible to take a random sample. Moreover, it would have been somewhat inappropriate because the study focuses on the more important members of the Resistance. The subsequent analysis is, therefore, based on a selection of the available material. In drawing from the records, I tended to choose those activists who had engaged in significant clandestine acts. Overall, I stressed the selection of those who had obtained positions of responsibility. Nevertheless, the size of the sample seems large enough to infer the social and political characteristics of the various resistance strata. The main criterion for inclusion was participation in resistance activities.

I used the official files because they supplied more background data than I could obtain through interviews, correspondence, and newspaper articles, or by any direct contact with the surviving resisters and because their information was relatively accurate. Unfortunately, the quality of evidence was uneven. Although the data for some indicators (e.g., sex, age) were satisfactory for the entire sample, no evidence existed in a large number of cases for other relevant variables. I detected no significant instances of incorrect personal data or of intentional inaccuracy. However, the court and Gestapo records contained many false or arbitrary evaluations and descriptions.

Seven sources provided data on the persons under scrutiny: The People's Court (629 entries), the *Oberlandesgericht* (320 entries), the Gestapo (719 entries), the *Landgericht* and *Sondergericht* (108 entries), the *Reichskriegsgericht* (26 entries), published studies (553 entries), and various other sources (690 entries largely from secondary sources). The biographical material on 60 percent of the entries comes directly from the official Nazi records and was based on the information furnished by those apprehended and interrogated by the authorities. Similarly, the authors of the publications usually compiled their information from the Gestapo and court records. Although the sample is mostly composed of those activists whom the Nazis arrested, I detected no significant differences between the apprehended and nonapprehended resisters.[3]

RESISTANCE AFFILIATES

I have sorted the data into nine empirical categories on the basis of political-ideological commitment: (1) the Communist Party of Austria (KPÖ); (2) the Revolutionary Socialists and Social Democrats (RS); (3) Factory-based cells (F); (4) Legitimists (L); (5) Traditionalists (T); (6) Military (M); (7) the Jehovah's Witnesses (JW); (8) All-Austrians (AA); (9) Home-Fronters (HS). Table 1 sharply illuminates some of the characteristics of the sample and subsamples. To check the sample's bias and my subjective evaluations, I used files of documentary data, including those on less significant subversive activities such as paying illegal membership fees and helping resisters' families.[4]

Although the differences among these main resistance affiliates generally stood out clearly, in some cases, I may have incorrectly categorized resisters because the evidence was inadequate. The KPÖ and RS groups were easily classifiable. The old pre-1934 Socialist cadres were listed under the RS. In many cases I coded the cells as part of the KPÖ network because of their KP

Table 1. Resistance Affiliates (N = 2,795)

Formations	Percentage
KPÖ	44.5%
RS	5.0
Factory cells	2.8
Legitimists	6.5
Traditionalists	16.1
Military	3.8
Jehovah's Witnesses	2.9
All-Austrians	17.7
Home-Fronters	0.7
	100.0%

connections. The factory-based clandestine cells were usually closely associated with the Communist underground. The absence of direct KP propaganda, the existence of a line of communication to the KPÖ, and the participants' SPÖ background characterized these cells. Under the Legitimists I listed the supporters of the Habsburg restoration. I included as Traditionalists politically oriented non-Socialists, who formed important segments of the Austrian People's Party (ÖVP) founded in 1945. Under Traditionalists I usually listed not only former Christian Socials and Catholics but also liberal elements (e.g., the Moldens). In the All-Austrian patriotic conspiracy, I counted non-party followers motivated by Austrian patriotism (such as the Tyrolian partisans).[5]

The data summarized in Table 1 permit some general conclusions. Together with its sympathizers in the factories, the KPÖ almost equaled the membership for the non-Marxist groups. Its numerical strength accounted for the Party's central role in the Resistance during the first four years of Nazi rule. Whereas the left was overwhelmingly represented by the KPÖ, the amorphous democratic center and right, despite their very respectable showing, were badly fragmented. No one formation became the major rallying point for the non-Communists. If we omit the special JW group, the political composition of the sample is balanced, although it leans slightly toward the left (52.3 to 44.8 percent). However, because of the vast political gulf between the RS and the KPÖ, the democratic forces enjoyed a small majority. Conversely, the most conservative element, the HS, was conspicuously insignificant. The major formations of the centrist democratic forces were the AA and T, which tended to coalesce in the closing months of the war. The RS were conspicuous by their relative weakness, although Socialist officials exercised considerable influence over the politically conscious leaders of the Resistance who believed that the SPÖ would reclaim its important political role after the liberation. The Legitimists remained a traditional force, not without influence, but numerically weak.

Common to all tendencies was their espousal of the democratic form of the future state. No predictable pattern emerged to explain why persons defied the regime. The effect of the occupation was to throw the hardy RS, KPÖ, and Christian Social militants back on to their own initiative. Their adherence to the Resistance became more a matter of character, past experience, and temperament than of party orthodoxy.

VARIABLES

For the purposes of this investigation, I have observed forty-six discrete variables, including sex, date of birth, place of birth and of residence, marital status, nationality, religion, education, military service, social and occupational classification, income group, father's occupation, unemployment, trade union membership, political affiliation before and after 1934 and after 1938, father's political affiliation, political imprisonment before and after 1938, year of joining the Resistance, Resistance political-ideological affiliation, and resistance activities.[6] Unfortunately, I have not been able to collect sufficient information to analyze some of the variables, such as income group, participation in World War I and in February 1934 uprising, father's occupation and political affiliation, and trade union membership. Here, the number of observations was too small to produce meaningful results for the entire Resistance population. I will clarify some of my classifications in the relevant sections below. Usually the data in the entries are from the official records, to which individuals themselves supplied the information. Only in a few cases, when information was missing or the attributes were unclear, have I based the compilation on indirect evidence. Because of discrepancies between the terminology of the sources, I did not entirely avoid inconsistent coding.

The analytical procedure consists of three parts. First, I grouped all forty-six variables to provide a broad picture of the sample. Second, for purposes of cross-tabulation, I divided the sample into nine categories, according to resistance affiliation and cross-tabulated these with nineteen variables. Third, to furnish a sharper profile of each of the nine resistance categories and to compare with the attributes of the general profile, I analyzed the composition of each category using forty-six variables. I used the principal tendencies of the general Resistance sample as a standard against which I evaluated the distinctive characteristics of the nine affiliations. I attempted to compare both the general Resistance sample and the individual affiliates with the Austrian population as a whole.

THE RESISTANCE MEMBERSHIP

Sex, Marital Status, Race

Although women showed considerable gifts for clandestine work, they had some difficulties in entering what was supposedly a man's world. But they could contribute inconspicuously, which Austrian men could not. They were active as couriers, organizers, transmitter operators, providers of shelter and safe houses, and trusted helpers of their husbands. Primarily in the Communist underground, a sizable proportion of female resisters exercised considerable power, often directing networks after the imprisonment or killing of the male leaders. A few, mostly single young women, devoted their lives to the Communist cause. But these were exceptions. Generally, women could not aspire to positions of responsibility and leadership, above all in the non-Communist networks, where many female participants seemed to have had no special interest in politics, beyond a deep emotional attachment to their homeland and a desire to serve it. Within the Resistance they often participated on a virtually equal basis with men; yet their contribution to the Resistance was relatively minor and far from representative of the female proportion of the population (51.9 percent) (Table 2). The proportion of women in the Resistance sample was only 11.6 percent.[7] However, whereas 42.3, 20.1, 10.4, and 10.1 percent of all the female resisters worked for the KPÖ, T, AA, and JW, respectively—the four groups with the highest number of women—the percentage of women in these samples was 11.5, 15.1, 7.1, and 42.0 percent. The percentage figure in both the RS and L exceeded that in the KPÖ. The disparity between males and females was striking in all the groups with the exception of the JW, and most marked in the largest group, the KPÖ, despite its claims to champion the public role of women.[8]

Very close similarity in marital status existed between the Resistance sample and the total population—53.9 and 52.2 percent respectively were married, and 40.3 and 38.8 percent were single.[9] There are, however, curious dissimilarities between the national percentages and those of the L and T movements, 32.7 and 25.5 percent married and 57.2 and 69.4 single. The KPÖ, RS, and JW attracted an above national average portion of the married persons, 62.4, 73.7, and 64.5 percent.

When Hitler occupied Austria in 1938, over 220,000 ethnic Jews resided in the country. Emigration and deportations reduced their number to fewer than 10,000 by December 1942. Racial persecution made Jewish participation in clandestine activities hazardous both for the Jews and for the underground.

Jews in the Resistance (N = 3,019)

Race	Percentage
Non-Jews	97.9%
Jews (those with three or four Jewish grandparents)	0.4
Half-Jews	1.5
Second-degree Jews (with one Jewish grandparent)	0.2

Age

More than half of the resisters were born between 1890 and 1909 (Table 3)[10] Persons aged 40 and under constituted 64 percent of the sample,

Table 2. Cross-Tabulation of Resistance Affiliation by Sex (N = 2,795)[a]

	KPÖ	RS	L	T	AA	Factory-Based	Military	JW	Home-Front	Total
Men[b]	1,099	116	152	380	457	78	105	47	18	2,452 = 87.7%
	44.8%	4.7%	6.2%	15.5%	18.6%	3.2%	4.3%	58.0%	1.9%	0.7%
	88.4	83.5	83.5	84.6	92.3	98.7	98.1		90.0	
	39.3	4.2	5.4	13.6	16.4	2.8	3.8	1.7	0.6	
Women	143	23	30	68	35	1	2	34	2	338 = 12.1%
	42.3%	6.8%	8.9%	20.1%	10.4%	0.3%	0.6%	10.1%	0.6%	
	11.5	16.5	16.5	15.1	7.1	1.3	1.9	42.0	10.0	
	5.1	0.8	1.1	2.4	1.3		0.1	1.2	0.1	5 (errors)
	1,243	139	182	449	495	79	107	81	20	2,795
	44.5%	5.0%	6.5%	16.1%	17.7%	2.8%	3.8%	2.9%	0.7%	100%

[a]The percentages for the whole sample of 3,058 cases are 88.4 percent men and 11.6 percent women.

[b]The first row gives the male or female membership of each group.

The second row expresses the male or female membership of each group as a percentage of the total male or female membership of all groups (44.8% of the total male membership of 2,452 belonged to the KPÖ).

The third row expresses the male or female membership as a percentage of the total (male and female) membership of that particular group (88.4% of all KPÖ members were male).

The fourth row expresses the male or female membership as a percentage of the total (male and female) membership of all groups (39.3% of the 2,795 persons were male KPÖ members).

Table 3. Age Distribution of Resistance Affiliates (10-Year Periods)

Year of Birth	Total[a] Population	Total Resist. (N = 1,961) 100% valid entries	KPÖ (1,148) (58.5% of valid entries)	T (309) 15.8%	L (159) 9.1%	RS (112) 5.7%	AA (86)	F (49)	M (12)	JW (47)	HS (20)
1880-89	12.42%	8.0%	5.7%	10.0%	10.7%	13.4	14.0	8.2	16.7	10.6	10.0
1890-99	14.53	25.9	25.8	18.4	27.5	37.5	20.9	49.0	16.7	36.2	10.0
1900-09	17.54	30.6	36.4	15.9	18.0	38.4	20.9	38.8	16.7	34.0	15.0
1910-19	14.28	17.8	19.3	20.7	17.4	7.1	14.0	4.1	25.0	4.3	30.0
1920-29	16.71	16.3	12.4	33.0	21.9	1.8	26.7	—	25.0	4.3	35.0

[a]Bundesamt, eds., *Die Ergebnisse*, 1936, p. 12.

which appears predominantly composed of youthful cohorts. In particular, the age distribution of the 1980-99 and 1900-09 cohorts varied significantly from the overall age structure of the total population. The Resistance sample stands out with its higher percentage of mature adults.

When one compares the age structures of the age cohorts for the four largest affiliates, the ages of the KPÖ and of the sample are roughly equally distributed. In contrast, the youngest cohort is overrepresented in the T, AA, and L categories. In particular, a strikingly large proportion of the T affiliate is in the youngest cohort, twice as large as that of the whole sample. Molded by their ideological experiences in various youth groups during the Schuschnigg regime, the core of the non-Communist anti-Nazi youth opposition apparently joined the T and L. Despite the Dollfuss-Schuschnigg regime's authoritarian nature, its ideology encouraged an inchoate Austrian consciousness among its youthful sympathizers and so politicized some that they became heavily involved in the Resistance. It is equally revealing that 89.3 percent of the RS category was older than 30 years of age. The data also suggest that the KPÖ commanded the support of the younger age cohorts.

Regional Distribution

Austria's dissolution after 1938 helped emotionally fuel the Resistance's promotion of Austrian self-consciousness. Table 4 presents in percentages the provincial distribution of the Resistance and of its five largest affiliates. The imbalances in the regional distribution of the categories are due to biases that the samples exhibited largely because of unavailable evidence (e.g., Burgenland, Carinthia) and because of missing birth and residence data for some RS, T, and L members. However, these distortions and disproportions do not change "the plausibility of the relationships" uncovered.[11]

The regional composition of the Resistance reflected political differences between the nine Austrian Länder. Especially significant were the residential percentages for the provinces. Greater Vienna, drawing adherents from Lower Austria, was the capital of the Resistance. The dominant position of the metropolis within the Resistance shows the dissatisfaction of some segments of the urban population with the regime. The position of Vienna in the Resistance evolved as special, almost separate, in Austria. Influenced by the steady importation of people and life-styles from other provinces and neighboring countries, the city's more cosmopolitan Resistance was linked to every corner of the country.

As the differences between the regional residential and birthplace figures in Table 4 show, persons were generally active in clandestine activities within the provinces where they were born. Evidently, strong regional roots explain the correlation; this did not hold true for Lower Austria, which served as a recruiting base for Vienna. Vienna's overly strong representation in the sample, a much larger percentage of the Resistance members

Table 4. Provincial Distribution of Members of the Resistance

Provinces	Total Population in Austria[a]	Place of Birth						Place of Residence					
		Resistance[b] Total	KPÖ	RS	L	T	AA	Resistance[c] Total	KPÖ	RS	L	T	AA
(1) Vienna	27.72%	39.9%	46.1%	50.0%	51.1%	35.7%	8.1%	52.6%	55.4%	64.2%	78.1%	64.3%	21.0%
(2) Lower Austria	22.32	14.6	17.8	7.4	9.1	19.7	4.2	8.4	9.7	0.0	1.7	9.2	10.4
(3) Upper Austria	13.34	4.9	2.4	6.6	11.4	10.7	2.7	4.9	2.2	2.2	8.4	6.4	4.4
(4) Salzburg	3.63	3.0	2.8	10.7	0.0	1.2	1.9	3.3	2.7	14.0	0.0	3.2	1.9
(5) Styria	15.01	13.0	19.0	3.3	6.3	2.5	11.1	12.9	22.8	2.2	3.9	3.4	8.7
(6) Carinthia	5.99	4.3	2.1	6.6	0.6	3.3	16.0	2.7	1.2	5.2	0.0	1.4	8.9
(7) Tyrol	5.16	9.5	0.8	4.1	6.8	11.9	45.4	10.4	0.7	4.5	6.2	10.3	37.6
(8) Vorarlberg	2.29	2.1	0.6	2.5	0.0	2.9	8.8	2.0	0.7	3.7	0.0	1.1	6.6
(9) Burgenland	4.42	1.3	2.2	0.0	0.0	0.4	0.4	1.5	3.1	0.0	0.6	0.0	0.2
Foreign	6.6	6.6	6.4	9.1	14.2	11.8	1.5	0.9	1.2	3.0	1.1	0.7	0.4
	100.0	100.0	100.0	100.0	100.0	100.0	100.0	100.0	100.0	100.0	100.0	100.0	100.0

[a]The distribution of the population in Austria in 1934. Bundesamt für Statistik, ed., Statistisches Handbuch, 1936, p. 5.

[b]The sample contains 1,965 cases; the subsamples for the five main affiliates list respectively 1,052 (53.5 percent), 122 (6.2), 176 (9.0), 244 (12.4), and 262 (13.3) cases. I used the pre-1938 territorial division of Austria into nine provinces as a yardstick and disregarded the Nazi administration's division of Austria into seven Länder.

[c]The sample contains 2,709 cases; the subsamples list 1,208 (44.6 percent), 134 (4.9), 178 (6.6), 437 (16.1) 482 (17.8) cases. The places of residence for the remaining four affiliates in the nine provinces are as follows: F (70 cases): 1-70 percent; 2-8.6; 3-5.7; 4-2.9; 5-2.9; 7-8.6; M (100 cases): 1-48 percent; 2-9.0; 3-18.0; 5-3.0; 6-1.0; 7-13.0; 8-4.0; JW (80 cases): 1-56.3; 2-3.8; 3-20.0; 4-1.3; 6-2.5; 7-15.0; HS (20 cases): 1-40.0 percent; 4-50.0; 5-10.0.

resided in the city than were born there, did not seem to affect significantly the almost constant incidence of indigenous regionalism in the provincial Resistance.[12] The other strong regions were Styria and Tyrol.[13]

The concentration of the underground in Greater Vienna and Tyrol was above the proportion of the total population residing in the two provinces-—an example of similar opinions existing almost independently in two distant Länder. This similarity, however, tends to obscure some differences. In contrast to Vienna, where every resistance formation, with the exception of the AA, was disproportionately strong, the Resistance in Styria and Tyrol was overwhelmingly composed of a single formation. Every fifth member of the Communist underground and every third member of the patriotic AA resided, respectively, in Styria and Tyrol. The main formations usually recruited in Vienna and in a few other Länder. Elsewhere they tended to be weak. Surprisingly, a relatively large number of resisters were born outside of Austria, mostly in Czechoslovakia (Table 5).

Table 5. Foreign-born Resisters

Place of Birth	Resistance total	KPÖ	RS	L	T	AA	Residence total
Czechoslovakia	3.1%	2.9%	6.6%	6.8%	3.3%	—	0.1%
Hungary	0.8	1.0	—	1.1	0.4	0.4	—
Germany	1.2	0.8	2.5	0.6	3.3	0.4	0.3
Yugoslavia	0.8	0.7	—	2.3	1.2	—	0.5
South Tyrol	0.7	0.2	—	1.7	1.6	0.4	—
Other	1.0	0.8	—	1.7	2.0	0.4	—
	6.6	6.4	9.1	14.2	11.8	1.6	

In presenting the rural-urban distribution, Table 6 shows that the Resistance was predominantly an urban phenomenon, and that the rural share steadily declined. This migration to the city was particularly true in the largest Austrian cities.[14] The recruits came not only from urban centers but usually from the largest urban centers. The concentration of the Resistance in urban areas also reflected the relative weakness of the guerrilla movement. However, as every fifth resistance member resided in rural areas, the rural participants' share was respectable.[15]

Nationality

The Resistance was ethnically homogeneous (Table 7). Its ethnic composition agreed with the ethnic distribution of the population although the proportion of non-Austrian nationals, especially of Czechs and Slovenes, was slightly higher in the sample. In contrast, the Croats were much less represented.[16] The proportion of non-Austrians was relatively higher (7.1 percent) in the Communist movement than in the others, owing to the size of the Czech segment (4.2 percent). It was also higher in the Legitimists (7.8), because of the presence of Sudeten Germans (4.4). The Slovenes were mainly grouped in the AA formation (4.7).

Table 6. Rural-Urban Distribution

	Community of Origin (N = 1,873)	Place of Residence (N = 2,851)
Vienna	43.7%	53.3%
Provincial Capitals	5.9	10.8
Towns over 5,000	12.1	13.1
Countryside	38.0	22.4
Large Cities Abroad	0.3	0.4

Table 7. Nationality Distribution

Nationality	Total Population	Resistance (N = 1,786)
Austrian	97.4%	94.6%
Reich German		0.3
Slovene	0.4	1.0
Czech	0.7	1.6
Hungarian		0.2
Croat	0.6	0.3
Sudeten German		1.0
Stateless, other		0.7
Italian		0.3

Religion

Rather surprisingly, Roman Catholics were much less represented in the sample than in the population, as Table 8 shows.[17] Persons with no denomination and "God believers" totaled much larger percentages of the sample than they did in the total population. The findings in Table 9, which confirm this breakdown, indicate that more than half of the RS sample and more than one-quarter of the Communist sample were individuals without religious affiliation. Similarly, the percentage of the Evangelics in these two affiliates is twice as large as the national figure. Conversely, the non-

Table 8. Religious Affiliation

Religion	Percentage Total Population	Resistance (N = 973)
Roman Catholic	90.4%	65.4%
Old Catholic	0.5	1.8
Evangelic	4.3	5.2
Greek Orthodox		0.3
Jewish		0.6
Jehovah's Witnesses		8.4
Other sects		0.2
No denomination	1.5	9.5
God believers[a]		8.5

[a]The Nazis introduced this new category in 1938. Vienna occupied first place among the provinces, with 6.4 percent of God believers.

Marxist affiliates had a larger than national percentage of Roman Catholics. The JW, all of whose members naturally shared the same denomination, presented a special case, as the authorities had prohibited their sect.

Table 9. Distribution of Religious Denominations Among Resistance Groups

Religion	KPÖ (N = 460)	RS (80)	L (126)	T (130)	JW (81)	AA (31)
Roman Catholic	60.9%	32.5%	96.0%	97.8%	—	100.0%
Old Catholic	2.6	7.5				
Evangelic	8.0	6.3	3.2	0.7	—	—
Greek Catholic	0.4					
Jewish	1.1		0.8			
Sects					100.0	
No denomination	12.0	42.5				
God believers	15.0	11.3				

Education

Education is an important index of family social status. Unlike in the Anglo-American world where there were two different types of education, private and public, an excellent uniform public school system existed in Central Europe. I coded the five main levels of school education to find out the highest level of education that the Resistance aggregate attained.[18]

Level of Education (highest level attended)

Educational Level	(N = 796)
Elementary (5 years) and High School (3 or 4 years)	6.2%
Vocational (incl. trade schools, commercial schools, apprenticeship)	30.2
Secondary (Mittelschule), including incomplete education	12.2
University or other higher schools attended but without degree	17.2
University degree or equivalent	34.3

The sample reflects the predominantly high educational level of the Resistance. The intelligentsia clearly outnumbered members with lower educational training. As in Poland or France, the better-educated strata in society supported the non-Communist cadres, in proportions far above their share of the total population. The educational distribution shows a very low proportion of those with only primary education. Skilled workers with less than secondary education and university-trained individuals formed the two largest groups. In all, the Resistance members seemed to be better educated and more literate than the national average. Their school environment perhaps partly accounted for their anti-Nazi commitment.

There appears to be a significant difference in the educational levels attained by the Resistance affiliates. Table 10 shows the political effect of education differences. Members of the various groups were recruited from different social strata. The lower educational level and social status of members of the Communist groups compare significantly with the predominance of secondary-educated members of the L and HS, and of university-educated members in the T and M groups. Although the RS members are more evenly spread among the five educational levels than are the Communists, nearly half of them entered vocational training. The RS who left school at the primary level formed the largest contingent of all affiliates to leave at that level. These great differences in education not only indicate the relative social status of the groups, but also reflect their distinctive political attitudes.

Table 10. Level of Education among Resistance Affiliates

Level of Education	KPÖ (251 cases)	RS (30)	L (103)	T (205)	M (35)	AA (108)	HS (20)
Elementary and High School	11.2%	16.7%	6.8%	—	—	5.6%	5.0%
Vocational	74.9	46.7	22.3	3.9	—	1.9	20.0
Secondary	3.2	10.0	40.8	15.6	—	0.9	50.0
University education without degree	4.4	10.0	16.5	21.0	54.3	24.1	15.0
University degree or equivalent	6.4	16.7	13.6	59.5	45.7	67.6	10.0

Occupational Profile

I have grouped the sample into two tables. In Table 12 I have used the standard international classifications (1968) for economic activities.[19] As my sources used empirical classificatory procedures different from those of the international standard classification, I have had to construct a system of occupational classifications for Table 11.[20] To portray the occupational and economic characteristics of the Resistance, I have cross-tabulated the affiliates by occupation and economic activity.

The important finding from Table 11 is the relatively high proportion of workers who contributed—49.1 percent—which almost matches their 51 percent share of the total population. For the most part, the Resistance attracted the skilled and better educated workers. The KPÖ recruited almost eight of every ten workers who joined the Resistance. The respective figures for the RS, which was approximately ten times smaller, and for the F are 46.5 and 95 percent. The overall representation of white-collar workers in many affiliates contrasted with their high percentages in the RS and L. The white-collar worker category failed to conform to its distribution within the Austrian population, where it showed twice as large a percentage as in the sample.

The civilian-military servants accounted for a large percentage of the AA and T. The police and gendarmerie were strongly represented in the AA, although the largest number of policemen joined the KPÖ. The N.C.O.s and officers were mainly grouped in the military organizations. The artisan category was strongly represented in the L and T, but one of every four members joined the KPÖ. Over 65 percent of the free professions were entrenched in the ranks of the T and AA. Rather surprisingly, the occupational complexion of the T revealed a striking number of students. In all, student representation in the Resistance was substantial and was notably stronger on the political center and right than on the left. The efforts of the Resistance to expand its rural underground did not meet with success. Only the AA showed a strong rural composition. Housewives were more evenly distributed between the democratic groups and the KPÖ. The rather pitiable proportion of recruits from high income groups (managers, businessmen, landowning aristocracy) was largely associated with the T.

As Table 11 makes clear, the Resistance encountered difficulty in recruiting teachers, whereas the percentage of the priests and members of religious order seems to be relatively higher.[21] The data on economic activities in Table 12 further enlarge our knowledge of the socioeconomic characteristics of the Resistance. The components of the sample reveal an urban character, with the sole exception of the AA, whose strength in rural areas was based on the guerrilla contingent. The resisters clustered heavily in the "community, social and personal services" and the "transport and communication" categories. In each of the two categories, one political group held the dominant position, and each of these two categories had a greater representation within the sample than on the national level. Over 63 percent of the recruits of the four largest non-Marxist groups were in the first category. On the other hand, the KPÖ, RS, and F were concentrated in the second category, where the KPÖ enlisted more than one-third of its followers. The differences in social background between the two camps thus essentially correspond to the economic dimensions shown in Table 12.

The figures in Tables 11 and 12 show the political polarization of the underground, that is, the wide differences in social background and economic activities between the left and right. The greater participation of workers and middle-class intellectuals in the underground contrasted with the extremely low participation of farmers and housewives and with the low participation of the white-collar workers. Both tables indicate similar political patterns with regard to the economic activities and professions of the main social groups. A comparison of the political tendencies of the affiliates with the social characteristics of their members shows the Resistance as a closed functional elite, whose social composition differed from that of the country. By primarily enlisting workers and the intelligentsia, the Resistance reduced its isolation from the urban population, but its influence became increasingly attenuated as one moved from industrial centers into the rural hinterlands. The Resistance was urban and homogeneous; it was younger, better educated, better trained, more professional, more industry-

Table 11. Occupational Breakdown of the Resistance (N = 2,307)[a]

Occupation[b]	KPÖ (N = 1,141)	RS (112)	F (79)	L (174)	T (340)	M	JW	AA	HS	Resistance Total	Gainful Employment[c] Total Population
Agricultural Worker	—	—	—	—	—	—	—	—	—	0%	
Unskilled Worker	113 81.3% 9.4 4.9	3 2.2% 2.7 0.1	4 2.9% 5.1 0.2	3 2.2% 1.7 0.1	8 5.8% 2.3 0.3	—	6 4.3% 13.3 0.3	1 0.7% 0.3 —	1 0.7% 5.0	139 6.1%	51.06%
Skilled Worker	774 78.1% 67.8 33.6	49 4.9% 43.8 2.1	71 7.2% 89.9 3.1	23 2.3% 13.2 1.0	21 2.1% 6.1 0.9	—	9 0.9% 20.0 0.4	43 4.3% 14.0 1.9	1 0.7% 5.0	991 43.0%	
Disabled, Old Age Pension	2 40.0% 0.2 0.1	1 20.0% 0.9	—	1 20.0% 0.6	—	—	1 20.0% 2.2	—		5 0.2%	
White-Collar Worker (Angestellte)	79 43.9% 6.9 3.4	27 15.0% 24.1 1.2	2 1.1% 2.5 0.1	28 15.6% 16.1 1.2	26 1.1% 2.4 0.1	2 1.1% 2.4 0.1	—	14 7.8% 4.6 0.5	2 1.1% 10.0 0.1	180 7.8%	14.51%
Non-Commissioned Officers (N.C.O.s)	—	—	—	—	—	41 80.4% 49.4 1.8	—	10 19.6% 3.3 0.4	—	51 2.2%	
Civil Servant	28 18.8% 2.5 1.2	11 7.4% 9.8 0.5	—	14 9.4% 8.0 0.6	58 38.9% 16.8 2.5	—	1 0.7% 2.2 —	35 23.5% 11.4 1.5	2 1.3 10.0 —	149 6.5%	

Table 11 (Continued)

Occupation[b]	KPÖ (N = 1,141)	RS (112)	F (79)	L (174)	T (340)	M	JW	AA	HS	Resistance Total	Gainful Employment[c] Total Population
Teacher	7	4	1	4	17	—	—	7	—	40	
	17.5%	10.0%	2.5%	10.0%	42.5%			17.5%		1.7%	
	0.6	3.6	1.3	2.3	4.9			2.3			
	0.3	0.2	—	0.2	0.7			0.3			
Police, Gendarmerie	32	—	—	3	9	—	—	30	—	74	
	43.2			4.1%	12.2%			40.5%		3.2%	
	2.8			1.7	2.6			9.8			
	1.4			0.1	0.4			1.3			
Military Officer (including retired)	—	—	—	7	13	38	—	20	—	78	
				9.0%	16.7%	48.7%		25.6%		3.4%	
				4.0	3.8	45.8		6.5			
				0.3	0.6	1.6		0.9			
Independent, Artisan, Craftsman, Retailer	20	2	—	18	18	—	8	12	—	78	
	25.6	2.6		23.1	23.1		10.3	15.4		3.4%	
	1.8	1.8		10.3	5.2		17.8	3.9			
	0.9	0.1		0.8	0.8		0.3	0.5			
Free professions	19	5	—	9	37	2	1	33	1	107	
	17.8	4.7		8.4	34.6	1.9	6.9	30.8	6.9	4.6%	
	1.7	4.5		5.2	10.7	2.4	2.2	10.7	5.0		
	0.8	0.2		1.6	0.1	0.0	1.4	—			
Student	17	1	—	32	88	—	—	19	10	159	
	10.7	0.6		20.1	50.3			11.9	6.3	6.9%	
	1.5	0.9		18.4	23.1			6.2	50.0		
	0.7	0.0		1.4	3.5			0.8	0.4		

Table 11 *(Continued)*

Occupation[b]	KPÖ (N = 1,141)	RS (112)	F (79)	L (174)	T (340)	M	JW	AA	HS	Resistance Total	Gainful Employment[c] Total Population
Priest, member of religious orders	—	—	—	12 / 38.7 / 6.9 / 0.5	13 / 41.9 / 3.8 / 0.6	—	—	5 / 16.1 / 1.6 / 0.2	1 / 3.2 / 5.0 / —	31 / 1.3%	
Manager	—	—	—	—	6 / 75.0 / 1.7 / 0.3	—	—	2 / 25.0 / 0.7 / 0.1	—	8 / 0.3%	
Businessman, independent	—	—	—	2 / 15.4 / 1.1 / 0.1	10 / 76.9 / 2.9 / 0.4	—	—	1 / 7.7 / 0.3 / —	—	13 / 0.6	
Farmer	3 / 4.3 / 0.3 / 0.1	—	—	2 / 2.9 / 1.1 / 0.1	3 / 4.3 / 0.9 / 0.1	—	1 / 1.4 / 2.2 / —	60 / 87.0 / 19.5 / 2.6	—	69 / 3.0%	
Housewife	43 / 40.6 / 3.8 / 1.9	39 / 8.5 / 8.0 / 0.4	—	7 / 6.6 / 4.0 / 0.3	18 / 17.0 / 5.2 / 0.8	—	13 / 12.3 / 28.9 / 0.6	14 / 13.2 / 4.6 / 0.6	2 / 1.9 / 10.0 / 0.1	106 / 4.6%	32.70%
Hausbesorgerin, Bedienerin, Köchin	2 / 18.2 / 0.2 / 0.1	—	—	5 / 45.5 / 2.9 / 0.2	2 / 18.2 / 0.6 / 0.1	—	2 / 18.2 / 4.4 / 0.1			11 / 0.5%	

Table 11 (Continued)

Occupationᵇ	KPÖ (N = 1,141)	RS (112)	F (79)	L (174)	T (340)	M	JW	AA	HS	Resistance Total	Gainful Employmentᶜ Total Population
Upper Class Aristocracy, etc.	—	—	—	3	7	—	—	1	—	11	
				27.3	63.6			9.1		0.5%	
				1.7	2.0			0.3			
				0.1	0.3			—			
	1141	112	79	174	346	83	45	307	20	2307	
	49.5	4.9	3.4	7.5	15.0	3.6	2.0	13.3	0.9	100%	

ᵃIn this table, the first row gives the membership of each Resistance affiliate from each occupational classification. The second row expresses the membership of each affiliate from each occupational classification (e.g., 81.3 percent of all unskilled workers were KPÖ members). The third row expresses the membership of each affiliate from each occupational classification as a percentage of each affiliate's total membership. The fourth row indicates the membership of each affiliate from an occupational classification as a percentage of the total sample.

ᵇBecause of slight coding errors, percentages and subtotals may not total designated figures. Seven entries were coded as belonging to nonexisting categories. The differences are statistically unimportant.

ᶜFor the gainfully employed, see Statistisches Handbuch, 1936, pp. 11-13.

Table 12.[a] Economic Activities of Resistance Members by Affiliation (N = 1,638)[b]

Economic Activities	KPÖ	RS	F	L	T	M	JW	AA	HS	Resistance Total	Gainful Employment[c] Total Population
Agriculture	4 5.2% 0.6% 0.2%	—	—	5 6.5% 3.7 0.3	6 7.8% 2.3 0.4	—	2 2.6 6.5 0.1	60 77.9 23.3 3.7	—	77 4.7%	31.66%
Forestry	1 14.3 0.1 0.1	—	—	—	2 28.6 0.8 0.1	—	1 14.3 3.2 0.1	3 42.9% 1.2 0.2	—	7 0.4%	
Metal Ore Mining	7 77.8 1.0 0.4	—	—	—	—	—	—	2 22.2 0.8 0.1	—	9 0.5%	
Other Mining	19 82.9 2.7 1.2	1 4.3 1.2 0.1	—	1 4.3 0.7 0.1	1 4.3 0.4	—	—	1 4.3 0.4 0.1	—	23 1.4%	
Manufacture of food, beverages, and tobacco	7 36.8 1.0 0.4	1 5.3 1.2 0.1	—	1 5.3 0.7 0.1	4 21.1 1.5 0.2	—	2 10.5 6.5 0.1	4 21.1 1.6 0.2	—	19 1.2%	
Textile wearing apparel, and leather	47 65.3 6.7 2.9	1 1.4 1.2 0.1	—	9 12.5 6.7 0.5	6 8.3 2.3 0.4	—	5 6.9 16.1 0.3	4 5.6 1.6 0.2	—	72 4.4%	8.8%

Table 12 (Continued)

	KPÖ	RS	F	L	T	M	JW	AA	HS	Resistance Total	Gainful Employment Total Population
Manufacture of wood and furniture	13	—	—	1	1	—	1	1	—	17	
	76.5			5.9	5.9		5.9	5.9		1.0%	
	1.8			0.7	0.4		3.2	0.4			
	0.8			0.1	0.1		0.1	0.1			
Manufacture of paper, printing and publishing	34	3	4	—	10	—	—	2	—	53	
	64.2	5.7	7.5		18.9			3.8		3.2%	
	4.8	3.6	5.6		3.8			0.8			
	2.1	0.2	0.2		0.6			0.1			
Manufacture of chemicals, petroleum, and coal	5	—	—	—	2	—	—	2	—	9	
	55.6				22.2			22.2		0.5%	
	0.7				0.8			0.8			
	0.3				0.1			0.1			
Nonmetallic mineral products (glass, pottery, china)	3								3		
	100.0									0.2%	
	0.4										
	0.2										
Rubber and fabricated metal products, and machinery	91	6	9	4	2	—	2	—	—	114	
	79.8	5.3	7.9	3.5	1.8		1.8			7.0%	6.8%
	12.9	7.2	12.7	3.0	0.8		6.5				
	5.6	0.4	0.5	0.2	0.1		0.1				
Other manufacturing industries	4	—	—	—	2	—	1	—	—	7	
	57.1				28.6		14.3			0.4%	
	0.6				0.8		3.2				
	0.2				0.1		0.1				

Table 12 *(Continued)*

	KPÖ	RS	F	L	T	M	JW	AA	HS	Resistance Total	Gainful Employment Total Population
Electricity, gas and water	38	—	23	3	4	—	—	1	—	69	
	55.1		33.3	4.3	5.8			1.4		4.2%	0.3%
	5.4		32.4	2.2	1.5			0.4			
	8.3		1.4	0.2	0.2			0.1			
Construction	29	—	—	3	7	—	—	4	3	46	
	63.0			6.5	15.2			8.7	6.5	2.8%	
	4.1			2.2	2.7			1.6	30.0		
	1.8			0.2	0.4			0.2	0.2		
Wholesale and retail trade, restaurants, and hotels	37	9		16	35		2	5		104	
	35.6	8.7		15.4	33.7		1.9	4.8		6.3%	11.0%
	5.3	10.8		11.9	13.3		6.5	1.9			
	2.3	0.5		1.0	2.1		0.1	0.3			
Transport, storage, and communication	258	28	29	9	10	1	2	31	2	370	
	69.7	7.6	7.8	2.4	2.7	0.3	0.5	8.4	0.5	22.6%	4.6%
	36.0	33.7	40.8	6.7	3.8	1.2	6.5	12.1	20.0		
	15.8	1.7	1.8	0.5	0.6	0.1	0.1	1.9	0.1		
Financing, insurance, real estate, and business services	15	6	—	10	14	—	—	5	1	51	
	29.4	11.8		19.6	27.5			9.8	2.0	3.1%	
	2.1	7.2		7.5	5.3			1.9	10.0		
	0.9	0.4		0.6	0.9			0.3	0.1		

Table 12 (Continued)

	KPÖ	RS	F	L	T	M	JW	AA	HS	Resistance Total	Gainful Employment Total Population
Community, social and personal services (public administration, defense, sanitary, social, cultural, recreational, and household)	84	20	5	61	152	83	13	131	4	553	
	15.2	3.6	0.9	11.0	27.5	15.0	2.4	23.7	0.7	33.8%	14.0%
	11.9	24.1	7.0	45.5	57.6	98.8	41.9	51.0	40.0		
	5.1	1.2	0.3	3.7	9.3	5.1	0.8	8.0	0.2		
Not adequately defined	2	8	—	10	6	—	—	—	—	26	
	7.7	30.8		38.5	23.1					1.6%	
	0.3	9.6		7.5	2.3						
	0.1	0.5		0.6	0.4						
	704	83	71	134	264	84	31	257	10	1638	
	43.0%	5.1	4.3	8.2	16.1%	5.1	1.9	15.7	0.6	100.0%	

[a]See note a under Table 10.

[b]Subtotals and percentages may not total designated figures because nine cases (0.69), including those of four coal miners, were misplaced in nonexisting categories. The differences are statistically unimportant. For the gainfully occupied, including employed and unemployed, see *Statistisches Handbuch*, 1936, pp. 11-13. Some contingents, such as coal miners, have been underrepresented because of the lack of detailed documentation.

oriented, and more politically conscious and socially concerned than the population as a whole.

Political Affiliation

An important factor in prompting people to become active was past political association. The various groups had distinctive appeals to former party members or voters who volunteered for the anti-Nazi cause. Past affiliation and political conviction, as well as social origin or some personal cause for commitment (friendship, etc.), were important considerations in selecting an underground group. By focusing more narrowly on the political experiences of resisters in the years following the constitution of the Republic in 1918, I have been able to display in Table 13 the evolutionary process that led to an individual's joining a given underground formation after 1938. I posited in each case two stages of the process, selecting the uprising of February 1934 as the dividing point.

Table 13.[a] Political Affiliation Before and After 1934

Pre-1934 (N = 530)			1934-38 (N = 483)[b]		
KPÖ	6.2%	} 7.3%	17.0%	} 24.3%	
KJV	1.1		6.2		
Rote Hilfe			1.1		
SPÖ-RS	66.0	} 75.3%	24.8	} 25.2%	
SPD	0.8		0.4		
Schutzbund	8.5				
Christian Socials	5.7	} 9.3%	8.6	} 20.7%	
Catholic Organization	3.6		12.1		
Heimwehr (Home Front, HF)	3.6		9.7		
NSDAP, SA, SS, HJ	1.6		3.6		
Legitimists	2.8		3.4		
Veterans organizations	0.2				
Ostmärkische Sturmscharen (OS)			3.5	} 11.7%	
Jungvolk (JV)			4.3		
Bündisch youth			3.9		

[a]Percentages do not total 100 percent because I left out some unimportant categories. The figures are illustrative, and, because of the small size of the sample, which overrepresents the leftist tendency, only give an order of magnitude.

[b]If we add the sample figures for the Christian Socials, Catholics, Heimwehr, OS, Jungvolk, and Bündisch youth, we get 42.1 percent in the post-1934 stage as against 12.9 percent before 1934.

In the post-1934 period, the sharp decline in the number of SPÖ-RS members reflects both the KPÖ's success in integrating some of the RS, and the average SPÖ-RS member's reluctance to join the underground struggle. In sharp contrast, every other group greatly increased its share in that period. Although 3 of every 4 activists in the sample were Socialists before 1934, the ratio dropped sharply to 1 of every 4 after 1934. The KPÖ seemed to have benefited most from this marked change. The supporters of the Dollfuss-Schuschnigg government scored high in the sample. Of all resisters who launched their political careers before 1938, more than 4 of every 10 supported the corporate regime. Those who opted for Austrian self-identity after 1934—the KPÖ and the Catholic and traditionalist forces—emerged in 1938 hostile to the National Socialist regime and subsequently engaged in active resistance. The RS with their consistent all-German line initially failed to understand the importance of Austrian patriotism.

As Table 14 shows, the massive influx of Socialists into the KPÖ after 1934 marked an important turn in the KPÖ's membership policies. It widened its popular base. Some 85 percent of the 1938-1945 Communist Resistance sample had been enlisted in the SPÖ before 1934. Thus there was obviously a considerable carryover of Socialist experience into the Communist Resistance. These fluctuations reflect the shifting heterogeneous nature of the KPÖ membership after 1938, when it had to assimilate former Social Democrats.

Table 14.[a] Political Affiliation of the KPÖ Resistance Before 1938

	Pre-1934 (291 cases out of 1,243)		1934-38 (140 cases out of 1,243)	
KPÖ	10.7%		52.1%	
KJV	2.1	} 12.8%	19.3	} 74.3%
Rote Hilfe			2.9	
SPÖ-RS	73.9		13.5	
SPD	0.7	} 85.3%		
Schutzbund	10.7			
Christian Socials	1.0		1.4	
Home Front, Catholics, Jungvolk, OS			4.2	
NSDAP	0.7		2.1	
SA	0.3	} 1.0%	1.4	} 4.2%
HJ			0.7	

[a]Regard the percentages as orders of magnitude. A number of cases in the two samples overlap. The available figures are of uncertain value and insufficient data somewhat distorted the sample. The percentages do not equal 100 percent because I have not included all the categories.

Despite the presence of large numbers of pre-1934 SPÖ adherents, that almost three-quarters of the core of the post-1938 Communist Resistance were recruited from its own ranks implies a strong element of organizational continuity and political stability. Some of this large-scale internal shift after 1934 resulted from the rejuvenation of the KPÖ, which prided itself on winning the support of the younger generations. With its meteoric rise, the Party youth undoubtedly brought to the illegal structure different political expectations and experiences. Both the young and the former SPÖ members probably joined the KPÖ after 1934 more out of ideological enthusiasm than from a desire to endorse the Stalinist principles. The KPÖ sent its members into the ranks of the NSDAP, SA, and HJ to penetrate the

Nazis from within their own organizations. The increased enrollment of adherents of the Schuschnigg corporate system paralleled this development. Although I could not determine the nature of this process, it led to a situation in which almost one-tenth of the KPÖ activists were former members of the Nazi, semi-Fascist, or rightist movements.

The KPÖ's impressive efforts to expand its constituency and to recruit new members after 1934 differed sharply from the uninspiring policies of the RS, in whose party politically alien elements were conspicuously absent from the sample drawn from pre-1934 and post-1934 Socialist members.[22] The RS's development of a remarkable inbred character coincided with the shift of its former supporters to the KPÖ. Apparently strong ties with the Socialist Party past and the absence of nonparty elements fostered a less imaginative approach that thwarted political initiative.

Because of insufficient data, I can make only tentative conclusions about the political past of the members of the other main resistance formations L, T, AA) (Table 15).[23] The Christian Socials in the T and AA samples showed significant continuity in their recruitment pattern. The evolutionary pattern of the sample members was highly erratic throughout their last twenty years. Young people provided an important source of recruits. They were increasingly drawn from the ranks of the Catholic youth and students, from the Bündisch youth groups, and from the former pro-Schuschnigg organizations.[24] Apparently their presence markedly affected the development of the Resistance because of their preoccupation with furthering Austrian awareness. The shifting, amorphous, youth-oriented, pro-Schuschnigg elements became, in varying degrees, the core of the non-Marxist Resistance.[25]

Recapitulation

The pattern emerging from the samples testified that the dominant position of the KPÖ, which accounted for less than one-half of the resisters, was mainly due to its recruitment of former Socialist cadres. The AA and T became the leading formations of the non-Communist forces. The Resistance was essentially a male movement; its female share was woefully weak. The members showed a youthful profile. Most members were German-speaking Austrians. A relatively larger percentage than for the population as a whole embraced non-Roman Catholic denominations or were without religious ties.

Overwhelmingly, the members of the Resistance came from skilled labor and the intellectual segments of the middle classes, giving the Resistance its dominantly urban character. Members had attained high levels of education, and a considerable proportion had university training. Vienna was the focal point of the Resistance, followed by Styria and Tyrol as the regional strongholds.

TIME OF RECRUITMENT

Table 16 establishes the different phases at which the volunteers entered the underground. During the *first phase* from 1938 to the end of 1940, the KPÖ, RS, L, T, and JW reached their peak rather early in 1938-39 and rapidly declined in 1940-41. In general, in the *interim phase* of 1941-42, the M and AA increased their growth. In the *final phase* from 1943 to 1945, these two formations, undoubtedly encouraged by the course of the war, continued to grow and recorded their highest level in 1944. The three stages of joining clearly corresponded to the changing tides of the war. Those groups in which the influx of recruits peaked in 1938-40 were partly wrecked by the Gestapo in 1939-41.

FORMS OF ACTIVITIES

The resisters engaged in various types of activities. To gain closer insight into their operations, I classified the recruits in terms of the tasks they performed. Defining activity classifications was a task less precise and more subjective than that of defining the social and political backgrounds of the membership. A person might have been engaged in several activities or just in one. Although it was difficult to distinguish precisely all activities in which individuals were involved, the background material generally permitted a reasonably correct assessment. For Table 17, I have constructed eight categories of activities based on the available data.

1) The first category combines assignments related to the organization and administration of the Resistance: creating clandestine organizations, recruiting new adherents, setting up safe houses, providing shelters and material assistance, arranging systems of communication, paying membership fees, listening to foreign broadcasts, and similar activities. (2) Category two includes writing subversive political propaganda and working in the underground press. (3) The gathering and transmitting of information, which includes collecting military, economic, and political information, and the writing of situation reports for domestic purposes form the core of the third category. (4) The fourth category comprises preparations for sabotage, acts of sabotage, and delivery of arms and explosives. (5-6) Categories five and six include preparing and participating in guerrilla activities and organizing armed actions. There is no clear dividing line between the two. Category five includes the activities of insurgents living underground in remote areas. Category six includes the actions of the clandestine military groups, carrying out armed acts or preparing for a final insurrection in cooperation with the advancing Allied troops. This category also includes the actions of teams of armed civilians who operated in the urban areas

Table 15. Political Affiliation of the Three Largest Non-communist Groups Pre-1934, Post-1934

	L Pre-1934 (44 cases)	L Post-1934 (99 cases)	T Pre-1934 (31 cases)	T Post-1934 (83 cases)	AA Pre-1934 (13)	AA Post-1934 (14)
RS	2.3%	—	3.2%	1.2%	53.9%	21.4%
Christian Social	9.1	3.0	51.6	34.9	38.5	35.7
Catholic adult organizations	2.3	1.0	12.9	6.0	—	—
Catholic youth	2.3	34.3	—	8.4	—	—
Catholic students	15.9	1.0	9.7	—	—	14.3
Home Front	27.3	31.3	16.1	9.6	—	7.1
NSDAP, HJ, SA, SS	4.6	3.0	6.4	8.4	—	7.1
Legitimists	34.1	16.2	—	—	—	—
OS, Jungvolk, Bündisch youth	—	10.1	—	30.1	—	14.2

Table 16.[a] Years of Recruitment into the Resistance

	Resistance (2,459 cases)	KPÖ (936)	RS (139)	L (172)	T (324)	M (106)	JW (81)	AA (477)
1938	20.8%	25.1%	34.6%	46.5%	18.8%	0.9%	63.0%	2.9%
1939	18.1	20.1	48.5	23.3	27.5	3.8	13.6	4.8
1940	15.3	21.3	2.9	10.5	15.1	1.9	17.8	6.3
1941	9.2	13.4	1.5	11.0	7.4	5.7	3.7	5.0
1942	8.3	9.2	5.9	3.5	7.7	10.4	—	10.3
1943	11.5	8.0	2.9	5.2	7.7	27.4	—	19.9
1944	10.9	2.7	3.7	—	12.0	28.3	—	29.1
1945	5.7	—	—	—	3.7	21.7	—	21.4

[a]I have not included the pre-1938 years and have left out two small groups, the F and HS. The sample is somewhat underrepresented in the post-1942 period. Sometimes, but not very often, I had to make an educated guess about dates of affiliation.

Table 17.[a] Underground Activities (N = 3,058 cases)

Forms of Activities	Resistance	KPÖ 1,243 cases	F 79	L 182	T 449	M 107	JW 81	AA 495	HS 20	RS 139
1. Organizational-administrative	90.4%	98.2%	96.2%	97.3%	99.1%	87.9%	98.8%	73.7%	100%	75.5%
2. Writing propaganda	20.7	29.1	17.7	37.9	6.9	0.9	81.5	5.5	60%	23.7
3. Gathering information and preparing situation reports	3.3	2.4	—	2.2	5.8	8.4	—	3.8	—	9.4
4. Acts of sabotage including their preparation, collecting arms	10.6	6.8	2.5	0.5	6.9	37.4	—	22.8	—	5.0
5. Guerrilla activities including support	7.3	2.1	1.3	3.8	1.8	16.8	—	26.7	—	—
6. Armed activity	6.5	1.9	—	1.1	2.9	24.3	—	22.4	—	—
7. Communicating with foreign intelligence, including contacting foreign powers and parachuted agents	7.2	5.1	—	11.0	7.6	18.7	—	8.9	—	7.2
8. Other activities	18.7	16.7	—	17.0	18.7	48.6	—	29.5	—	10.1

[a]As entries in the sample have been assigned various activities, Table 17 gives the relative instead of adjusted frequency. Naturally, double counting is involved, as numerous individuals participated in several activities.

toward the end of the war. (7) The seventh category comprises the establishing of communications with foreign intelligence networks or with the authorities of foreign intelligence networks or with the authorities of foreign governments abroad, the transmitting of intelligence data, and the staging of operations within Austria by foreign agents parachuted into the country. (8) The eighth category embraces all of the remaining activities (forging papers, etc.), including those for which information was incomplete.

Table 17 shows the consistently high incidence of the organizational-administrative activity. The creation and administration of the groups was the most essential task of any clandestine work. Isolated individuals did not thrive in the underground, dependent as they were on guidance, communication, information, material, and assistance. In general, political propaganda (publication and distribution of newspapers, pamphlets, leaflets) constituted the second most widely shared activity. The record of the Resistance in gaining intelligence was noteworthy, although not outstanding. Making contact with Allied officials and agents stood out in all occupied countries as the most pressing task.[26] Without outside help, sabotage was largely ineffective, and the actual damage that the underground inflicted was slight. Some saboteurs claimed many unverifiable clerical "errors" and acts of negligence. They also claimed to have proposed a go-slow attitude among employees to impair the war effort. No mass direct action took place, because Nazi repression was not indiscriminate enough to drive the people to arms. The primarily political commitment to protecting the safety of the population made immediate action an important but still subordinate part of the political efforts of the national liberation movement.

The substantial differences in underground activities among the groups are revealing. Analysis of Table 17 shows that the AA and M outdid the others in the militant categories four and seven. The largest formation, the AA, became the most active group in the post-1943 phase. The composite picture of the AA actions suggests an aggressive combative cluster of patriotic organizations. Similarly, the military men displayed an aggressive attitude, accounting for the largest share of the most militant categories, while not surprisingly having the lowest percentage engaged in political propaganda. Generally, the sabotage and arms collecting records of the Resistance were good. The KPÖ was primarily political in character but did engage in sabotage and in developing foreign contacts. In categories three to eight, the T tended to exhibit a pattern similar to that of the KPÖ, showing, however, more strength in intelligence.

The percentages for the KPÖ, L, and T in armed and guerrilla actions were disproportionately low, reflecting the moderation of the leaders, who stressed political warfare. An astonishing 18.7 percent of the sample of military men directly or indirectly communicated with an Allied power. On our scale of activities, the most active were those groups that exhibited the largest number of members active in categories four to eight.[27]

Judged by the indexes of activism, the Resistance as a whole was predominantly engaged in recruiting and in organizing its networks, and in highly risky and perilous political propaganda. It emphasized the collecting of intelligence and of arms, and the undertaking of sabotage. The M and AA alone accounted, respectively, for over sixty and forty percent of the sabotage and armed actions. Occupational and regional indicators appear important background elements in determining where and how extensively the Resistance concentrated its activities. Generally, the main five formations performed most of these activities.

NOTES

1. Harold D. Lasswell defines the elite as those who exercise the most influence in a given situation, but I do not believe that this definition applies to the Austrian Resistance. Harold D. Lasswell and Daniel Lerner, eds., *World Revolutionary Elites* (Cambridge, Mass., 1965), p. 8. The definition that Marshall R. Singer proposes seems more useful, although still not quite sufficient for my purpose. He defines the elite as a "leadership group" consisting "of those persons in any community who possess in extraordinary degree one (quality) or a combination of generally desired qualities. The elite possesses power, respect, wealth, and skill in combination or singly," *The Emerging Elite; A Study of Political Leadership in Ceylon* (Cambridge, Mass., 1964), p. 5. However, none of these criteria fully apply to the Resistance.

2. One could refer to the Resistance as a counter-elite, which does not possess the usual qualities of eliteness such as wealth, power, influence, intelligence, or respect. In identifying the Resistance elite, civic and moral concerns are the determining factors. At the individual level, the hopes for future professional opportunities usually blended with moral rectitude and ideological justification, qualities that legitimized the underground activities.

3. Political prisoners, 19 percent of whom were sentenced to death, accounted for 62.4 percent of the total entries. The proportion of prisoners may be inflated as many resisters, who were not arrested, were not included because no records were available.

4. The computer results consisting of 524 pages which Tulane Computer Laboratory prepared on November 18, 1977, are deposited in Tulane University Library, New Orleans, La. 70118.

5. The coding raised some difficulties, as distinctions between the T and AA formations were not always clear-cut. Under the heading of religious-oriented resistance I counted exclusively the Jehovah's Witnesses. Another coding problem involved the difference between the non-partisan All-Austrian and Military resistance movements. Whenever in doubt, I enlisted the individual in the All-Austrian formation. Basically, I listed under military only those servicemen and their associates who were recruited from among their units or joined an organization designated military. Former professional soldiers who participated in an underground organization I listed under that organization.

6. At the end of the data-collecting process, I designed the codebook and transferred the data from the sources to data sheets. Then the information was punched on IBM cards. I prepared twenty-three questions for the computer to correlate and cross-tabulate. A Tulane University graduate student of history, Edward A. Allen, who handled all the computer programming with competence and great skill, aided me.

7. Regard this figure as a general rather than a specific indicator of the level of female participation in the Resistance. I used the census of March 1934 for population figures. Bundesamt für Statistik, ed., *Die Ergebnise der österreichischen Volkszählung vom 22. März 1934. Tabellenheft* (Vienna, 1935), p. 2.

8. The otherwise well-informed M. R. D. Foot asserted that women participated in the Resistance "on terms of perfect equality with men," *Resistance; European Resistance to Nazism 1940-1945* (New York, 1977), p. 13. Foot doubtless had in mind the situation in France, where women became effective leaders of the networks. For example, see the major eyewitness account by the leader of the Alliance network, Marie-Madeleine Fourcade, *Noah's Ark* (London, 1973). For a description of the part women played in Austria, see Tilly Spiegel, *Frauen und Mädchen im österreichischen Widerstand,* and the dissertation by Brauneis, "Widerstand der Frauen." The percentage of women in the French movement "Franc-Tireur" was around 10 percent. Dominique Veillon, *Le Franc-Tireur. Un journal clandestin, un mouvement de résistance (1940-1944)* (Paris, 1977), pp. 256-57.

9. Bundesamt für Statistik, ed., *Statistisches Handbuch für den Bundesstaat Österreich* (Vienna, 1936), 16:5. The sample lists 1,239 entries.

10. There were 2,099 valid observations in the sample, which contained only four persons born before 1870, and 27 persons (1.3 percent) born in 1870-79.

11. See the discussion in Peter H. Merkl, *Political Violence under the Swastika; 581 Early Nazis* (Princeton, 1975), pp. 19-21. Greater Vienna, which had been abundantly documented and whose territory had been greatly enlarged in 1938, may be slightly overrepresented in the samples.

12. I define regionalism as the coincidence of the place of birth and the place of residence. Although I use the traditional names for the provinces of Lower and Upper Austria, I am aware of the different territorial composition of the two provinces under the new names, Lower- and Upper Danube after 1938.

13. In the provinces bordering a non-German state with a German minority (Italy, Czechoslovakia, Yugoslavia, Hungary), national rivalry with the ethnically different neighbor made some of the native population receptive to racist ideology and all-German ideas. It apears, however, that the persons listed in the sample attached no significance to this borderland nationalism.

14. For our purposes, the percentages may be considered as orders of magnitude.

15. Obviously, some persons living in rural areas commuted to work in towns and cities and therefore did not properly belong to rural elements.

16. However, one has to consider the underrepresentation in the sample of Burgenland where the Croatian group resided.

17. Roman Catholics were probably consistently underrepresented in the sample because the documents tended to emphasize disproportionately individuals who professed other religions and failed to provide information when the person professed the religion of the great majority. Nevertheless, the Catholic underrepresentation does not overly distort the picture that Table 8 gives.

18. I have coded the Volks-, Bürger- and Hauptschulen as elementary and high schools, and the military academies as universities. I employed the secondary and university categories regardless of whether the individual finished the school in question. The sample is relatively small and biased. Undoubtedly, those with university education were inclined to report that information, and those with little education were inclined not to mention their education. As a result, the data on education are incomplete. However, the bias operated on all categories of resisters. Therefore, the comparisons are valid, even though the percentages may be imprecise.

19. International Labour Office, *Year Book of Labour Statistics 1974* (Geneva, 1974), pp. 761-62.

20. Ibid., pp. 769-71. I encountered problems of coding reliability because my sources used different categories and imprecise terminology. Lack of definition and blurred demarcation between occupations such as white-collar worker *(Angestellte)* and civil-servant *(Beamte)* caused the greatest difficulties. To minimize these coding problems, I used the less strictly constructed occupational labels of my sources. Most vocational labels caused no confusion. Some subjective evaluations were unavoidable in my coding. For instance, I usually place a shoemaker in the blue-collar worker category but in the independent artisan category if he had been

self-employed. I have included train-drivers, tram- and train-conductors, and train superintendents among skilled workers; and railway traffic superintendents, accountants, and office clerks among white-collar workers. I listed public, bank, Trade-Union and private officials *(Beamten)* as civil servants. Generally, I have followed the Austrian terminology in the occupational compilations. The identification with occupational groups by the members themselves or by the authorities constituted the basis for the listing of occupations. Thus, I list a railway employee as a blue-collar worker and a postal employee as a white-collar worker. Among the military men I also include all those professional soldiers who attained officer rank before or after 1918 and retired before 1938 or did not serve in the Wehrmacht after 1938. Fortunately, the sources did not conceive of the occupational groups as social classes and avoided using umbrella terms such as *Mittelstand.*

21. They were recruited from some 8,000 members. Luža, *Austro-German Relations,* p. 191.

22. There were 93 and 90 cases out of 139. I have included a person in both categories if he or she adhered to the SPÖ before 1934 and to the RS after 1934.

23. The same person may be listed in both the pre- and post-1934 categories.

24. I have not used the sample of 811 cases designed to register political affiliation in 1938-45 because adequate data were not available. The non-Marxist groups have been grossly underrepresented, and I could not make any well-founded statements about their political distribution. However, the percentages generally reflect the trends and patterns described in the text.

25. Among the most interesting features of the composition of Resistance groups would have been the size of the enrollment of members of the NSDAP, its affiliates, and auxiliaries. Unfortunately, no data concerning this group were available. The sample of 811 entries suggests a figure of slightly below 5 percent for the NSDAP and HJ. From the auxiliaries, the NSV (the National Socialist Public Welfare Organization) made up a substantial 60 percent of the small subsample of 62 entries listing National Socialist auxiliaries and affiliates.

First World War experiences left deep imprints on the minds of many men, which tended to sharpen their commitment to the Austrian cause after 1938. Over 20 percent of the small sample of 237 cases had been drafted into military service in 1914-18, and about 10 percent of the sample had earned high decorations in combat. The war of 1939 involved a substantial proportion of another sample of 376 cases who served in the Wehrmacht. Finally, almost 20 percent of the sample of 212 cases took part in the February 1934 events (13.7 fought for the SPÖ and 6.1 percent defended the regime). However, the two samples are biased and too small to allow for more definite conclusions.

26. I included the activities of parachuted agents and of their contacts in category seven. Some overlapping occurs between category three and seven. I included members in the latter category if they had been, directly or indirectly, involved with the Allied powers.

27. I define the nature and intensity of activism by the degree and scope of participation in the eight categories of activities. Thus the more active groups had a high percentage of their members involved in armed, sabotage, and intelligence operations.

BIBLIOGRAPHY

Bibliography

PRIMARY SOURCES

Unpublished Documents

Bundesarchiv, Koblenz
  Reichsinnenministerium — R 18 and R 18 Rep. 320
  Reichsjustizministerium — R 22
  Reichskommissar für die Wiedervereinigung Österreichs mit dem Deutschen Reich — R 104
  Reichssicherheitshauptamt — R 58
  Sammlung Schumacher
Dokumentationsarchiv des österreichischen Widerstandes, Vienna
  Files and records, 1-16635
  Sammlung illegaler Flugschriften
Institut für Zeitgeschichte der Universität Wien
  Privatarchiv Otto Molden. Zur Geschichte der österreichischen Widerstandsbewegung
    gegen Hitler 1938-1940
  Volksgerichtshof, Akten — Oberlandesgericht Wien, Akten
National Archives of the United States, Washington, D.C.
  Records of Headquarters, German Armed Forces, High Command, T-77
  Records of the Reich Ministry of Economics, T-71
  Records of the NSDAP, T-81
  Records of Private Austrian, Dutch, and German Enterprises, T-83
  Miscellaneous German Collections, T-84
  Records of the Reich Leader of the SS and Chief of German Police, T-175
Österreichische Nationalbibliothek, Vienna
  Flugschriftensammlung. Weltkrieg 1939-1945
Österreichisches Staatsarchiv-Allgemeines Verwaltungsarchiv
  Reichskommissar für die Wiedervereinigung Österreichs mit dem Deutschen Reich.
    Materienregistratur 1-402
Österreichisches Staatsarchiv — Kriegsarchiv
  Deutsche Division 177. Feldgerichtsurteile 1939-1945
Roosevelt, Franklin D. Library, Hyde Park, New York
  PSF OSS. Container 170-171
Staatliches Archivlager, Göttingen

Zwölf Nürnberger U.S. — Militärgerichtsprozesse. Documents.
Tulane University Library
R. Luža, The Austrian Resistance 1938 to 1945. Incidence of Variables, November 18, 1977.
Verein für Geschichte der Arbeiterbewegung, Vienna
SPÖ Partei-Archiv, Mappe 70.

Published Documents

Bundesamt für Statistik. *Die Ergebnisse der österreichischen Volkszählung vom 22. März 1934. Bundesstaat. Tabellenheft.* Vienna, 1935.

_____. *Statistisches Handbuch für den Bundesstaat Österreich.* Vols. 16-17. Vienna, 1936-1937.

Dokumentationsarchiv des österreichischen Widerstandes.
Katalog Nos. 1-10. Vienna, 1963-1975.

_____. ed. *Widerstand und Verfolgung in Wien 1934-1945.*
Eine Dokumentation. Vols. 2-3 *1938-1945.* Vienna, 1975.

_____. ed. *Widerstand und Verfolgung in Burgenland 1934-1945.*
Eine Dokumentation. Vienna, 1979.

_____. ed. *Widerstand und Verfolgung in Oberösterreich 1934-1945.*
Eine Dokumentation. 2 vols. Vienna, 1982.

Ellwood, David W., and Miller, James E., eds. *Introductory Guide to American Documentation of the European Resistance Movement in World War II.* Vol. I: *Public records.* Turin, 1975.

Generaldirektion der Staatlichen Archive Bayerns, ed. *Widerstand und Verfolgung in Bayern 1933-1945. Archivinventare* I-III. 3 vols. Munich, 1975.

Janeček, Oldřich, ed. "Depeše mezi Prahou a Moskvou 1939-1941," *Příspěvky k dějinám KSČ* 3 (1967): 375-433.

International Labour Office. *Year Book of Labour Statistics 1974.* Geneva, 1974.

Ministerium für Auswärtige Angelegenheiten der UdSSR. *UdSSR-Österreich 1938-1979. Dokumente und Materialien.* Moscow, 1980.

Österreichisches Statistisches Zentralamt, ed. *Statistisches Handbuch für die Republik Österreich.* Vols. 2-4. Jahrgang. Vienna, 1951-1953.

Rüter-Ehlermann. Adelheid L. and Rüter, C. F., eds. *Justiz und NS-Verbrechen. Sammlung deutscher Strafurteile wegen nationalsozialistischer Tötungsverbrechen 1945-1966.* Vols. I-11. Amsterdam, 1968-1974.

Secrétairerie d'État de Sa Sainteté. *Actes et documents du Saint Siège relatifs à la Seconde guerre mondiale.* Vol. 6: *Le Saint Siège et les victimes de la guerre, mars 1939-décembre 1940.* Vatican City, 1972.

[U.S.A.] Foreign Relations of the United States. *Diplomatic Papers.* Vol. 3: *European Advisory Commission; Austria; Germany.* Washington, D.C., 1968.

U.S. Department of State. *Documents on German Foreign Policy 1918-1945. From the Archives of the German Foreign Ministry.* Series D. Vol 1. Washington, D.C., 1949-1966.

SECONDARY SOURCES

Books

Adam, Uwe Dietrich. *Judenpolitik im Dritten Reich.* Düsseldorf, 1972.

Adler, H. G. *Der verwaltete Mensch. Studien zur Deportation der Juden aus Deutschland.* Tübingen, 1974.

Aichinger, Wilfried. "Sowjetische Österreichpolitik 1943-1945." Ph.D. dissertation, University of Vienna, 1977.

Altmann, Peter, et al. *Der deutsche antifaschistische Widerstand 1933-1945. In Bildern und Dokumenten.* Frankfurt a.M., 1975.

American Friends of German Freedom. "Inside Germany Reports." Mimeographed, New York. October 1940-August 1943.

Archiv Peter für historische und zeitgeschichtliche Dokumentation, ed. *Spiegelbild einer Verschwörung. Die Kaltenbrunner Berichte . . . über das Attentat vom 20. Juli 1944. . . .* Stuttgart, 1961.

d'Astier, Emmanuel. *Sept fois sept jours.* Paris, 1947

[Austria] Bundesministerium für Unterricht und Kunst. *März 1938-35 Jahre danach.* Vienna, 1973.

Balfour, Michael, and Frisby, Julian. *Helmuth von Moltke. A Leader against Hitler.* London, 1972.

Balzer, Karl. *Der 20. Juli und der Landesverrat. Eine Dokumentation über Verratshandlungen im deutschen Widerstand.* Preussisch Oldendorf, 1971.

Banny, Leopold. "Ihre Namen sind verweht . . . Österreicher bei Geheimunternehmen in ihrer Heimat während des 2. Weltkrieges, 1938-44." Manuscript. DÖW.

Barker, Elisabeth. *Austria 1918-1972.* London, 1973.

Barker, Thomas M. *The Slovenes of Carinthia. A National Minority Problem.* New York, 1960.

Bärnthaler, Irmgard. *Die Vaterländische Front. Geschichte und Organisation.* Vienna, 1971.

Bauer, Otto. *Die illegale Partei.* Paris, 1939.

Bauer, Yehuda. *A History of the Holocaust.* New York, 1982.

Bayern, Prinz Konstantin von. *Ohne Macht und Herrlichkeit. Hohenzollern, Wittelsbach, Habsburg.* Munich, 1961.

Becker, Hans. *Österreichs Freiheitskampf. Die Widerstandsbewegung in ihrer historischen Bedeutung.* Vienna, 1946.

Benz, Wolfgang, ed. *Miscellanea. Festschrift für Helmut Krausnick zum 75. Geburtstag.* Stuttgart, 1980.

Berczeller, Richard, and Leser, Norbert. *. . . mit Österreich verbunden. Burgenlandschicksal 1918-1945.* Vienna-Munich, 1975.

Bernard, Henri. *Histoire de la résistance européenne. La "quatrième force" de la guerre 39-45.* Verviers, 1968.

_____. *L'autre Allegmagne. La Résistance allemande à Hitler 1933-1945.* Bruxelles, 1976.

Binder, Gerhart. *Irrtum und Widerstand. Die deutschen Katholiken in der Auseinandersetzung mit dem Nationalsozialismus.* Munich, 1968.

Blenk, Gustav. *Leopold Kunschak und seine Zeit. Porträt eines christlichen Arbeiterführers.* Vienna, 1966.

Blöchl, Johann. *Meine Lebenserinnerungen.* Linz, 1976.

Bludau, Kuno. *Gestapo-geheim! Widerstand und Verfolgung in Duisburg 1933-1945.* Bonn-Bad Godesberg, 1973.

Boberach, Heinz, ed. *Berichte des SD und der Gestapo über die Kirchen und Kirchenvolk in Deutschland 1934-1944.* Mainz, 1971.

_____, ed. *Meldungen aus dem Reich. Auswahl aus den geheimen Lageberichten des Sicherheitsdienstes der SS 1939-1944.* Neuwied-Berlin, 1965.

Bögl, Hans. *Burgenland. Ein Bericht zur Geschichte.* Vienna, 1974.

Böhm, Johann. *Erinnerungen aus meinem Leben.* Vienna, 1964.

Born, Ludger, S.J. *Die erzbischöfliche Hilfstelle für nichtarische Katholiken in Wien.* Edited by Lothar Gruppe. In Wiener Katholische Akademie. Miscellanea No. 62. Vienna, 1979.

Botz, Gerhard. *Wien vom "Anschluss" zum Krieg.* Vienna, 1978.

Botz, Gerhard, et al., eds. *Bewegung und Klasse. Studien zur österreichischen Arbeitergeschichte. 10 Jahre Ludwig Boltzmann Institut für Geschichte der Arbeiterbewegung.* Vienna, 1978.

Boveri, Margret. *Der Verrat im 20. Jahrhundert.* 4 vols. Hamburg, 1956-1960.

Bracher, Karl Dietrich. *Die deutsche Diktatur. Entstehung, Struktur, Folgen des Nationalsozialismus.* Cologne-Berlin, 1969.

Brandenburg, Hans-Christian. *Die Geschichte der HJ. Wege und Irrwege einer Generation.* Cologne, 1968.

Brauneis, Inge. "Widerstand von Frauen in Österreich gegen den Nationalsozialismus 1938-1945." Ph.D. dissertation, University of Vienna, 1974.

Bretschneider, Heike. *Der Widerstand gegen den Nationalsozialismus in München 1933 bis 1945.* Munich, 1968.

Broszat, Martin, et al., ed. *Bayern in der NS-Zeit.* 4 vols. Munich, 1977-1981.

Brousek, Karl M. *Wien und seine Tschechen. Integration und Assimilation einer Minderheit im 20. Jahrhundert.* Vienna, 1980.

Brown, Anthony Cave. *The Secret War Report of the OSS.* New York, 1976.

Büchel, Regine. *Der Deutsche Widerstand im Spiegel von Fachliteratur und Publizistik seit 1945.* Munich, 1975.

Buchinger, Josef. *Das Ende 1000 jährigen Reiches. Dokumentation über das Kriegsgeschehen in der Heimat.* 2 vols. Vienna, 1972.

Bund sozialistischer Freiheitskämpfer und Opfer des Faschismus. *30 Jahre nach der Befreiung Österreichs. Eine Dokumentation.* Vienna, 1975.

Burghardt, Anton, und Matis, Herbert. *Die Nation — Werdung Österreichs. Historische und soziologische Aspekte.* Vienna, 1976.

Buttinger, Joseph. *Das Ende der Massenpartei. Am Beispiel Österreichs.* Frankfurt a.M., 1953.

Cole, Marley. *Jehovah's Witness. The New World Society.* New York, 1955.

Conference Group for Social and Administrative History. Transactions. Vol. 4. Mimeographed. Oshkosh, Wisc., 1974.

Conway, John S. *The Nazi Persecution of the Churches 1933-45.* London, 1968.

Czeike, Felix. *Wien und seine Bürgermeister. Sieben Jahrhunderte Wiener Stadtgeschichte.* Vienna, 1974.

Czernetz, Karl. *The Underground Movement in Austria. A Sober and Informed Account of Revolutionary Organisation under Nazism.* London, 1942.

Danimann, Franz, ed. *Finis Austriae. Österreich, März 1938.* Vienna, 1978.

Dawidowicz, Lucy S. *The War against the Jews 1933-1945.* New York, 1975.

Deutsch, Harold C. *The Conspiracy against Hitler in the Twilight War.* Minneapolis, 1968.

Dokumentationsarchiv des österreichischen Widerstandes und Dokumentationsstelle für neuere österreichische Literatur. *Österreicher im Exil 1934 bis 1945. Protokoll des Internationalen Symposiums zur Erforschung des österreichischen Exils von 1934 bis 1945.* Vienna, 1977.

Drimmel, Heinrich. *Die Häuser meines Lebens. Erinnerungen eines Engagierten.* Vienna-Munich, 1975.

Duczynska, Ilona. *Workers in Arms. The Austrian Schutzbund and the Civil War of 1934.* New York and London, 1978.

Duhnke, Horst. *Die KPD von 1933 bis 1945.* Cologne, 1972.

Dusek, Peter. *Der vergessene Widerstand.* Vienna, 1978.

Ebert, Theodor. *Gewaltfreier Aufstand. Alternative zum Bürgerkrieg.* Freiburg i.B., 1968.

Edinger, Lewis J. *German Exile Politics. The Social Democratic Executive Committee in the Nazi Era.* Berkeley, 1956.

Ehlers, Dieter. *Technik und Moral einer Verschwörung. Der Aufstand am 20. Juli 1944.* Bonn, 1964.

Engel-Janosi, Friedrich. *. . . . aber ein stolzer Bettler. Erinnerungen aus einer verlorenen Generation.* Graz-Vienna-Cologne, 1974.

European Resistance Movements 1939-1945. Vol. 1: *First International Conference on the History of the Resistance Movements Held at Liège-Bruxelles-Breendonk, 14-17 September 1958.* Oxford, 1960. Vol. 2: *Proceedings of the Second International Conference on the History of the Resistance Movements Held at Milan 26-29 March 1961.* Oxford, 1964.

Exenberger, Herbert. "Die illegale Presse in Österreich 1938-1945." Mimeographed. Vienna, 1979.

Fein, Erich. *Die Steine reden. Gedenkstätten des österreichischen Freiheitskampfes. Mahnmale für die Opfer des Faschismus. Eine Dokumentation.* Vienna, 1975.

Ferenc, Tone. *Quellen zur nationalsozialistischen Entnationalisierungspolitik in Slowenien 1941-1945.* Maribor, 1980.

Fiereder, Bruno. "Die Reichswerke 'Hermann Göring' in Österreich 1938 bis 1945. Zur Gründungsgeschichte der Vereinigten Österreichischen Eisen — und Stahlwerke (VÖEST)." Ph.D. dissertation, University of Salzburg, 1979.

Fischer, Ernst. *Das Ende einer Illusion. Erinnerungen 1945-1955.* Vienna, 1973.

_____. *Erinnerungen und Reflexionen.* Reinbek bei Hamburg, 1969.

Flanner, Karl. *Widerstand im Gebiet von Wiener Neustadt 1938-1945.* Vienna, 1973.

Foot, M. R. D. *Resistance: European Resistance to Nazism 1940-1945.* New York, 1977.

_____. *SOE in France. An Account of the Work of the British Special Operations Executive in France 1940-1944.* London, 1966.

Forschungsinstitut der Friedrich-Ebert-Stiftung. "Stand und Problematik der Erforschung des Widerstandes gegen den Nationalsozialismus. Studien und Berichte aus dem Forschungsinstitut der Friedrich-Ebert-Stiftung." Mimeographed. Bad Godesberg, 1965.

Frei, Bruno. *Der kleine Widerstand.* Vienna, 1978.

Frenay, Henri. *La nuit finira.* Paris, 1973.

Fried, Jakob. "Mein Leben in der Nazizeit." Miscellanea aus dem Kirchenhistorischen Institut d. Kath.-Theo. Fakultät, Vienna, 1970.

_____. *Nationalsozialismus und katholische Kirche in Österreich.* Vienna, 1947.

Fürnberg, Friedl. *Österreichische Freiheitsbataillone-Österreichische Nation.* Vienna, 1975.

Gaiswinkler, Albrecht. *Sprung in die Freiheit.* Vienna-Salzburg, 1947.

Gardiner, Muriel, and Buttinger, Joseph. *Damit wir nicht vergessen. Unsere Jahre 1934-1947 in Wien, Paris und New York.* Vienna, 1978.

Genner, Michael. *Mein Vater Laurenz Genner. Ein Sozialist im Dorf.* Vienna, 1979.

The German Resistance to Hitler. Berkeley and Los Angeles, 1970.

Göhring, Walter. "Der illegale Kommunistische Jugendverband Österreichs." Ph.D. dissertation, University of Vienna, 1971.

Goldinger, Walter. *Die Geschichte der Republik Österreich.* Vienna, 1962.

Goldner, Franz. *Die österreichische Emigration 1938 bis 1945.* Vienna-Munich, 1972.

Görlich, Ernst Joseph. *Die österreichische Nation und der Widerstand.* Vienna, 1967.

Görlich, Ernst J., and Romanik, Felix. *Geschichte Österreichs.* Innsbruck, 1970.

Grand, Anselm J. *"Turm A ohne Neuigkeit"! Erleben und Bekenntnis eines Österreichers. Ein Komponist, Maler und Schriftsteller schildert das KZ.* Vienna-Leipzig, 1946.

Grasmann, Peter. *Sozialdemokraten gegen Hitler 1933-1945.* Munich, 1976.

Grobauer, Franz Joseph. *Feuer auf den Tempeldachern (Reichskristallnacht 1938).* Vienna, 1978.

Groscurth, Helmuth. *Tagebücher eines Abwehroffiziers 1938-1940.* Stuttgart, 1970.

Gross, Jan Tomasz. *Polish Society under German Occupation. The Generalgouvernement, 1938-1944.* Princeton, 1979.

Gruber, Karl. *Ein politisches Leben. Österreichs Weg zwischen den Diktaturen.* Vienna, 1976.

_____. *Zwischen Befreiung und Freiheit. Der Sonderfall Österreichs.* Vienna, 1953.

Die Guillotinierten. Namensliste der durch das Fallbeil im Wiener Landesgericht durch die Nazihenker Ermordeten. n.d., n.p. [Vienna, 1945].

Gulick, Charles A. *Austria from Habsburg to Hitler.* 2 vols. Berkeley and Los Angeles, 1948.

Haas, Hanns, and Stuhlpfarrer, Karl. *Österreich und seine Slowenen.* Vienna, 1977.

Haestrupp, Jorgen. *European Resistance Movements, 1939-1945: A Complete History.* Westport, Conn., 1981.

Hájková, Alena. *Strana v odboji.* Prague, 1975.

Hammerstein, Kunrat Freiherr von. *Spähtrupp.* Stuttgart, n.d. [1963?].

Harriman, Helga H. *Slovenia under Nazi Occupation, 1941-1945.* New York-Washington, D.C., 1977.

Hautmann, Hans, and Kropf, Rudolf. *Die österreichische Arbeiterbewegung vom Vormärz bis 1945. Sozialökonomische Ursprünge ihrer Ideologie und Politik.* Vienna, 1974.

Heer, Friedrich. *Challenge of Youth.* n.p., 1974.

Heinisch, Theodor. *Österreichs Arbeiter für die Unabhängigkeit 1934-1945.* Vienna, 1968.

Heissenberger, Franz. *The Economic Reconstruction of Austria 1945-1952.* Washington, D.C., 1953.

Helwig, Werner. *Die Blaue Blume des Wandervogels. Vom Aufstieg, Glanz und Sinn einer Jugendbewegung.* Gütersloh, 1960.

Hillegeist, Friedrich. *Mein Leben im Wandel der Zeiten. Eine Selbstbiographie mit kritischen Betrachtungen.* Vienna, 1974.

Hindels, Josef. *Österreichs Gewerkschaften im Widerstand 1934-1945.* Vienna, 1976.

Hindinger, Gabriele. *Das Kriegsende und der Wiederaufbau demokratischer Verhältnisse in Oberösterreich im Jahre 1945.* Vienna, 1968.

Hirsch, Bettina, ed. *Anton Proksch und seine Zeit.* Vienna, 1977.

Hiscocks, Richard. *The Rebirth of Austria.* London, 1953.

Historische Kommission beim ZK der KPÖ, ed. *Aus der Vergangenheit der KPÖ. Aufzeichnungen und Erinnerungen zur Geschichte der Partei.* Vienna, 1961.

_____. *Beiträge zur Geschichte der Kommunistischen Partei Österreichs.* Vienna, 1976.

Hochmuth, Ursel, and Meyer, Gertrud. *Streiflichter aus dem Hamburger Widerstand 1933-1945. Berichte und Dokumente.* Frankfurt a.M., 1969.

Hoekema, Anthony A. *The Four Major Cults. Christian Science—Jehovah's Witnesses —Mormonism—Seventh-day Adventism.* Grand Rapids, Mich., 1963.

Hofer, Josef Theodor. *Weggefährten. Vom österreichischen Freiheitskampf 1933 bis 1945.* Vienna, 1946.

Hoffmann, Peter. *Widerstand—Staatsstreich—Attentat. Der Kampf der Opposition gegen Hitler.* Munich, 1969.

Holtmann, Everhard. *Zwischen Unterdrückung und Befriedung, Sozialistische Arbeiterbewegung und autoritäres Regime in Österreich 1933-1938.* Vienna, 1978.

Holzer, Willibald I. *Im Schatten des Faschismus. Der österreichische Widerstand gegen den Nationalsozialismus (1938-1945).* Vienna, 1978.

_____. "Die österreichischen Bataillone im Verbande der NOV i POJ. Die Kampfgruppe Avantgarde/Steiermark. Die Partisanengruppe Leoben-Donawitz. Die Kommunistische Partei Österreichs im militanten politischen Widerstand." Ph.D. dissertation, University of Vienna, 1971.

Holzner, Johann. "Untersuchungen zur Überwindung des Nationalsozialismus in Österreich." Ph.D. dissertation, University of Vienna, 1971.

_____, et al., eds. *Zeugen des Widerstandes. Eine Dokumentation über die Opfer des Nationalsozialismus in Nord-, Ost- und Südtirol von 1938 bis 1945.* Innsbruck, 1977.

Hörbiger, Paul. *Ich hab für euch gespielt. Erinnerungen.* Munich-Berlin, 1979.

Hostache, René. *Le Conseil National de la Résistance. Les institutions de la clandestinité.* Paris, 1958.

Huber, Wolfgang, ed. *Franz Rehrl. Landeshauptmann von Salzburg 1922-1938.* Salzburg, 1975.

Huebmer, Hans. *Von gestern bis morgen. Von Menschen und Ländern.* Bregenz, 1949.

Hurdes, Felix. *Vater Unser. Gedanken aus dem Konzentrationslager.* Vienna, 1950.

Hymoff, Edward. *The OSS in World War II.* New York, 1972.

Institut für Marxismus-Leninismus beim Zentralkomitee der SED. *Geschichte der deutschen Arbeiterbewegung.* Vol. 5: *Von Januar 1933 bis Mai 1945.* Berlin, 1966.

Janeček, Oldřich, ed. *Z počátků odboje.* Prague, 1969.

Jedlicka, Ludwig. *Der 20. Juli 1944 in Österreich.* Vienna-Munich, 1965.

_____. *Vom alten zum neuen Österreich. Fallstudien zur österreichischen Zeitgeschichte 1900-1975.* St. Pölten, 1975.

Kalmar, Rudolf. *Zeit ohne Gnade.* Vienna, 1946.

Kammerstätter, Peter. "Materialsammlung über die Widerstands- und Partisanenbewegung

Willy- Fred Freiheitsbewegung im oberen Salzkammergut-Ausseerland 1943-1945." Typewritten. 2 vols. 1978.

Karner, Stefan. *Kärntens Wirtschaft 1939-1945. Unter besonderer Berücksichtigung der Rüstungsindustrie.* Klagenfurt, 1976.

Käs, Ferdinand. *Wien im Schicksalsjahr 1945.* Vienna, 1965.

Kästner, Erich. *Notabene 45. Ein Tagebuch.* Zurich, 1961.

Katholische Sozialakademie Österreich. *"Kirche und Widerstand Österreichs im Dritten Reich," Österreichische Zeitgeschichte 6.* Vienna, 1969.

Kattwig, Franz, ed. *Sämtlich Slowenen—Versuch einer Dokumentation.* Klagenfurt, 1978.

Kaut, Josef. *Der steinige Weg. Geschichte der sozialistischen Arbeiterbewegung im Lande Salzburg.* Vienna, 1961.

Keller, Fritz. *Gegen den Strom. Fraktionskämpfe in der KPÖ. Trotzkisten und andere Gruppen 1919-1945.* Vienna, 1978.

Kempner, Benedicta Maria. *Priester vor Hitlers Tribunalen.* Munich, 1966.

Kerschbaumer, Marie-Therese. *Der weibliche Name des Widerstandes. Sieben Berichte.* Olten and Freiburg im/B., 1980.

Khol, Andreas et al., eds. *Um Parlament und Partei. Alfred Maleta zum 70. Geburtstag.* Graz-Vienna-Cologne, 1976.

Kittel, Franz. *Nacht über Österreich.* Vienna, 1945.

Klessman, Christoph and Pingel, Falk, eds. *Gegner des Nationalsozialismus. Wissenschaftler und Widerstandskämpfer auf der Suche nach historischer Wirklichkeit.* Frankfurt a.M., 1980.

Klotzbach, Kurt. *Gegen den Nationalsozialismus. Widerstand und Verfolgung in Dortmund 1930-1945. Eine historischpolitische Studie.* Hannover, 1963.

Klusacek, Christine. *Die österreichische Freiheitsbewegung. Gruppe Roman Karl Scholz.* Vienna, 1968.

_____. *Österreichs Wissenschaftler und Künstler unter dem NS-Regime.* Vienna, 1966.

Koch, Magdalena. "Der Widerstand der Kommunistischen Partei Österreichs gegen Hitler von 1938 bis 1945." Ph.D. dissertation, University of Vienna, 1964.

Kocka, Jürgen. *Unternehmensverwaltung und Angestelltenschaft am Beispiel Siemens 1847-1914.* Stuttgart, 1969.

Kollman, Eric C. *Theodor Körner. Militär und Politik.* Vienna, 1973.

Konrad, Helmut. "KPÖ und KSČ zur Zeit des Hitler-Stalin-Paktes." Ph.D. dissertation, University of Vienna, 1972.

_____. *Widerstand an Donau und Moldav. KPÖ und KSČ zur Zeit des Hitler-Stalin-Paktes.* Vienna, 1978.

_____, ed. *Sozialdemokratie und "Anschluss," Historische Wurzeln Anschluss 1918 und 1938 Nachwirkungen.* Vienna, 1978.

Koref, Ernst. *Die Gezeiten meines Lebens.* Vienna, 1980.

8. Koroški kulturni dne . . . 17.-19. Februar 1977. Klagenfurt, 1977.

[KPÖ]. *Die Kommunisten im Kampf für die Unabhängigkeit Österreichs. Sammelband.* Vienna, 1955.

_____. *Die Kommunistische Partei zur nationalen Frage Österreichs, 1937-1945.* Vienna, 1945.

_____. *Unsterbliche Opfer. Gefallen im Kampf der Kommunistischen Partei für Österreichs Freiheit.* Vienna, n.d. [1946].

_____. Historische Kommission beim ZK der KPÖ, ed., *Geschichte der Kommunistischen Partei Österreichs 1918-1955. Kurzer Abriss.* Vienna, 1977.

_____. *Die KPÖ im Kampf für Unabhängigkeit, Demokratie und Sozialistische Perspektive. Sammelband.* Vienna, 1978.

Kraushaar, Luise. *Berliner Kommunisten im Kampf gegen den Faschismus 1936 bis 1942. Robert Uhrig und Genossen.* East Berlin, 1981.

Krebs, Albert. *Fritz Dietlof Graf von der Schulenburg. Zwischen Staatsraison und Hochverrat.* Hamburg, 1964.

Kreissler, Felix. La prise de conscience de la nation autrichienne de 1938 à 1945 et ses effets durables. Un processus d'identification nationale. Habilitation. Université Paris 3, 1978.

Kreuzberg, Heinrich. *Franz Reinisch: ein Martyrer unserer Zeit.* Limburg, 1953.

Kühmayer, Ignaz Christoph. *Auferstehung.* Vienna, 1947.

Kühnrich, Heinz. *Der Partisanenkrieg in Europa 1939-1945.* Berlin, 1968.

[Kurfürst, Richard.] *West. Als Wien in Flammen stand. Der grosse Erinnerungsbericht über die Apriltage von 1945.* Vienna, 1960.

Kykal, Inez and Stadler, Karl R. *Richard Bernaschek. Odyssee eines Rebellen.* Vienna, 1976.

des Bezirkes Linz-Land. 1934-1954. Wels, 1955.

Lakenbacher, Ernst. *Die österreichischen Angestelltengewerkschaften. Geschichte und Gegenwart.* Vienna, 1967.

Langbein, Hermann. *Menschen in Auschwitz.* Vienna, 1972.

Laqueur, Walter Z. *Young Germany. A History of the German Youth Movement.* New York, 1962.

Leber, Annedore. *Conscience in Revolt. Sixty-four Stories of Resistance in Germany 1933-45.* London, 1975.

Le Chêne, Evelyn. *Mauthausen. The History of a Death Camp.* London, 1971.

Leichter, Otto. *Zwischen zwei Diktaturen. Österreichs Revolutionäre Sozialisten 1934-1938.* Vienna, 1968.

Leimlehner, Erich. "Das Kriegsende und der Wiederaufbau demokratischer Verhältnisse im Mühlviertel 1945." Lizentiatsarbeit. University of Zürich, 1972.

Leithäuser, Joachim G. *Wilhelm Leuschner. Ein Leben für die Republik.* Cologne, 1962.

Lenz, Johann M. *Christus in Dachau oder Christus der Sieger.* Vienna, 1957.

Leser, Norbert, ed. *Werk und Widerhall. Grosse Gestalten des österreichischen Sozialismus.* Vienna, 1964.

Lipgens, Walter, ed. *Europa-Föderationspläne der Widerstandsbewegungen 1940-1945.* Munich, 1968.

Lipset, Seymour Martin. *Political Man. The Social Bases of Politics.* Garden City, N.Y., 1960.

Littell, Franklin H., and Locke, Hubert G., eds. *The German Church Struggle and the Holocaust.* Detroit, 1974.

Löffler-Bolka, Dietlinde. *Vorarlberg 1945. Das Kriegsende und der Wiederaufbau demokratischer Verhältnisse in Vorarlberg im Jahre 1945.* Bregenz, 1975.

Loidl, Franz. *Festschrift zum 65. Geburtstag.* 3 vols. Vienna, 1969-71.

_____, ed. *Auftrag und Verwirklichung. Festschrift zum 200-Jährigen Bestand der kirchenhistorischen Lehrkanzel seit der Aufhebung des Jesuitenordens 1773.* Vienna, 1974.

Maass, Walter B. *The Years of Darkness. The Austrian Resistance Movement 1938-1945.* Vienna, 1975.

_____. *Country without a Name. Austria under Nazi Rule 1938-1945.* New York, 1979.

Mackowitz, R. *Kampf um Tirol. Entscheidende Taten zur Befreiung Innsbrucks im Frühjahr 1945.* Innsbruck, 1945.

Mader, Julius. *Der Banditenschatz. Ein Dokumentarbericht über Hitlers geheimen Gold- und Waffenschatz.* Berlin, 1966.

Magaziner, Alfred. *Ein Sohn des Volkes. Karl Maisel erzählt sein Leben.* Vienna, 1977.

Maimann, Helene. *Politik im Wartesaal. Österreichische Exilpolitik in Grossbritannien 1938 bis 1945.* Vienna, 1975.

Mair, John. *Austria in Four Power Control in Germany and Austria 1945-1946. Survey of International Affairs 1939-1946.* London, 1956.

Maršalek, Hans. *Die Geschichte des Konzentrationslagers Mauthausen. Dokumentation.* Vienna, 1974.

Marschall, Karl. "Volksgerichtsbarkeit und Verfolgung von nationalsozialistischen Gewaltverbrechen in Österreich (1945 bis 1972). Eine Dokumentation." Mimeographed. Vienna, 1977.

Matthias, Erich. *Sozialdemokratie und Nation. Ein Beitrag zur Ideengeschichte der sozialdemokratischen Emigration in der Prager Zeit des Parteivorstandes 1933-1938.* Stuttgart, 1952.

Mayenburg, Ruth von. *Blaues Blut und rote Fahnen. Ein Leben unter vielen Namen.* Vienna, 1969.

Merkl, Peter H. *Political Violence under the Swastika. 581 Early Nazis.* Princeton, N.J., 1975.

Merl, Edmund. *Besatzungszeit im Mühlviertel. Anhand der Entwicklung im politischen Bezirk Freistadt.* Linz, 1980.

Metzler, G. *Heimführen werd ich euch von überall her. Aufzeichnungen am Rande des Zeitgeschehens.* Vienna, 1959.

Michel, Henri. *La guerre de l'ombre. La Résistance en Europe.* Paris, 1970.

_____. *Histoire de la Résistance en France (1940-1944).* Paris, 1975 ed.

Micklem, Nathaniel. *National Socialism and the Roman Catholic Church. Being an Account of the Conflict between the National Socialist Government of Germany and the Roman Catholic Church 1933-1938.* London, 1939.

Minott, Rodney G. *The Fortress that Never Was.* New York, 1964.

Mitteräcker, Hermann. *Kampf und Opfer für Österreich. Ein Beitrag zur Geschichte des österreichischen Widerstandes 1938 bis 1945.* Vienna, 1963.

Molden, Fritz. *Fepolinski und Waschlapski auf dem berstenden Stern. Bericht einer unruhigen Jugend.* Vienna, 1976.

_____. *Exploding Star. A Young Austrian Against Hitler.* New York, 1979. This is the American version of the Fepolinski book.

Molden, Otto. *Der Ruf des Gewissens. Der österreichische Freiheitskampf 1938-1945.* Vienna, 1958.

Moltke, Freya von; Balfour, Michael; and Frisby, Julian. *Helmuth James von Moltke, 1907-1945. Anwalt der Zukunft.* Stuttgart, 1975.

Mörl, Anton. *Erinnerungen aus bewegter Zeit Tirols 1932-1945.* Innsbruck, 1955.

Muchitsch, Max. *Die Partisanengruppe Leoben-Donawitz.* Vienna, 1966.

Muckermann, Friedrich. *Im Kampf zwischen zwei Epochen. Lebenserinnerungen.* Mainz, 1973.

Mueller, Ralph, and Turk, Jerry. *Report after Action. The Story of the 103rd Infantry Division.* Innsbruck, 1945.

Müller, Josef. *Bis zur letzten Konsequenz. Ein Leben für Frieden und Freiheit.* Munich, 1975.

Mussener, Helmut. *Exil in Schweden. Politische und kulturelle Emigration nach 1933.* Munich, 1974.

Nebgen, Elfriede. *Jakob Kaiser. Der Widerstandskämpfer.* Stuttgart, 1967.

Nerdinger, Eugen, ed., *Flamme unter Asche.* Augsburg, 1979.

Neugebauer, Wolfgang. *Bauvolk der kommenden Welt. Geschichte der sozialistischen Jugendbewegung in Österreich.* Vienna, 1975.

Neuhäusler, Johann. *Kreuz und Hakenkreuz. Der Kampf des Nationalsozialismus gegen die katholische Kirche und der kirchliche Widerstand.* Munich, 1946.

Noguères, Henri, et al. *Histoire de la Résistance en France de 1940 à 1945.* 4 vols. Paris, 1967-1976.

Nollau, Günther and Zindel, Ludwig. *Gestapo ruft Moskau. Sowjetische Fallschirmagenten im 2. Weltkrieg.* Munich, 1979.

Novák, Oldřich, et al., eds. *KSČ proti nacismu. KSČ v dokumentech nacistických bezpečnostnich a zpravodajských orgánů.* Prague, 1971.

Novick, Peter. *The Resistance versus Vichy. The Purge of Collaborators in Liberated France.* New York, 1968.

Nutall, Carylyn Gwyn. "An Exercise in Futility: The Austrian Resistance to the Nazis, 1938-1940." M.A. thesis, Emory University, 1972.

Olschewski, Malte. "Die psychologische Kriegsführung und Propaganda der Titopartisanen in Kärnten und Slowenien." Ph.D. dissertation, University of Vienna, 1966.

Die Österreichische Freiheitsfront (ÖFF) und die Österreichische Freiheitsbewegung (ÖF) in den Jahren 1938 bis 1945. Ein Tätigkeitsbericht. . . . Vienna, 1946.

Österreichische Widerstandsbewegung. *Österreichs Beitrag zu seiner Befreiung.* Vienna, 1968.

_____. *Österreichische Widerstandsbewegung.* Vienna, n.d.

Pelinka, Anton. *Stand oder Klasse? Die Christliche Arbeiterbewegung Österreichs 1933 bis 1938.* Vienna, 1972.

Pelinka, Peter. *Erbe und Neubeginn. Die Revolutionären Sozialisten in Österreich 1934-1938.* Vienna, 1981.

Persico, Joseph E. *Piercing the Reich. The Penetration of Nazi Germany by American Secret Agents during World War II.* New York, 1979.

Peterson, Eward N. *The Limits of Hitler's Power.* Princeton, 1969.

Pfaundler, Wolfgang. "Zum Problem des Freiheitskampfes 1938-1945 an Hand von Beispielen, insbesondere des Widerstandes eines Tiroler Tales." Ph.D. dissertation, University of Innsbruck, 1950.

Pfeifer, Edda. "Beiträge zur Geschichte der österreichischen Widerstandsbewegung des konservativen Lagers 1938-1940. Die Gruppen Karl Roman Scholz, Dr. Karl Lederer und Dr. Jakob Kastelic." Ph.D. dissertation, University of Vienna, 1963.

Pirker, Paul. *Citadelle Bregenz.* Bregenz, 1946.

Plieseis, Sepp. *Vom Ebro zum Dachstein. Lebenskampf eines österreichischen Arbeiters.* Linz, 1946.

Pross, Harry. *Jugend-Eros-Politik. Die Geschichte der deutschen Jugendverbände.* Bern, 1964.

Prušnik-Gašper, Karl. *Gemsen auf der Lawine. Der Kärntner Partisanenkampf.* Klagenfurt, 1980.

Rauchensteiner, Manfried. *1945. Entscheidung für Österreich. Eine Bilddokumentation.* Vienna, 1975.

————. *Krieg in Österreich 1945.* Vienna, 1970.

————. *Der Sonderfall. Die Besetzungszeit in Österreich 1945 bis 1955.* Graz, 1979.

Rausch, Josef. *Der Partisanenkampf in Kärnten im Zweiten Weltkrieg.* Vienna, 1979.

Reichhold, Ludwig. *Arbeiterbewegung jenseits des totalen Staates. Die Gewerkschaften und der 20. Juli 1944.* Vienna, 1965.

————. *Geschichte der ÖVP.* Graz, 1975.

Reimann, Viktor. *Innitzer. Kardinal zwischen Hitler und Rom.* Vienna, 1967.

Reingrabner, Gustav. *Protestanten in Österreich. Geschichte und Dokumentation.* Vienna, 1981.

Reisberg, Arnold. "Chronik zur Geschichte der Kommunistischen Partei Österreichs 1935-1939." Manuscript. 1976. DÖW.

Renner, Karl. *Österreich von der Ersten zur Zweiten Republik.* Vienna, 1953.

Report of Operation. The Seventh United States Army in France and Germany 1944-1945. 3 vols. Restricted. n.d., n.p.

Revolutionäre Bewegungen in Österreich. Vienna, 1981.

Rieger, Hans. *Verurteilt zum Tod. Dokumentarbericht. Seelsorge im Gefängnis des Wiener Landgerichts 1942-1944.* Wuppertal, 1967.

Riepl, Hermann. *Fünfzig Jahre Landtag von Niederösterreich.* 2 vols. Vienna, 1972-1973.

Rings, Werner. *Leben mit dem Feind—Anpassung und Widerstand in Hitler's Europa 1939-1945.* Zurich, 1979.

Ritschel, Karl Heinz. *Julius Raab. Der Staatsvertrags Kanzler.* Salzburg, 1975.

Ritter, Gerhard. *Carl Goerdeler und die Deutsche Widerstandsbewegung.* Stuttgart, 1955.

Romanik, Felix. *Der Leidensweg der österreichischen Wirtschaft 1933-1945.* Vienna, 1957.

————, Wollinger, Johann. *Der Anteil der Akademikerschaft am österreichischen Freiheitskampf.* Vienna, n.d.

Roon, Ger van. *German Resistance to Hitler, Count von Moltke and the Kreisau Circle.* New York, 1971.

Rosenkranz, Herbert. *Verfolgung und Selbstbehauptung. Die Juden in Österreich 1938-1945.* Vienna, 1978.

Rot-weiss-rot-Buch. Darstellungen. Dokumente und Nachweise zur Vorgeschiche und Geschichte der Okkupation Österreichs (nach amtlichen Quellen). Vienna, 1946.

Rothfels, Hans. *The German Opposition to Hitler. An Assessment.* London, 1961.

Rudolf, Karl. *Aufbau im Widerstand. Ein Seelsorge-bericht aus Österreich 1938-1945.* Salzburg, 1947.

Rusinow, Dennison I. *Nationalism Today: Carinthia's Slovenes.* American Universities Field Staff, Inc. Field Staff Reports. Southeast Europe Series 23, Nos. 4-5, 23. Hanover, N.H., 1977-1978.

Sachs, Franz. *"Ich glaube, ich hätte noch viel leisten können . . . " Aufzeichnungen eines österreichischen Freiheitskämpfers.* Vienna, n.d.

Schambeck, Herbert, ed. *Kirche und Staat. Fritz Eckert zum 65. Geburtstag.* Berlin, 1976.

Schärf, Adolf. *April 1945 in Wien.* Vienna, 1948.

_____. *Österreichs Erneuerung 1945-1955. Das erste Jahrzehnt der Zweiten Republik.* Vienna, 1955.

Schärf, Paul. *Otto Haas. Ein revolutionärer Sozialist gegen das Dritte Reich.* Vienna, 1967.

Schausberger, Norbert. *Der Griff nach Österreich. Der Anschluss.* Vienna-Munich, 1978.

Scheffler, Wolfgang. *Judenverfolgung im Dritten Reich 1933-1945.* Berlin, 1960.

Schmitthenner, Walter, und Buchheim, Hans, eds. *Der deutsche Widerstand gegen Hitler.* Cologne-Berlin, 1966.

Schnabel, Raimund. *Die Frommen in der Hölle.* Frankfurt, a.M., 1965.

Scholl, Inge. *Die Weisse Rose.* Frankfurt, a.M., 1953.

Scholz, Roman Karl. *Goneril. Die Geschichte einer Begenung.* Vienna, 1947.

Schröter, Heinz. *Geheime Reichssache 330.* Klagenfurt, 1969.

Schütte-Lihotzky, Margarete. "Erlebnisse 1940-1945." Manuscript. DÖW.

Schwager, Ernst. "Die österreichische Emigration in Frankreich in der Zeit vom "Anschluss" Österreichs an das Deutsche Reich im März 1938 bis zum Kriegsende 1945." Ph.D. dissertation, University of Vienna, 1979.

Schwarz, Robert. *"Sozialismus" der Propaganda. Das Werben des "Völkischer Beobachters" um die österreichische Arbeiterschaft 1938/1939.* Vienna, 1975.

Simon, Joseph T. *Augenzeuge.* Vienna, 1979.

Slapnicka, Harry. *Oberösterreich-als es "Oberdonau" hiess (1938-1945).* Linz, 1978.

Slavik, Felix. *Wien. Am Beispiel einer Stadt.* Vienna, 1974.

Smith, R. Harris. *OSS. The Secret History of America's First Central Intelligence Agency.* Berkeley, 1972.

Sozialistische Jugend Österreichs. *Sozialismus das Ziel. Kampf und Arbeit der Sozialistischen Jugend Österreichs.* Vienna, 1950.

Spiegel, Tilly. *Frauen und Mädchen im österreichischen Widerstand.* Vienna, 1967.

_____. *Österreicher in der belgischen und französischen Resistance.* Vienna, 1969.

Stadler, Karl R. *Opfer verlorener Zeiten. Die Geschichte der Schutzbund-Emigration 1934.* Vienna, 1974.

_____. *Österreich 1938-1945 im Spiegel der NS-Akten.* Vienna-Munich, 1966.

Stafford, David. *Britain and European Resistance 1940-1945. A Survey of the Special Operations Executive with Documents.* Toronto, 1980.

Steinberg, Hans-Josef. *Widerstand und Verfolgung in Essen 1933-1945.* Hannover, 1969.

Steiner, Herbert. *Gestorben für Österreich. Widerstand gegen Hitler.* Vienna, 1964.

_____. "März, 1938 und der Widerstand." Mimeographed. Vienna, 1967.

_____, ed. *Käthe Leichter. Leben und Werk.* Vienna, 1973.

_____. *Zum Tode verurteilt. Österreicher gegen Hitler. Eine Dokumentation.* Vienna, 1964.

Stiefel, Dieter. *Entnazifizierung in Österreich.* Vienna, 1981.

Stiftung für die Pflege der Tradition der christlichen Arbeiterbewegung. *Die christlichen Gewerkschaften in Österreich.* Vienna, 1975.

Stillfried, Alfons. *Die österreichische Widerstandsbewegung und ihr Rückhalt im Volk. Vortrag im grossen Musikvereinssaal gehalten am 17.6.1946.* Vienna, 1946.

Strafdivision 999. Erlebnisse und Berichte aus dem antifaschistischen Widerstandskampf. Berlin, 1965.

Symposium 14. und 15. März 1938-Anschluss 1938. Mimeographed. Vienna, 1978.

Szecsi, Maria, and Stadler, Karl. *Die NS-Justiz in Österreich und ihre Opfer.* Vienna-Munich, 1962.

Tesarek, Anton. *Unser Seitz. Zu seinem achtzigsten Geburtstag. Beitrag zu einer Biographie.* Vienna, 1949.

Tidl, Marie. *Die Roten Studenten. Dokumente und Erinnerungen 1938-1945.* Vienna, 1976.

Tilt, Notburga. *The Strongest Weapon.* Elms Couth, Devon, 1972.

Toland, John. *The Last Days.* New York, 1966.

Trost, Ernst. *Figl von Österreich.* Vienna, 1972.

Tschol, Helmut. *Pfarrer Otto Neururer. Priester und Blutzeuge.* Innsbruck, 1963.

Tuider, Othmar. *Die Kämpfe im Vorgelande der Fischbacher Alpen 1945.* Vienna, 1971.

_____. *Die Wehrkreise XVII und XVIII 1938-1945.* Vienna, 1975.

[U.S.A.]. Military Affairs/Aerospace Historian Instant Publishing Series. "Special Operations: AAF Aid. European Resistance Movements 1943-1945." Manhattan, Kansas. [n.d.]

Ústav dějin KSČ. "Materiály z vědecké konference věnované 50. výročí Československé republiky." I. Prague, 1968.

Ústav marxismu-leninismu ÚV KSSS, ed. *Komunistická Internacionála.* Prague, 1972.

Vasari, Emilio. *Dr. Otto Habsburg oder die Leidenschaft für Politik.* Vienna-Munich, 1972.

Veillon, Dominique. *Le Franc-Tireur. Un journal clandestin, un mouvement de Résistance 1940-1944.* Paris, 1977.

Verein für Geschichte der Stadt Wien. *Wien 1938. Forschungen und Beiträge zur Wiener Stadtgeschichte,* Vol. 2. Vienna, 1978.

Vetiška, Rudolf. *Skok do tmy.* Prague, 1966.

Vistel, Alban. *La nuit sans ombre.* Paris, 1970.

Vogelmann, Karl. "Die Propaganda der österreichischen Emigration in der Sowjetunion für einen selbständigen österreichischen Nationalstaat (1938-1945)." Ph.D. dissertation, University of Vienna, 1973.

Vogl, Friedrich. *Österreichs Eisenbahner im Widerstand.* Vienna, 1968.

_____. *Widerstand im Waffenrock. Österreichische Freiheitskämpfer in der Deutschen Wehrmacht 1938-1945.* Vienna, 1977.

Vollmer, Bernhard. *Volksopposition im Polizeistaat. Gestapo-und Regierungsberichte 1934-1936.* Stuttgart, 1957.

Wachs, Walter. *Kampfgruppe Steiermark.* Vienna, 1968.

Wagner, Albrecht. *Die Umgestaltung der Gerichtsverfassung und des Verfahrens—und Richterrechts im nationalsozialistischen Staat. Die deutsche Justiz und der Nationalsozialismus,* Vol. 16/I. Stuttgart, 1968.

Wagner, Karl. Erinnerungen an Neustift. Beitrag zur Geschichte des antifaschistischen Widerstandes 1942 bis 1945 in Neustift/Stubai. Typescript. Karlsruhe, 1979.

Wagner, Walter. *Der Volksgerichtshof im nationalsozialistischen Staat. Die deutsche Justiz und der Nationalsozialismus,* vol. 3. Stuttgart, 1974.

Walser, Gaudentius P. *Carl Lampert. Ein Leben für Christus und die Kirche, 1894-1944.* Dornbirn, 1964.

Wanner, Gerhard. *Kirche und Nationalsozialismus in Vorarlberg.* Dornbirn, 1972.

Weber, Friedrich. "Die linken Sozialisten 1945-1948. Parteiopposition im beginnenden Kalten Krieg." Ph.D. dissertation, University of Salzburg, 1977.

Weber, Wilhelm, ed. *Österreichs Wirtschaftsstruktur gestern—heute-morgen.* 2 vols. Berlin, 1961.

Weinberger, Lois. *Tatsachen, Begegnungen und Gespräche. Ein Buch um Österreich.* Vienna, 1948.

Weinert, Wilhelm. "Grundlagen und Praxis des Widerstandkampfes der österreichischen Arbeiterklasse gegen den Nationalsozialismus (1938-1945)." Ph.D. dissertation, Vienna, 1976.

Weinkauff, Hermann. *Die deutsche Justiz und der Nationalsozialismus. Ein Überblick.* Teil I: *Die deutsche Justiz und der Nationalsozialismus. Quellen und Darstellungen zur Zeitgeschichte,* Vol. 16/I. Stuttgart, 1968.

Weinzierl, Erika, and Skalnik, Kurt, eds. *Österreich. Die Zweite Republik.* 2 vols. Graz, 1972.

_____, and Stadler, Karl R., eds. *Justiz und Zeitgeschichte.* Vol. 1. Vienna, 1977.

_____. *Zu wenig Gerechte. Österreicher und Judenverfolgung.* Graz, 1969.

Weisenborn, Günther. *Der lautlose Aufstand. Bericht über die Widerstandsbewegung des deutschen Volkes 1933-1945.* Hamburg, 1962 ed.

West, Franz. *Die Linke im Ständestaat Österreich. Revolutionäre Sozialisten und Kommunisten 1934-1938.* Vienna, 1978.

Wetz, Ulrike. "Geschichte der Wiener Polizeidirektion vom Jahre 1945 bis zum Jahre 1955 mit Berücksichtigung der Zeit vor 1945." Ph.D. dissertation, University of Vienna, 1971.

Winzer, Otto. *Zwölf Jahre Kampf gegen Faschismus und Krieg. Ein Beitrag zur Geschichte der Kommunistischen Partei Deutschlands 1933 bis 1945.* Berlin, 1955.

Wisshaupt, Walter. *Wir kommen wieder! Eine Geschichte der Revolutionären Sozialisten Österreichs 1934-1938.* Vienna, 1967.

Zahn, Gordon C. *German Catholics and Hitler's Wars. A Study in Social Control.* New York, 1962.

_____ . *In Solitary Witness: The Life and Death of Franz Jägerstätter.* New York, 1964.

Zeder, Heinrich. *Judas sucht einen Bruder. Schicksale aus dem Freiheitskampf Österreichs.* Vienna, 1947.

Zeller, Eberhard. *The Flame of Freedom. The German Struggle Against Hitler.* Coral Gables, Florida, 1969.

Ziak, Karl, ed. *Widergeburt einer Weltstadt. Wien 1945-1965.* Vienna, 1965.

Zinnhobler, Rudolf, ed. *Das Bistum Linz im Dritten Reich.* Linz, 1979.

Zipfel, Friedrich. *Kirchenkampf in Deutschland 1933-1945.* Berlin, 1965.

Zucker-Schilling, Erwin. *Er diente seiner Klasse. Johann Koplenig, 1891-1968.* Vienna, 1971.

Articles

Bollmus, Reinhard. "Österreichs Unabhängigkeit im Widerstreit. Neuere Arbeiten über das politische Exil der Österreicher in Grossbritannien und der Sowjetunion 1938-1945." *Zeitgeschichte* 4 (November 1976): 56-75.

Burchardt, Lothar. "Die Auswirkungen der Kriegswirtschaft auf die deutsche Zivilbevölkerung im Ersten und im Zweiten Weltkrieg." *Militärgeschichtliche Mitteilungen* 15, No. 1 (1974): 65-97.

Danimann, Franz. "Österreichs Arbeiter unter dem Hakenkreuz." *Arbeit und Wirtschaft* No. 12 (1963): 23-28.

Eckert, Fritz. "Vor 25 Jahren . . . ." *Die österreichische Nation* 22, No. 7/8 (July-August 1970): 98-103.

Fischer, Ernst. "Der Weg der Provisorischen Regierung." *Weg und Ziel* 4, No. 1 (January 1946): 1-19.

Frass-Ehrfeld, Claudia. "Kärnten 1945—Von Neubeginn und Bewältigung." *Österreich in Geschichte und Literatur* 20 (March-April, 1976): 100-109, 100-103.

Garscha, Winfried R. "KPÖ und nationale Frage." *Fortschrittliche Wissenschaft* Nos. 1/2 (1979): 44-54.

Heeresgeschichtliches Museum—Militärwissenschiftliches Institut, "Die Bevölkerungsverluste Österreichs während des Zweiten Weltkrieges." *Österreichische Militärische Zeitung* No. 2 (1974): 219-20.

Hohenecker, Leopold. "Das Kriegsende 1945 im Raum Fischbach." *Österreich in Geschichte und Literatur* 19, No. 4 (1975): 193-225.

Holzer, Willibald I. "Internationalismus und Widerstand." *Österreichische Zeitschrift für Politikwissenschaft* 6 (1977): 163-82.

_____ . "Die österreichische Bataillone in Jugoslawien 1944-1945. Zur Widerstandsstrategie der österreichischen kommunistischen Emigration." *Zeitgeschichte* 4, No. 2 (November 1976): 39-55.

Engel-Janosi, Friedrich. "Remarks on the Austrian Resistance, 1938-1945." *Journal of Central European Affairs* 13 (July 1953): 105-22.

Jedlicka, Ludwig. "Dokumente zur Geschichte der Ereignisse in Wien im April 1945." *Österreich in Geschichte und Literatur,* No. 3 (1961): 127-32.

Kater, Michael, H. "Die Ernsten Bibelforscher im Dritten Reich." *Vierteljahrshefte für Zeitgeschichte* 27 (April 1969): 181-218.

Keller, Fritz. "KPÖ und nationale Frage." *Österreichische Zeitschrift für Politikwissenschaft* 6 No. 2 (1977): 183-91.

King, Jonathan, H. "Emmanuel d'Astier and the Nature of the French Resistance." *Journal of Contemporary History* 8 (October 1973): 25-45.

Knoeringen, Waldemar von. "Der sozialistische Widerstand und die illegale Partei." *Der Kochel-Brief* 14 (December 1963): 81-87.

Kocka, Jürgen. "The First World War and the 'Mittelstand': German Artisans and White-Collar Workers." *Journal of Contemporary History* 8 (January 1973): 101-23.

Koplenig, Hilde. "Alfred Klahr (1904-1943)." *Zeitgeschichte* 3 (January 1976): 97-111.

Laschitza, Horst. "Faschismus und Widerstand—Fälschung und Wirklichkeit—Auseinandersetzung mit Auffassungen der westdeutschen Historiker Hans Rothfels und Walther Hofer." *Zeitschrift für Geschichtswissenschaft* 9 (1961): 1847-60.

Leichter, Otto. "Für ein unabhängiges Österreich. Eine Denkschrift aus dem Jahr 1939." *Die Zukunft* Nos. 1/2 (Jänner 1973): 29-34.

Loidl, Franz. "Von den in Wien als ns.-Opfer 1943/45 hingerichteten geistlichen Personen." *Beiträge zur Wiener Diözesangeschichte* 7 (May 1966): 29-30.

_____. "Zum Siebziger des Kirchen-und Lokalhistorikers (Rückblick und Rechtfertigung) Dr. Franz Loidl." Miscellanea aus dem Kirchenhist. Institute d. Kath.-Theol. Fakultät Wien, 75 (1975). Mimeographed.

_____. "Entweihte Heimat. KZ Ebensee." Miscellanea aus dem Kirchenhist. Institut d. Kath.-Theol. Fakultät Wien, 13 (1971). Mimeographed.

_____. "Kaplan Dr. Dr. Heinrich Maier, ein Hauptopfer des nationalsozialistischen Gewaltsystems." Miscellanea aus dem Kirchenhist. Institut d. Kath.-Theol. Fakultät Wien, 12 (1970): 1-20.

Luža, Radomir. "Nazi Control of the Austrian Catholic Church, 1939-1941." *The Catholic Historical Review* 63 (October 1977): 537-72.

Marek, Franz. "Im Kampf gegen den deutschen Faschismus." *Weg und Ziel* No. 12 (December 1954): 866-84.

Mastny, Vojtech. "Soviet War Aims at the Moscow and Teheran Conferences of 1943." *Journal of Modern History,* 47 (September 1975): 481-504.

Mittendorfer, Johann. "Oberösterreichische Priester in Gefängnissen und Konzentrationslagern zur Zeit des Nationalsozialismus (1938-1945)." *72. Jahresbericht des Bischöflichen Gymnasiums und Diözesanseminars am Kollegium Petrinum.* Linz. Schuljahr 1975/76, 77-102; *73. Jahresbericht 1976/77,* 39-194.

Neugebauer, Wolfgang. "Der Widerstand der österreichischen Arbeiterbewegung 1938 bis 1945." Antifaschismus und Widerstand. Protokoll zur Tagung 19.-21. January 1973, 87-120.

_____. "Widerstandsforschung in Österreich." In *Politik und Gesellschaft im alten und neuen Österreich. Festschrift für Rudolf Neck zum 60. Geburtstag,* edited by Isabella Ackerl et al., pp. 363 ff. Vol. 2, Vienna, 1981.

_____. "Der österreichische Widerstand unter besonderer Berücksichtigung seiner Beziehungen zur Sowjetunion. Referat für die Tagung: Österreich und die Sowjetunion 1938-1955. Typescript (November 27, 1980).

_____, and Steiner, Herbert. "Widerstand und Verfolgung in Österreich (im Zeitraum vom 12. Februar 1938 bis zum 10. April 1938)." In *Anschluss 1938. Protokoll des Symposiums in Wien am 14. und 15. März 1978,* edited by Rudolf Neck and Adam Wandruszka, pp. 86-108. Vienna, 1981.

Otruba, Gustav. "Zur Geschichte der 'Angestellten' und ihrer wachsenden Bedeutung in Österreich bis 1918 (Im Vergleich zu Deutschland)." *Österreich in Geschichte und Literatur* 21 (March-April 1977): 74-102.

[ÖVP]. "Aus der Vorgeschichte des neuen Österreichs: Unter den Augen der Gestapo. Wie

Österreichs Bauern ihre Organisation vorbereiteten." *Der "Österreichischer Bauernbündler,"* August 1, 1945.

Pittermann, Bruno. "Österreichs Befreiung und Wiederaufbau." *Zeitgeschichte* 2, No. 7 (April 1975): 174-76.

Plum, Günter. "Widerstand und Antifaschismus in der marxistisch—leninistischen Geschichtsauffassung." *Vierteljahrshefte für Zeitgeschichte* 9 (January 1961): 50-65.

Rausch, Josef. "Der Partisanenkampf in Kärnten im Zweiten Weltkrieg." *Österreichische Osthefte* 23, No. 1 (1981): 53-76.

Romoser, George K. "The Politics of Uncertainty: The German Resistance Movement." *Social Research* 31 (Spring 1964): 73-93.

Steiner, Herbert. "Einige Probleme des Widerstandes gegen den Nationalsozialismus in Österreich (1938-1945)." *Studien und Berichte aus dem Forschungsinstitut der Friedrich-Ebert-Stiftung, Widerstand, Verfolgung und Emigration,* Bad Godesberg, 1967, pp. 3-14.

_____. "Die Jugoslawische Kommunistische Partei im Mai 1940." *Zeitgeschichte* 7 (October 1979): 1-8.

Suchy, Viktor. "Der Kampf des Dritten Reiches gegen die österreichische Kultur und Österreichs Widerstand." In Polish Academy of Sciences. Committee of Historical Sciences. Institute of History, *Interarma non silent Musae. The War and the Culture 1939-1945,* pp. 245-64. Warsaw, 1977.

Szokoll, Karl. "Der österreichische Widerstand und seine Zusammenarbeit mit der russischen Befreiungs-Armee." *Die österreichische Nation* 23 (June 1970): 83-87.

Weinzierl-Fischer, Erika. "Österreichs Katholiken und der Nationalsozialismus." *Wort und Wahrheit* 28 (1963): 493-526.

_____, "Christen und Juden nach der NS-Machtergreifung in Österreich." In *Anschluss 1938. Protokoll des Symposiums in Wien am 14. und. 15. März 1978,* edited by Rudolf Neck and Adam Wandruszka, pp. 175-205. Vienna, 1981.

Williams, Maurice. "The Aftermath of Anschluss: Disillusioned Germans or Budding Austrian Patriots." *Austrian History Yearbook* 14 (1978): 130-44.

Illegal Periodicals

Arbeitermacht
Die Einheit
Der freie Österreicher
Freies Österreich
Gegen den Strom
Hammer und Sichel
Jung-Österreich
KPÖ-Nachrichten
Mitteilungsblatt der KPÖ
Mitteilungen des Auslandsbüros österreichischer Sozialdemokraten, Paris
Der Österreichische Freiheitskämpfer
Der Pionier
Die Rote Fahne
Der rote Kurier
Die Rote Jugend
Das Signal
Der Soldatenrat
Der sozialistische Kampf, Paris
Der Vorposten
Die Wahrheit
Weg und Ziel

Other Sources

Interview with Erwin Altenburger
Interview with Herbert Baumann
Interview with Father Ludger Born, S.J.
Interview with Antonia Brůha
Interview with Hans Christian
Interview with Dr. Herbert Crammer
Interview with Karl Czernetz
Interview with Dr. Franz Danimann
Interview with Dr. Johann Dostal
Interview with Johannes Eidlitz
Interview with Alfred Ellinger
Interview with Professor Anselm Grand
Interview with Dr. Wilhelm Grimburg
Interview with Dr. Karl Gruber
Interview with Dr. Otto von Habsburg
Interview with Professor Walter Hacker
Interview with Karl Hartl
Interview with Theodor Heinisch
Interview with Josef Hindels
Interview with Alois Hradil
Interview with Anton Hyross
Interview with Dr. Hubert Jurasek
Interview with Msgr. Dr. Alfred Kostelecky
Interview with Julius Kretschmer
Interview with Leopold Kuhn
Interview with Hermann Langbein
Interview with Dr. Franz Latzka
Interview with Bertha Lauscher
Interview with Josef Lauscher
Interview with Hans Leinkauf
Interview with Dr. Ernst Lemberger
Interview with Univ.-Professor Dr. Franz Loidl
Interview with Karl Maisel
Interview with Dr. Alfred Maleta
Interview with Hans Maršalek
Interview with Heinz Mayer
Interview with Dr. Alfred Migsch
Interview with Fritz Molden
Interview with Dr. Otto Molden
Interview with Rudolfine Muhr
Interviews with Dr. Wolfgang Neugebauer
Interview with Frieda Nödl
Interview with Dr. Wolfgang Pfaundler
Interview with Msgr. Josef Pinzenöhler
Interview with Dr. Bruno Pittermann
Interview with Raimund Poukar
Interview with Anton Proksch
Interview with Dr. Viktor Reimann
Interview with Prof. Ludwig Reichhold
Interview with Prof. Dr. Felix Romanik
Interview with Erwin Scharf

Interview with Dr. Paul Schärf
Interview with Dr. Peter Schramke
Interview with Dr. Kurt Schuschnigg
Interview with Felix Slavik
Interview with Bruno Sokoll
Interview with Dr. Ludwig Soswinski
Interview with Dr. Josef Staribacher
Interviews with Dr. Herbert Steiner
Interview with Dr. Ludwig Steiner
Interview with Major Carl Szokoll
Interview with Edwin Tangl
Interview with Dr. Erich Thanner
Interview with Wilhelm Turn und Taxis
Interview with Roman Weinstabl
Interview with Dr. Josef Windisch
Interview with Dr. Stefan Wirlandner
Interview with Fritz Würthle
Letters to author from Leopold Banny
Letter to author from Dr. Franz Danimann
Letter to author from Dokumentationsarchiv des österreichischen Widerstandes
Letter to author from Dr. Heinrich Gleissner
Letter to author from Dr. Karl Gruber
Letters to author from Dr. Wolfgang Neugebauer
Letter to author from Charles A. Shaughnessy, National Archives, Military Archives Division, Washington, D.C.
Letter to author from Professor Dr. Theodor Veiter

INDEX

Index

Abwehr: in Vienna, 30, 41*n*; in Milan, 213
Adlon: 05 group, 217, 225*n*
Agency, Archiepiscopal Relief: aid to Jews, 72
Aigen: cell in, 261
Air Force: infiltration of, in Klagenfurt, 37; District Command XVII, cell in, 230
Alexander, Franz: in Ötz Valley, 246
Alge, Josef: and Müller group, 33
All-Austrians, AA: 37; underground, 281, 292-320 *passim;* coding difficulties and, 320*n*
Allen, Edward A., 320*n*
All-German: nationalism, 7; tradition, 7; ideology, 8; revolution, 82
Allied: powers, 3, 90; aid, 4; strategy, 11; lack of assistance, 11; occupation of Italy, 11; diplomacy, 51; agents, 225*n*
Allies: help of, 11; Karasek and, 41*n;* and missions, 219-21, 225*n*, Molden and, 213, 214; in 1945, 231. *See also* Contacts; 05; OSS; F. Molden
ALÖS. *See* Foreign Bureau of Austrian Social Democrats
Alt Aussee: Weihs von Mainprugg in, 168; art treasures in, 202, 209*n*, cells in, 202; arrests in, 203
Altenburger, Erwin: and Christian Democratic Resistance, 179, 187*n*
American. *See* United States
Amstetten: cells in, 230, 262
Andreasch, Otto: and Jewish group, 168

Andreatta, Artur: and 05, 255*n*
Angermann, Josef: and KPÖ, 108, 113*n*; and Gestapo, 220
Anschluss, 3, 4, 6, 7, 8, 13, 14, 16*n*, 44, 46
Anti-Fascist Freedom Movement of Austria: 36, 37; leaflets of, 37
Anti-Fascist Party of Austria: group of half-Jews, 168
Anti-Hitler Movement: and KPÖ, 146-48
Antl, Paul: and Communist group, 56, 61*n*
Arckel, Gerhard van: and OSS Bern, 213, 221*n*
Arlberg tunnel, 257*n*, 267
Armament Inspection, Vienna: cell in, 224*n*
Army. *See* Wehrmacht
Army Medical Service Center: cell in, 162
Army Medical Service Section 17: cell in, 161
Artillery Reserve and Training Unit 109: group in, 171, 230, 262
Artillery Reserve Unit 96: cell in, 262
Astra: network, 168
ATA: network, 171
Attnang-Puchheim: group in, 176*n*
Auer, Alexander: and Legitimist cell, 32
Augsburg: RSÖ group in, 89
Austria, Republic of, 1918-1938: foundation of, 3; inhabitants of, 3, 16; factories in, 3; politics of, 3-7; plebiscite in, 7; occupation of, 7, 8
Austria, 1938-1945: and NSDAP, 11; concentration camps in, 18*n*

345

246, 248, 250, 251, 252; and coding, 320*n*
Military Police of Greater Vienna: group in, 167, 168, 227
Mitterndorf: cell in, 201, 202
Moik, Wilhelmine: group of, 84
Molden, Ernst, 210, 212, 214, 222*n*
Molden, Fritz: arrested, 45; and Maier-Messner group, 170, 221*n*, 222*n*; and 05, 210, 211, 212, 213, 214, 215, 222*n*, 223*n*, 224*n*; and military Resistance, 212, 214, 215, 223*n*, 229; and escape route, 221*n*, 255*n*; and funds, 223*n*; 05 in Tyrol and, 248, 254*n*; and K. Gruber, 256*n*
Molden, Otto: and Free Corps Leaders' Group, 44, 48*n*; and OSS, 216, 222*n*; in Salzburg, 223*n*; on military Resistance, 231; in Tyrol, 247, 248, 249
Moltke, Helmuth James von: and German Resistance, 188*n*
Monarchist. *See* Legitimist
Montafone Valley: cells in, 266, 267
Moosbierbaum: cell in, 143*n*, 166*n*
Mörl, Anton von: and July 20 coup, 183, 188*n*
Moscow: and KPÖ in, 101, 114, 115, 116, 123*n*, 141, 150, 151, 197, 220; Schütte in, 122*n*; Gabler left, 126; Hudomalj and, 147; and Austrian battalions, 197-98; and Styrian Group, 198; Honner in, 207*n*, 208*n*; and missions, 219-21. *See also* Soviet Union
Moscow Declaration of 1943: and Austria, 83, 153, 159, 164, 197, 220, 284
Moser, Hans: in Resistance, 203
Moser: and military cell in Vienna, 230
Moser, Josef: military Resistance in Tyrol and, 250, 256*n*
Motor Car Reserve and Training Unit 17: cell in, 262
Motorcycle Unit, Vienna: cell in, 230
Mountain Communication Reserve and Training Unit 18, Bludenz: cell in, 267
Mountain Troops Reserve Battalion 136, Tyrol: cell in, 245, 246, 249
Mraz, Hildegard: KPÖ parachutist, 147
Mrhar, Stane: and guerrilla warfare, 193
Muchitsch, Willi: and Leoben group, 197
Muhr, Rudolfine: and RS, 84, 87*n*
Muigg, Josef: and unified Resistance in Tyrol, 256*n*
Mukarovski, Geza: and Legitimists, 32, 33

Müller, Johann: group of, 32-33, 34, 40*n*; and other Legitimist groups, 32, 33; and Social Democrats, 32; travels of, 40*n*; sentence of, 41*n*
Müller, Josef: contacts with Vatican, 67; and Resistance, 188*n*
Müller, Leopold: and KPÖ, 130
Müllern, Hans: group of, 176*n*
Müllner, Viktor: group of, 163
Munich: attempt at Hitler's life in, 33; bündisch youth in, 48*n*; RSÖ network in, 89
Mürzzuschlag: KPÖ in, 115, 120, 138; cell in, 173, 263
Mussolini, Benito, 6

Nagel, Mathias: in Mauthausen, 123*n*
Nakowitz, Franz: and KPÖ, 129
National Socialism: in Germany, 4; in Austria before 1938, 6, 7, 46; after 1938, 9, 27, 29, 47, 79, 80, 81, 125; and Catholic Church, 66, 67, 69, 70, 74*n*; and Evangelical Church, 72*n*; and clemency appeals, 117, 118; and numerical strength of, 286*n*
National Socialist German Workers' Party (NSDAP) in Austria: pre-1938, 4, 5, 6
—post-1938: existence of, 11, and SD, 14, 15; control of Austria, 4, 10, 14, 15, 47*n*, 79, 80; and Catholics, 79; Socialists, 79; and Communists, 100, 127; and Resistance, 195, 314-15, 322*n*
National Socialists. *See* National Socialist German Workers' Party
Navis Valley: cells in, 249
Nazi-Soviet Pact, 1939: 107, 108, 122*n*
Nazis. *See* National Socialist German Workers' Party
Nazism. *See* National Socialism
Nebenführ, Johann: and Catholic bündisch activities, 46, 48*n*
Nebgen, Elfriede: and Austrian Resistance, 187*n*, 188*n*
Neu Beginnen, group, 19, 88
Neugebauer, Wolfgang: and source materials, 287*n*
Neuhäusler, Josef: reports to Vatican, 67
Neuhold, Elfriede: and KPÖ, 115
Neuhold, Josef: and KPÖ, 115, 120
Neuland Bund: after 1938, 46
Neulengbach: group in, 161
Neururer, Otto: assassinated, 70
Neustadtl, Adolf: and KPÖ, 135, 136, 142*n*

Radomir Luza, born in Prague, was active in the Czechoslovak Resistance during World War II. Arrested by the Gestapo in 1941, he lived underground from September 1942 until May 9, 1945, ending the war as deputy commander of the Partisan Brigade. After the war, he studied at Masaryk University in Brno and at New York University, where he earned his doctorate in 1959. Luza is now professor of history at Tulane University. His books include *The Transfer of the Sudeten Germans: A Study of Czech-German Relations, 1933-1962* and *Austro-German Relations in the Anschluss Era.*

96785

D
802
.A9
L89
1984

LUZA, RADOMIR
    RESISTANCE IN AUSTRIA, 1938-1945.

DATE DUE	
NOV 15 1993	

Fernald Library
Colby-Sawyer College
New London, New Hampshire

GAYLORD   PRINTED IN U.S.A.